Bringing the State Back In

Until recently, dominant theoretical paradigms in the comparative social sciences did not highlight states as organizational structures or as potentially autonomous actors. Indeed, the term "state" was rarely used. Current work, however, increasingly views the state as an agent which, although influenced by the society that surrounds it, also shapes social and political processes. The contributors to this volume, which includes some of the best recent interdisciplinary scholarship on states in relation to social structures, make use of theoretically engaged comparative and historical investigations to provide improved conceptualizations of states and how they operate.

Each of the book's major parts presents a related set of analytical issues about modern states, which are explored in the context of a wide range of times and places, both contemporary and historical, and in developing and advanced-industrial nations. The first part examines state strategies in newly developing countries. The second part analyzes war making and state making in early modern Europe, and discusses states in relation to the post-World War II international economy. The third part pursues new insights into how states influence political cleavages and collective action. In the final chapter, the editors bring together the questions raised by the contributors and suggest tentative conclusions that emerge from an overview of all the articles.

As a programmatic work that proposes new directions for the analysis of modern states, the volume will appeal to a wide range of teachers and students of political science, political economy, sociology, history, and anthropology.

Sponsored by three committees of the
SOCIAL SCIENCE RESEARCH COUNCIL

Committee on States and Social Structures
Joint Committee on Latin American Studies
Joint Committee on Western European Studies

Bringing the State Back In

Edited by

PETER B. EVANS,
Brown University

DIETRICH RUESCHEMEYER,
Brown University

THEDA SKOCPOL,
The University of Chicago

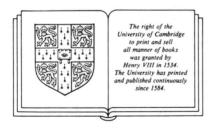

The right of the
University of Cambridge
to print and sell
all manner of books
was granted by
Henry VIII in 1534.
The University has printed
and published continuously
since 1584.

CAMBRIDGE UNIVERSITY PRESS

Cambridge

London   New York   New Rochelle

Melbourne   Sydney

Published by the Press Syndicate of the University of Cambridge
The Pitt Building, Trumpington Street, Cambridge CB2 1RP
32 East 57th Street, New York, NY 10022, USA
10 Stamford Road, Oakleigh, Melbourne 3166, Australia

First published 1985
Reprinted 1986

Printed in the United States of America

Library of Congress Cataloging in Publication Data

Main entry under title:

Bringing the state back in.

1. Policy sciences – Addresses, essays, lectures.
2. State, The – Addresses, essays, lectures.   1. Evans,
Peter B., 1944–   II. Rueschemeyer, Dietrich.
III. Skocpol, Theda.
H97.B733   1985   361.6'1   85-4703
ISBN 0 521 30786 4 hard covers
ISBN 0 521 31313 9 paperback

Contents

Preface

Like society itself, the social sciences undergo continual change, and it is the mission of the Social Science Research Council (SSRC) to identify and further emerging research agendas. This volume is the first publication of the council's Research Planning Committee on States and Social Structures. Established in 1983, the committee aims to foster sustained collaborations among scholars from several disciplines who share in the growing interest in states as actors and as institutional structures.

Until recently, dominant theoretical paradigms in the comparative social sciences did not highlight states as organizational structures or as potentially autonomous actors. Indeed, the term "state" was rarely used. Current work, however, increasingly views the state as an actor that, although obviously influenced by the society surrounding it, also shapes social and political processes. There is a recognized need, therefore, to improve conceptualizations of the structures and capacities of states, to explain more adequately how states are formed and reorganized, and to explore in many settings how states affect societies through their interventions – or abstentions – and through their relationships with social groups.

Most of the essays collected here were originally drafted for a conference entitled "Research Implications of Current Theories of the State" held at Mount Kisco, New York, in February 1982. The conference was sponsored by the Joint Committees on Latin American Studies and on Western Europe of the SSRC and the American Council of Learned Societies (ACLS). It brought together an unusually wide range (though certainly not exhaustive set) of scholars who have been at the forefront of theorizing and comparative research on states in societal and world contexts. Participants included political scientists, sociologists, economists, and historians, and there were both theoretical generalists and area specialists familiar with Europe, Latin America, and East Asia. After the 1982 conference, eight of its participants – the three of us who edited this volume, along with Albert O.

Hirschman, Peter Katzenstein, Ira Katznelson, Stephen Krasner, and Charles Tilly – continued discussions under SSRC auspices in order to lay the basis for the Committee on States and Social Structures.

Like the conference out of which it grew, and along with the Committee on States and Social Structures itself, this book aims to further dialogues across areas of scholarship that usually proceed in comfortable insulation from one another. Thus, each of its major parts poses a related set of analytical issues about modern states and includes essays that explore those issues for quite different times and places. Part I, "States as Promoters of Economic Development and Social Redistribution," brings together discussions of state strategies in newly industrializing countries, especially Latin American nations and Taiwan, with an exploration of various patterns of Keynesianism in advanced industrial democracies. Part II, "States and Transnational Relations," ranges even more broadly, especially through time. It includes an analysis of war making and state making in early modern Europe and discussions of states in relation to the post–World War II international economy for both developing and advanced industrial nations. Finally, Part III, "States and the Patterning of Social Conflicts," moves from England and the United States in the nineteenth century to present-day Yorubaland in northern Nigeria and to the "southern cone" nations of Latin America in pursuit of new insights about how states influence political cleavages and collective action.

Not only does this volume bridge the concerns of area specialties delimited by time and place; it also attempts to mediate between general theoretical debates and the specific evidence that in-depth case studies and comparisons can provide about *variations* in state organizations, public policies, and their roots and consequences. As we editors explain more fully in the introductory and concluding essays, a methodological strategy of "analytical induction" – doing comparative and historical studies to address theoretically relevant questions – seems the best way to move toward improved social scientific understandings of state structures and state activities.

Clearly, the time has come to move beyond highly speculative theoretical debates about whether the "modern state" or the "state in capitalism" has an independent impact on the course of social change. Heuristically, at least, it is fruitful to assume *both* that states are potentially autonomous and, conversely, that socioeconomic relations influence and limit state structures and activities. The challenge for researchers is to identify, conceptualize precisely, and explain variations through time and space. Well-focused hypotheses must be formulated about conditions favoring or impeding state autonomy, about the determinants of the effectiveness of state interventions, about the unintended consequences of state activities, and about the impact of state policies and structures on social conflicts.

Theoretical inspiration must be drawn from many sources as the important work of conceptualization and description, of hypothesis generation and hypothesis testing, proceeds. Yet it seems obviously premature to attempt a grand new theoretical synthesis on the interrelations between states and social structures. Glib overgeneralizations from partial evidence, along with what might be called "fallacies of misplaced abstraction" that obscure temporal and comparative variations, have all too often plagued macroscopic social science. It may in the end prove more theoretically fruitful to lay the groundwork for sound generalizations through the rewarding complexities of comparative-historical research.

All of the authors whose work is gathered into this volume are theoretically engaged in, as well as empirically well informed about, happenings in at least one area of the world and era of history. As the reader proceeds through the book, he or she will witness a dialogue among theoretical positions and hypotheses derived with deliberate eclecticism from many sources, but especially from Max Weber, Alexis de Tocqueville, Otto Hintze, and both classical and contemporary Marxists. Moreover, the reader will notice that the confrontations between these theoretical ideas and concrete historical patterns generate new questions and suggest new hypotheses as often as they provide answers. We editors have taken great pleasure in this, and in the final essay we have tried to pull together some of the questions as well as tentative conclusions that emerge from an overview of all the chapters. Yet our concluding essay is advisedly entitled "On the Road toward a More Adequate Understanding of the State." This signals where we find ourselves, and it is also meant to invite all the readers of this collection to join us in the journey.

A few words should be added to acknowledge those who helped on the first leg of the journey, toward the publication of this book. The volume is not simply a collection; it is a collective product. All of the participants in the 1982 Mount Kisco conference helped to shape the ideas of the various authors along with our editorial conceptions. Fellow members of the Committee on States and Social Structures and over a hundred other scholars who made comments and suggestions on the committee's agenda also profoundly influenced the arguments found here. The support and interest of members of the ACLS/SSRC Committees on Latin America and Western Europe sustained this effort from the time of the conference through the production of the manuscript. As staff associates for these committees, Reid Andrews and Bob Gates provided invaluable encouragement and advice in the early stages; this volume would not exist without their faith in 1981 that the emerging ideas were worth pursuing. And in the past two years, Martha Gephart, staff associate for the Committee on States and Social Structures, has unstintingly offered practical assistance and sound counsel. She deserves a good deal of the credit for keeping the project going.

Susan Allen-Mills at Cambridge University Press facilitated the publication of the book from start to finish. In the months between the 1982 conference and the submission of the manuscript, John Ikenberry, then a Ph.D.

candidate in Political Science at the University of Chicago, and Jane Szurek, a Ph.D. candidate in Anthropology at Brown University, provided crucial editorial assistance. We would also like to thank Louise Lamphere, Marilyn Rueschemeyer, and Bill Skocpol, both for their intellectual contributions and for putting up with all the lengthy phone calls among us as we jointly edited this volume and coordinated related SSRC activities. In fact, one of the most rewarding aspects of putting this volume together has been the collective character of the editorial process. From the beginning, our joint editorship meant more than administrative convenience or a simple division of labor. It was an opportunity for intellectual collaboration, and in the actual process the collaboration proved to be an extraordinarily fruitful experience.

August 1984

Peter B. Evans
Dietrich Rueschemeyer
Theda Skocpol

Introduction

1.   Bringing the State Back In: Strategies of Analysis in Current Research

Theda Skocpol

A sudden upsurge of interest in "the state" has occurred in comparative social science in the past decade. Whether as an object of investigation or as something invoked to explain outcomes of interest, the state as an actor or an institution has been highlighted in an extraordinary outpouring of studies by scholars of diverse theoretical proclivities from all of the major disciplines. The range of topics explored has been very wide. Students of Latin America, Africa, and Asia have examined the roles of states in instituting comprehensive political reforms, helping to shape national economic development, and bargaining with multinational corporations.[1] Scholars interested in the advanced industrial democracies of Europe, North America, and Japan have probed the involvements of states in developing social programs and in managing domestic and international economic problems.[2] Comparative-historical investigators have examined the formation of national states, the disintegration and rebuilding of states in social revolutions, and the impact of states on class formation, ethnic relations, women's rights, and modes of social protest.[3] Economic historians and political economists have theorized about states as institutors of property rights and as regulators and distorters of markets.[4] And cultural anthropologists have explored the special meanings and activities of "states" in non-Western settings.[5]

No explicitly shared research agenda or general theory has tied such diverse studies together. Yet I shall argue in this essay that many of them have implicitly converged on complementary arguments and strategies of analysis. The best way to make the point is through an exploration of the issues addressed in a range of comparative and historical studies – studies that have considered states as weighty actors and probed how states affect political and social processes through their policies and their patterned relationships with social groups. First, however, it makes sense to underline the paradigmatic reorientation implied by the phrase "bringing the state back in."[6]

From Society-Centered Theories to a Renewed Interest in States

There can be no gainsaying that an intellectual sea change is under way, because not long ago the dominant theories and research agendas of the social sciences rarely spoke of states. This was true even – or perhaps one should say especially – when politics and public policy making were at issue. Despite important exceptions, society-centered ways of explaining politics and governmental activities were especially characteristic of the pluralist and structure–functionalist perspectives predominant in political science and sociology in the United States during the 1950s and 1960s.[7] In these perspectives, the state was considered to be an old-fashioned concept, associated with dry and dusty legal-formalist studies of nationally particular constitutional principles. Alternative concepts were thought to be more compatible with scientific, generalizing investigations.[8] "Government" was viewed primarily as an arena within which economic interest groups or normative social movements contended or allied with one another to shape the making of public policy decisions. Those decisions were understood to be *allocations* of benefits among demanding groups. Research centered on the societal "inputs" to government and on the distributive effects of governmental "outputs." Government itself was not taken very seriously as an independent actor, and in comparative research, variations in governmental organizations were deemed less significant than the general "functions" shared by the political systems of all societies.

As often happens in intellectual life, the pluralist and structure–functionalist paradigms fostered inquires that led toward new concerns with phenomena they had originally de-emphasized conceptually. When pluralists focused on the determinants of particular public policy decisions, they often found that governmental leaders took initiatives well beyond the demands of social groups or electorates; or they found that government agencies were the most prominent participants in the making of particular policy decisions. Within pluralist theoretical premises, there were but limited ways to accommodate such findings.[9] In the classic pluralist studies of New Haven politics, Mayor Richard Lee's strong individual initiatives for urban renewal were extensively documented but not grounded in any overall state-centered analysis of the potential for certain kinds of mayors to make new uses of federal funding.[10] In major works about "bureaucratic politics" such as Graham Allison's *Essence of Decision* and Morton Halperin's *Bureaucratic Politics and Foreign Policy*, government agencies were treated individually, as if they were pure analogues of the competing societal interest groups of classical pluralism.[11] The structure and activities of the U.S. state as a whole receded from view and analysis in this approach.[12]

Like the pluralists, yet on a broader canvas, when structure–functionalist students of comparative political development set out to "apply" their grand theories to Western European history or to particular sets of non-Western polities, they often found poor fits between historical patterns and sequences and those posited by the original concepts and assumptions. "Political development" (itself found to be an overly evolutionist conception) ended up having more to do with concrete international and domestic struggles over state building than with any inherent general logic of socioeconomic "differentiation." Most telling in this regard were the historically oriented studies encouraged or sponsored by the Social Science Research Council's Committee on Comparative Politics toward the end of its life span of 1954–72.[13] In many ways, the ideas and findings about states to be reviewed here grew out of reactions set in motion by such confrontations of the committee's grand theories with case-study and comparative-historical evidence.

Especially among younger scholars, new ideas and findings have also arisen from an alternative theoretical lineage. From the mid-1960s onward, critically minded "neo-Marxists" launched a lively series of debates about "the capitalist state." By now, there are conceptually ramified and empirically wide-ranging literatures dealing especially with the roles of states in the transition from feudalism to capitalism, with the socioeconomic involvements of states in advanced industrial capitalist democracies, and with the nature and role of states in dependent countries within the world capitalist economy.[14] Neo-Marxists have, above all, debated alternative understandings of the socioeconomic functions performed by the capitalist state. Some see it as an instrument of class rule, others as an objective guarantor of production relations or economic accumulation, and still others as an arena for political class struggles.

Valuable concepts and questions have emerged from these neo-Marxist debates, and many of the comparative and historical studies to be discussed here have drawn on them in defining researchable problems and hypotheses. Yet at the theoretical level, virtually all neo-Marxist writers on the state have retained deeply embedded society-centered assumptions, not allowing themselves to doubt that, at base, states are inherently shaped by classes or class struggles and function to preserve and expand modes of production.[15] Many possible forms of autonomous state action are thus ruled out by definitional fiat. Furthermore, neo-Marxist theorists have too often sought to generalize – often in extremely abstract ways – about features or functions shared by *all* states within a mode of production, a phase of capitalist accumulation, or a position in the world capitalist system. This makes it difficult to assign causal weight to variations in state structures and activities across nations and short time periods, thereby undercutting the usefulness of some neo-Marxist schemes for comparative research.[16]

So far the discussion has referred primarily to paradigms in American social science in the period since World War II; yet the reluctance of pluralists and structure–functionalists to speak of states, and the unwillingness even of critically minded neo-Marxists to grant true autonomy to states, resonate with proclivities present from the start in the modern social sciences. These sciences emerged along with the industrial and democratic revolutions of Western Europe in the eighteenth and nineteenth centuries. Their founding theorists quite understandably perceived the locus of societal dynamics – and of the social good – not in outmoded, superseded monarchical and aristocratic states, but in civil society, variously understood as "the market," "the industrial division of labor," or "class relations." Founding theorists as politically opposed as Herbert Spencer and Karl Marx (who now, not entirely inappropriately, lie just across a lane from one another in Highgate Cemetery, London) agreed that industrial capitalism was triumphing over the militarism and territorial rivalries of states. For both of these theorists, nineteenth-century British socioeconomic developments presaged the future for all countries and for the world as a whole.

As world history moved – via bloody world wars, colonial conquests, state-building revolutions, and nationalist anticolonial movements – from the Pax Britannica of the nineteenth century to the Pax Americana of the post–World War II period, the Western social sciences managed to keep their eyes largely averted from the explanatory centrality of states as potent and autonomous organizational actors.[17] It was not that such phenomena as political authoritarianism and totalitarianism were ignored, just that the preferred theoretical explanations were couched in terms of economic backwardness or the unfortunate persistence of non-Western "traditional" values. As long as capitalist and liberal Britain, and then capitalist and liberal America, could plausibly be seen as the unchallengeable "lead societies," the Western social sciences could manage the feat of downplaying the explanatory centrality of states in their major theoretical paradigms – for these paradigms were riveted on understanding modernization, its causes and direction. And in Britain and America, the "most modern" countries, economic change seemed spontaneous and progressive, and the decisions of governmental legislative bodies appeared to be the basic stuff of politics.

As the period after World War II unfolded, various changes rendered society-centered views of social change and politics less credible. In the wake of the "Keynesian revolution" of the 1930s to the 1950s national macroeconomic management became the norm and public social expenditures burgeoned across all of the advanced industrial capitalist democracies, even in the United States. The dismantlement of colonial empires gave birth to dozens of "new nations," which before long revealed that they would not simply recapitulate Western liberal democratic patterns in their political organization or policy choices. Finally, and perhaps most importantly, by the mid-1970s, both Britain and the United States were unmistakably becoming hard-pressed in a world of more intense and uncertain international economic competition. It is probably not surprising that, at this juncture, it became fashionable to speak of states as actors and as society-shaping institutional structures.

Social scientists are now willing to offer state-centered explanations, not just of totalitarian countries and late industrializers, but of Britain and the United States themselves. Fittingly, some recent arguments stress ways in which state structures have distinctively shaped economic development and international economic policies in Britain and America and also ponder how the British and U.S. states might fetter or facilitate current efforts at national industrial regeneration.[18] In short, now that debates about large public sectors have taken political center stage in all of the capitalist democracies and now that Britain and the United States seem much more like particular state–societies in an uncertain, competitive, and interdependent world of many such entities, a paradigmatic shift seems to be underway in the macroscopic social sciences, a shift that involves a fundamental rethinking of the role of states in relation to economies and societies.

The Revival of a Continental European Perspective?

In the nineteenth century, social theorists oriented to the realities of social change and politics on the European continent refused (even after industrialization was fully under way) to accept the de-emphasis of the state characteristic of those who centered their thinking on Britain. Even though they might positively value liberal ideals, Continental students of social life, especially Germans, insisted on the institutional reality of the state and its continuing impact on and within civil society. Now that comparative social scientists are again emphasizing the importance of states, it is perhaps not surprising that many researchers are relying anew – with various modifications and extensions, to be sure – on the basic understanding of "the state" passed down to contemporary scholarship through the widely known writings of such major German scholars as Max Weber and Otto Hintze.

Max Weber argued that states are compulsory associations claiming control over territories and the people within them.[19] Administrative, legal, extractive, and coercive organizations are the core of any state. These organizations are variably structured in different countries, and they may be embedded in some sort of constitutional–representative system of parliamentary decision making and electoral contests for key executive and legislative posts. Nevertheless, as Alfred Stepan nicely puts it in a formulation that captures the biting edge of the Weberian perspective:

The state must be considered as more than the "government." It is the continuous administrative, legal, bureaucratic and coercive systems that attempt not only to structure relationships *between* civil society and public authority in a polity but also to structure many crucial relationships within civil society as well.[20]

In this perspective, the state certainly does not become everything. Other organizations and agents also pattern social relationships and politics, and the analyst must explore the state's structure and activities in relation to them. But this Weberian view of the state does require us to see it as much more than a mere arena in which social groups make demands and engage in political struggles or compromises.

What is more, as the work of Otto Hintze demonstrated, thinking of states as organizations controlling territories leads us away from basic features common to all polities and toward consideration of the various ways in which state structures and actions are conditioned by historically changing transnational contexts.[21] These contexts impinge on individual states through geopolitical relations of interstate domination and competition, through the international communication of ideals and models of public policy, and through world economic patterns of trade, division of productive activities, investment flows, and international finance. States necessarily stand at the intersections between domestic sociopolitical orders and the transnational relations within which they must maneuver for survival and advantage in relation to other states. The modern state as we know it, and as Weber and Hintze conceptualized it, has always been, since its birth in European history, part of a system of competing and mutually involved states.

Although a refocusing of social scientific interests significantly informed by the Weber–Hintze understanding of states may be upon us, the real work of theoretical reorientation is only beginning to be done. This work is understandably fraught with difficulties, because attempts are being made to think about and investigate state impacts against a background of deeply rooted theoretical proclivities that are stubbornly society-centered. Recent attempts by neo-Marxists and (what might be called) neopluralists to theorize in very general terms about "state autonomy" have not offered concepts or explanatory hypotheses rich enough to encompass the arguments and findings from various comparative-historical studies.[22]

Rather than dwell on the shortcomings of such general theories, however, the remainder of this essay will be devoted to an exploration of what some selected historical and comparative studies have to tell us about states in societal and transnational contexts. Two somewhat different, but equally important tendencies in current scholarship will claim our attention. First, we shall examine arguments about *state autonomy* and about the *capacities of states* as actors trying to realize policy goals. Then we shall explore arguments about the *impacts of states on the content and workings of politics*. The overall aim of this exercise is not to offer any new general theory of the state or of states and social structures. For the present, at least, no such thing may be desirable, and it would not in any event be feasible in the space of one essay. Rather, my hope is to present and illustrate a conceptual frame of reference, along with some middle-range issues and hypotheses that might inform future research on states and social structures across diverse topical problems and geocultural areas of the world.

The Autonomy and Capacity of States

States conceived as organizations claiming control over territories and people may formulate and pursue goals that are not simply reflective of the demands or interests of social groups, classes, or society. This is what is usually meant by "state autonomy." Unless such independent goal formulation occurs, there is little need to talk about states as important actors. Pursuing matters further, one may then explore the "capacities" of states to implement official goals, especially over the actual or potential opposition of powerful social groups or in the face of recalcitrant socioeconomic circumstances. What are the determinants of state autonomy and state capacities? Let us sample the arguments of a range of recent studies that address these questions.

States as Actors

Several lines of reasoning have been used, singly or in combination, to account, for why and how states formulate and pursue their own goals. The linkage of states into transnational structures and into international flows of communication may encourage leading state officials to pursue transformative strategies even in the face of indifference or resistance from politically weighty social forces. Similarly, the basic need of states to maintain control and order may spur state-initiated reforms (as well as simple repression). As for who, exactly, is more likely to act in such circumstances, it seems that organizationally coherent collectivities of state officials, especially collectivities of career officials relatively insulated from ties to currently dominant socioeconomic interests, are likely to launch distinctive new state strategies in times of crisis. Likewise, collectivities of officials may elaborate already established public policies in distinctive ways, acting relatively continuously over long stretches of time.

The extranational orientations of states, the challenges they may face in maintaining domestic order, and the organizational resources that collectivities of state officials may be able to draw on and deploy – all of these features of the state as viewed from a Weberian–Hintzean perspective can help to explain autonomous state action. In an especially clear-cut way, combinations of these factors figure in Alfred Stepan's and Ellen Kay Trimberger's explanations of what may be considered extreme instances of autonomous state action – historical situations in which strategic elites use military force to take control of an entire national state and then employ bureaucratic means to enforce reformist or revolutionary changes from above.

Stepan's book *The State and Society: Peru in Comparative Perspective* investigates attempts by state elites in Latin America to install "inclusionary" or "exclusionary" corporatist regimes.[23] A key element in Stepan's explanation of such episodes is the formation of a strategically located cadre of officials enjoying great organizational strength inside and through existing state organizations and also enjoying a unified sense of ideological purpose about the possibility and desirability of using state intervention to ensure political order and promote national economic development. For Brazil's "exclusionary" corporatist coup in 1964 and for Peru's "inclusionary" corporatist coup in 1968, Stepan stresses the prior socialization of what he calls "new military professionals." These were career military officers who, together, passed through training schools that taught techniques and ideas of national economic planning and counterinsurgency, along with more traditional military skills. Subsequently, such new military professionals installed corporatist regimes in response to perceived crises of political order and of national economic development. The military professionals used state power to stave off or deflect threats to national order from nondominant classes and groups. They also used state power to implement socioeconomic reforms or plans for further national industrialization, something they saw as a basic requisite for improved international standing in the modern world.

Ellen Kay Trimberger's *Revolution from Above* focuses on a set of historical cases – Japan's Meiji restoration, Turkey's Ataturk revolution, Egypt's Nasser revolution, and Peru's 1968 coup – in which "dynamically autonomous" bureaucrats, including military officials, seized and reorganized state power. Then they used the state to destroy an existing dominant class, a landed upper class or aristocracy, and to reorient national economic development.[24] Like Stepan, Trimberger stresses the formation through prior career interests and socialization of a coherent official elite with a statist and nationalist ideological orientation. She also agrees with Stepan's emphasis on the elite's concern to contain any possible upheavals from below. Yet, perhaps because she is in fact explaining a more thoroughly transformative version of autonomous state action to reshape society, Trimberger places more stress than Stepan on the role of foreign threats to national autonomy as a precipitant of "revolution from above." And she highlights a structural variable that Stepan ignored: the relationship of the state elite to dominant economic classes. As Trimberger puts it, "A bureaucratic state apparatus, or a segment of it, can be said to be relatively autonomous when those who hold high civil and/or military posts satisfy two conditions: (1) they are not recruited from the dominant landed, commercial, or industrial classes; and (2) they do not form close personal and economic ties with those classes after their elevation to high office."[25] Trimberger also examines the state elite's relationship to dominant economic classes in order to predict the extensiveness of socioeconomic changes a state may attempt in response to "a crisis situation – when the existing social, political, and economic order is threatened by external forces and by upheaval from below."[26] State-initiated authoritarian *reforms* may occur when bureaucratic elites retain ties to existing dominant classes, as, for example, in Prussia in 1806–1814, Russia in the 1860s, and Brazil after 1964. But the more sweeping structural changes that Trimberger labels "revolution from above," including the actual dispossession of a dominant class, occur in crisis situations only when bureaucratic state elites are free of ties or alliances with dominant classes.[27] As should be apparent, Trimberger has given the neo-Marxist notion of the relative autonomy of the state new analytical power as a tool for predicting the possible sociopolitical consequences of *various* societal and historical configurations of state and class power.[28]

State Autonomy in Constitutional Polities

Stepan and Trimberger deal in somewhat different, though overlapping, terms with extraordinary instances of state autonomy – instances in which nonconstitutionally ruling officials attempt to use the state as a whole to direct and restructure society and politics. Meanwhile, other scholars have teased out more circumscribed instances of state autonomy in the histories of public policy making in liberal democratic, constitutional polities, such as Britain, Sweden, and the United States.[29] In different forms, the same basic analytical factors – the international orientations of states, their domestic order-keeping functions, and the organizational possibilities for official collectivities to formulate and pursue their own policies – also enter into these analyses.

Hugh Heclo's *Modern Social Politics in Britain and Sweden* provides an intricate comparative-historical account of the long-term development of unemployment insurance and policies of old-age assistance in these two nations.[30] Without being explicitly presented as such, Heclo's book is about autonomous state contributions to social policy making. But the autonomous state actions Heclo highlights are not all acts of coercion or domination; they are, instead, the intellectual activities of civil administrators engaged in diagnosing societal problems and framing policy alternatives to deal with them. As Heclo puts it:

Governments not only "power" (or whatever the verb form of that approach might be); they also puzzle. Policy-making is a form of collective puzzlement on society's behalf; it entails both deciding and knowing. The process of making pension, unemployment, and superannuation policies has extended beyond deciding what "wants" to accommodate, to include problems of knowing who might want something, what is wanted, what should be wanted, and how to turn even the most sweet-tempered general agreement into concrete collective action. This process is political, not because all policy is a by-product of power and conflict but because some men have undertaken to act in the name of others.[31]

According to Heclo's comparative history, civil service administrators in both Britain and Sweden have consistently made more important contributions to social policy development than political parties or interest groups. Socioeconomic conditions, especially crises, have stimulated only sporadic demands from parties and interest groups, argues Heclo. It has been civil servants, drawing on "administrative resources of information, analysis, and expertise" who have framed the terms of new policy elaborations as "corrective[s] less to social conditions as such and more to the perceived failings of previous policy" in terms of "the government bureaucracy's own conception of what it has been doing."[32] Heclo's evidence also reveals that the autonomous bureaucratic shaping of social policy has been greater in Sweden than in Britain, for Sweden's premodern centralized bureaucratic state was, from the start of industrialization and before the full liberalization and democratization of national politics, in a position to take the initiative in diagnosing social problems and proposing universalistic solutions for administering to them.

Heclo says much less than he might about the influences shaping the timing and content of distinctive state initiatives. He does, however, present evidence of the sensitivity of civil administrators to the requisites of maintaining order in the face of dislocations caused by industrial unemployment. He also points to the constant awareness by administrators of foreign precedents and models of social policy. Above all, Heclo demonstrates that collectivities of administrative officials can have pervasive direct and indirect effects on the content and development of major government policies. His work suggests how to locate and analyze autonomous state contributions to policy making, even within constitutional polities nominally directed by legislatures and electoral parties.

Along these lines, it is worth looking briefly at two works that argue for autonomous state contributions to public policy making even in the United States, a polity in which virtually all scholars agree that there is less structural basis for such autonomy than in any other modern liberal capitalist regime. The United States did *not* inherit a centralized bureaucratic state from preindustrial and predemocratic times. Moreover, the dispersion of authority through the federal system, the division of sovereignty among branches of the national government, and the close symbiosis between segments of the federal administration and Congressional committees all help to ensure that state power in the twentieth-century United States is fragmented, dispersed, and everywhere permeated by organized societal interests. The national government, moreover, lacks such possible underpinnings of strong state power as a prestigious and status-conscious career civil service with predictable access to key executive posts; authoritative planning agencies; direct executive control over a national central bank; and public ownership of strategic parts of the economy. Given such characteristics of the U.S. government, the concept of state autonomy has not often been used by scholars to explain American policy developments.

Nevertheless, Stephen Krasner in his *Defending the National Interest* does use the concept to explain twentieth-century continuities in the formulation of U.S. foreign policy about issues of international investments in the production and marketing of raw materials.[33] A clever heuristic tactic lies behind Krasner's selection of this "issue area" for systematic historical investigation: It is an issue area located at the intersection of properly geopolitical state interests and the economic interests of (often) powerful private corporations. Thus, Krasner can ask whether the short-term push and pull of business interests shapes the definition of the U.S. "national interest" with respect to raw materials production abroad or whether an autonomous state interest is consistently at work. He finds the latter pattern and attributes it to actors in a special location within the otherwise weak, fragmented, and societally permeated U.S. government:

For U.S. foreign policy the central state actors are the President and the Secretary of State and the most important institutions are the White House and the State Department. What distinguishes these roles and agencies is their high degree of insulation from specific societal pressures and a set of formal and informal obligations that charge them with furthering the nation's general interests.[34]

Unfortunately, Krasner does not expand on the concept of "insulated" parts of the state. In particular, he does not tell us whether various organizational features of state agencies make for greater or lesser insulation. Instead, Krasner primarily emphasizes the degree to which different parts of the federal executive are subject to Congressional influences.[35] And he cannot fully dispel the suspicion that the Presidency and the State Department may simply be subject to class-based rather than interest-based business influences.[36] Nevertheless, he does show that public policies on raw materials have been most likely to diverge from powerful corporate demands precisely when distinctively geopolitical issues of foreign military intervention and broad ideological conceptions of U.S. world hegemony have been involved. Thus, Krasner's study suggests that distinctive statelike contributions to U.S. policy making occur exactly in those instances and arenas where a Weberian–Hintzean perspective would insist that they should occur, no matter how unpropitious the overall governmental potential for autonomous state action. As J. P. Nettl once put it, "Whatever the state may or may not be internally, . . . there have . . . been few challenges to its sovereignty *and* its autonomy in 'foreign affairs.' "[37]

My own work with Kenneth Finegold on the origins of New Deal agricultural policies also suggests that autonomous state contributions to domestic policy making can occur within a "weak state." Such autonomous state contributions happen in specific policy areas at given historical moments, even if they are not generally discernible across all policy areas and even if they unintentionally help to create political forces that subsequently severely circumscribe further autonomous state action.[38] Finegold and I argue that, by the period after World War I, the U.S. Department of Agriculture was "an island of state strength in an ocean of weakness."[39] We attribute the formulation of New Deal agricultural interventions – policies that responded to a long-standing "agrarian crisis" but *not* simply in ways directly demanded by powerful farm interest groups – to the unique resources of administrative capacity, prior public planning, and practical governmental experience available to federal agricultural experts at the dawn of the New Deal. Our argument resembles Hugh Heclo's findings about innovative civil officials in Britain and Sweden. Essentially, we found a *part* of the early-twentieth-century U.S. national government that allowed official expertise to function in a restricted policy area in ways that were similar to the ways it functioned in Sweden, or in Britain between 1900 and 1920.

In addition, however, we trace the political fate of the New Deal's administrative interventions in agriculture. We show that, in the overall context of the U.S. state structure, this initially autonomous state intervention inadvertently strengthened a particular lobbying group, the American Farm Bureau Federation, and gave it the final increments of electoral and administrative leverage that it needed to "capture" preponderant influence over post-1936 federal agricultural policies. Subsequent state planning efforts, especially those that implied redistribution of economic, racial, or social-class power, were then circumscribed and destroyed by the established commercial farming interests championed by the Farm Bureau.

In short, "state autonomy" is not a fixed structural feature of any governmental system. It can come and go. This is true not only because crises may precipitate the formulation of official strategies and policies by elites or administrators who otherwise might not mobilize their own potentials for autonomous action. It is also true because the very *structural potentials* for autonomous state actions change over time, as the organizations of coercion and administration undergo transformations, both internally and in their relations to societal groups and to representative parts of government. Thus, although cross-national research can indicate in general terms whether a governmental system has "stronger" or "weaker" tendencies toward autonomous state action, the full potential of this concept can be realized only in truly historical studies that are sensitive to structural variations and conjunctural changes within given polities.

Are State Actions "Rational"?

An additional set of comments must be made about the rationality of autonomous state actions. Often such actions are considered more capable of addressing "the capitalist *class* interest" or "society's general interests" or "the national interest" than are governmental decisions strongly influenced by the push and pull of demands from interest groups, voting blocs, or particular business enterprises.[40] In such perspectives, state officials are judged to be especially capable of formulating holistic and long-term strategies transcending partial, short-sighted demands from profit-seeking capitalists or narrowly self-interested social groups. But scholars skeptical about the notion of state autonomy often respond that state officials' own self-legitimating arguments, their claims to know and represent "general" or "national" interests, should not be taken at face value. State officials have no privileged claims to adequate knowledge of societal problems or solutions for them, argue the skeptics. Besides, their legitimating symbols may merely mask policies formulated to help particular interests or class fractions.

Surely such doubts about the superior rationality of state actions deserve respectful attention; yet we need not entirely dismiss the possibility that partially or fully autonomous state actions *may* be able to address problems and even find "solutions" beyond the reach of societal actors and those parts of government closely constrained by them. Partly, the realization of such possibilities will depend on the availability and (even more problematically) the appropriate use of sound ideas about what the state can and should do to address societal problems. Partly, it will depend on the fit (or lack thereof) between the *scope* of an autonomous state organization's authority and the scale and depth of action appropriate for addressing a given kind of problem. Planning for coordinated systems of national transportation, for example, is unlikely to be achieved by state agencies with authority only over particular regions or kinds of transportation, no matter how knowledgeable and capable of autonomous official action those agencies may be. In sum, autonomous official initiatives can be stupid or misdirected, and autonomous initiatives may be fragmented and partial and work at cross-purposes to one another. Notwithstanding all of these possibilities, however, state actions may sometimes be coherent and appropriate.

Still, no matter how appropriate (for dealing with a given kind of crisis or problem) autonomous state activity might be, it can never really be "disinterested" in any meaningful sense. This is true not only because all state actions necessarily benefit some social interests and disadvantage others (even without the social beneficiaries' having worked for or caused the state actions). More to the point, autonomous state actions will regularly take forms that attempt to reinforce the authority, political longevity, and social control of the state organizations whose incumbents generated the relevant policies or policy ideas. We can hypothesize that one (hidden or overt) feature of all autonomous state actions will be the reinforcement of the prerogatives of collectivities of state officials. Whether rational policies result may depend on how "rational" is defined and might even be largely accidental. The point is that policies different from those demanded by societal actors will be produced. The most basic research task for those interested in state autonomy surely is to explore why, when, and how such distinctive policies are fashioned by states. Then it will be possible to wonder about their rationality for dealing with the problems they address – and we will be able to explore this issue without making starry-eyed assumptions about the omniscience or disinterestedness of states.

Can States Achieve Their Goals?

Some comparative-historical scholars not only have investigated the underpinnings of autonomous state actions, but have also tackled the still more challenging task of explaining the various *capacities* of states to implement their policies. Of course, the explanation of state capacities is closely connected to the explanation of autonomous goal formation by states, because state officials are most likely to try to do things that seem feasible with the means at hand. Nevertheless, not infrequently, states do pursue goals (whether their own or those pressed on them by powerful social groups) that are beyond their reach. Moreover, the implementation of state policies often leads to unintended as well as intended consequences, both when states attempt tasks they cannot complete and when the means they use produce unforeseen structural changes and sociopolitical reactions. Thus, the capacities of states to implement strategies and policies deserve close analysis in their own right. Here, I will not attempt any comprehensive survey of substantive findings in this important area of research. Instead, I shall simply indicate some promising ideas and approaches embodied in current investigations of state capacities.

A few basic things can be said about the general underpinnings of state capacities. Obviously, sheer sovereign integrity and the stable administrative–military control of a given territory are preconditions for any state's ability to implement policies.[41] Beyond this, loyal and skilled officials and plentiful financial resources are basic to state effectiveness in attaining all sorts of goals. It is not surprising that histories of state building zero in on exactly these universal sinews of state power.[42] Certain of these resources come to be rooted in institutional relationships that are slow to change and relatively impervious to short-term manipulations. For example, do state offices attract and retain career-oriented incumbents with a wide array of skills and keen motivation? The answer may well depend on historically evolved relationships among elite educational institutions, state organizations, and private enterprises that compete with the state for educated personnel. The best situation for the state may be a regular flow of elite university graduates, including many with sophisticated technical training, into official careers that are of such high status as to keep the most ambitious and successful from moving on to nonstate positions. But if this situation has not been historically established by the start of the industrial era, it is difficult to undo alternative patterns less favorable to the state.[43]

Factors determining a state's financial resources may be somewhat more manipulable over time, though not always. The amounts and forms of revenues and credit available to a state grow out of structurally conditioned, yet historically shifting political balances and bargains among states and between a state and social classes. Basic sets of facts to sort out in any study of state capacities involve the sources and amounts of state revenues and the degree of flexibility possible in their collection and deployment. Domestic institutional arrangements and international situations set difficult to change limits within which state elites must maneuver to extract taxes and obtain credit: Does a state depend on export taxes (for example, from a scarce national resource or from products vulnerable to sudden world market fluctuations)?[44] Does a nonhegemonic state's geopolitical position allow it to reap the state-building benefits of military aid, or must it rely on international bankers or aid agencies that insist on favoring nonpublic investments and restrict the domestic political options of the borrower state?[45] What established authority does a state have to collect taxes, to borrow, or to invest in potentially profitable public enterprises? And how much "room" is there in the existing constitutional–political system to change patterns of revenue collection unfavorable to the state?

Finally, what authority and organizational means does a state have to deploy whatever financial resources it does enjoy? Are particular kinds of revenues rigidly "earmarked" for special uses that cannot easily be altered by official decision makers?[46] Can the state channel (and manipulate) flows of credit to particular enterprises and industrial sectors, or do established constitutional–political practices favor only aggregate categorical expenditures? All of these *sorts* of questions must be asked in any study of state capacities. The answers to them, taken together, provide the best general insight into the direct and indirect leverage a state is likely to have for realizing any goal it may pursue. A state's means of raising and deploying financial resources tell us more than could any other single factor about its existing (and immediately potential) capacities to create or strengthen state organizations, to employ personnel, to coopt political support, to subsidize economic enterprises, and to fund social programs.[47]

State Capacities to Pursue Specific Kinds of Policies

Basic questions about a state's territorial integrity, financial means, and staffing may be the place to start in any investigation of its capacities to realize goals; yet the most fruitful studies of state capacities tend to focus on particular policy areas. As Stephen Krasner puts it:

There is no reason to assume *a priori* that the pattern of strengths and weaknesses will be the same for all policies. One state may be unable to alter the structure of its medical system but be able to construct an efficient transportation network, while another can deal relatively easily with getting its citizens around but cannot get their illnesses cured.[48]

Those who study a comprehensive state-propelled strategy for change, such as a "revolution from above" or a major episode of bureaucratically sponsored reforms, may need to assess the overall capacity of a state to realize transformative goals across multiple spheres. Moreover, as Krasner points out, it may be useful to establish that "despite variations among issue areas within countries, there are modal differences in the power of the state among [for example] the advanced market-economy countries."[49] Nevertheless, such overall assessments are perhaps best built up from sectorally specific investigations, for one of the most important facts about the power of a state may be its *unevenness* across policy areas. And the most telling result, even of a far-reaching revolution or reform from above, may be the *disparate* transformations produced across sociopolitical sectors.

Thus, in a provocative article, "Constitutionalism, Class and the Limits of Choice in U.S. Foreign Policy," Ira Katznelson and Kenneth Prewitt show how U.S. policies toward Latin America have been partly conditioned by the uneven capacities of the American national government: strongly able to intervene abroad, yet lacking the domestic planning capacities necessary "to direct the internal distribution of costs entailed by a less imperialist foreign policy."[50] To give another example, Alfred Stepan draws many of his most interesting conclusions about the contradictory and unintended results of Peru's episode of "inclusionary corporatism" from a careful analysis of the regime's uneven successes in restructuring the political involvements of various social groups and redirecting the course of economic development in various sectors.[51]

Many studies of the capacities of states to realize particular kinds of goals use the concept of "policy instrument" to refer to the relevant means that a state may have at its disposal.[52] Cross-national comparisons are necessary to determine the nature and range of institutional mechanisms that state officials may conceivably be able to bring to bear on a given set of issues. For example, Susan and Norman Fainstein compare the urban policies of northwest European nations with those of the United States. Accordingly, they are able to conclude that the U.S. national state lacks certain instruments for dealing with urban crises that are available to European states, instruments such as central planning agencies, state-controlled pools of investment capital, and directly administered national welfare programs.[53]

Analogously, Peter Katzenstein brings together a set of related studies of how six advanced industrial-capitalist countries manage the international trade, investment, and monetary involvements of their economies.[54] Katzenstein is able to draw fairly clear distinctions between the strategies open to states such as the Japanese and the French, which have policy instruments that enable them to apply policies at the level of particular industrial sectors, and other states, such as the British and U.S., which must rely on aggregate macroeconomic manipulations of fiscal and monetary parameters. Once again, as in the Fainstein study, it is the juxtaposition of different nations' approaches to a given policy area that allows relevant policy instruments to be highlighted. Neither study, however, treats such "instruments" as deliberate short-term creations of state managers. Both studies move out toward macroscopic explorations of the broad institutional patterns of divergent national histories that explain why countries now have, or do not have, policy instruments for dealing with particular problems or crises.

States in Relation to Socioeconomic Settings

Fully specified studies of state capacities not only entail examinations of the resources and instruments that states may have for dealing with particular problems; they also necessarily look at more than states as such. They examine states *in relation to* particular kinds of socioeconomic and political environments populated by actors with given interests and resources. One obvious use of a relational perspective is to investigate the power of states over domestic or transnational nonstate actors and structures, especially economically dominant ones. What capacities do states have to change the behavior or oppose the demands of such actors or to transform recalcitrant structures? Answers lie not only in features of states themselves, but also in the balances of states' resources and situational advantages compared with those of nonstate actors. This sort of relational approach is used by Stephen Krasner in his exploration of the efforts of U.S. policy makers to implement foreign raw materials policy in interactions with large corporations, whose preferences and established practices have frequently run counter to the state's definition of the national interest.[55]

This is also the sort of approach used by Alfred Stepan to analyze the successes and failures of Peruvian military leaders in using state power to change the patterns of foreign capital investments in their dependent country.[56] Stepan does a brilliant job of developing a consistent set of causal hypotheses to explain the diverse outcomes across industrial sectors: sugar, oil, and manufacturing. For each sector, he examines regime characteristics: degree of commitment to clear policy goals, technical capacities, monitoring abilities, state-controlled investment resources, and the state's international position. He also examines the characteristics of existing investments and markets as they impinge on the advantages that either Peru or foreign multinational corporations might hope to attain from any further investments. The entire argument is too complex to reproduce here, but its significance extends well beyond the foreign investment issue area and the Peruvian case. By taking a self-consciously relational approach to the balances of resources that states and multinational corporations may bring to bear in their partially symbiotic and partially conflictual dealings with one another, Stepan has provided an important model for further studies of state capacities in many policy areas.

Another, slightly different relational approach to the study of state capacities appears in Peter Katzenstein's *Between Power and Plenty*, where (as indicated earlier) the object of explanation is ultimately not state *power over* nonstate actors, but nations' strategies for managing "interdependence" within the world capitalist economy. One notion centrally invoked in the Katzenstein collection is that of a "policy network" embodying a patterned relationship between state and society. In Katzenstein's words:

The actors in society and state influencing the definition of foreign economic policy objectives consist of the major interest groups and political action groups. The former represent the relations of production (including industry, finance, commerce, labor, and agriculture); the latter derive from the structure of political authority (primarily the state bureaucracy and political parties). The governing coalitions . . . in each of the advanced industrial states find their institutional expression in distinct policy networks which link the public and the private sector in the implementation of foreign policy.[57]

Katzenstein argues that the definition and implementation of foreign economic policies grow out of the nexus of state and society. Both state goals and the interests of powerful classes may influence national policy orientations. And the implementation of policies is shaped not only by the policy instruments available to the state, but also by the organized support it receives from key societal groups.

Thus, policy objectives such as industrial reorganization might be effectively implemented because a central state administration controls credit and can intervene in industrial sectors. Yet it may be of equal importance that industries are organized into disciplined associations willing to cooperate with state officials. A complete analysis, in short, requires examination of the organization and interests of the state, specification of the organization and interests of socioeconomic groups, and inquiries into the complementary as well as conflicting relationships of state and societal actors. This is the sort of approach consistently used by the contributors to *Power and Plenty* to explain the foreign economic objectives of the United States, Britain, Germany, Italy, France, and Japan. The approach is also used to analyze the capacities of these nations' policy networks to implement existing, or conceivable alternative, economic strategies.

The relational approaches of Stepan's *State and Society* and Katzenstein's *Power and Plenty* drive home with special clarity some important points about all current research on states as actors and structures. Bringing the state back in to a central place in analyses of policy making and social change does require a break with some of the most encompassing social-determinist assumptions of pluralism, structure–functionalist developmentalism, and the various neo-Marxisms. But it does not mean that old theoretical emphases should simply be turned on their heads: Studies of states alone are not to be substituted for concerns with classes or groups; nor are purely state-determinist arguments to be fashioned in the place of society-centered explanations. The need to analyze states in relation to socioeconomic and sociocultural contexts is convincingly demonstrated in the best current research on state capacities. And we are about to examine yet another cluster of studies in which a fully relational approach to states and societies is even more essential.

States and Patterns of Politics

The previous section focused on the state as a set of organizations through which collectivities of officials may be able to formulate and implement distinctive strategies or policies. When the state comes up in current social scientific discourse, non-Marxists, at least, are usually referring to it in this sense: as an *actor* whose independent efforts may need to be taken more seriously than heretofore in accounting for policy making and social change. But there is another way to think about the sociopolitical impact of the state, an alternative frame of reference not often articulated but perhaps even more important than the view of the state as an actor. This second approach might be called "Tocquevillian," because Alexis de Tocqueville applied it masterfully in his studies *The Old Regime and the French Revolution* and *Democracy in America*.[58] In this perspective, states matter not simply because of the goal-oriented activities of state officials. They matter because their organizational configurations, along with their overall patterns of activity, affect political culture, encourage some kinds of group formation and collective political actions (but not others), and make possible the raising of certain political issues (but not others).

To be sure, the "strengths" or "weaknesses" of states as sites of more or less independent and effective official actions constitute a key aspect of the organizational configurations and overall patterns of activity at issue in this perspective. This second approach is entirely complementary to the ideas we explored in the previous section, but here the investigator's modus operandi is not the same. When the effects of states are explored from the Tocquevillian point of view, those effects are *not* traced by dissecting state strategies or policies and their possibilities for implementation. Instead, the investigator looks more macroscopically at the ways in which the structures and activities of states unintentionally influence the formation of groups and the political capacities, ideas, and demands of various sectors of society. Thus, much of Tocqueville's argument about the origins of the French Revolution dealt with the ways in which the French absolutist monarchy, through its institutional structure and policy practices, unintentionally undermined the prestige and political capacities of the aristocracy, provoked the peasantry and the urban Third Estate, and inspired the intelligentsia to launch abstract, rationalist broadsides against the status quo. Effects of the state permeated Tocqueville's argument, even though he said little about the activities and goals of the state officials themselves.

Comparative Studies of State Structures and Politics in Industrial-Capitalist Democracies

A good way to demonstrate the contemporary fruitfulness of such macroscopic explorations of the sociopolitical effects of states is to sketch some of the findings of comparative-historical scholars who have focused on differences among and within Western advanced industrial-capitalist nations. Analogous effects have been, or could be, found among other sets of countries – for example, among peripheral or "newly industrializing" capitalist nations or among the "state-socialist" countries – but the analytically relevant points would be similar. Thus, I shall confine myself to comparisons among the United States and some European nations, drawing on a number of works to sketch ideas about how the structures and activities of states affect political culture, group formation and collective political action, and the issue agendas of politics.

In a highly unusual and path-breaking essay for its decade, "The State as a Conceptual Variable," J. P. Nettl delineated a series of instutional and cultural differences in the "stateness" of the United States, Britain, and the continental European nations.[59] Some of his most telling contrasts referred to dimensions of political culture, that is, widely held ideas about the nature and locus of political power and notions about what can be attained in politics and how. In their essay entitled "Constitutionalism, Class, and the Limits of Choice in U.S. Foreign Policy," Ira Katznelson and Kenneth Prewitt apply and extend some of these ideas from Nettl.

Owing to the different historical paths their governmental systems have traversed, argued Nettl, continental Europeans think of "sovereignty" as residing in centralized administrative institutions; Britons focus on political parties in Parliament; and U.S. citizens refuse to designate any concrete body as sovereign, but instead attribute sovereignty to the law and the Constitution. In Europe, according to Nettl, the administrative order is instantly recognizable as an area of autonomous action, and both supporters and opponents of the existing order orient themselves to working through it as the agent of the public good. But in the United States, as Katznelson and Prewitt nicely spell out:

> The Constitution does not establish . . . [an administratively centralized] state that in turn manages the affairs of society toward some clear conception of the public welfare; rather, it established a political economy in which the public welfare is the aggregate of private preferences. . . . The United States is a government of legislation and litigation. . . . Politics becomes the struggle to translate social and economic interests into law. . . . *The political culture defines political power as getting a law passed.*
>
> Dissatisfaction most frequently takes the form of trying to force a new and more favorable interpretation of the Constitution. . . . Never in this endless shuffling does the Constitution itself become the target. Rather, constitutional principles legitimate claims for a fair share of "the American way of life," and constitutional interpretations and reinterpretations are the means for forcing reallocations.[60]

In short, various sorts of states not only conduct decision-making, coercive, and adjudicative activities in different ways, but also give rise to various conceptions of the meaning and methods of "politics" itself, conceptions that influence the behavior of all groups and classes in national societies.

The forms of collective action through which groups make political demands or through which political leaders seek to mobilize support are also partially shaped in relation to the structures and activities of states. This point has been richly established for Western countries by scholars dealing with causes and forms of social protest, with "corporatism" as governmentally institutionalized interest consultation, and with political parties as mediators between electorates and the conduct of state power.

Charles Tilly and his collaborators have investigated changing forms of violent and nonviolent collective protest in France and elsewhere in the West since the seventeenth century. In the process, they have pointed to many ways in which state structures, as well as the actions of state officials, affect the timing, the goals, and the forms of collective protest. Inexorable connections between war making and state making in early modern Europe meant, according to Tilly, that most "collective contention" in those days entailed attempts, especially by regional elites and local communities, to defend established rights against royal tax collectors and military recruiters.[61] Later, nationwide networks of middle- and working-class people in industrializing Britain created the innovative protest forms of the associational "social movement" through interactions with the parliamentary, legal, and selectively repressive practices of the British state.[62] Variations on social-movement "repertoires" of collective action, always adapted to the structures and practices of given states, also spread across many other modern nations. Many additional examples of state effects on collective action could be given from Tilly's work. For many years, he has been a powerful proponent of bringing the state back in to the analysis of social protest, an area of political sociology that was previously dominated by social systems and social psychological approaches.[63]

If studies of collective action are a perennial staple in sociology, studies of interest groups have a comparable standing in political science. Recently, as Suzanne Berger points out, students of Western European countries have ceased to view "interest groups as reflections of society." Instead, they find that "the timing and characteristics of state intervention" affect "not only organizational tactics and strategies," but "the content and definition of interest itself," with the result that each European nation, according to the historical sequence and forms of the state's social and economic interventions, has a distinctive configuration of interests active in politics.[64] In addition, students of interest groups in Western Europe have vigorously debated the causes and dynamics of "corporatist" patterns, in which interest groups exclusively representing given functional socioeconomic interests attain public status and the right to authoritative participation in national policy making. Some scholars have directly stressed that state initiatives create corporatist forms. Others, more skeptical of such a strong state-centered view, nevertheless analyze the myriad ways in which particular state structures and policies foster or undermine corporatist group representation.[65]

Key points along these lines are driven home when the United States is brought into the picture. In a provocative 1979 essay, Robert Salisbury asked, "Why No Corporatism in America?" and Graham K. Wilson followed up the query in 1982.[66] Both scholars agree that such basic (interrelated) features of the U.S. state structure as federalism, the importance of geographic units of representation, nonprogrammatic political parties, fragmented realms of administrative bureaucracy, and the importance of Congress and its specialized committees within the national government's system of divided sovereignty all encourage a proliferation of competing, narrowly specialized, and weakly disciplined interest groups. In short, little about the structure and operations of the American state renders corporatism politically feasible or credible, either for officials or for social groups. Even protest movements in the United States tend to follow issue-specialized and geographically fissiparous patterns. State structures, established interest groups, and oppositional groups all may mirror one another's forms of organization and scopes of purpose.

Along with interest groups, the most important and enduring forms of collective political action in the industrial-capitalist democracies are electorally competing political parties. In a series of brilliant comparative-historical essays, Martin Shefter demonstrates how such parties have come to operate either through patronage or through programmatic appeals to organized voter blocs.[67] Shefter argues that this depended in large part on the forms of state power in existence when the democratic suffrage was established in various nations. In Germany, for example, absolutist monarchs had established centralized administrative bureaucracies long before the advent of democratic elections. Vote-getting political parties, when they came into existence, could not offer the "spoils of office" to followers, because there was an established coalition (of public officials tied to upper and middle classes oriented to using university education as a route to state careers) behind keeping public bureaucracies free of party control. Thus, German political parties were forced to use ideological, programmatic appeals, ranging from communist or socialist to anti-Semitic and fascist.[68] In contrast, Shefter shows how the territorial unevenness of predemocratic central administration in Italy and the absence of an autonomous federal bureaucracy in nineteenth-century U.S. democracy allowed patronage-wielding political parties to colonize administrative arrangements in these countries, thereby determining that voters would be wooed with nonprogrammatic appeals, especially with patronage and other "distributive" allocations of publicly controlled resources.

The full scope of Shefter's work, which cannot be further summarized here, also covers Britain, France, and regional contrasts within the twentieth-century United States. With analytical consistency and vivid historical detail, Shefter shows the influence of evolving state administrative structures on the aims and organizational forms of the political parties that mediate between public offices, on the one hand, and socially rooted electorates, on the other. Unlike many students of voting and political parties, Shefter does not see parties merely as vehicles for expressing societal political preferences. He realizes that they are also organizations for claiming and using state authority, organizations that develop their own interests and persistent styles of work. Lines of determination run as much (or more) from state structures to party organizations to the content of electoral politics as they run from voter preferences to party platforms to state policies.

Structures of public administration and political party organizations, considered together, go a long way toward "selecting" the *kinds* of political issues that will come onto (or be kept off) a society's "political agenda." In his book on policy making in relation to air pollution in U.S. municipal politics, Matthew Crenson develops this argument in a manner that has implications beyond his own study.[69] Boss-run, patronage-oriented urban machines, Crenson argues, prefer to highlight political issues that create *divisible* benefits or costs to be allocated differentially in discrete bargains for support from particular businesses or geographic sets of voters. Air pollution controls, however, generate indivisible *collective* benefits, so machine governments and patronage-oriented parties will try to avoid considering the air pollution issue. Entire political agendas, Crenson maintains, may be dominated by similar types of issues: either mostly "collective" or mostly "specific"/distributional issues. This happens, in part, because the organizational needs of government and parties will call forth similar issues. It also happens because, once political consciousness and group mobilization are bent in one direction, people will tend to make further demands along the same lines. Once again, we see a dialectic between state and society, here influencing the basic issue content of politics, just as previously we have seen state–society interrelations at work in the shaping of political cultures and forms of collective action.

States and the Political Capacities of Social Classes

With so many aspects of politics related to nationally variable state structures, it should come as no surprise that the "classness" of politics also varies in relation to states, for the degree to which (and the forms in which) class interests are organized into national politics depends very much on the prevailing political culture, forms of collective action, and possibilities for raising and resolving broadly collective (societal or class) issues. Marxists may be right to argue that classes and class tensions are always present in industrial societies, but the political expression of class interests and conflicts is never automatic or economically determined. It depends on the capacities classes have for achieving consciousness, organization, and representation. Directly or indirectly, the structures and activities of states profoundly condition such class capacities. Thus, the classical wisdom of Marxian political sociology must be turned, if not on its head, then certainly on its side.

Writing in direct critical dialogue with Marx, Pierre Birnbaum argues that the contrasting ideologies and attitudes toward politics of the French and British working-class movements can be explained in state-centered terms.[70] According to Birnbaum, the centralized, bureaucratic French state, sharply differentiated from society, fostered anarchist or Marxist orientations and political militancy among French workers, whereas the centralized but less differentiated British "establishment" encouraged British workers and their leaders to favor parliamentary gradualism and private contractual wage bargaining.

Analogous arguments by Ira Katznelson in *City Trenches* and by Martin Shefter in an essay entitled "Trades Unions and Political Machines: The Organization and Disorganization of the American Working Class in the Late Nineteenth Century" point to the specifically state-centered factors that account for the cross-nationally very low political capacity of the U.S. industrial working class.[71] Democratization (in the form of universal suffrage for white men) occurred in the United States right at the start of capitalist industrialization. From the 1830s onward, electoral competition incorporated workers into a polity run, not by a national bureaucracy or "establishment," but by patronage-oriented political parties with strong roots in local communities. In contrast to what happened in many European nations, unions and workers in the United States did not have to ally themselves with political associations or parties fighting for the suffrage in opposition to politically privileged dominant classes and an autonomous administrative state. Common meanings and organizations did not bridge work and residence in America, and the early U.S. industrial working class experienced "politics" as the affair of strictly local groups organized on ethnic or racial lines by machine politicians. Work-place struggles were eventually taken over by bread-and-butter trade unions. "In this way," Katznelson concludes, "citizenship and its bases were given communal meaning separate from work relations. The segmented pattern of class understandings in the United States . . . was caused principally by features of the polity created by the operation of a federal constitutional system."[72]

State structures influence the capacities not only of subordinate but also of propertied classes. It is never enough simply to posit that dominant groups have a "class interest" in maintaining sociopolitical order or in continuing a course of economic development in ways congruent with their patterns of property ownership. Exactly how – even whether – order may be maintained and economic accumulation continued depends in significant part on existing state structures and the dominant-class political capacities that those structures help to shape. Thus, in my 1973 discussion of Barrington Moore's *Social Origins of Dictatorship and Democracy*, I argued that the "reformism" of key landed and bourgeois groups in nineteenth-century Britain was not simply a product of class economic interests. It was also a function of the complexly balanced vested political interests those groups had in decentralized forms of administration and repression and in parliamentary forms of political decision making.[73] Likewise, much of the argument in my *States and Social Revolutions* about causes of revolutionary transformations in certain agrarian states rests on a comparative analysis of the political capacities of landed upper classes as these were shaped by the structures and activities of monarchical bureaucratic states.[74]

Again, the point under discussion can be brought home to the United States. Along with the U.S. industrial working class, American capitalists lack the political capacity to pursue classwide interests in national politics. This is one of the reasons invoked by Susan and Norman Fainstein to explain the incoherence and ineffectiveness of contemporary U.S. policy responses to urban crises, which northwest European nations have handled more effectively, to the benefit of dominant and subordinate classes alike.[75] Historically, America's relatively weak, decentralized, and fragmented state structure, combined with early democratization and the absence of a politically unified working class, has encouraged and allowed U.S. capitalists to splinter along narrow interest lines and to adopt an antistate, laissez faire ideology.[76] Arguably, American business groups have often benefited from this situation. Yet American business interests have been recurrently vulnerable to reformist state interventions that they could not strongly influence or limit, given their political disunity or (as at the height of the New Deal) their estrangement from interventionist governmental agencies or administrations.[77] And American business has always found it difficult to provide consistent support for national initiatives that might benefit the economy as a whole.

Obviously, industrial workers and capitalists do not exhaust the social groups that figure in the politics of industrial democracies. Studies of the effects of state structures and policies on group interests and capacities have also done much to explain, in historical and comparative terms, the political involvements of farmers and small businesses. In addition, important new work is now examining relationships between state formation and the growth of modern "professions," as well as related concerns about the deployment of "expert" knowledge in public policy making.[78] Yet without surveying these literatures as well, the basic argument of this section has been sufficiently illustrated.

Politics in all of its dimensions is grounded not only in "society" or in "the economy" or in a "culture" – if any or all of these are considered separately from the organizational arrangements and activities of states. The meanings of public life and the collective forms through which groups become aware of political goals and work to attain them arise, not from societies alone, but at the meeting points of states and societies. Consequently, the formation, let alone the political capacities, of such apparently purely socioeconomic phenomena as interest groups and classes depends in significant measure on the structures and activities of the very states the social actors, in turn, seek to influence.

Conclusion

This essay has ranged widely – although, inevitably, selectively – over current research on states as actors and as institutional structures with effects in politics. Two alternative, though complementary, analytical strategies have been discussed for bringing the state back in to a prominent place in comparative and historical studies of social change, politics, and policy making. On the one hand, states may be viewed as organizations through which official collectivities may pursue distinctive goals, realizing them more or less effectively given the available state resources in relation to social settings. On the other hand, states may be viewed more macroscopically as configurations of organization and action that influence the meanings and methods of politics for all groups and classes in society.

Given the intellectual and historical trends surveyed in the introduction to this essay, there can now be little question whether states are to be taken seriously in social scientific explanations of a wide range of phenomena of long-standing interest. There remain, however, many theoretical and practical issues about how states and their effects are to be investigated. My programmatic conclusion is straightforward: Rather than become embroiled in a series of abstruse and abstract conceptual debates, let us proceed along the lines of the analytical strategies sketched here. With their help, we can carry through further comparative and historical investigations to develop middle-range generalizations about the roles of states in revolutions and reforms, about the social and economic policies pursued by states, and about the effects of states on political conflicts and agendas.

A new theoretical understanding of states in relation to social structures will likely emerge as such programs of comparative-historical research are carried forward. But this new understanding will almost certainly not resemble the grand systems theories of the structure–functionalists or neo-Marxists. As we bring the state back in to its proper central place in explanations of social change and politics, we shall be forced to respect the inherent historicity of sociopolitical structures, and we shall necessarily attend to the inescapable intertwinings of national-level developments with changing world historical contexts. We do not need a new or refurbished grand theory of "The State." Rather, we need solidly grounded and analytically sharp understandings of the causal regularities that underlie the histories of states, social structures, and transnational relations in the modern world.

Notes

This chapter is a revision of "Bringing the State Back In: False Leads and Promising Starts in Current Theories and Research," originally prepared for a Social Science Research Council conference entitled "States and Social Structures: Research Implications of Current Theories," held at Seven Springs Center, Mt. Kisco, New York, February 25–27, 1982. I benefited greatly from conference discussions. Subsequently, reactions from Pierre Birnbaum, David Easton, Harry Eckstein, Kenneth Finegold, and Eric Nordlinger also helped me to plan revisions of the conference paper, as did access to prepublication copies of Stephen Krasner's "Review Article: Approaches to the State: Alternative Conceptions and Historical Dynamics," *Comparative Politics* 16 (2) (January 1984), 223–46 and Roger Benjamin and Raymond

Duvall's "The Capitalist State in Context," forthcoming in *The Democratic State*, ed. R. Benjamin and S. Elkin (Lawrence: University of Kansas Press, 1985). Most of all, I am intellectually indebted to discussions and exchanges of memos with all of my fellow members of the 1982–83 Social Science Research Council Committee on States and Social Structures: Peter Evans, Albert Hirschman, Peter Katzenstein, Ira Katznelson, Stephen Krasner, Dietrich Rueschemeyer, and Charles Tilly.

1. Important examples include Alice Amsden, "Taiwan's Economic History: A Case of Etatism and a Challenge to Dependency Theory," *Modern China* 5 (1979): 341–80; Pranab Bardhan, "The State, Classes and Economic Growth in India," 1982–83 Radhakrishnan Memorial Lectures, All Souls College, Oxford; Douglas Bennett and Kenneth Sharpe, "Agenda Setting and Bargaining Power: The Mexican State versus Transnational Automobile Corporations," *World Politics* 32 (1979): 57–89; Peter B. Evans, *Dependent Development: The Alliance of Multinational, State, and Local Capital in Brazil* (Princeton, N.J.: Princeton University Press, 1979); Nora Hamilton, *The Limits of State Autonomy: Post-Revolutionary Mexico* (Princeton, N.J.: Princeton University Press, 1982); Steven Langdon, *Multinational Corporations in the Political Economy of Kenya* (London: Macmillan, 1981); Hyun-chin Lim, "Dependent Development in the World System: The Case of South Korea, 1963–1979" (Ph.D. diss., Harvard University, 1982); Richard Sklar, *Corporate Power in an African State: The Political Impact of Multinational Mining Companies in Zambia* (Berkeley: University of California Press, 1975); Alfred Stepan, *The State and Society: Peru in Comparative Perspective* (Princeton, N.J.: Princeton University Press, 1978); and Ellen Kay Trimberger, *Revolution from Above: Military Bureaucrats and Development in Japan, Turkey, Egypt and Peru* (New Brunswick, N.J.: Transaction Books, 1978).

2. Important examples include Douglas Ashford, *British Dogmatism and French Pragmatism: Central-Local Policymaking in the Modern Welfare State* (London: Allen & Unwin, 1983); Pierre Birnbaum, *The Heights of Power: An Essay on the Power Elite in France*, trans. Arthur Goldhammer (Chicago: University of Chicago Press, 1982); David Cameron, "The Expansion of the Public Economy: A Comparative Analysis," *American Political Science Review* 72 (1978): 1243–61; Kenneth Dyson and Stephen Wilks, eds., *Industrial Crisis: A Comparative Study of the State and Industry* (New York: St. Martin's Press, 1983); Peter Hall, "Policy Innovation and the Structure of the State: The Politics–Administration Nexus in France and Britain," *Annals of the American Academy of Political and Social Science* 466 (1983): 43–59; Peter A. Hall, "Patterns of Economic Policy among the European States: An Organizational Approach," in *The State in Capitalist Europe*, ed. Stephen Bornstein, David Held, and Joel Krieger (London: Allen & Unwin, forthcoming); Hugh Heclo, *Modern Social Politics in Britain and Sweden* (New Haven, Conn.: Yale University Press, 1974); Chalmers Johnson, *MITI and the Japanese Miracle: The Growth of Industrial Policy, 1925–1975* (Stanford, Calif.: Stanford University Press, 1982); Peter Katzenstein, ed., *Between Power and Plenty: Foreign Economic Policies of Advanced Industrial States* (Madison: University of Wisconsin Press, 1978); Steven Kelman, *Regulating America, Regulating Sweden: A Comparative Study of Occupational Health and Safety Policy* (Cambridge, Mass.: MIT Press, 1981); Stephen D. Krasner, *Defending the National Interest: Raw Materials Investments and U.S. Foreign Policy* (Princeton, N.J.: Princeton University Press, 1978); Theodore J. Lowi, "Public Policy and Bureaucracy in the United States and France," in *Comparing Public Policies: New Concepts and Methods*, ed.

Douglas E. Ashford, vol. 4 of *Sage Yearbooks in Politics and Public Policy* (Beverly Hills, Calif.: Sage, 1978), pp. 177–96; Leo Panitch, ed., *The Canadian State: Political Economy and Political Power* (Toronto: University of Toronto Press, 1977); Theda Skocpol and John Ikenberry, "The Political Formation of the American Welfare State in Historical and Comparative Perspective," *Comparative Social Research* 6 (1983): 87–148; S. Tolliday and J. Zeitlin, eds., *Shop Floor Bargaining and the State: Historical And Comparative Perspectives* (Cambridge and New York: Cambridge University Press, 1984); and John Zysman, *Political Strategies for Industrial Order: State, Market and Industry in France* (Berkeley: University of California Press, 1977).

3. Important examples include Michael Adas, "From Avoidance to Confrontation: Peasant Protest in Pre-Colonial and Colonial Southeast Asia," *Comparative Studies in Society and History* 23 (1981): 217–47; Betrand Badie and Pierre Birnbaum, *The Sociology of the State*, trans. Arthur Goldhammer (Chicago: University of Chicago Press, 1983); Pierre Birnbaum, "States, Ideologies, and Collective Action in Western Europe," *Social Science Journal* 32 (1980): 671–86; Jose Murilo de Carvalho, "Political Elites and State Building: The Case of Nineteenth-Century Brazil," *Comparative Studies in Society and History* 24 (1981): 378–99; Mounira Charrad, "Women and the State: A Comparative Study of Politics, Law, and the Family in Tunisia, Algeria, and Morocco" (Ph.D. diss., Harvard University, 1980); Daniel Chirot, *Social Change in a Peripheral Society: The Creation of a Balkan Colony* (New York: Academic Press, 1976); Stanley B. Greenberg, *Race and State in Capitalist Development* (New Haven, Conn.: Yale University Press, 1980); Michael Hechter, *Internal Colonialism: The Celtic Fringe in British National Development, 1536–1966* (Berkeley: University of California Press, 1975); Ira Katznelson, *City Trenches: Urban Politics and the Patterning of Class in the United States* (New York: Pantheon Books, 1981); Joel S. Migdal, *Peasants, Politics, and Revolution: Pressures toward Political and Social Change in the Third World* (Princeton, N. J.: Princeton University Press, 1974); Gianfranco Poggi, *The Development of the Modern State: A Sociological Introduction* (Stanford, Calif.: Stanford University Press, 1978); Joseph Rothschild, *Ethnopolitics: A Conceptual Framework* (New York: Columbia University Press, 1981); Theda Skocpol, *States and Social Revolutions: A Comparative Analysis of France, Russia, and China* (Cambridge and New York: Cambridge University Press, 1979); Stephen Skowronek, *Building a New American State: The Expansion of National Administrative Capacities, 1877–1920* (Cambridge and New York: Cambridge University Press, 1982); Ezra N. Suleiman, *Politics, Power, and Bureaucracy in France: The Administrative Elite* (Princeton, N. J.: Princeton University Press, 1974); Charles Tilly, ed., *The Formation of National States in Western Europe*, Studies in Political Development no. 8 (Princeton, N. J.: Princeton University Press, 1975); and Charles Tilly, *The Contentious French* (Cambridge: Harvard University Press, forthcoming).

4. See especially Douglass C. North, "A Framework for Analyzing the State in Economic History," *Explorations in Economic History* 16 (1979): 249–59; Douglass C. North, *Structure and Change in Economic History* (New York: Norton, 1981); and Robert H. Bates, *Markets and States in Tropical Africa: The Political Basis of Agricultural Policies* (Berkeley: University of California Press, 1981).

5. See especially Clifford Geertz, *Negara: The Theatre State in Nineteenth-Century Bali* (Princeton, N. J.: Princeton University Press, 1980).

6. Sociologists may recognize that the title of this chapter echoes the title of George

C. Homans's 1964 presidential address to the American Sociological Association, "Bringing Men Back In." Of course, the subject matters are completely different, but there is an affinity of aspiration for explanations built on propositions about the activities of concrete groups. This stands in contrast to the application of analytical conceptual abstractions characteristic of certain structure–functionalist or neo-Marxist "theories."

7. Among the most important exceptions were Samuel Huntington's path-breaking state-centered book, *Political Order and Changing Societies* (New Haven, Conn.: Yale University Press, 1968); Morris Janowitz's many explorations of state–society relationships, as in *The Military in the Political Development of New Nations* (Chicago: University of Chicago Press, 1964), and *Social Control of the Welfare State* (Chicago: University of Chicago Press, 1976); and James Q. Wilson's conceptually acute probings in *Political Organizations* (New York: Basic Books, 1973). In his many works in political sociology, Seymour Martin Lipset has always remained sensitive to the effects of various institutional structures of government representation. In addition, Reinhard Bendix consistently developed a state-centered Weberian approach to political regimes as a critical counterpoint to structure–functionalist developmentalism, and S. N. Eisenstadt and Stein Rokkan elaborated creative syntheses of functionalist and Weberian modes of comparative political analysis.

8. For clear paradigmatic statements, see Gabriel Almond, "A Developmental Approach to Political Systems," *World Politics* 16 (1965): 183–214; Gabriel Almond and James S. Coleman, eds., *The Politics of Developing Areas* (Princeton, N. J.: Princeton University Press, 1960); Gabriel Almond and G. Bingham Powell, Jr., *Comparative Politics: A Developmental Approach* (Boston: Little, Brown, 1966); David Easton, "An Approach to the Analysis of Political Systems," *World Politics* 9 (1957): 383–400; and David B. Truman, *The Governmental Process* (New York: Knopf, 1951).

9. Eric A. Nordlinger's *On the Autonomy of the Democratic State* (Cambridge: Harvard University Press, 1981) has stretched pluralist premises to their conceptual limits in order to encompass the possibility of autonomous actions by elected politicians or administrative officials. Tellingly, Nordlinger defines "state autonomy" purely in terms of the conscious preferences of public officials, who are said to be acting autonomously as long as they are not deliberately giving in to demands by societal actors. By insisting that public officials have wants and politically relevant resources, just as voters, economic elites, and organized interest groups do, Nordlinger simply gives officials the same dignity that all actors have in the fluid "political process" posited by pluralism. State autonomy, Nordlinger in effect says, is simply the creative exercise of political leadership. No matter what the organization or capacities of the state, any public official at any time is, by definition, in a position to do this. In my view, the value of Nordlinger's book lies, not in this rather inspid general conclusion, but in the researchable hypotheses about variations in state autonomy that one might derive from some of the typologies it offers.

10. See Robert Dahl, *Who Governs?* (New Haven, Conn.: Yale University Press, 1961); Raymond E. Wolfinger, *The Politics of Progress* (Englewood Cliffs, N. J.: Prentice-Hall, 1974); and Nelson W. Polsby, *Community Power and Political Theory* (New Haven, Conn.: Yale University Press, 1961). In thinking about the missing analytical elements in these studies, I have benefited from Geoffrey

Fougere's critical discussion in "The Structure of Government and the Organization of Politics: A Polity Centered Approach" (Department of Sociology, Harvard University, September 1978).

11. Graham Allison, *Essence of Decision: Explaining the Cuban Missile Crisis* (Boston: Little, Brown, 1971); and Morton S. Halperin, *Bureaucratic Politics and Foreign Policy* (Washington, D.C.: The Brookings Institution, 1971).

12. I have benefited from Stephen Krasner's discussion of the bureaucratic politics perspective in *Defending the National Interest*, p. 27. Krasner's own book shows the difference it makes to take a more macroscopic, historical, and state-centered approach.

13. See Leonard Binder, James S. Coleman, Joseph La Palombara, Lucian W. Pye, Sidney Verba, and Myron Weiner, *Crises and Sequences in Political Development*, Studies in Political Development no. 7 (Princeton, N. J.: Princeton University Press, 1971); Gabriel Almond, Scott C. Flanagan, and Robert J. Mundt, *Crisis, Choice, and Change: Historical Studies of Political Development* (Boston: Little, Brown, 1973); Tilly, ed., *Formation of National States*; and Raymond Grew, ed., *Crises of Political Development in Europe and the United States*, Studies in Political Development no. 9 (Princeton, N. J.: Princeton University Press, 1978). The Tilly and Grew volumes openly criticize the theoretical ideas advocated by the Committee on Comparative Politics that sponsored these projects, and Tilly calls for the kind of approach now embodied in the mission of the Committee on States and Social Structures.

14. A sampling of the most important neo-Marxist works includes Perry Anderson, *Passages from Antiquity to Feudalism* (London: New Left Books, 1974) and *Lineages of the Absolutist State* (London: New Left Books, 1974); Gösta Esping-Andersen, Roger Friedland, and Erik Olin Wright, "Modes of Class Struggle and the Capitalist State," *Kapitalistate*, no. 4–5 (1976): 186–220; John Holloway and Simon Picciotto, eds., *State and Capital: A Marxist Debate* (London: Arnold, 1978); Ralph Miliband, *The State in Capitalist Society* (New York: Basic Books, 1969); Nicos Poulantzas, *Political Power and Social Classes*, trans. Timothy O'Hagen (London: New Left Books, 1973); Claus Offe, "Structural Problems of the Capitalist State," *German Political Studies* 1 (1974): 31–57; Göran Therborn, *What Does the Ruling Class Do When It Rules?* (London: New Left Books, 1978); and Immanuel Wallerstein, *The Modern World System*, vols. 1 and 2 (New York: Academic Press, 1974, 1980).

Some excellent overviews of the neo-Marxist debates are those of Martin Carnoy, *The State and Political Theory* (Princeton, N. J.: Princeton University Press, 1984); David A. Gold, Clarence Y. H. Lo, and Erik Olin Wright, "Recent Developments in Marxist Theories of the Capitalist State," *Monthly Review* 27 (1975), no. 5: 29–43; no. 6: 36–51; Bob Jessop, "Recent Theories of the Capitalist State," *Cambridge Journal of Economics* 1 (1977): 353–73; Bob Jessop, *The Capitalist State: Marxist Theories and Methods* (New York: New York University Press, 1982); and Ralph Miliband, *Marxism and Politics* (Oxford: Oxford University Press, 1977).

15. Of all those engaged in the neo-Marxist debates, Fred Block goes the farthest toward treating states as truly autonomous actors. See his "The Ruling Class Does Not Rule: Notes on the Marxist Theory of the State," *Socialist Revolution* 7 (1977): 6–28; and "Beyond Relative Autonomy," in *The Socialist Register 1980*, ed. Ralph Miliband and John Saville (London: Merlin Press, 1980), pp. 227–42. For congruent positions, see also Trimberger, *Revolution from Above*, as well as

my own *States and Social Revolutions* (Cambridge and New York: Cambridge University Press, 1979) and "Political Response to Capitalist Crisis: Neo-Marxist Theories of the State and the Case of the New Deal," *Politics and Society* 10 (1980): 155–201. Block and I are jointly criticized for overemphasizing state autonomy in Carnoy, *State and Political Theory*, chap. 8; and Block, Trimberger, and I are all critically discussed in Ralph Miliband, "State Power and Class Interests," *New Left Review*, no. 138 (1983): 57–68.

16. The scope of many neo-Marxist propositions about states makes them more applicable/testable in comparisons *across* modes of production, rather than across nations within capitalism. Therborn, in *Ruling Class*, is one of the few theorists to attempt such cross-mode comparisons, however.

17. I do not mean to imply pure continuity. Around the World Wars and during the 1930s depression, when both British and U.S. hegemony faltered, there were bursts of more state-centered theorizing, including such works as Harold Lasswell's "The Garrison State," *American Journal of Sociology* 46 (1941): 455–68; and Karl Polanyi's *The Great Transformation* (Boston: Beacon Press, 1957; originally 1944).

18. For some suggestive treatments, see Stephen D. Krasner, "United States Commercial and Monetary Policy: Unravelling the Paradox of External Strength and Internal Weakness," in *Between Power and Plenty*, ed. Katzenstein, pp. 51–87; Stephen Blank, "Britain: The Politics of Foreign Economic Policy, the Domestic Economy, and the Problems of Pluralistic Stagnation," in *Between Power and Plenty*, ed. Katzenstein, pp. 89–138; Andrew Martin, "Political Constraints on Economic Strategies in Advanced Industrial Societies," *Comparative Political Studies* 10 (1977): 323–54; Paul M. Sacks, "State Structure and the Asymmetrical Society: An Approach to Public Policy in Britain," *Comparative Politics* 12 (1980): 349–76; and Dyson and Wilks, eds., *Industrial Crisis*.

19. For Max Weber's principal writings on states, see *Economy and Society*, ed. Guenther Roth and Claus Wittich (New York: Bedminster Press, 1968; originally 1922), vol. 2, chap. 9; vol. 3, chaps. 10–13.

20. Stepan, *State and Society*, p. xii.

21. See *The Historical Essays of Otto Hintze*, ed. Felix Gilbert (New York: Oxford University Press, 1975; originally 1897–1932).

22. For discussion of the most important neopluralist theory of state autonomy, see note 9. The works by Poulantzas and Offe cited in note 14 represent important neo-Marxist theories of state autonomy. Poulantzas's approach is ultimately very frustrating because he simply posits the "relative autonomy of the capitalist state" as a necessary feature of the capitalist mode of production as such. Poulantzas insists that the state is "relatively autonomous" regardless of varying empirical ties between state organizations and the capitalist class, and at the same time he posits that the state must invariably function to stabilize the capitalist system as a whole.

23. Stepan, *State and Society*, chaps. 3 and 4. See also Alfred Stepan, "The New Professionalism of Internal Warfare and Military Role Expansion," in *Authoritarian Brazil*, ed. A. Stepan (New Haven, Conn.: Yale University Press, 1973), pp. 47–65.

24. Trimberger, *Revolution from Above*.

25. Ibid., p. 4.

26. Ibid., p. 5.

27. Thus, in commenting on Stepan's work, Trimberger argues that he could have

explained the repressive and "exclusionary" nature of the Brazilian coup (in contrast to Peru's "inclusionary" reforms, which included mass political mobilization and expropriation of hacienda landlords) by focusing on the Brazilian military's ties to Brazilian and multinational capitalists. In fact, Stepan does report ("The New Professionalism," p. 54) that Brazilian military professionals received their training alongside elite civilians, including industrialists, bankers, and commercial elites, who also attended the Superior War College of Brazil in the period before 1964.

28. Trimberger's work thus speaks to the problems with Nicos Poulantzas's theory discussed in note 22.

29. For France, there is an especially rich literature on state autonomy, its consequences and its limits. I am deliberately leaving it aside here, because France is such an obvious case for the application of ideas about state autonomy. See the works, however, by Birnbaum, Hall, Suleiman, and Zysman cited in notes 2 and 3, along with Stephen Cohen, *Modern Capitalist Planning: The French Experience* (Berkeley: University of California Press, 1976); and Richard F. Kuisel, *Capitalism and the State in Modern France: Renovation and Economic Management in the Twentieth Century* (Cambridge and New York: Cambridge University Press, 1981).

30. Heclo, *Modern Social Politics.*

31. Ibid., p. 305.

32. Ibid., pp. 305–6, 303.

33. Krasner, *Defending the National Interest.*

34. Ibid., p. 11.

35. See also Krasner, "United States Commercial and Monetary Policy, pp. 51–87.

36. Thus, Krasner has the most difficulty in distinguishing his argument for "state autonomy" from the structural Marxist perspective according to which the state acts for the class interests of capital as a whole. His solution, to stress "nonrational" ideological objectives of state policy as evidence against the class-interest argument, does not strike me as being very convincing. Could an imperialist ideology not be evidence of class consciousness as well as of state purpose: One might stress, instead, the perceived geopolitical "interests" at work in U.S. interventions abroad. "Free-world" justifications for such interventions are not obviously irrational, given certain understandings of U.S. geopolitical interests.

37. J. P. Nettl, "The State as a Conceptual Variable," *World Politics* 20 (1968), 563–64.

38. Kenneth Finegold and Theda Skocpol, "Capitalists, Farmers, and Workers in the New Deal – The Ironies of Government Intervention" (Paper presented at the annual meeting of the American Political Science Association, Washington, D.C., August 31, 1980). Part of this paper was subsequently published as Theda Skocpol and Kenneth Finegold, "State Capacity and Economic Intervention in the Early New Deal," *Political Science Quarterly* 97 (1982): 255–78.

39. Skocpol and Finegold, "State Capacity," p. 271.

40. In contrasting ways, both Krasner's *Defending the National Interest* and Poulantzas's *Political Power and Social Classes* exemplify this point.

41. Or perhaps one should say that any state or state-building movement preoccupied with sheer administrative–military control will, at best, only be able (as well as likely) to implement policies connected to that overriding goal. This

principle is a good guide to understanding many of the social changes that accompany state-building struggles during revolutionary interregnums.

42. See Tilly, ed., *Formation of National States;* Michael Mann, "State and Society, 1130–1815: An Analysis of English State Finances," *Political Power and Social Theory* (Greenwich, Conn.: JAI Press, 1980), vol. 1, pp. 165–208; and Stephen Skowronek, *Building a New American State: The Expansion of National Administrative Capacities* (Cambridge and New York: Cambridge University Press, 1982).

43. See Bernard Silberman's important comparative-historical work on alternative modes of state bureaucratization in relation to processes of professionalization: "State Bureaucratization: A Comparative Analysis" (Department of Political Science, the University of Chicago, 1982).

44. Windfall revenues from international oil sales, for example, can render states *both* more autonomous from societal controls and, because social roots and political pacts are weak, more vulnerable in moments of crisis. I argue along these lines in "Rentier State and Shi'a Islam in the Iranian Revolution," *Theory and Society* 11 (1982): 265–83. The Joint Committee on the Near and Middle East of the American Council of Learned Societies and the Social Science Research Council currently has a project entitled "Social Change in Arab Oil-Producing Societies" that is investigating the impact of oil revenues on state–society relationships.

45. See Robert E. Wood, "Foreign Aid and the Capitalist State in Underdeveloped Countries," *Politics and Society* 10(1) (1980): 1–34. Wood's essay primarily documents and discusses the anti-state-building effects of most foreign aid, but it also notes that "the 'overdeveloped' military institutions fostered by aid can provide a springboard for statist experimentation unintended by aid donors" (p. 34). Taiwan and South Korea would both seem to be good examples of this.

46. See John A. Dunn, Jr., "The Importance of Being Earmarked: Transport Policy and Highway Finance in Great Britain and the United States," *Comparative Studies in Society and History* 20(1) (1978): 29–53.

47. For "classic" statements on the social analysis of state finances, see especially Lorenz von Stein, "On Taxation," and Rudolf Goldscheid, "A Sociological Approach to Problems of Public Finance," both in *Classics in the Theory of Public Finance,* ed. Richard A. Musgrave and Alan T. Peacock (New York: Macmillan, 1958), pp. 202–13 and 28–36, respectively.

48. Krasner, *Defending the National Interest,* p. 58.

49. Ibid.

50. Ira Katznelson and Kenneth Prewitt, "Constitutionalism, Class, and the Limits of Choice in U.S. Foreign Policy," in *Capitalism and the State in U.S.–Latin American Relations,* ed. Richard Fagen (Stanford, Calif.: Stanford University Press, 1979), p. 38.

51. Stepan, *State and Society,* chaps. 5–8.

52. This concept is discussed by Peter Katzenstein in *Between Power and Plenty,* pp. 16, 297–98.

53. Susan S. and Norman I. Fainstein, "National Policy and Urban Development," *Social Problems* 26 (1978): 125–46; see especially pp. 140–41.

54. Katzenstein, ed., *Between Power and Plenty.*

55. Krasner, *Defending the National Interest,* especially parts 2 and 3.

56. Stepan, *State and Society,* chap. 7.

57. Katzenstein, ed., *Between Power and Plenty,* p. 19.

58. I am indebted to Jeff Weintraub for pointing out the affinities of this second approach to Tocqueville's political sociology.
59. Nettl, "The State as a Conceptual Variable," pp. 559–92. A recent work pursuing related issues is Kenneth Dyson's *The State Tradition in Western Europe: A Study of an Idea and Institution* (New York: Oxford University Press, 1980).
60. Ira Katznelson and Kenneth Prewitt, "Limits of Choice," in *Capitalism and the State*, ed. Fagen, pp. 31–33.
61. Charles Tilly, *As Sociology Meets History* (New York: Academic Press, 1981), pp. 109–44.
62. Ibid., pp. 145–78.
63. For an overview of Tilly's approach to collective action in critical response to earlier sociological approaches, see *From Mobilization to Revolution* (Reading, Mass.: Addison-Wesley, 1978).
64. Suzanne Berger, "Interest Groups and the Governability of European Society," *Items* (Newsletter of the Social Science Research Council) 35 (1981): 66–67.
65. See Suzanne Berger, ed., *Organizing Interests in Western Europe: Pluralism, Corporatism, and the Transformation of Politics* (Cambridge and New York: Cambridge University Press, 1981); Philippe C. Schmitter and Gerhard Lehmbruch, eds., *Trends toward Corporatist Intermediation*, vol. 1 of *Contemporary Political Sociology* (Beverly Hills, Calif.: Sage, 1979), and Gerhard Lehmbruch and Philippe C. Schmitter, eds., *Patterns of Corporatist Policy-Making*, vol. 7 of *Modern Politics Series* (Beverly Hills, Calif.: Sage, 1982).
66. Robert H. Salisbury, "Why No Corporatism in America?" in *Corporatist Intermediation*, ed. Schmitter and Lehmbruch, pp. 213–30; and Graham K. Wilson, "Why Is There No Corporatism in the United States?," in *Corporatist Policy-Making*, ed. Lehmbruch and Schmitter, pp. 219–36.
67. See Martin Shefter's "Party and Patronage: Germany, England, and Italy," *Politics and Society* 7 (1977): 403–51; "Party, Bureaucracy, and Political Change in the United States," in *The Development of Political Parties: Patterns of Evolution and Decay*, ed. Louis Maisel and Joseph Cooper, vol. 4 of *Sage Electoral Studies Yearbook* (Beverly Hills, Calif.: Sage, 1979), pp. 211–65, and "Regional Receptivity to Reform: The Legacy of the Progressive Era," *Political Science Quarterly* 98 (1983): 459–83.
68. In fact, Shefter shows ("Party and Patronage," p. 428) that parties in the Weimar Republic that might have preferred to use patronage appeals to garner peasant votes were prodded into ideological appeals because bureaucratic autonomy was so great. Thus, they resorted to anti-Semitic and nationalist "ideas" to appeal to the peasantry, a class that is often supposed to be inherently oriented to patronage appeals.
69. Matthew Crenson, *The Un-Politics of Air Pollution: A Study of Non-Decisionmaking in the Cities* (Baltimore, Md.: Johns Hopkins University Press, 1971), especially chaps. 5 and 6.
70. Pierre Birnbaum, "States, Ideologies and Collective Action in Western Europe," *International Social Science Journal* 32 (1980): 671–86.
71. Katznelson, *City Trenches*; and Martin Shefter, "Trades Unions and Political Machines: The Organization and Disorganization of the American Working Class in the Late Nineteenth Century," forthcoming in *Working Class Formation: Nineteenth Century Patterns in Western Europe and the United States*, ed. Ira Katznelson and Aristide Zolberg (Princeton, N. J.: Princeton University Press).

72. Katznelson and Prewitt, "Limits of Choice," p. 30.
73. Theda Skocpol, "A Critical Review of Barrington Moore's Social Origins of Dictatorship and Democracy," *Politics and Society* 4 (1973): 1–34.
74. Skocpol, *States and Social Revolutions*.
75. Fainstein and Fainstein, "National Policy and Urban Development."
76. Ibid., pp. 39–40; and David Vogel, "Why Businessmen Distrust Their State: The Political Consciousness of American Corporate Executives," *British Journal of Political Science* 8 (1978): 45–78.
77. See David Vogel, "The 'New' Social Regulation in Historical and Comparative Perspective," in *Regulation in Perspective*, ed. Thomas McGraw (Cambridge: Harvard University Press, 1981), pp. 155–85.
78. See Gerald L. Geison, ed., *Professions and the French State, 1700–1900* (Philadelphia: University of Pennsylvania Press, 1984); Arnold J. Heidenheimer, "Professions, the State, and the Polic(e)y Connection: How Concepts and Terms Evolved over Time and across Language Boundaries" (Paper presented at a panel, Professions, Public Policy and the State, Twelfth World Congress, International Political Science Association, Rio de Janeiro, Brazil, August 12, 1982); Terry Johnson, "The State and the Professions: Peculiarities of the British," in *Social Class and the Division of Labour*, ed. Anthony Giddens and Gavin Mackenzie (Cambridge and New York: Cambridge University Press, 1982), pp. 186–20; Dietrich Rueschemeyer, *Lawyers and Their Society: A Comparative Study of the Legal Profession in Germany and the United States* (Cambridge: Harvard University Press, 1973); Dietrich Rueschemeyer, "Professional Autonomy and the Social Control of Expertise," in *The Sociology of the Professions*, ed. R. Dingwall and P. Lewis (London: Macmillan, 1983); Bernard Silberman, "State Bureaucratization"; and Deborah A. Stone, *The Limits to Professional Power: National Health Care in the Federal Republic of Germany* (Chicago: University of Chicago Press, 1980).

Part I

States as Promoters of Economic Development and Social Redistribution

Modern national states have taken on tasks ranging from war making to the provision of welfare services, and they have purposefully or unintentionally reshaped many aspects of their social surroundings. Yet interventions into economic processes have been the kind of state activities most fascinating to modern social scientists from Adam Smith to contemporary neo-Marxists. Again and again social scientists have asked how, and to what effect, states influence market and class relations at regional, national, and global levels.

All too often, however, discussions of "the state" in relation to "the economy" have been distracted from the difficult business of explaining historical and cross-national variations. This has happened in one or both of two ways. In the first place, much writing about the modern state has been normatively preoccupied with what it should or should not do – above all, what it should or should not do in or "to" the "free market." When analytical rather than normative concerns have emerged, moreover, scholars have repeatedly resorted to very abstract theoretical models that derive transhistorical logics of state intervention, or abstention, from functional requisites of "the market" or of "capital accumulation."

Nevertheless, some scholars have proceeded analytically rather than primarily normatively, and among those, some have examined the state's role in economic development in historically grounded ways, with sensitivity to various institutional forms and social effects. This kind of scholarship has focused especially on the contributions of states to the original capitalist industrialization of Europe and North America. The essays in this part of *Bringing the State Back In* draw many conceptual insights from such giants of this literature as Alexander Gerschenkron, Barrington Moore, Jr., and Karl Polanyi; yet they focus on substantive questions of more contemporary reference than European industrialization. They reflect the recent growth of social scientific interest in Third World economic development and in the dynamics of Keynesian macroeconomic management in the advanced industrial democracies.

State interventions to promote agricultural development and industrialization in what are often called the "newly industrializing nations" of
the twentieth-century Third World are the focus of the essay by Dietrich
Rueschemeyer and Peter Evans and of the essay by Alice Amsden. In
"The State and Economic Transformation" Rueschemeyer and Evans offer many hypotheses and heuristic questions about conditions favorable
and unfavorable to "state autonomy" and to "state capacities" for furthering economic transformations. To shift attention away from the problematic issue of state action versus market functioning – an issue that has
often dominated normative and abstract theoretical discussions of the
state – Rueschemeyer and Evans zero in on concrete aspects of state bureaucracies and on relationships between states and dominant social
classes. Taken together, such patterns may help to explain variations in
the effectiveness with which Third World national states have pursued
capital accumulation and associated social redistributions.

Rueschemeyer and Evans sensitize us to cross-cutting and contradictory tendencies that may operate simultaneously or in sequence, both to
further and to undercut state capacities. For example, states often need,
at once, centralized policy coordination and decentralized capacities for
gathering information and pursuing policy goals in disparate concrete
settings. The effectiveness of states that have such contradictory needs
will depend on temporally and nationally varying unstable "solutions" to
the enduringly intractable dilemma of balancing opposed tendencies.
Rueschemeyer and Evans repeatedly pose such dilemmas and sketch alternative ways in which state structures and state ties to dominant
classes may condition ways of handling them. They illustrate their conceptual points with examples ranging from the Tanzanian state's ineffectual efforts to increase agricultural productivity to more and less successful state-owned economic enterprises in several Latin American countries
and in Taiwan.

In "The State and Taiwan's Economic Development," Alice Amsden
also has broad comparative insights to offer about the conditions for effective state economic interventions throughout the Third World, but her
essay primarily probes in depth one special case of remarkably successful
recent economic development. What features of the structure, history,
social context, and geopolitical circumstances of the Taiwanese state, she
asks, can help us to understand not only Taiwan's "economic miracle"
since the 1960s, but also the occurrence of this miracle under the auspices
of a regime dominated by unusually conquest-oriented militarists? How
could a state ruled by Mainland Chinese dedicated to autarkic self-sufficiency and the accumulation of arms, soldiers, and foreign support to retake the Mainland from the Communists end up using state interventions to encourage export-led capitalist industrialization?

As it turns out in Amsden's account, some of the economically effective measures taken by the state in Taiwan were possible precisely because a conquest state had more autonomy from preexisting dominant
agrarian interests than most Third World states normally have. Yet she
shows that other state-sponsored measures favoring economic growth in
Taiwan were stumbled into or devised only as changing international cir-

cumstances and domestic economic improvements "weaned" the Guomindang regime away from some (not all) of its militaristic goals and organizational features.

That states normally play very active roles in promoting economic development in the contemporary Third World tends to be taken for granted, even by many professional economists. For the established industrial-capitalist nations, however, ever since the heyday of laissez faire economics in the nineteenth century, many kinds of state interventions have been considered unnecessary or inappropriate. This was especially true before the 1930s in the Anglo-American world and in the areas of the world economy under Anglo-American influence. And the precepts of laissez faire economics may even now be reemerging in the same centers, as the "Keynesian era" seems to be drawing to a close, or at least coming to a fundamental watershed, in the advanced industrial nations. Yet the "Keynesian era" since the 1930s has been a phase of Western industrial capitalism in which state activism in relation to economic growth and associated social distribution has been both expected and celebrated. This has been true even though the kinds of state interventions in question are distinct from many of those, such as state-owned enterprises or enforced agrarian land reforms, that Third World states have used to try to facilitate economic development.

Keynesian economics, like the classical liberal paradigms that preceded it, looks to private business and market dynamics as the mainsprings of economic growth. Still, the "Keynesian revolution" in public policy making and in academic economics was remarkable for the explicit rationale it offered for deliberate fiscal and monetary interventions by public authorities. National state officials – advised, of course, by economic experts in or out of governmental employ – have been theoretically authorized to coordinate their politically necessary concern about maintaining employment with new roles for government in ensuring the proper parameters for steady capitalist economic growth. Keynesian policy makers have been enjoined to deploy or develop the capacities to monitor national economic aggregates and to devise strategies for adjusting public spending, tax levels, and monetary regulations in the pursuit of national economic growth accompanied by maximal employment.

The essay by Margaret Weir and Theda Skocpol examines the historical origins of Keynesian-style macroeconomic interventions in capitalist-industrial democracies and pays careful attention to some of the cross-national variations in the timing and form by which such strategies were adopted. Why was Sweden rather than Britain the first industrial democracy to adopt deficit-financed public works as a deliberate way of simultaneously pursuing goals of reemployment and national economic recovery in the Great Depression? And why, despite overall similarities in their domestic reforms during the 1930s, did Sweden adopt "social Keynesianism," melding active macroeconomic management with high levels of public spending for social welfare purposes, whereas the United States ended up with "commercial Keynesianism," which de-emphasized public spending in favor of tax cuts and "automatic stabilizers"? To answer these questions, Weir and Skocpol analyze state structures and public "policy legacies" (that is, patterns of prior government intervention), arguing that these influenced both official responses to the economic crisis of the 1930s and the political demands for such responses formulated by social groups and political parties.

The three essays of this part build on (and also extend into more complex sets of issues) some of the analytical strategies already surveyed in Chapter 1. They deal not simply with pre-given policies that may or may not "succeed" in some short-term sense, but with the myriad and often contradictory ways in which particularly structured states may contribute, inadvertently as well as intentionally, to long-term economic transformations – or to watershed policy transitions, such as the advent of Keynesianism or the turn from "import-substituting" to "export-led" industrialization.

The importance of studying state contributions to economic transformations over relatively long stretches of time in concrete settings is underlined both by Rueschemeyer and Evans and by Amsden. The former authors stress that although strong, effective state interventions in economic processes may grow initially out of coherent bureaucracies relatively autonomous from dominant social interests, those very interventions are likely to lead in time to diminished state autonomy and capacities for further interventions, because affected groups will mobilize to pressure state authorities or penetrate relevant parts of the state apparatus. This suggestion can be pinned down only by a dissection and comparison of many temporal sequences involving particular kinds of state interventions through various sorts of state structures. Amsden, meanwhile, demonstrates for her special case of Taiwan the indispensability of long-term historical analysis, for neither the contributions of Japanese colonialism to later state capacities in Taiwan, nor the "feedback" effects of some economic growth on the Mainlander dictatorship's will to pursue more growth through reoriented organizations and policies would have emerged in a study that looked at Taiwan only in the 1960s and after.

These essays illustrate the value of macroscopic institutional as well as temporal investigations. Rueschemeyer and Evans argue that the construction of state bureaucracies is the basis for state capacities to act on economic problems from a possibly more "general and inclusive vision" than is available to private enterprises or sectional social interests. Yet such "state building" cannot be understood only as short-term efforts at deliberate organizational engineering, for the construction and reconstruction of particular state bureaucracies take place within the overall institutional structure of the state and in the context of established relations between state officials and groups in society (or on the transnational scene). Often, in fact, it is not possible to create new state organizations when new problems emerge, and states may try to adapt existing organizations. These, in turn, often have limited ranges of adaptability. Either their internal organizational structures might be inappropriate, or their embeddedness in class or political relations prevents them from accepting or implementing new policy goals.

Weir and Skocpol later explore comparative variations in accounting for state adaptability in response to a sudden and massive economic crisis. They probe the placement of particular state organizations within overall state structures and the relationships among states, political parties, and intellectual experts in order to explain the inability of the British to move from disbursing unemployment benefits toward Keynesian macroeconomic management versus the ability of the Swedes to adapt public works administration to a new economic recovery strategy. Also, Amsden deals with the adaptability of state capacities in Tawain, where the structure of the Guomindang regime was partly rooted in the island's past and partly in the party's past on the Chinese Mainland. After 1949, Amsden argues, the Guomindang regime benefited from the strong state capacities to encourage agricultural growth inherited from the period of Japanese colonial control of Taiwan. Yet, at the same time, the Guomindang military dictatorship, once newly transplanted to Taiwan from the Mainland, could not and would not immediately plan industrialization, because economic technocrats were shunted away from any central role in public policy.

On this fascinating issue of the adaptability of state organizations built up for one set of purposes to new challenges, and on a number of other equally important issues, as the reader will see, the historical essays of this section make cross-national comparisons and intranational comparisons of different aspects of state economic intervention that flesh out the analytical questions posed by Rueschemeyer and Evans. The interest of these essays is enhanced by the many ways in which the lead conceptual piece and the following historical investigations echo one another's insights. Together, these essays certainly pose complementary questions. They do not provide complete answers that can be automatically generalized to different aspects of state intervention in other countries and times. Nevertheless, the essays are richly suggestive of hypotheses about the causes and consequences of state economic interventions that might be explored for earlier historical times than the twentieth century and for countries other than the ones that these authors have investigated in depth.

2. The State and Economic Transformation: Toward an Analysis of the Conditions Underlying Effective Intervention

Dietrich Rueschemeyer
and Peter B. Evans

Effective state intervention is now assumed to be an integral part of successful capitalist development. The classic interpretations of Polanyi and Gerschenkron[1] have brought the state to the fore in the analysis of European industrialization, puncturing the myth of the original industrial revolution as a purely private process. In the Third World, where the capacity of the private entrepreneurial class to undertake industrialization was always viewed with a more skeptical eye, even conventional economic analysis has acknowledged the importance of the role of the state. In both early and late industrialization, state policy is assumed to affect the forms and the rate of capital accumulation and to play a major role in determining whether the negative distributional effects that normally accompany capitalist industrialization will be mitigated or made worse.

There are a number of theoretical arguments as to why state intervention should be necessary for economic transformation in a capitalist context. They are worth reiterating briefly. Insofar as economic transformation involves the institutionalization of market exchange or its extension to land and labor, even the narrowest neoclassical model has space for the state. As Durkheim argued so effectively in his polemics against utilitarianism, the market requires a strong set of normative underpinnings in order to function at all. Without effectively institutionalized guarantees of these normative underpinnings, "transaction costs" will be exorbitant and the market will not allocate resources efficiently.[2] The state role derived from this argument is strictly limited and pertains most critically to the period in which capitalist exchange is struggling for predominance over precapitalist economic forms, but it is a critical role nonetheless.

Another argument, similarly critical for the establishment of a capitalist order, can be constructed by focusing on class structure. Given a dominant class that has no structured interest in the transformation of the means of production, a split between this class and those who control the state apparatus is likely to become an important element in the struggle to initiate a process of accumulation. Because all states operate now in an international context in which political–military survival depends in large part on attaining a competitive level of economic productivity, state managers are almost compelled to become involved in conflicts with such a dominant class. Skocpol's historical discussion of the problems of agrarian bureaucracies offers some instructive examples of this sort of conflict between the state apparatus and the dominant class.[3]

Arguments for the necessity of state intervention are not, however, limited to the imposition of market exchange or the overthrow of precapitalist elites. Even in an idealized market model, the "sheep on the common" problem persists.[4] Collective goods will be inadequately provided, negative externalities will not be controlled, and the rate of accumulation will suffer correspondingly in the absence of some institutionalized mechanism for imposing a less atomized rationality. As long as the market approaches the ideal typical model of competition this is a relatively limited role, but again it is a critical one.

The difficulties created by leaving accumulation in the hands of private decision makers disciplined only by the market increase dramatically as market structures deviate from ideal typical standards. In advanced "monopoly capitalist" economies, where basic industries are likely to be tight oligopolies and financial or corporate organizations are likely to cut across a number of different markets, the theoretical justification for relying on "market signals" to promote capital accumulation fades. In Third World countries, where smaller markets and imported technology make oligopolies even more pervasive,[5] the decisions of even the most carefully calculating profit maximizers may not mesh into an optimal strategy for industrialization.[6]

Once the assumption of a competitive market is relaxed, it is no longer possible to rely on the market to both stimulate and discipline entrepreneurial behavior. If the predominant economic actors are comfortable oligopolists, as is the case in major sectors of advanced capitalist economies, the state may have to intrude in order to interject entrepreneurship.[7] In the Third World the problem is compounded. The dominant class is likely to include a tightly knit set of oligopolists, some of whose primary interests are transnational rather than local, and an equally tightly knit agrarian elite, whose interests are as much patrimonial in character as they are profit-oriented. Furthermore, the extent to which Third World industrial elites are made up of risk-taking profit maximizers rather than monopoly-seeking security maximizers is questionable. The need for some additional agent of accumulation is difficult to deny under these circumstances.

In short, even without Marxist assumptions regarding the tendency of the rate of profit to fall or the inherent irrationality of accumulation based on private ownership of the means of production, there are strong theoretical reasons for believing that state intervention is necessary if capitalist economies are to sustain capital accumulation and reach higher levels of productivity. Some form of a rather direct assertion of collectively oriented administrative rationality as underpinning and counterpoint to the individualized rationality aggregated in the market must be seen as a "normal" feature of capital accumulation in both advanced and industrializing countries.

If distribution rather than accumulation is at issue, the necessity for some "extramarket" agent is even more clear-cut. Given the empirically unavoidable assumption that market exchange is instituted under conditions of preexisting inequality, there is no reason to expect inequality to diminish, even less so if the markets involved are "imperfect" ones. Indeed, there are good reasons, empirical as well as theoretical, to expect it to become worse in the absence of some allocational criteria and mechanisms that channel and counteract market forces. To the degree that one accepts Marxist predictions of proletarianization and immiseration, the projected distributional consequences of the unfettered market become much more negative. Given actually existing market structures and the historical conditions under which they have arisen, however, even those who would argue that competitive markets arising in conditions of relative equality might produce equitable distributional results will have a difficult time dismissing the case for state intervention on behalf of distributional goals.

Arguments for the necessity of state intervention could be rehearsed at great length, but that is not the aim here. As long as debate is focused exclusively on the question of state action versus market functioning, a number of interesting and, in fact, quite critical issues regarding the state itself remain unexplored. It is one thing to argue that state intervention is necessary; it is quite another to specify the conditions under which effective state intervention will be possible.

Starting instead from the working assumption that both the "invisible hand" and its visible private counterparts are sufficiently flawed as agents of accumulation or distribution to require the introduction of some additional agent, we shall try not to fall into the functionalist trap of assuming that because the state is "necessary" it will therefore have the inclination and capacity to fill the required role. Instead, we shall focus on problems concerning the nature of the state structures required to undertake effective intervention and the social structural conditions likely to facilitate such intervention.[8] There is already a substantial amount of good scholarship that speaks to these issues, but it is a literature that badly needs integration and synthesis. Our work here is intended to be a preliminary contribution to such a synthesis.

An Outline of the Approach

Our working definition of the state is essentially a Weberian one: We consider the state to be a set of organizations invested with the authority to make binding decisions for people and organizations juridically located in a particular territory and to implement these decisions using, if necessary, force. We have not chosen this definition because we see the state as a simple bureaucracy. On the contrary, precisely because we see the state as simultaneously expressing several contradictory tendencies, we adopt a definition that does not prejudge the way in which these tensions will be resolved in a given historical situation.

The state cannot escape being an instrument of domination. The inter-relations between the various parts of the state apparatus, on the one hand, and the most powerful classes or class fractions, on the other, will determine the character of the overall "pact of domination." At the same time, the state's role as an instrument of domination inevitably implies a second role, that of corporate actor. As Cardoso observes, one cannot see the state "just as the expression of class interests, without recognizing that such an expression requires an organization which, since it cannot be other than a social network of people, exists in its own right and possesses interests of its own."[9] Coherent state action will be a concern of state elites, a concern for which they can mobilize outside support and that may come to stand in conflict even with dominant interests.

The state's presence as a corporate actor is made problematic, however, by a number of factors. Despite their obvious interest in unified action, state managers are likely to be divided on substantive goals. Equally important, the state's ability to act in a unified way is strictly circumscribed by the fact that it is simultaneously an arena of social conflict. Unless social domination is monolithic, state apparatuses of any consequence in the real life of a society will inevitably become arenas of social conflict. Various groups, both dominant and subordinate, will try to use the state as a means of realizing their particular interests. In the extreme, such attempts can lead to fragmentation and paralysis of the state as a corporate actor due to a "balkanization" of state organizations in response to divergent outside forces.

Standing in opposition to the divergent pressures imposed on the state by the fact that it is an arena of social conflict is a fourth and no less real aspect of the state's role: its necessary claim to being the guardian of the universal interests of the society over which it has jurisdiction. Although such a claim provides one means of preserving the state's unity and capacity for corporate action, it also contradicts the state's role as an autonomous corporate actor, since it presumes that the goals of state activities are not generated inside the state apparatus but dictated to it by the general interests of civil society. Even more fundamentally, the state's claim to represent universal interests contradicts its role as an instrument of domination.

Nonetheless, such claims should not be simply dismissed as ideological. As O'Donnell puts it, "Tension between the underlying reality of the state as guarantor and organizer of social domination on the one hand, and as agent of a general interest which, though particularized and limited, is not fictitious, on the other, is characteristic of any state."[10] It is the need for organized collective action which transcends individual capabilities and yet is necessary for individual interests that lies at the core of such a state mission in the general interest. Maintaining sovereignty, defense, and an institutional infrastructure that secures internal peace and facilitates individual and group activities represents tasks any viable state will undertake. These core issues provide a springboard for more elaborate conceptions of the "common good." If such elaborations are much more likely to be contested as favoring partial interests, it must be recognized that state action in support of core tasks quite likely has partial implications, too. For example, Horwitz has shown how the judicial transformation of law in nineteenth-century America not only laid the institutional foundations for economic growth, but also systematically shifted economic burdens from capitalist entrepreneurs to farmers, workers, and consumers.[11] Nevertheless, pursuit of the "general interest" constitutes a nearly universal state role, one that attracts commitments of different strength from state managers as well as outside groups.

To recapitulate, although our definition of the state is cast in formal terms of authority and enforcement, we recognize that across a range of historical circumstances – in ways that vary substantially – the state *tends* to be an expression of pacts of domination, to act coherently as a corporate unit, to become an arena of social conflict, and to present itself as the guardian of universal interests. Clearly, these tendencies stand in contradiction to each other and cannot all at once come into their own. Our preoccupation with effective intervention naturally focuses attention on the state as a corporate actor and for precisely this reason tends to highlight the ways in which this role is problematic. The crucial underlying point is that the efficacy of the state will always depend on the pattern in which these contradictory tendencies are combined, both in its internal structure and in its relation to the social structure as a whole.

The body of our analysis of the conditions underlying effectiveness is divided into two parts. The first focuses on variations in the structuring of the state apparatus itself; the second on variations in the relation between the state and the dominant class. In each case we have built our discussion on the foundation of a general proposition, salient in the literature and plausible in common-sense terms, not so much in order to test these propositions as to trace some of their more interesting implications.

In looking at the internal structuring of the state, we have continued in the Weberian vein, building on the classic proposition that to be effective the state must have at its disposal a well-developed bureaucratic apparatus. Here we begin by suggesting that Weber's requirement is more stringent than it first appears. The construction of a cohesive bureaucracy should not be taken as a simple instrumental project requiring only the creation of a set of formal organizational ties joined with a cooresponding structure of incentives. Instead, the existence of an adequate bureaucratic machinery depends on a more delicate, long-term process of institution building, which makes it much less probable that a given state will have the bureaucracy it needs when it needs it. At the same time, we argue that, as the state becomes more deeply involved in promoting economic transformation, nonbureaucratic modes of interrelation among the parts of the state apparatus become increasingly important. Since direct involvement in the market exemplifies the expansion of state attempts at intervention, we have used a discussion of state-owned enterprises as a vehicle for analyzing the contradictions involved in nonbureaucratic modes of structuring the state.

In the second major segment of the analysis we try to build on the proposition that the state must acquire a certain degree of "relative autonomy" from the dominant class in order to promote economic transformation effectively, though what is meant by "relative autonomy" varies substantially depending on the theoretical context in which it is embedded. The same idea, broadly conceived, is found in some form in Marxist, classic pluralist, and more recently state-centric approaches.[12] Indeed, many of the arguments in support of this proposition parallel general arguments for the necessity of state interventions. We take the importance of relative autonomy to be as established as the need for a bureaucratic apparatus, arguing in particular that a certain autonomy is necessary not only to formulate collective goals but to implement them as well. Therefore, most of our discussion focuses on the social structural conditions likely to promote autonomy. At the same time, we have tried to set out several substantial qualifications to the hypothesized relation between autonomy and efficacy.

The two major sections of the analysis are brought together in the concluding section, which looks at the interaction between the extent to which the state realizes its role as corporate actor, the degree to which it may be considered autonomous from the dominant class, and its efficacy as an agent of economic transformation. Our main purpose in this last section is to argue against the view that these three characteristics are simply mutually reinforcing. It is tempting to see the development of bureaucratic machinery as enhancing autonomy, autonomy as facilitating the state's ability to operate as a corporate actor, both as enhancing possibilities for effective intervention, and both as being reinforced in turn by the expansion of state intervention. The result is an image of the state as an evermore self-aggrandizing juggernaut. We argue instead for a more double-edged relationship between these characteristics, suggesting that the state's very success in building its role as a corporate actor may undercut its ability to remain autonomous and that effective intervention may increase the extent to which the state becomes an arena of social conflict.

Throughout the discussion "economic transformation" is treated primarily as capital accumulation. At various points, however, we have tried to examine the special logic that is involved in state intervention on behalf of distributive goals. The differences between efforts at promoting accumulation and efforts at promoting distribution are, of course, particularly salient when the consequences of autonomy are in question, but they cannot be ignored in discussions of the construction of bureaucratic and nonbureauratic state structures.

Despite the generality of our discussion, its scope is circumscribed in several important ways. We have framed most of the discussion in terms of interests and the ways in which they might be realized, neglecting issues related to the ideological construction of political goals. We have also neglected the organizational impact of political parties, both on the state structure itself and in mediating relations between the state and other social actors. Most of our examples are drawn from the so-called semiperiphery, the larger and richer less developed countries that are considered "newly industrializing." Consideration of advanced capitalist countries is sporadic, and states in which capitalist relations of production are absent or only beginning to be institutionalized have been neglected almost completely. Our focus on semiperipheral states is not fortuitous. These countries represent the most interesting contemporary cases of economic transformation, even though closer consideration of the historical process of industrialization in currently advanced countries might well have modified our conclusions.

Finally, we have restricted the discussion here to domestic considerations. By leaving aside the international context, we lose the opportunity of looking at the sphere in which the state is probably most able to present itself as the guardian of universal interests. The failure to consider the role of international elites also removes an important dimension from the discussion of relative autonomy, especially in the semiperiphery. Despite these costs, we decided that our arguments were already sufficiently complex and that a separate discussion of the international sphere would be more appropriate.[13]

What follows, then, is a general, but circumscribed attempt to bring together some suggestive ideas from the existing literature regarding the ways in which variations in the structure of the state and its relation to the class structure inhibit or enhance the state's capacity to intervene.

State Structure and the Capacity to Intervene

Which features of the state apparatus make state intervention more effective? The classic answer is Max Weber's: Bureaucratic organization is the most efficient form of organizing large-scale administrative activities. The existence of an extensive, internally coherent bureaucratic machinery is the first prerequisite for effective state action. Weber's ideal type identified a number of critical issues: corporate cohesion of the organization, differentiation and insulation from its social environment, unambiguous location of decision making and channels of authority, and internal features fostering instrumental rationality and activism (in particular, suitable hiring and promotion practices as well as organizational designs that minimize obstacles to personnel replacement and to the restructuring of roles and bureaus as needed).

An effective bureaucratic machinery is the key to the state's capacity to intervene. In order for the capitalist state to engage in economic transformation, however, the workings of this machinery must link up with the workings of the market. At some point the analysis of state structures must therefore be joined with an analysis of market structures. In the consideration that follows we begin with some issues intrinsic to the functioning of state bureaucracies: the problematic nature of their institutional foundations, organizational competence for specific tasks and the distinctive perspectives of state elites, and problems of cohesion and decentralization. The problem of decentralization leads directly to an examination of the interaction of state organizations and markets, a question we have broached primarily through consideration of the activities of state enterprises. But the starting point remains a Weberian appreciation of the extent to which the state's first project must be the construction of an adequate bureaucracy.

Constructing Bureaucratic Machinery

To understand how much an inadequately developed bureaucracy limits the state's capacity to intervene, it is necessary to recognize the long-term nature of the task of constructing such machinery. Beyond the material resources required to sustain a large bureaucracy and the accumulation of expertise necessary for its functioning, there is a less tangible but equally critical side to building a bureaucratic state apparatus. Any institution building requires transcending individual rational-instrumental behavior. The "noncontractual elements of contract," which Durkheim insisted underlie the system of market exchange, have their analogue in bureaucratic organization. An effective process of institution building must reshape the goals, priorities, and commitments of core participants and inculcate shared assumptions and expectations on which a common rationality can be based.[14] The growth of a distinctive esprit de corps among pivotal civil servants is an essential aspect of this process, which in turn is often coupled with the emergence of (higher) civil servants as a "status group" distinguished by a particular social prestige as well as privileged association and exclusiveness. Such institutional constructions are likely to require decades, if not generations, to become established.

A first implication of taking seriously the problems of institution building and collectivity formation involved in constructing a fully developed bureaucratic machine is obvious. In a state without a fully developed bureaucratic apparatus, construction of any specific administrative organ must be considered a long-term institutional problem rather than a short-term organizational one. Even if state elites make a correct diagnosis of the kind of intervention that is indicated and have the political will and command over the material resources necessary to undertake the action, they may not be able to carry it out, simply because the required bureaucratic machinery cannot be created in time. The literature on Third World states is rife with examples, and the problem has also been noted in twentieth-century America.[15]

The converse of this observation is equally important. A state apparatus approaching bureaucratic forms may have been created in fortuitous historical developments, whereas the fruits of such institution building in the form of a capacity for effective interventions in the economy may appear only after a substantial lag. Thus, for example, one may argue that the construction of colonial administrations in Korea and Taiwan by the Japanese served later as a resource for the construction of effective state organizations, which helped integrate these countries advantageously into the world capitalist economy.

The implicit assumption in this argument that bureaucratic organizations are fungible tools for any state action whatsoever suggests important problems that deserve discussion in their own right. It is true that bureaucratic organizations can serve as a crucial institutional resource for endeavors quite different from those for which they were originally created. However, bureaucratic organizations are geared to do certain things relatively well and, *as organizations,* cannot easily switch to or expand into other fields of action. Organizational structures tend to mesh with specific sets of policy instruments and form a fairly stable amalgam. For example, an effective military apparatus is not necessarily able to collect taxes efficiently or to run public enterprises. (This, perhaps, suggests a particular affinity between military regimes and "free-enterprise" economic policies, which do not require specialized state interventions that are difficult to make effective.) The observation is not, of course, limited to the military. The effective administration of public enterprises is no guarantee of a good educational system or even successful agricultural development policies.

Furthermore, the processes just indicated, which turn a set of heterogeneous officials and offices into a coherent organization with shared orientations and assumptions, also stabilize certain policy inclinations among the state managers. The intricate meshing of expertise with a given personnel and organizational form gives these inclinations a powerful influence. This was recognized at the statewide level as an issue of critical importance by observers as different as Lenin and Weber;[16] it can apply with almost equal force to specific ministries and agencies. Although by design bureaucracies may only implement policies, in actuality they shape them, too. It is the very same processes that constitute the institutional foundations and the operational capacity of bureaucratic organization that also set limits to the range of policy options for which the state apparatus is a willing and effective instrument.

A set of issues paralleling that of the state elite's fundamental orientations pertains to the expertise and knowledge required for effective state action. We cannot assume that even a well-organized bureaucratic apparatus will have sufficient knowledge to intervene effectively in the complex interrelations of socioeconomic processes and patterns. For economic and social interventions by the state, relevant and sufficiently specific theory often does not exist. Equally important, data about particular social and economic conditions as well as about the effects of past interventions have to be gathered and are difficult to come by. Especially when market signals cannot be taken as an appropriate basis for policy formation and implementation, information gathering itself requires tremendous organizational capacity.[17]

If state elites cannot be *assumed* to have superior knowledge and insight, do they have, by reason of their structural position, the chance to develop *different* insights? Do they develop particular points of view, perspectives, and problem formulations that set them apart from other elites? We are inclined to think so.

The classic argument for state managers having a perspective distinct from that of private members of the dominant class is their structural removal from concern with short-run profit considerations. Shared technocratic training may also generate a distinctive outlook. Ideologically, the state's tendency to present itself as the guardian of universalistic interests is likely to give state managers a distinctive affinity for ideological formulations that can be phrased in universalistic terms, an affinity that will in turn shape more concrete preferences. Although certain bureaucratic elites may be more exposed to short-run profit considerations (i.e., executives of state enterprises) or subject to cooptation in a way that precludes the development of an outlook distinctive from that of their constituencies, the potential for a distinctive outlook among state managers remains an important aspect of state structure, both because it may provide policies different from and occasionally superior to those espoused by private elites and because a distinctive outlook is critical to the state's ability to realize, even partially, its role as a corporate actor.

Organizational Capacity and Distribution Policies

Effective bureaucratic organization as well as the issue competence and factual knowledge required for intervention are perhaps nowhere more put to the test than in attempts at income redistribution. Agencies aiming by direct intervention at income redistribution must almost by definition become involved in relations between dominant and subordinate groups. They typically cannot – as most agencies implementing policies aimed at accumulation are able to – rely on the information processing and coordination accomplished by the mechanisms of the market, but must seek equivalent results with administrative means. Nor can they legitimate their activities in terms of performing well by market criteria as state enterprises can, and their interventions often stand in conflict with established social norms embedded in custom as well as in the policies pursued by other state institutions. In short, income redistribution policies must typically work against the grain of both the market and social norms.

A classic example is INCRA, the Brazilian agency charged with promoting colonization in the Amazon. Given the responsibility for one of the Brazilian regime's few distributive policies, to provide new land in the Amazon to peasants coming from the Northeast, the agency proved incapable of producing results.[18] It could not find a way of making the colonists' production economically rewarding, nor could it surmount the obstacles embedded in legal procedures that prevented colonists from gaining clear title to their land. In the end its activities benefited surveying companies and large landholders as much as, or more than, landless Northeasterners.

The problems of redistributive agencies, such as INCRA, are not simply problems of insufficient autonomy from the dominant class. They are also problems of the bureaucratic capacity required to engage in activities that run counter both to the logic of the market and to fundamental societal institutions, such as the legal system. Directly restructuring patterns of distribution requires a thoroughgoing intrusion into social and economic processes. Such intrusions would be extremely difficult to implement even if autonomy could be taken for granted.

The difficulties encountered by Tanzania in restructuring its economy provide another case in point. Those who criticize the Tanzanian regime from the left[19] assume, noting the weakness of private capital, that the limited effect collective agricultural programs had in improving the life of the peasantry must be taken as an indicator of the degree to which those within the state apparatus are acting in a self-interested fashion, that is, becoming a "bureaucratic bourgeoisie." Although there may be some truth to such criticism, it overlooks the enormous capacity, both informational and bureaucratic, that would be required to implement such a program of social change.[20] The more a given policy of economic change attempts to operate independently of market processes, the greater the need for efficient information processing and for a successful shaping of individual behavior through political and administrative means. In short, the obstacles to deeply penetrating state interventions, such as those aimed directly at redistribution, may lie as much in the greater bureaucratic and political capacities they require as in the opposition of dominant classes.

Any viable state must be able to extract sufficient resources for its functioning from private actors. This, too, involves deeply intrusive state interventions in civil society, especially when revenue creation takes the form of income taxation. And, indeed, we are likely to find developed organizational capacity of the state, if at all, in this area. As revenue extraction expands with expanding state activities to the point of comprising a substantial fraction of the total domestic income, the state becomes involved in the societal distribution of income whether or not that is intended. Policies aimed at reducing income inequality, even if they use income transfers and not only differential taxation, can then build on existing organizational capacities without encountering the problems of building effective institutions for direct intervention in income-generating processes as just discussed. This does not, of course, mean that such policies will be adopted or that they will be implemented with success if adopted. Although a lack of organizational capacity is a particularly serious obstacle to effective intervention in the processes shaping the distribution of income, the impact of dominant interests, the balance of class power, and the issues of state autonomy are also specially important in this area, more important than in interventions aimed at economic growth.

Centralization and Decentralization

In our opening remarks specifying some initial theoretical perspectives on the state, we pointed to inherent antinomies between the state as a corporate actor and the state as an arena of social conflict. Effective state action requires a minimum of coherence and coordination within and among different state organizations, and that in turn presupposes a minimum of autonomy from forces in civil society. This is not only or even primarily a question of combating dual employment, careers that lead incumbents to anticipate private roles, and "nepotism," that is, of freeing individual officials from entanglement in outside socioeconomic obligations. Equally and perhaps more important is the responsiveness of whole organizational parts of the state apparatus to internal guidance and coordination of state action rather than to outside interests and demands.

This problem is made more serious by the fact that many types of state action require decentralization for maximum efficiency. The issues of an inadequate knowledge base for developing and implementing rational policies discussed earlier are exacerbated in highly centralized bureaucracies by the loss of information and distortion of commands incurred as both pass through the hierarchy.[21] Subordination to a centralized chain of command deprives subunits of taking initiatives of their own and using the information about particular conditions available to them. For maximum efficiency, decision making must be – so runs a prescriptive conclusion of organizational theory – optimally aligned with the availability of intelligence about the varied relevant conditions.

The "decoupling" of subunits is critical not only on grounds of efficient information use and situational decision making, but also because of the political role that must be played by the leadership of these subunits. Weber himself insisted on the essentially political nature of leadership at the top of the central bureaucracy.[22] The necessity of negotiating with threatened interests and building support among potential constitutents applies also to state organs at a lower level. The more the state wishes to penetrate social and economic life, the less can the leaders of lower-level operative units afford to act simply as subordinates in a bureaucratic chain of command. Both in order to ensure efficient decision making and in order to allow for more effective political relations, the state must decentralize its activities, insulating certain aspects of the operation of its subunits from the control of the central bureaucracy.

Yet by giving such autonomy to subunits, a state creates serious problems of corporate cohesion and coordination, especially when strong and divergent forces in civil society are bent on capturing parts of the state apparatus and using them for their purposes. The state then is in danger of dissipating its own special contribution, which must lie in its ability to operate on the basis of a more general and inclusive vision than is feasible for private actors embedded in the market. If decentralization destroys the ability of the state to act coherently in ways reflecting general goals and diagnoses, then the unique character of its contribution is lost. This leads to the critical question of whether there are countervailing integration mechanisms that make it possible to combine coherence and effective coordination with a decentralization that is more than a geographic dispersion of offices.

A few indications about such mechanisms must suffice. We need only mention that a distinctive esprit de corps among higher civil servants can function as a fluid form of coordination combining relative autonomy for officials with a shared sense of purpose, which is reinforced by identification with the group. This distinctive sense of identity, especially when it coalesces with the emergence of civil servants as a status group, can further act as a barrier to outside influence. However, when status groups and the related patterns of social association and exclusion extend beyond the state managers, they link them to certain outside elites and make them particularly accessible to outside influence.

Planning at the center and central control of financial resources for decentralized agencies may achieve coordination, but central resource control is often difficult to balance with real delegation of decision making. Another integration mechanism is the creation of dual bureaucratic structures in which a strand of offices more responsive to intentions of the center parallels the operative main-line organizations, serving to inform the center as well as acting to control and guide the main body of the bureaucracy through sanctions and normative appeals. Such dual lines of control can take many forms, among them ideologically informed parties, army units with a particular esprit de corps, or even parties based on complex patronage relations; Katzenstein's analysis of party control over the state apparatus in postwar Austria could also be interpreted along these lines.[23] Such dual organizational forms can significantly improve coordination, but they can also themselves become a source of tension and create coordination problems of their own.

Issues of decentralization come to a head when the state apparatus moves to intervene in market processes. State action may suspend the operation of the market mechanism and substitute administrative direction and coordination. The state may transfer economic resources from one income group to another by way of taxation and subsidy. Finally, the state may itself engage in capital formation; this can take the form of raising funds for infrastructural investments in schools, roads, and bridges or the increasingly important form of public enterprises operated for profit. We have chosen this last type of state activity for somewhat more detailed discussion. It does not represent the most intrusive form of state intervention in the economy, but it is instructive for exploring the interrelations of state action and market operation and it highlights further the issues of decentralization and coherence of state action.

State-Owned Enterprises

With public enterprises the state becomes an active participant in production and market exchange and partially supersedes the way in which the market meshes knowledge, incentives, and economic power. Even if state enterprises behave very much like private firms, they represent a significant state intervention: Through them the state supplants private capital accumulation and becomes itself an agent of the accumulation of capital. This is classically justified by the need to overcome impediments to private investments created by externalities. More recent analyses suggest that it may be more important for the state to supply entrepreneurship when a new balance of risks and inducements has to be achieved before private capital will act.[24] In addition, the state may, in an oligopolized market, engage in provocative competition designed to elicit entrepreneurial behavior from otherwise too comfortable oligopolists.[25] The creation of state-owned enterprises has been a central part of state policy in newly industrializing countries. Indeed, for them the existence of a strategically located set of state-owned enterprises probably constitutes a prerequisite for effective intervention in the economy. The phrase "strategically located" is critical here: The way in which market structures mesh with state initiatives is crucial for the effectiveness of state enterprises.

Empirically, state-owned enterprises tend to be located in sectors where high capital requirements and longer payback periods suggest that only a few powerful actors will share the market.[26] It makes sense for the state to insert itself in such markets because they lend themselves to the functioning of large bureaucratized organizations and because the disciplines and incentives of competition cannot be counted on to produce optimal behavior on the part of private capital. The effects of state participation can be further enhanced if such sectors have important forward or backward linkages. Finally, the evidence suggests that the existence of technological "disciplines" within the sector will facilitate the possibility of the state enterprise remaining insulated from the central bureaucracy but still making an efficient contribution to the process of accumulation.[27]

Some examples will illustrate the sorts of structural locations in which state enterprises appear to have been effective. Generating electrical power tends to be highly concentrated if not monopolistic by nature, imposes technological discipline on the firms involved in it, and has important forward linkages in the form of lowering costs to manufacturing industries. State companies have traditionally played important roles in this sector.[28] Steel is another classic locus where the state may play a role in the process of accumulation.[29] Petroleum refining and mineral extraction in general again tend to be monopolistic or at least highly concentrated, to have important linkages because of their revenue-generating capacity, and to provide semiperipheral states with important sources of leverage over the process of accumulation.[30] The petrochemical industry is dominated by a small number of firms, is intimately connected to the (normally) state-controlled petroleum sector, is subject to stringent technological discipline, and has important forward linkages to a diverse set of manufacturing industries.[31] State intervention in sectors with these characteristics is by no means assured success, as the failures of Argentina and Venezuela in petrochemicals show, but the chances of intervening successfully are much greater than they would be if the state attempted to penetrate a sector normally characterized by atomistic competition.

A brief consideration of contrasting strategies with regard to agriculture will further illustrate the importance of meshing the form of intervention with the nature of the market. Agricultural production tends to be fragmented; even concentrated agriculture seems dispersed when compared with the sort of industrial sectors just considered. Direct state intervention in the agricultural production process is problematic even for socialist countries and would be practically impossible in the capitalist semiperiphery. Intervention in the marketing process, especially at the international level, may be effective.[32] The state may also intervene effectively by changing the structure of landholdings. But entrepreneurial interventions are likely to be more effective if indirect. The fertilizer industry, for example, lends itself nicely to the participation of state enterprises and provides a strong base for shaping accumulation in agriculture. The Taiwanese development strategy in agriculture used precisely this combination:[33] Agriculture, restructured by land reform, remained private, but both surplus extraction and the promotion of accumulation were managed through state control of the fertilizer industry.

State-owned enterprises not only allow the state to participate directly in the process of accumulation, but also diminish certain of the risks of decentralization. The market, even an oligopolistic one, sets some limits on the possibilities of inefficiency and corruption; it also provides a metric (prices, production, and profits) that allows the central bureaucracy to keep rough track of performance. Nonetheless, insertion into the market increases certain other kinds of control problems. Obviously, it does make it difficult for the state to use the enterprise as an instrument of policy goals other than accumulation. In addition, insofar as state enterprises coexist with private capital, they are likely to become integrated into an oligopolistic community that places primacy on accumulation within the sector itself, possibly at the expense of accumulation more generally.[34]

Profitable state enterprises have both a claim on resources that are independent of the central budgetary process and a legitimacy based on their apparent efficiency in market terms. If they find, in addition, political allies in a sectorally based oligopolistic community, they are likely to have a great deal of "relative autonomy" vis-à-vis the central bureaucracy. State structures that include a highly developed state enterprise sector are likely to end up, in Abranches's terms,[35] "segmented," that is, consisting of different components that operate semiindependently and are integrated only at the very highest level of policy formation, if at all.

The problematic character of state structures designed primarily for effective insertion into the market is even more apparent when distribution rather than accumulation is the focus. State enterprises, like large oligopolistic firms in general, reinforce normal market tendencies toward unequal distribution. They tend to favor capital-intensive methods of production, operate often in regions where income is already concentrated, and tend to take advantage of their market power in setting prices. Thus, it is difficult to find evidence for a positive relation between the expansion of the state enterprise sector and improvements in the income distribution.[36]

State Structure: Implications and Conclusions

We have borrowed the starting point of our discussion of state structure and the capacity to intervene from Weber: Effective state intervention is predicated on the existence of a well-developed bureaucratic apparatus. A first conclusion of our review of the ways in which state structure limits effective intervention is straightforward and follows directly Weberian lines of thought, though we cast it in Durkheimian terms. Building the "nonbureaucratic foundations of bureaucratic functioning," that is, creating the noninstrumental sources of cohesion of the bureaucratic apparatus and especially of its elite, is a long-term enterprise. Such bases cannot be laid ad hoc, within the short time spans of shifting political urgencies, just because the need for powerful and effective administrative intervention presents itself. In addition, these developments have far-reaching consequences for the range of tasks and policies for which a given bureaucratic machine is a willing and capable instrument. The historical character of the bureaucratic apparatus must be taken into account in any attempt to explain its capacity, or lack of capacity, to intervene.

A second conclusion, closely related but analytically distinct, is equally critical to the orientation of future work in the area. The assumption that the state will emerge as a corporate actor capable of cohesive intervention is highly problematic. By this we do not mean simply that "bureaucratic politics" and differences in the bounded rationality of actors within the state apparatus will lead to fissiparous tendencies, though this is clearly true. We mean that cohesion must always be seen to have been constructed – constructed through long-term processes of institution building rather than merely by the creation of a set of formal organizational ties joined with a corresponding structure of incentives. It is particularly incumbent on those who take the state's role as a social actor seriously to raise the issue of corporate cohesiveness. Otherwise, what may be the most important single limitation on the possibility of effective state intervention remains unanalyzed.

We have tried to spell out the ways in which active intervention itself makes coherent corporate action of the state apparatus problematic. Deeply penetrating state actions make necessary a decentralization that goes beyond the internal imperatives of large-scale administrative organization. Interventions that address circumstantially varied problems and affect different constellations of interests require a large measure of *political* independence for the decentralized units rather than merely administrative differentiation. This in turn invites attempts to capture and coopt these units for the goals of divergent interests. The state apparatus becomes an arena of social conflict. As a consequence of state intervention, then, the antinomies of civil society tend to reproduce themselves within the state,[37] undermining the state's capacity for coherent corporate action.

Deeply penetrating state action requires effective interorganizational relations that respond to the fundamental contradiction between the need for decentralization and the necessity of preserving a general coherence of state action. State enterprises operating in a market economy represent one such pattern, though by no means a uniformly successful one. Understanding the successful use of public enterprises as tools of state intervention requires, first, an analysis of contrasting market structures as the context for this kind of state intervention and for its relations to private capital; second, it requires analysis of how state enterprises fit into and interact with the rest of the state structure. Central to both kinds of investigation are, again, the contradictions between the prerequisites of the capacity for coherent corporate action and the unique potential contribution of the state to economic development, on the one hand, and those of effective action in variegated settings, effective intervention in market relations, and effective influence on private capital, on the other hand.

State Action and Class Relations

We start from the proposition that state autonomy is a prerequisite for effective state action. Given the individualist "sheep on the common" bias inherent in capitalist elites, it must be possible to sacrifice the interests of certain segments of capital in the pursuit of policies that maintain the viability of the socioeconomic system and preserve the general rate of return. These problems are aggravated in highly monopolized capitalist economies by the vastly increased power of divergent partial interests. In the marginal case, for which Katzenstein's analysis of Switzerland[38] is perhaps a suggestive example, these issues may be tackled by a political directorate outside the state. Such an "executive committee of the bourgeoisie" in a literal sense would have to be sufficiently autonomous and united, oriented to systemically required collective goals, and in control of an effective bureaucratic apparatus. Normally, these tasks will devolve on that institutional structure which can claim to represent collective interests vis-à-vis international forces, is capable of making binding collective decisions internally, and can enforce them, if need be, by coercion – that is, the state.

The state offers, in the context of a capitalist economy, a contribution that is both unique and necessary – unique because it transcends the logic of the competitive market and necessary because a capitalist economy requires, for its development as well as its maintenance in the face of changing conditions, the supply of "collective goods" that cannot be provided by the competitive actors in the economy. Both for the conception of appropriate policy goals and for their implementation, at least some corporate coherence of the state apparatus is necessary. Without a minimum degree of autonomy the state's contribution would therefore lose its unique character and fail to serve systemic needs of the capitalist political economy.[39]

Lest this thesis be misunderstood, we shall return to and elaborate certain caveats already noted in the discussion of state structure. State managers are not omniscient, omnipotent demiurges in the service of Hegelian reason. They often lack the knowledge necessary for formulating "correct" policies aimed at the promotion of accumulation and system maintenance. Furthermore, even if state managers hit on an essentially "correct" policy, they will not be able to implement it unless they have at their disposal a previously constructed bureaucratic machinery with appropriate capacities for action.

Although their structural position favors more comprehensive orientations than one can expect of entrepreneurs who stand in competition with each other and are concerned with short-run profit maximization, state managers may also be so concerned with short-term political support as to justify Marx's epithet of "parliamentary cretinism."[40] Insofar as they have a vested interest in the salience of concerns that can be portrayed as universalistic, state managers may also be prone to pursuing ideological goals to a degree incompatible with maximizing accumulation.[41]

Finally, there are policies inspired simply by the state elite's own immediate interests, seeking, for instance, an expansion of the state bureaucracy for its own sake. In its early development the state is likely to have a thoroughly parasitic and even predatorial character. Greater autonomy of such a predatorial state is likely to have negative rather than positive consequences for economic transformation. Under these circumstances, reducing the autonomy of the state, trying to make it the "handmaiden" of dominant economic elites, should also make it a more effective agent of accumulation.[42] Only when the state has become thoroughly capitalist in its orientation is the positive relation between state autonomy and accumulation likely to be strong.

Even once such a structural integration of orientation and overall purpose has been achieved, there are no guarantees that state interventions will match appropriately the historically changing systemic problems. In the extreme, there looms the specter of autonomous state elites creating "collective disaster" rather than providing the systemically required "collective goods." The opportunities for such radical interventions must not, however, be overestimated. Strict limits are imposed on the autonomy of any capitalist state. In the succinct formulation of Block, "Those who manage the state apparatus – regardless of their own political ideology – are dependent on the maintenance of some reasonable level of economic activity" both for financing state operations and for maintaining political support, and "in a capitalist economy the level of economic activity is largely determined by the private investment decisions of capitalists. This means that capitalists, in their collective role as investors, have a veto over state policies."[43] This constraint is the more effective as state activities, and thus also the state's revenue needs, have vastly expanded in all advanced industrial countries. Corporate power furthermore is enhanced by increasing oligopolization and monopolization of strategic markets.

State autonomy in non-core states is even more constrained. Even in countries where the state appears to be in the strongest position relative to private capital, "state capitalism" is not the dominant mode of accumulation.[44] The state remains dependent on private capital, foreign and domestic, not only to promote accumulation but also to produce a surplus in which the state itself may share. The strict limits under which the state must operate in a dependent capitalist political economy are grimly indicated by the severe problems confronted by social democratic regimes such as those of Salvador Allende in Chile and Michael Manley in Jamaica. Even the Mexican PRI (Partido Revolucionario Institucional) regime witnessed dramatic changes in the flow of investment when its policies did not meet with the approval of capital.[45] The evidence suggests generally that the particular policy interests of dominant classes will get a hearing even in the most autonomous states and that it is virtually impossible for the state to substitute its actions for the working of the market.

The assertion that autonomy is a prerequisite of effective state intervention must then be qualified in three fundamental ways. First, we do not expect the positive relation to apply to precapitalist states. Second, autonomy does not necessarily imply superior knowledge and capability; state interventions may be unsuccessful or even disastrous because of wrong assumptions and insufficient information or because of deficient state organization. Finally, autonomy remains very relative; the handmaiden role remains an inescapable part of the repertoire of even the most autonomous modern state. Within these limits, however, a positive connection between increased autonomy and state intervention remains plausible, and the social structural conditions that might increase the likelihood of autonomy remain correspondingly worth exploring.

Conditions Leading to Greater Autonomy

The most obvious social structural condition favoring greater autonomy is division within the dominant class. In Latin America, for example, the state's role during the period of hegemony of agricultural export elites was focused primarily on the traditional task of dealing with the international environment. As a more complex elite structure that included urban and industrial groups emerged, the state expanded its intervention in the domestic economy.[46] Likewise, the current division in the industrial elite between foreign and local capital offers the state space to expand its role.

Because divisions among private elites are such an important precondition for autonomy, evaluation of what constitutes a divided dominant class should be done with great care. The work of Zeitlin and his associates on pre-Allende Chile provides a good illustration.[47] Their research produced no evidence of the conventionally assumed split between agrarian and industrial capital. Quite to the contrary, they discovered that precisely those individuals who integrated agrarian and industrial interests in their personal networks were likely to assume the political leadership of the dominant class. Likewise, the supposed split between foreign and local capital must be analyzed concretely rather than assumed.[48]

Increased pressure from subordinate classes is a second source of increased state autonomy vis-à-vis the dominant class. Oddly, increasing levels of class conflict probably enhance the state's autonomy vis-à-vis society in general. As the state apparatus is called on to take a more active role in repressing subordinate groups, it becomes more willing to move against dominant groups as well. O'Donnell's portrayal of the bureaucratic authoritarian state becoming "deaf" to the demands of the local bourgeoisie during the initial and most repressive phase of its rule is a case in point.[49] The consequences of its role in suppressing rural unrest for the politicization of the Peruvian military is another example. The military not only took control of the state apparatus, but then used the state against the rural elite.[50]

This pattern stands in contrast to the classic analysis of "Bonapartism" as a basis of state autonomy. In the Bonapartist model, the state is propelled into a leading position by a balance of class forces combined with the inability of subordinate classes (classically the peasantry) to exercise control over their supposed representatives in the state apparatus. Typically, the state uses the leverage gained to preserve both the status quo and the interests of the dominant class. It does not "turn a deaf ear," as in O'Donnell's case.

Situations in which increased pressure from subordinate classes leads to increased autonomy should not be confused with the possibility of an inverted instrumentalism in which subordinate groups might eventually acquire sufficient power to use the state for their ends. This possibility is, of course, the basis of the democratic socialist vision of the state engaging in redistributive and other activities at odds with dominant interests.[51] It is central as well to the Leninist theory of the dictatorship of the proletariat, in which, before it withers away, the state becomes the instrument of the previously subordinate class. It should be noted that these cases can also be taken as other examples of situations in which the handmaiden state, in this case the handmaiden of the working class, might be seen to be more effective than the autonomous state. Inverted instrumentalism is not, however, of central interest at this point. It merely underlines the fact that a social structure in which the dominant interests are monolithic drastically narrows the room for state autonomy, regardless of the content of those interests.

The most likely conditions for increased state autonomy are constellations in which the pact of domination has serious cleavages within it, in which threats from below induce the dominant classes to grant greater autonomy to the state, or in which subordinate classes acquire sufficient power to undo monolithic political control by the dominant classes. A wide variety of such constellations can be envisioned, and each of them may serve as a basis for increased state autonomy. However, we cannot assume an automatic tendency of such social structural cleavages to enhance state autonomy. Divisions within the dominant class and pressures from subordinate classes offer opportunities for enhanced autonomy, but such divisions may also lead to a capture of different parts of the state apparatus by different interests and result in a "balkanization" of the state. Which of these contradictory outcomes is more likely depends on the internal relations of control and coordination within the state structure, on the relative strength of the state apparatus and outside forces, and on the specifically political patterns and processes mediating between the state and the interest structure of society that have not been considered here.

Even if the balance of these factors does not favor state autonomy, complete paralysis of coherent state action due to multiple veto powers is not the most likely result. Far more likely are compromises among the major contending forces that persist over some time and set down broad directions and constraints for state action. They may range from de facto stalemates reluctantly uncontested to explicitly recognized regime pacts.[52] Such compromises tend to concede, virtually by necessity, a certain space for autonomous action to the state apparatus, providing at least that minimum of coherence understood to be necessary for successful implementation of any set of policies. Such a limited autonomy space can become the basis for attempts to widen the state machine's independence as changing circumstances provide the opportunity.

Socioeconomic crises and even less severe accumulations of new policy problems may present such opportunities. The Achilles' heel of sociopolitical compromises is that they tend to preserve the historical constellation of their origin. They represent not only the power balance, but also the policy conceptions of the past and may be burdened to the breaking point by unprecedented policy problems. In crisis situations with which even well-functioning regime pacts may not be able to cope, the state apparatus – needed as much as ever – has new chances to enhance its autonomy.

All of our arguments thus far have assumed that the major cleavages in a social structure are based on interests. However, the potentially positive relation of interest-based divisions to state autonomy must be contrasted with the consequences of ethnic and religious cleavages. Conflict between interest-based groups is more susceptible to the material inducements and means of coercion at the disposal of the state. Ethnic or religious solidarities and exclusions, in contrast, tend to be diffuse and all-embracing rather than instrumental and therefore respond less readily to state policy. In addition, the state's claim to be the embodiment of universalistic interests – and therefore its legitimacy – are particularly difficult to sustain in an ethnically and religiously divided society. A number of specific examples might be cited in support of this proposition, ranging from Lebanon as an extreme example of a state debilitated by primordial cleavages, to Japan as a strong state the relatively autonomous role of which is facilitated by the fact of operating in an ethnically homogeneous society. Unfortunately, however, the role of ethnicity in relation to state autonomy is not quite as straightforward as this argument would imply.

Although primordial cleavages may debilitate the state, either because they penetrate the state apparatus itself or because they make legitimacy all but impossible, ethnic and religious divisions may, under certain circumstances, play exactly the opposite role. When ethnic cleavages are hierarchically ordered and when a single ethnic group manages to gain continuous control over the state apparatus, ethnic cleavages may enhance state autonomy. The relative autonomy of the Afrikaner state vis-à-vis the Anglo economic elite in South Africa is perhaps the most obvious example, but the relation between the Guomingdang state and the Taiwanese landlords might also be considered a case in point. Autonomy may, in short, be enhanced either by fissures within the external groups that might control the state or by special loyalties that bind together those who control the state apparatus and separate them from powerful external constituencies.

Since autonomy is generally an important prerequisite for effective intervention, these same conditions are likely to facilitate intervention. At the same time, however, we would argue that, even without specially favorable structural conditions enhancing autonomy, effective intervention must not be ruled out completely. A brief analysis of possible state interventions on behalf of redistribution will illustrate the point.

Autonomy and Distribution

Some insulation from direct control by the dominant class would seem more critical to state interventions aimed at redistribution than to interventions aimed at promoting accumulation. Unless the state has at least the minimal autonomy necessary to extract a share of the surplus from the dominant class, even its attempts at maintaining itself must be based on regressive extraction from subordinate groups. Even above this lower limit, the opposition of the dominant class to obviously redistributive policies will be much more consistent and intense than its resistance to the expansion of the state's role in the process of accumulation. As indicated by our earlier discussion of the state structures required for direct interventions aimed at income redistribution, such agencies are especially unlikely to be equipped for their complex administrative and political tasks and at the same time are particularly vulnerable to attempts at capture and cooptation.

Direct attempts at redistribution would have most demanding requirements for both state autonomy and the state's coherence as a corporate actor, but this does not necessarily mean that there is no possibility of effective intervention in this area. The degree of autonomy required may be reduced significantly if the effects of state action on distribution are indirect.

If we have stressed repeatedly that states cannot be presumed to act coherently on the basis of adequate knowledge, the same must be said of social classes, even of dominant classes. The most effective opposition to redistributive policies should therefore be expected wherever the connection between state action and redistribution is direct and plainly visible and wherever opposition can be effective at the local and individual level and does not require coordination into a single class action. Conversely, we find in this proposition suggestions as to where effective opposition to redistributive policies from the dominant class is less likely to exist. Insofar as redistributive outcomes are uncertain, they may not be apparent to the dominant class at all. This is especially the case if redistributive outcomes are by-products of policies initiated and justified on other grounds. Indirect redistributive approaches should therefore require a much lower degree of autonomy than direct, explicit approaches.

Again, Taiwan may be taken as an example. The improvements in income distribution experienced in Taiwan, though admittedly built on the foundation of an explicitly redistributive agricultural policy (the land reform of the early 1950s), seem to have been enhanced by policies chosen for other reasons.[53] Labor-absorbing manufacturing industries were initiated in order to improve Taiwan's export performance but had the eventual effect of raising real wages and improving the income distribution. Knight has suggested analogous possibilities for Brazil.[54] A policy designed to stimulate more labor-intensive branches of industry would, he argues, be energy conserving, be consistent with the expansion of manufactured exports, and have the effect of strengthening local rather than foreign capital. Such policies might therefore be attractive to Brazilian capital regardless of their redistributive implications.

Another, quite different group of indirectly redistributive policies also deserves mention. Policies that have the effect of strengthening the bargaining position of subordinate groups may be undertaken by the state largely with the aim of dampening social conflict and building political support for the regime. The Peruvian case is a prime example.[55] Peasant cooperatives were organized partially in the hope of creating rural allies for the regime. The cooperatives had the effect, not of successful corporatist cooptation, but of increasing the political militancy not just vis-à-vis the largely displaced rural landowners but vis-à-vis the state apparatus itself. The formation of "industrial communities" had the effect, not of integrating workers into cooperative relations with industrial capital, but of increasing strikes and other industrial conflict.[56] (These effects seem quite similar to those observed in advanced countries.)[57] Unless they are undermined by subsequent events (as has been largely the case in Peru), such policies create a political and organizational basis for future redistribution, a basis quite different from that intended by those who initiated the policy.[58]

Speculations regarding possibilities for indirectly redistributive state policies might appear trivial in the context of more advanced industrial societies where the level of organization of the working class and other subordinate groups is sufficient to provoke on occasion directly redistributive strategies. In the context of the capitalist semiperiphery a discussion of distribution limited to attempts at direct transfer of resources would have little to offer beyond an analysis of a few attempts at land reform. Focusing on indirect approaches not only is useful as a means of clarifying the degree of autonomy necessary for state efforts on behalf of redistribution, but may also be the best way of moving beyond paralyzing accounts of why the state can never be sufficiently autonomous to promote redistribution.[59]

What this suggests in terms of future research is a closer analysis of the dynamics of class relations in cases of redistribution. Are they cases best understood in terms of the state as an arena of social conflict, examples of increasingly organized and militant subordinate groups forcing the state to be more responsive (and consequently more autonomous from the dominant class)? Or are they cases in which the logic of accumulation happened to offer certain redistributive possibilities and the state, while remaining thoroughly wedded to the interests of the dominant class, was able to use its capacity as a corporate actor to take advantage of them?

Autonomy is necessary for effective state intervention. Nothing in our discussion negates this general proposition. What we have tried to suggest is that it would be a mistake to rest content with the general proposition. It must be qualified and embedded in the context of a larger discussion of the conditions under which greater and lesser degrees of autonomy are required, as well as the conditions under which greater or lesser degrees of autonomy may be expected. In addition, we have tried to set out some of the reasons why autonomy is not in itself sufficient for effective state action. Although the discussion has been anything but exhaustive, we hope that it has demonstrated the fruitfulness of focusing on variations in autonomy rather than arguing about whether or not it exists. In the concluding section we shall try to go a step farther and look at the interaction between state autonomy and state capacity.

Conclusions

In advanced industrial countries and in the "semiperiphery," growing state activities and an increasingly deep penetration of economy and society by state interventions seem to have played a critical part in enabling capitalist political economies to foster economic growth and manage socioeconomic conflicts. Yet the internal structure of the state and the state's relation to the class structure of society limit the state's capacity to intervene in civil society in pursuit of the goals of economic growth and income redistribution.

The analysis here has focused on two propositions concerning the conditions under which these limitations may be overcome. First, in order to undertake effective interventions, the state must constitute a bureaucratic apparatus with sufficient corporate coherence. Second, a certain degree of autonomy from the dominant interests in a capitalist society is necessary not only to make coherent state action in pursuit of any consistent policy conception possible, but also because some of the competing interests in economy and society, even structurally dominant ones, will have to be sacrificed in order to achieve systemically required "collective goods" that cannot be provided by partial interests. Although our energies have been devoted primarily to modifying these propositions, they have remained substantially supported.

In this closing section, we shall round out the analysis by briefly examining the consequences of state intervention for autonomy and the state's capacity to behave as a coherent corporate actor. An image of mutual reinforcement is tempting. Indeed, we would argue that mutual reinforcement not only occurs, but often predominates. The experience of intervention builds the capacity of the state bureaucracy and enhances its ability to behave as a corporate actor. By augmenting the resources under the state's control, intervention diminishes the state's reliance on privately generated resources and thereby enhances autonomy. Were this the only form of reciprocal effect, a progression of increasing autonomy, capacity, and intervention would follow smoothly. Autonomy and capacity for coherent corporate action would enhance in turn the capacity for future intervention, and the cycle would be repeated. We would suggest, however, that there are strong antinomies in the interaction between increasing state intervention, state autonomy, and state capacity.

Autonomy and coherence as a corporate actor may contribute to the efficacy of the state as an agent of economic transformation without intervention in turn reinforcing the state's autonomy or even its capacity to intervene in the future. As state action moves beyond guaranteeing minimal institutional conditions of social and economic life in the direction of substantial intervention in socioeconomic processes, the state's own character as well as its relation to civil society changes fundamentally.

The state's claim to being a "guardian of universal interests" is intrinsically problematic even if its activities-are confined to providing an infrastructure for invidualized competitive activities,[60] but this claim becomes manifestly questionable with broader and deeper interventions. State interventions, in contrast to the workings of the market or other institutions that are considered quasi-natural, continually raise the problem of justifying and legitimating results that seem willful and particularistic, at least to those not favored by these results.[61] Undermining the state's claim to represent the universal interest, deeper interventions thereby weaken one of the major bases from which state managers can defend state autonomy.

The effects of deeply penetrating interventions on state autonomy transcend the realm of ideology and cultural legitimation. Increased penetration of civil society by the state activates political responses and increases the likelihood that societal interests will attempt to invade and divide the state. Increasing intervention makes the state more clearly an arena of social conflict and makes its constituent parts more attractive targets for takeover. In other words, the contradictions of civil society become more embedded in the state as the state more deeply penetrates civil society,[62] potentially undermining both its coherence as a corporate actor and its autonomy.

Taking a more double-edged view of the consequences of intervention for the state helps to dispel two misleading visions of the evolution of the state's role. The prediction of smooth mutual reinforcement leads directly to the view of the state's power vis-à-vis the rest of society expanding indefinitely once it passes a certain threshold. Such a view is not only empirically unjustified and theoretically suspect, but also likely to engender a distorted set of policy prescriptions in which limiting state capacity and autonomy becomes the paramount policy objective of private elites.

A conception of simple reciprocal reinforcement is also likely to generate misleading expectations with regard to states that lack the minimal capacity and autonomy necessary to undertake interventions, suggesting that the inability to intervene will make it impossible to develop the minimally requisite levels of autonomy and capacity. A more double-edged view, though recognizing that such problems are real, suggests that states which have not yet embarked on significant degrees of intervention may also have certain advantages in constructing the bases of autonomy and coherent corporate action.

As long as the consequences of effective intervention for autonomy and capacity are seen to be potentially both positive and negative, predictions of the evolution of the state's role will not collapse into these mirror images of vicious circles. It is, of course, also true that such a double-edged view complicates the possibilities of making general predictions, but this is precisely the point.

Although we hope to have provided some suggestive substantive insights regarding the factors that underlie effective state intervention, we are equally anxious to make a programmatic argument regarding the way in which questions of state autonomy and capacity should be approached in future research. Debates over relative autonomy and the capacity of the state to intervene in the process of accumulation are too often carried on in terms of categorical theoretical pronouncements rather than focusing on an analysis of historical variation. Here, we have tried to emphasize throughout that specific outcomes cannot be predicted by an overarching theory of capitalism, nor do they follow an even more all-embracing logic of industrial society. They must be viewed as complexly contingent, explicable only by the basis of careful comparative-historical research.

Appendix:
A Note on the Character of Target Social Relations

Research on the effectiveness of legal sanctions[63] has confirmed the utility of the distinction – going back to classic sociological theory[64] – between rational instrumental behavior and "expressive" behavior embedded in emotion and style of life. Other things being equal, rational instrumental behavior, especially if institutionalized in separate roles and organizational arrangements, responds more readily to legal actions and material inducements than expressive behavior, especially, again, if the latter is culturally approved and socially institutionalized. Thus, legal actions are much more effective in bringing about change in the sanctions of business firms than in behavior related to family and sex roles.

This is a proposition of considerable reach; yet it has to be hedged with certain qualifications. Some qualifications are immediately obvious; others are more subtle. The *ceteris paribus* clause first of all refers to the intensity and strength of opposing interests involved in a given contest and to the resulting balance of power. The rationality induced and supported by instrumental concerns can, in fact, be an asset in such struggles. Clearly, powerful corporations with strong interests opposed to certain policy goals are not an easy target for state intervention; yet the conclusion that it is power rather than the character of the target behavior that counts would be erroneous: Deeply ingrained and firmly institutionalized expressive behavior patterns may resist attempts at state-sponsored change even with an extremely unfavorable distribution of power resources.[65]

A more subtle qualification is that normative appeals must be considered in addition to coercion and material inducements; they can be effective directly, and, perhaps more importantly, they can modify significantly the impact of sanctions and the strength of resistance through processes of legitimation and delegitimation.

Finally, it seems important not to lose sight of the fact that state interventions, as well as other changes, often affect behavior not so much by their direct impact as by altering the overall situation in such a way that old motivations and social arrangements lead to new results and are then perhaps changed themselves. Although this type of cause–effect path may be very important indeed for any systematic understanding of social change, it is clear that such indirect effects are exceedingly difficult to anticipate and plan and thus are only a very uncertain basis for state intervention.

Even with all these qualifications, however, there are several interesting implications and extensions of the basic proposition. The more that social relations – in a society, in a subpopulation, or in a functional realm of social life – approach contractual market exchange and bureaucratic organization, the greater is the likelihood of effective state intervention, since market exchange and bureaucratic organization are major institutional forms that encourage instrumental behavior and protect it by institutional differentiation and insulation. This is not to deny that rational behavior must not be underestimated in any context and that scarcity and intense interest are spurs that move people toward rational action even against such obstacles as custom, ignorance, and norms defining which options are reasonable and which are "unthinkable." However, rational behavior *is* impeded by such obstacles. Contract and bureaucratic organization aid rational action in many ways, but perhaps most importantly by institutionally separating some pursuits from entanglement with multiple heterogeneous goals, an entanglement that makes rational action difficult and in the extreme virtually impossible.

The increasing penetration of civil society by market exchange and bureaucratic organization provides a partial explanation for the greatly increased, if not unlimited, transformative capacity the modern state displays in contrast to patrimonial rule in agrarian societies. It is not, however, such a partial explanation of quasi-evolutionary generalizations that most interests us here, even if it concerns the long-term growth of the transformative capacity of state organizations. Rather, for us, the most important implications of the basic proposition are those that suggest differences in the likelihood of achieving policy goals between countries, sections of a country, functional target areas, and types of intervention.

The basic proposition does suggest that certain policy goals will be more difficult to attain than others. The most obvious suggestion is that changes in economic behavior that also require changes in family patterns will be less easily achieved than changes that do not involve such linkages. A less obvious implication concerns ethnic and related forms of social fragmentation and seems to be of special importance for uneven economic development and its consequences for income distribution. Ethnic solidarities and exclusions may constitute obstacles to developmental and distributive policies that are exceedingly difficult to overcome. Reformulated in terms of market exchange and bureaucratic organization, the proposition also indicates some conditions under which ethnic barriers to public policy can be overcome. Even such a deeply entrenched pattern as official segregation in the southern United States proved amenable to change when the relevant local decisions were left to the public officials and businessmen responding to legal sanctions as well as to the inducements of federal funds and market opportunities – when, in other words, interventions could be addressed to a network of bureaucratic and market relations structurally differentiated from substantive preoccupation with racial enmity.

Nonrational aspects of social life are not only important as loci of resistance and unresponsiveness to inducements and sanctions. Any institution building requires transcending individual rational-instrumental behavior. Durkheim's formula of the "noncontractual elements of contract" must be understood broadly, applying to any institution building and to collectivity formation as well.[66] Goals, priorities, and commitments – the elements of action that function as reference points in the rational calculus and thus tend to be taken for granted in utilitarian analysis – are reshaped in effective processes of institution building and collectivity formation, at least for the pivotal sets of actors. This very general theoretical argument has led us to a simple yet powerful proposition: Wherever state interventions require new institutions, we cannot simply assume that insight, political will, and resources of the state elites will lead to corresponding institutional creations, but must reckon with considerable difficulties, delays, and failures and look for particular social processes capable of forging new social identities and institutional forms. The building of state institutions themselves was a case in point. The conditions of effective state action reach, wherever they concern institutional patterns and collective identities, deep into the past, often so far that their analysis has little (and if any, primarily negative) relevance to policy planning.

Notes

1. Karl Polanyi, *The Great Transformation* (New York: Rinehart, 1944); Alexander Gerschenkron, *Economic Backwardness in Historical Perspective* (Cambridge: Harvard University Press, 1962).
2. Douglass C. North, "A Framework for Analyzing the State in Economic History," *Explorations in Economic History* 16 (1979): 249–59.
3. Theda Skocpol, *States and Social Revolutions* (Cambridge: Cambridge University Press, 1979).
4. See Mancur Olson, *The Logic of Collective Action: Public Goods and the Theory of Groups* (Cambridge: Harvard University Press, 1965).
5. M. Merhav, *Technological Dependence, Monopoly and Growth* (New York: Pergamon Press, 1969).
6. See Albert Hirschman, *The Strategy of Economic Development* (New Haven, Conn.: Yale University Press, 1958).

7. Stuart Holland, ed., *The State as Entrepreneur* (London: Weidenfeld & Nicolson, 1972).

8. At a different level of abstraction one can ask useful questions about the character of the social relations that are the target of state intervention and the way it affects the chances of success of such intervention. Since we prefer to keep our comments on the level of institutional and structural analysis, but at the same time want to refer on occasion to these more elementary and abstract theoretical arguments, we provide a brief sketch in the appendix.

9. F. H. Cardoso, "On the Characterization of Authoritarian Regimes in Latin America," in *The New Authoritarianism in Latin America*, ed. D. Collier (Princeton, N.J.: Princeton University Press, 1979), p. 51.

10. Guillermo O'Donnell, "Tensions in the Bureaucratic-Authoritarian State and the Question of Democracy," in *The New Authoritarianism*, ed. Collier, p. 290.

11. Morton J. Horwitz, *The Transformation of American Law, 1780–1860* (Cambridge: Harvard University Press, 1977).

12. See, for instance, Nicos Poulantzas, *Political Power and Social Classes* (London: NLB, 1973); Fred Block, "The Ruling Class Does Not Rule: Notes on the Marxist Theory of the State," *Socialist Revolution* 7(3) (1977): 6–28; Stephen D. Krasner, *Defending the National Interest: Raw Materials Investments and U.S. Foreign Policy* (Princeton, N. J.: Princeton University Press, 1978); Eric A. Nordlinger, *On the Autonomy of the Democratic State* (Cambridge: Harvard University Press, 1981).

13. Peter B. Evans, Chapter 6, this volume.

14. Dietrich Rueschemeyer, "Structural Differentiation, Efficiency and Power," *American Journal of Sociology* 83(1) (1977): 1–25.

15. Theda Skocpol, "Political Response to Capitalist Crisis: Neo-Marxist Theories of the State and the Case of the New Deal," *Politics and Society* 10 (1980): 155–201.

16. See Eric O. Wright, *Class, Crisis, and the State* (London: New Left Books, 1978).

17. See, for example, Gerd Spittler, "Administration in a Peasant State," *Sociologia Ruralis: Journal of the European Society for Rural Sociology* 23 (1983): 130–44; G. Spittler, "Abstraktes Wissen als Herrschaftsbasis," *Koelner Zeitschrift fuer Soziologie und Sozialpsychologie* 32 (1980): 574–604.

18. Stephen G. Bunker, "Power Structures and Exchange between Government Agencies in the Expansion of the Agricultural Sector," *Studies in Comparative International Development* 14 (1979): 56–75; S. G. Bunker, *Barreiras Burocraticas e Institucionais a Modernizacao: Um Caso da Amazonia*," *Pesquisa e Planejamento Economico* 10 (1980): 555–600; S. G. Bunker, "Policy Implementation in an Authoritarian State: A Case from Brazil," *Latin American Research Review* 18(1) (1983): 33–58.

19. See Issa Shivji, *Class Struggles in Tanzania* (New York: Monthly Review Press, 1977); Susanne Mueller, "Retarded Capitalism in Tanzania," in *The Socialist Register 1980*, ed. Ralph Miliband and John Saville (London: Merlin Press, 1980), pp. 203–26.

20. See Louis Putterman, "Agricultural Cooperation and Village Democracy in Tanzania," in *International Yearbook of Organizational Democracy*, vol. 2, *International Perspectives on Organizational Democracy*, ed. B. Wilpert and A. Sorge (New York: Wiley, 1984), pp. 473–93.

21. See O. E. Williamson, *Corporate Control and Business Behavior* (Englewood Cliffs,

N. J.: Prentice-Hall, 1970); O. E. Williamson, *Markets and Hierarchies* (New York: Free Press, 1975).

22. Max Weber, "Parliament and Government in a Reconstructed Germany: A Contribution to the Political Critique of Officialdom and Party Politics," reprinted in *Economy and Society*, ed. G. Roth and C. Wittich (New York: Bedminster, 1968, originally 1917); see also the discussion by Wright, *Class, Crisis, and the State*, mentioned earlier.

23. Peter J. Katzenstein, Chapter 7, this volume.

24. Albert Hirschman, *The Strategy of Economic Development* (New Haven, Conn.: Yale University Press, 1958); A. Hirschman, *Development Projects Observed* (Washington, D.C.: The Brookings Institution, 1967).

25. Holland, ed., *The State as Entrepreneur*, on the role of the Institute for Industrial Reconstruction (IRI).

26. See L. P. Jones and M. E. Mason, "The Role of Economic Factors in Determining the Size and Structure of the Public Enterprise Sector in Mixed Economy LDCs" (Paper presented at the Second Annual Boston Area Public Enterprise Group Conference, Boston, March 1980).

27. See Hirschman, *Development Projects Observed*, on the steel industry.

28. Judith Tendler, *Electric Power in Brazil: Entrepreneurship in the Public Sector* (Cambridge: Harvard University Press, 1968); Richard J. Newfarmer, *Transnational Conglomerates and the Economics of Dependent Development* (Greenwich, Conn.: JAI Press, 1980).

29. Werner Baer, *The Development of the Brazilian Steel Industry* (Nashville, Tenn.: Vanderbilt University Press, 1969).

30. Frank Tugwell, *The Politics of Oil in Venezuela* (Stanford, Calif.: Stanford University Press, 1975); T. H. Moran, *Multinational Corporations and the Politics of Dependence: Copper in Chile* (Princeton, N. J.: Princeton University Press, 1974); David G. Becker, "The New Bourgeoisie and the Limits of Dependency: The Social and Political Impact of the Mining Industry in Peru since 1968" (Ph.D. diss., University of California, Los Angeles, 1981).

31. F. Sercovich, "State-Owned Enterprises and Dynamic Comparative Advantages in the World Petrochemical Industry: The Case of Commodity Olefins in Brazil" (Development Discussion Paper 96, delivered at the Harvard Institute for International Development, Cambridge, 1980); Peter B. Evans, *Dependent Development: The Alliance of Multinational, State and Local Capital in Brazil* (Princeton, N. J.: Princeton University Press, 1979); P. B. Evans, "Collectivized Capitalism: Integrated Petrochemical Complexes and Capital Accumulation in Brazil," in *Authoritarian Capitalism: The Contemporary Economic and Political Development of Brazil*, ed. T. C. Bruneau and P. Faucher (Boulder, Colo.: Westview Press, 1981), pp. 85–125.

32. On the example of coffee, see Stephen D. Krasner, "Manipulating International Commodity Markets: Brazilian Coffee Policy 1906–1962," *Public Policy* 21(4) (1973): 493–523.

33. Alice Amsden, "Taiwan's Economic History: A Case of Etatisme and a Challenge to Dependency Theory," *Modern China* 5(3) (1979): 341–80; see also Chapter 3, this volume.

34. On steel in Brazil, see Sergio Abranches, "The Divided Leviathan: State and Economic Policy Formation in Authoritarian Brazil" (Ph.D. diss., Cornell Uni-

versity, 1978); on the petrochemical industry see Evans's "Collectivized Capitalism" and "Reinventing the Bourgeoisie: State Entrepreneurship and Class Formation in the Context of Dependent Capitalist Development," in *Marxist Inquiries: Studies of Labor, Class, and States,* ed. Michael Buroway and Theda Skocpol (*American Journal of Sociology,* suppl. 88, 1982: 210–47).

35. Abranches, *The Divided Leviathan.*

36. Werner Baer and A. Figueroa, "State Enterprises and the Distribution of Income," in *Authoritarian Capitalism,* ed. Burneau and Faucher, pp. 59–85.

37. See Claus Offe, *Strukturprobleme des kapitalistischen Staates* (Frankfurt: Suhrkamp, 1972); and Claudio Pozzoli, ed., *Rahmenbedingungen und Schranken staatlichen Handelns* (Frankfurt: Suhrkamp, 1976).

38. Peter Katzenstein, Chapter 7, this volume.

39. It is worthwhile noting here a point that Nordlinger emphasized in his discussion of state autonomy, *On the Autonomy of the Democratic State.* Situations in which policy choices of state managers and of political representatives of powerful groups coincide can be taken, not as evidence for lack of autonomy, but rather as instances of a special case of autonomy. Thus, the Japanese state, which would have to be judged as having a very low degree of autonomy if conflict with the dominant class were the principal criterion, is probably more accurately seen as a state with considerable autonomy in this broader sense. Using this logic may also elucidate the Swiss case further.

40. See Block, "The Ruling Class Does Not Rule."

41. On American foreign policy, see Krasner, *Defending the National Interest;* Herbert Franz Schurmann, *The Logic of World Power: An Inquiry into the Origins, Currents and Contradictions of World Politics* (New York: Pantheon, 1974).

42. We are grateful to Albert Hirschman for having drawn this point to our attention.

43. Block, "The Ruling Class Does Not Rule," p. 15.

44. See E. V. K. Fitzgerald, *The State and Economic Development: Peru Since 1968* (Cambridge: Cambridge University Press, 1976).

45. See Gary Gereffi and Peter B. Evans, "Transnational Corporations, Dependent Development, and State Policy in the Semiperiphery: A comparison of Brazil and Mexico," *Latin American Research Review* 16(3) (1981): 31–64.

46. See Nora Hamilton, "State Autonomy and Dependent Capitalism in Latin America," *British Journal of Sociology* 32(3) (1981): 305–29.

47. M. Zeitlin and L. A. Ewen, " 'New Princes' for Old? The Large Corporation and the Capitalist Class in Chile," *American Journal of Sociology* 80(1) (1974): 87–123; M. Zeitlin and R. Ratcliff, "Research Methods for the Analysis of the Internal Structure of Dominant Classes: The Case of Landlords and Capitalists in Chile," *Latin American Research Review* 10(3) (1975): 5–61; M. Zeitlin, W. L. Neuman, and R. Ratcliff, "Class Segments: Agrarian Property and Political Leadership in the Capitalist Class of Chile," *American Sociological Review* 41(6) (1976): 1006–29.

48. See Evans, *Dependent Development;* Newfarmer, *Transnational Conglomerates.*

49. O'Donnell, "Reflections on the Patterns of Change."

50. See Alfred Stepan, *The State and Society: Peru in Comparative Perspective* (Princeton, N. J.: Princeton University Press, 1978); Cynthia McClintock, *Peasant Co-*

operatives and Political Change in Peru (Princeton, N. J.: Princeton University Press, 1981).

51. See John D. Stephens, *The Transition from Capitalism to Socialism* (New York: Macmillan, 1979); Evelyne Huber Stephens and John D. Stephens, "The 'Capitalist State' and the Parliamentary Road to Socialism: Lessons from Chile?" (Paper delivered at the Latin American Studies Association Meeting, Bloomington, Ind., October 1980); E. H. Stephens and J. Stephens, "Democratic Socialism in Dependent Capitalism: An Analysis of the Manley Government in Jamaica, *Politics and Society* 12(3) (1983): 373–411.

52. See, for instance, Terry Karl, "Petroleum and Political Pacts: The Transition to Democracy in Venezuela" (Paper presented at a conference, Transitions from Authoritarianism and Prospects for Democracy in Latin America and Latin Europe, Woodrow Wilson International Center for Scholars, Smithsonian Institution, Washington, D.C., June 4–7, 1981).

53. John C. H. Fei, G. Ranis, and S. W. Y. Kuo, *Growth with Equity: The Taiwan Case* (New York: Oxford University Press, 1979).

54. Peter T. Knight, "Brazilian Socioeconomic Development: Issues for the Eighties," in *World Development* 9(11/12) (1981): 1063–82.

55. See Stepan, *State and Society*; Evelyne Huber Stephens, *The Politics of Worker Participation: The Peruvian Approach in Comparative Perspective* (New York: Academic Press, 1980); McClintock, *Peasant Cooperatives*.

56. E. H. Stephens, *Politics of Worker Participation*.

57. See, for example, Skocpol, "Political Response to Capitalist Crisis," on the Wagner Act; and J. D. Stephens, *Transition from Capitalism*, on the effects of leftist party incumbency on levels of union organizing.

58. There is an important caveat to be added to this last example. Although the state may have generated militancy instead of the corporatist cooptation it intended, the policies that it embarked on still stemmed from a situation of relatively high autonomy vis-à-vis the dominant class. The state was essentially intent on destroying the traditional rural landowning class and also wanted to limit the freedom of action of industrial capitalists (see Stepan, *State and Society*). In Mexico and Brazil, where the organization of subordinate groups was undertaken under conditions of closer relations between the state and the dominant classes, the results were much more conventionally corporatist and had fewer long-term redistributive implications.

59. See Albert Hirschman, *Journeys toward Progress* (New York: Anchor Books, 1965), on "reform mongering."

60. Horwitz, *Transformation of American Law*.

61. See Jürgen Habermas, *Legitimation Crisis* (Boston: Beacon Press, 1975); Offe, *Strukturprobleme des kapitalistischen Staates*.

62. Ulrich K. Preuss, "Zum Strukturwandel politischer Herrschaft im bürgerlichen Verfassungsstaat," in *Rahmenbedingungen und Schranken staatlichen Handelns*, ed. Pozzoli, pp. 71–88.

63. Yeheskel Dror, "Law and Social Change," *Tulane Law Review* 33 (1959): 749–801; Lawrence M. Friedman, *The Legal System: A Social Science Perspective* (New York: Russell Sage Foundation, 1975).

64. Max Weber, *Economy and Society*. See also Talcott Parsons, *The Social System* (Glencoe, Ill.: Free Press, 1951).

65. Gregory J. Massell, *The Surrogate Proletariat: Moslem Women and Revolutionary*

Strategies in Soviet Central Asia, 1919–1929 (Princeton, N. J.: Princeton University Press, 1974).

66. Emile Durkheim, *The Division of Labor* (New York: Free Press, 1964); see also Olson, *The Logic of Collective Action.*

3. The State and Taiwan's Economic Development

Alice H. Amsden

Two features of Taiwan's post–World War II history are striking. First, it is one of the few nonsocialist economies since Japan to rise from the grossest poverty and to enter the world of the "developed."[1] Second, the state in Taiwan has played a leading role in the process of capital accumulation. It has positioned itself to prevail on key economic parameters such as the size of the surplus extracted from agriculture and the rate of profit in industry. To understand Taiwan's economic growth, therefore, it is necessary to understand its potent state.

The challenge of understanding the role of the state in Taiwan's economic development is increased by the fact that the state's initial aims were so clearly military and geopolitical rather than economic. When Taiwan was occupied by the vanquished Nationalist government in 1949, the Guomindang was obsessed with one objective: military buildup in order to retake the Mainland. As Edwin Winckler bluntly put it, "The Jiang Jie-Shi forces, if they had had their own way, wouldn't have spent one penny on economic development."[2] Given that militarism and economic development must to some extent operate at cross-purposes, competing for the same scarce resources, Taiwan's success must seem somewhat paradoxical.

If the role of the state is critical to economic development, why should an economy under the heel of the military end up with a "good claim to be ranked as the most successful of the developing countries"?[3] One of the obvious factors mitigating the negative consequences of militarism in the Taiwan case was American aid, which diminished the extent of resource competition. I shall try to show, however, that this was not the only, or necessarily even the most important, factor in allowing economic growth to arise out of militarism. Rather, I shall argue that the reality of economic development itself both seduced the military away from its initial orientation and changed its position within the state apparatus, which then freed up the process of capital accumulation still further.

Although the Guomindang state in Taiwan's "economic miracle" is our central focus, it is necessary to take into account other factors that favored the island's economic development after World War II. One of the most important of these is the legacy of the Japanese colonial period. We shall begin, then, with a discussion of the colonial period and from there look at the Guomindang state itself, its role in agriculture and industry, and its gradual transformation from a state in which the preeminence of military aims was overwhelming to one in which military aims came to coexist with an evermore absorbing interest in economic growth.

The Colonial Heritage[4]

It is a misconception that the Taiwan miracle commenced with the export of labor-intensive manufactures and a reduction of government management of trade and monetary matters in the decade of the 1960s. Taiwan already enjoyed a relatively fast rising real gross domestic product (GDP) in the 1950s (Table 3.1). Agriculture was then the dominant sector, and the economic regime in industry, as in many other underdeveloped countries, was one of protection of infant industries. Growth was also rapid during the years of Japanese domination (1895–1945). Excluding the war years of 1941–45, the per capita income of the agricultural sector almost doubled in half a century. This is a rather impressive figure given that the population rose by approximately 43%.[5]

The economy that the Japanese fashioned in Taiwan was achieved by means of deliberate planning and government ownership of major resources (in partnership with private Japanese capitalists). The dominance of the Japanese colonial administration in Taiwan's economy mirrored the dominant role of the Meiji government in Japan proper, which distinguished it in important respects from the colonial offices of England and France.[6] The Jiang Jie-Shi forces benefited enormously from their inheritance of Japanese state monopolies, and the whole interventionist approach taken by the Japanese to the development of an occupied territory was not lost to the Guomindang.

From the start, Taiwan was regarded as an agricultural appendage to be developed as a complement to Japan. A two-crop economy (sugar and rice) was encouraged much in the classical imperial pattern. But one aspect that sets Taiwan's colonial experience apart from the rest is that primary production was not confined to a foreign enclave with limited spillover on subsistence agriculture. Many farmers with access to arable land produced rice for market to meet the ever-escalating needs of Japanese consumers. Although sugarcane is frequently cultivated on large plantations in some Third World countries, in Taiwan it was grown by small owner-operators and tenants as well as on large land tracts owned by Japanese sugar manufacturers. Thus, agriculture in Taiwan was quickly and generally commercialized.[7]

Table 3.1. *Indicators of Taiwan's Economic Performance-Average Annual Growth Rates*

Period	Popu- lation	Gross national product	Per capita GNP	Agricultural production	Industrial production	Transportation & communications	Consumer prices in Taiwan area	Wholesale prices in Taiwan area	Exports	Imports
1953–62	3.5	7.5	4.1	4.8	11.7	10.4	8.7	7.6	19.5	17.0
1963–72	2.9	10.8	8.1	4.0	18.6	15.7	2.9	1.8	29.9	23.5
1973–80	1.9	8.7	6.6	2.4	11.9	19.0	12.4	12.0	25.0	27.7

Note: Growth rates in the third through seventh columns are in real terms.
Source: Taiwan Statistical Data Book (Taibei: Council for Economic Planning and Development, 1981).

The Japanese remodeled the archaic "three-tier" tenancy system, expropriating the "great" landlords and making the second tier of tenant landlords the legal owners of the land and directly responsible for taxes. A flat tax on land replaced a proportional tax on output, giving landlords incentive to squeeze more production out of the tenants below them. Ground rents remained very high (commonly 50% or more), but the new structure allowed greater scope for the assimilation of new farming practices. The peasants who produced, on rented land, 65–70% of Taiwan's total crop[8] applied new seed strains and other technological advances proffered by state-supported research agencies. Thus, the colonial state set in motion the application of science to farming, which characterizes the rural economy of Taiwan today.[9]

An elaborate network of agricultural associations, under the aegis of the government and rich landlords, provided peasants with extension education, the cooperative purchase of fertilizers, warehousing, and other services. When persuasion failed, the police were employed to force modern techniques onto rural communities that resisted change.[10] The experience that small tenants gained in experimenting with new seed strains and their familiarization with scientific farming would also prove to be of immense usefulness to the later land reform efforts of the Chinese Nationalists. The extensive network of agricultural associations that the Japanese introduced was created to facilitate police surveillance and control over the local population. Today, these associations persist and are an important element in the government's management of agriculture.

In the 1930s, Japan reshaped its policy of transforming Taiwan into a source of food supply for the home market. The shift in policy can be understood only in the context of Japan's increasing militarism and expansionism in the Pacific. Belatedly and frantically, Japan sought to refashion Taiwan as an industrial adjunct to its own war preparations and ambitions in Southeast Asia and South China.

From a few industries with strong locational advantages before 1930 (e.g., sugar and cement), industry in Taiwan expanded in the 1930s to include the beginnings of chemical and metallurgical sectors, and as World War II cut off the flow of duty-free goods, some import substitution began. Japanese hopes of building Taiwan into an industrial bridgehead to Southeast Asia and South China, however, never materialized.[11] The policy was in effect for too short a time before it was halted by World War II. Although the last-minute efforts to construct transport and harbor facilities suited to military and industrial needs proved highly beneficial in postwar years, many projects remained on the drawing board when war erupted.

Thus, economic growth in Taiwan under Japanese rule went about as far as it could go, given the internal contradictions of imperialism. Growth included a rise in per capita income; indeed, the welfare of Taiwanese peasants in the first half of the twentieth century may have exceeded that of Japanese peasants – according to such welfare indices as type of wearing apparel, housing, local bank deposits, and the like.[12] The most enduring legacy of the Japanese occupation, however, was less the betterment of living standards than a relatively well educated population and the building of a foundation for subsequent development. Whereas much of the gain in per capita income was lost as a consequence of war and an influx of Mainlanders following the Communist victory in China (and was not regained until the 1950s and 1960s), a relatively high level of literacy and the economic structure implanted by the Japanese survived. The major lesson of the Japanese interlude, however, was that to exploit the economic potential of Taiwan required much more than a reliance on inexorable market forces. It required deliberate state policies, something that the invading force from the Mainland seemed very unlikely to be able to provide.

The Nature of the Guomindang State

The state that took over Taiwan from the Japanese was a highly militaristic bureaucracy dominated by a single leader, Jiang Jie-Shi. On this there is much agreement. But the internal structure of the state, the relative power of different groups within it, and even the extent to which it was a real bureaucracy in the positive Weberian sense are open to debate. The absence of descriptive material that would allow one to characterize the Taiwan state with confidence is well summed up by Winckler as follows:

> The basic nature of the political system remains undefined. If the island has been a military and political client of the United States, we know little about the international and inter-bureaucratic workings of the relationship. . . . If the island has been a dictatorship ruled by Chiang Kai-Shek [Jiang Jie-Shi] and his son . . . we do not have political biographies of either for their Taiwanese periods. . . . If the island has been a police state dominated by military interests, we lack institutional descriptions and political history of its internal and external security agencies. . . . If the island has been successful in managing its economic development, we do not have a political account of the persons, agencies, and interests involved. If the island has been ruled by the Kuomintang [Guomindang], we know little more about the party's politics and administration than its own glossy brochures tell us. . . . Finally, we need to know the relative weights of setting, personality, security, economics, and ideology, and how these elements fit together.[13]

Despite the accuracy of Winckler's laments, those who would try to examine the state's role have, of course, no choice but to sift through the available evidence and make the inferences that seem the most reasonable. The problem we are presently interested in exploring is the relationship between militarism and economic development. Hence, we are interested in the Taiwan state's military and technocratic dimensions. Concerning the latter, one view holds that Taiwan's new rulers were a competent group. Another view, rooted in an earlier historical period, is far less flattering. A quote from Simon Kuznets provides a summary of the positive view:

The governing group were largely newcomers to the island and had no substantial interest roots, no clear affiliation with any of the various Taiwanese interest groups. . . . They could, therefore, act as independent arbitrators attempting to achieve a long-term consensus and calling for sacrifices by some groups for the benefit of all. If we assume that there was substantial agreement among the decision-making groups and the larger groups that were being served, both islanders and mainlanders; that the historical and cultural community among all groups was an adequate basis for consensus; *and that the decision-making groups had enough experience and human capital for generating the required decisions promptly and efficiently*, we can argue that this combination of the islanders and the mainlanders was favorable for a poor, developing country like Taiwan [italics added].[14]

As Barbara Tuchman relates, a more sour impression of the "experience and human capital" of the Guomindang (KMT) was held by Joe Stilwell, U.S. general of the Pacific theater, who had the displeasure of dealing with Jiang Jie-Shi before and during World War II:

By keeping rivals off balance through a technique of "fear and favor," in Stilwell's phrase, [Jiang Jie-Shi] appeared strong and indispensable but he did not know how to make a government. Though long on experience, his mind was narrow and his education limited. His most serious handicap was the lack of competent government servants. He never allowed a really able man to reach an important post lest he become too strong. Because he made loyalty rather than ability the criterion of service, he was surrounded by mediocrities. His brother-in-law, . . . who as vice-president of the Executive Yuan headed the civil government and usually served as Finance Minister, was described by [the] representative of the Bank of England in China as having "the mentality of a child of 12. If I were to record his conversations with me about banking and play it back, nobody would ever take [J]iang's government seriously again."[15]

History, however, does not necessarily repeat itself, and it has been contended that old dogs do learn new tricks:

[J]iang's authority as a leader derived not only from his skill at political maneuver, but also from his selection of able officials for key positions. He was far more effective in this respect in Taiwan than he had been on the mainland, where a glaring weakness of the Nationalist government was his tendency to value loyalty above ability. Loyalty was important in Taiwan, too. . . . His military and civilian officials in Taiwan, therefore, had to be loyal, but many were also able.[16]

The U.S. Aid Mission to Taiwan, moreover, needed competent technocrats with whom to work, and the mission used its clout to shield the technocracy and to help it compete politically.[17]

Thus, we can speak of the existence fairly early on of an economic technocracy in Taiwan – albeit an embryonic one – and not make fools of ourselves, for the technocrats need not be equated with the rascals they once were in prewar Mainland China.

Nevertheless, the development-oriented technocracy was overshadowed in the early postwar period by the military. Most of the Nationalist cliques of the prewar period had disintegrated with the Communist victory, save one: the Whampoa military cadets. Studies of the Taiwan state in the early and late 1960s discuss the power plays centered around the then security administrator (Jiang Jie-Shi's son). For the purposes of understanding the policy orientation of the Taiwan state in the immediate postwar period, however, it is sufficient to note a consensus in the literature about Jiang Jie-Shi's unchallenged political supremacy and the fact that he, "more than any other person . . . was responsible for asserting and perpetuating the concept of mainland recovery. . . . He insisted on tighter authoritarian controls and a greater diversion of resources to military and security purposes."[18]

On the basis of this admittedly sketchy picture of the Guomindang state apparatus, the possibilities of the state serving as an effective instrument of economic development would seem bleak. Yet from the beginning of its reign, the Guomindang bureaucracy embarked on a set of policies that, though they appear to have been chosen for political as much as, or more than, for economic reasons, were crucial to the island's eventual economic growth. Nowhere is this more evident than in agriculture.

Agriculture

When the Guomindang regime arrived on Taiwan, agriculture was by far the most important sector economically. Its share of GDP was twice that of industry, and it accounted for 90% of exports. It was, in addition, important politically. The potential threat of an impoverished peasantry had been driven home to the Nationalists on the Mainland, and they were concerned with restructuring agriculture accordingly. From the beginning, Guomindang policy toward agriculture had two faces. On the one hand, state action was the key to increasing agricultural output. On the other hand, agriculture was consistently squeezed to provide the surplus necessary to finance the growth of other sectors. The cornerstone of both sides of state policy was the land reform initiated in 1949 and completed in 1953.

Agriculture was reformed in three stages. First, farm rent was limited to a maximum of 37.5% of the total main crop yield. Second, public land formerly owned by Japanese nationals was distributed on easy terms, with preference given to the tenant claimants. Third, landlords were obliged to divest themselves of their holdings above a minimal size and to sell out to their tenants under the Land-to-the-Tiller Act.[19] This end to landlordism and the creation of a class of small holders was the inspiration of Dr. Sun Yat-Sen. The Guomindang's Land-to-the-Tiller Program amounted to sheer rhetoric in China during the 1930s and 1940s because would-be expropriated landlords were stalwarts of the Nationalists. In Taiwan, by contrast, the Mainlander government was under no obligation to the rural Taiwanese elite. Although both were of Chinese origin, they were as different ethnically and socially as the French and the Americans. Landlords were given land bonds in kind and stocks in public enterprise in exchange for the compulsory divestiture of their holdings. Some landlords profited from their stock ownership and became successful industrialists. Others went into bankruptcy.[20] The landlord class, however, sank into social oblivion, as the great landlord class had done half a century earlier.

Thus, almost overnight the countryside in Taiwan ceased to be oppressed by a small class of large landlords and became characterized by a large number of owner-operators with extremely small holdings. By 1973, almost 80% of the agricultural population consisted of owner-cultivators and another tenth of part owners.[21] Only 6% of farm income accrued to landlords and money lenders.[22] This undoubtedly underscores the fact that income distribution (by household) in Taiwan is far less inequitable than in most other Third World countries and is more like the pattern in advanced capitalist countries, which is not to say, however, that income distribution is equitable.[23]

The years 1953–68 witnessed annual growth rates in agricultural output that were impressive by any standard. Equally impressive was the spillover effect on industry, for however tight the squeeze on agriculture under Japanese rule, it was even tighter under the Jiang Jie-Shi administration. Whereas net real capital outflow from agriculture had increased at a rate of 3.8% annually between 1911 and 1940, it rose on average by 10% annually between 1951 and 1960.[24] Fast growth and a transfer of agricultural resources to the towns, however, were neither the outcome of free market forces nor the automatic result of purely technical phenomena – the green revolution. Rather, they reflected the structure of ownership in the countryside and state management of almost every conceivable economic activity.

It is well known that in developing countries there have been substantial gains in income among the few (i.e., the bigger farmers) when the new technology associated with the green revolution has been introduced. By contrast, the green revolution in Taiwan has transformed the life of almost every peasant. Furthermore, such an extensive application of science appears to hinge on government control over capital accumulation. The state distributes resources equally among all peasants, as the market mechanism might not do. Hence, there have been large gains among the many. A small class of big landowners has not yet resurfaced (nor, consequently, has a potentially cohesive source of opposition to the state). It is, then, a defining characteristic of Taiwan's agriculture that a multiplicity of small peasant proprietors exists in conformity with the bourgeois model of individualistic family farming, whereas directing this drama is a highly centralized government bureaucracy.

This point was recognized by two anthropologists in a study of rice farming in three Taiwan villages:

In this small island with its geographically mobile population, the arm of the state reaches down to virtually every farmer – outside the mountainous regions. This is a basic social and administrative characteristic of agriculture in Taiwan that has been long in the making.

As a result of [land tenure reforms], the rural landlord social class in the villages disappeared. The power of the state could reach then direct to every villager. The tenants of the past pay land tax now to the state and water fees to the government directly.[25]

In 1965, government agencies or related credit institutions supplied 65% of all agricultural loans. Before land reform, private moneylenders accounted for 82% of credit.[26] With respect to such activities as agricultural education and marketing, the government exerts its control through the elaborate network of agricultural associations laid down by the Japanese.[27]

The state monopoly on fertilizers was perhaps the most important element both in stimulating production and in extracting the surplus from agriculture. The positive effects of the fertilizer monopoly on the peasantry are well summarized by Falcon:

> It permitted all farmers to obtain the key modern input. It provided a source of credit that was an alternative to rural moneylenders. And it reduced price risks to farmers. (Widespread emphasis on risk-reduction is evident in Taiwan's agricultural policies and seems to be one of its important lessons.)[28]

At the same time the fertilizer monopoly was the key to extracting surplus from agriculture. Fertilizer was bartered for rice, and the barter ratio was highly unfavorable to farmers. The price that Taiwanese farmers paid for 100 kilograms of ammonium sulfate in 1964–65 was higher by almost 40% than the price that Japanese, Dutch, Belgian, American, or Indian farmers paid.[29]

Other mechanisms were also used to transfer real net surplus out of agriculture: land taxes, compulsory rice purchases by the government, loan repayments, and repayment for land resold to tenants under the Land-to-the-Tiller Program. (See Table 3.3 for a comparison of the tax burden of farm and nonfarm families.) All such collections were made in kind. All amounted to "hidden rice taxes," because the government's purchase prices were considerably lower than implicit market prices. The government's gains through rice collection were enormous. The hidden rice tax exceeded total income tax revenue every year before 1963.[30]

Three classic problems typically prevent small peasant production from becoming a solid basis for capital accumulation. First, peasant production is generally unproductive because it is unscientific. Second (according to an argument popularized by Stalin in defense of collectivization), peasant production frustrates the extraction of a surplus by the state because, at a low level of per capita income, farmers are said to consume their incremental output rather than market it (i.e., they may be more resistant to exploitation). In land-scarce Taiwan, the Guomindang state managed to overcome both of these problems. State provision of educational and scientific infrastructure helped to resolve the first problem. The second problem resolved itself as scientific agriculture raised per capita income and forced the peasantry to part with its crop in order to obtain fertilizer and socially necessary items of consumption.

The third problem historically encountered in peasant production is described by Hla Myint. When peasants become full-time producers for the market,

[they] cease to be self-financing and have to borrow from the chief source available to them – the money-lenders who charge them high rates of interest. With their ignorance of the rapidly changing market conditions, they tend to get heavily into debt, and where land is alienable, they lose their land in default of loans and get reduced to the status of tenants.[31]

Economic history in Taiwan, by contrast, saw the state effectively preserve an agrarian structure of small peasant holdings by stabilizing prices and by making credit generally available (i.e., simulating a perfect credit market by having no market at all). The Jiang Jie-Shi government also dispensed with foreign middlemen, who typically exercise monopoly power in rural areas of other economies, by itself buying cash crops cheaply from the peasantry and selling them at high prices.[32]

Thus, a self-exploitative peasantry, working long hours to maximize production per hectare, and a superexploitative state, ticking along effectively to exact the fruits of the peasantry's labor, operated hand in hand in Taiwan to great advantage until the late 1960s.

The only question that remains is, to *whose* advantage in particular? For Taiwan is not a classless entity, and the state acted in the interests of an elite when it squeezed the countryside. Unfortunately, whereas a voluminous amount of statistical information is available about Taiwan, very little class analysis has been published. Clearly, however, the historical roots of the Guomindang's etatisme and its class affiliations are traceable not only to Japanese colonialism, but also to events on the Mainland. We may hypothesize that the system of "bureaucratic capitalism" of late imperial China, with its total interpenetration of public and private interests, was transplanted into Taiwan, along with the Mainlanders. Although historical conditions were unpropitious for economic development under bureaucratic capitalism in China, they were favorable in Taiwan. The 1953 land reform and subsequent agricultural development breathed new life into the Guomindang apparatus, and the bureaucratic capitalism of the Guomindang regime sustained the life of the reform and small-scale farming.

In summary, agriculture in Taiwan gave industrial capital a labor force, a surplus, and foreign exchange. Even during the immediate postwar years of economic chaos and a world record rate of population growth, agriculture managed to produce a food supply sufficient to meet minimum domestic consumption requirements as well as a residual for export.[33] Good rice harvests have been a major factor behind Taiwan's stunning price (and real wage) stability. The foreign exchange saved as a result of high productivity in agriculture has been equally important.[34] Agriculture also managed to provide an important source of demand for Taiwan's industrial output, particularly chemicals and tools, and a mass market for consumption goods. The agrarian structure provided a degree of political stability sufficient to draw the most timid of foreign firms to the island. Agriculture has even been sufficiently productive to set a floor on industrial wages. Factory women who returned home to the farm during the sharp depression of 1974–75 subsequently refused to return to wage employment at prevailing rates.[35] A labor shortage symbolizes Taiwan's introduction to the problems of capitalist development rather than underdevelopment, and it is to industrialization that attention is now turned.

Industrialization

Taiwan's industrialization has often been falsely characterized as exhibiting the efficacy of a "laissez faire" strategy. It has been argued that Taiwan's success is due to the fact that it, unlike most Third World countries, resisted the temptations of infant industry protection. A study published by the Organization for Economic Cooperation and Development (OECD) in 1970, comparing industrialization in Brazil, Mexico, Argentina, India, Pakistan, the Philippines, and Taiwan, made a start toward dispelling this illusion.[36] The study showed that a regime of import substitution preceded the export of labor-intensive manufactures in Taiwan. Nor was infant industry protection a trivial episode in Taiwan's economic history. The protection afforded to sales on the home market in 1966, the year under examination in the OECD report, far exceeded that which prevailed in Mexico, a country reputed to be highly protectionist.[37]

In the period from 1956 to 1961, the government introduced a package of reforms to reorient the Taiwan economy toward export-led growth. Monetary and fiscal policies were redesigned, the exchange rate was devalued and unified, inflation was brought under control, and exports were made highly profitable. These changes have earned the title "liberalization" and have been responsible for Taiwan's reputation for successful development with sound formulas. Nevertheless, what is not appreciated is that protection in Taiwan of key import substitutes never appears to have abated.[38] Whereas exporters were allowed to import their inputs duty free after "liberalization," critical second-stage import-substitute items continue to be shielded from foreign competition. These include intermediate inputs, consumer durables, and transportation equipment. Although machinery has received little tariff protection, it has not yet needed much. The level of sophistication of Taiwan machinery has been such that the competitive niche it occupies is different from that of American or European equipment. Indicative of the spirit of Taiwan's tariff system is the fact that machinery is technically freely importable – but, in the case of machinery that is locally available, only by machinery users and not distributors and except in the case of a handful of countries, which just happen to be those that constitute a genuine threat to local machinery builders, such as Japan and South Korea. Still another indication of the protectionist proclivities of the Taiwan government is the fact that most import tariffs are redundant, that is, higher than necessary.[39] This is the case despite the vigorous efforts of the liberalization lobby, to be discussed shortly, to wipe the tariff slate clean.

Buried in a dense amount of data in a World Bank study on the virtues of export-led growth is the revelation that governments in Third World countries not only have begun to subsidize exports, but have also continued to protect import substitutes, Taiwan being no exception.[40] Thus, average net effective subsidy rates for the manufacturing sector were 38% in Argentina, 10% in Colombia, 7% in Israel, −11% in Korea, −4% in Singapore, and 10% in Taiwan; such rates in Taiwan not only are relatively high by this reckoning, but also show the traditional pattern of escalation as one moves from lower to higher levels of transformation. Thus, not only in Taiwan, but also in other semiindustrialized countries, higher levels of transformation (read second-generation import substitutes) have far higher average net effective subsidy rates than those just reported. Quantitative import controls have also played an important role in the protection of manufacturing industries.[41]

Inward-oriented growth in Taiwan was introduced in 1949 partly by default (traditional agricultural exports no longer found protected or preferential markets in Japan and China) and partly by design (it was politically expedient to aid the class of small capitalists that had acquired a portion of the old Japanese facilities). Small enterprises were in serious trouble by 1949 as a result of the loss of the Mainland market and the reappearance of competitive Japanese goods.[42] Import, foreign exchange, and licensing controls were introduced by the government to salvage small establishments from extinction and to ease the critical balance of payments situation.

Inward-oriented growth in Taiwan's small domestic market, however, soon stalled. Although it conferred high profits to some, it conferred inflation, monopoly, excess capacity, a reliance on American donations of hard currency, and corruption to all. It was only after manufacturing had made a fair start, however, that the Taiwan government hesitantly charted a new course in the direction of export-led growth. Two points are worth stressing in this regard. First, "liberalization" should in no way be interpreted as a restoration in Taiwan of a "market economy." Government management of capital accumulation has continued, as evidenced, if by nothing else, by tariff protection. Second, although economists have viewed a regime of export-led growth as one that is more in keeping with liberal economic principles, the Taiwan government has not been guided by any theoretical orthodoxy to turn a profit. A civil servant writes:

Unorganized production and export often led to excessive production and cut-throat competition in foreign markets, which inevitably cause a sharp decline in price, deterioration in quality, and finally loss of the export market. To combat these shortcomings, the government has encouraged unified and joint marketing of exports in foreign markets through limitation of production by means of export quotas, improvement of quality, and unified quotation of export prices.[43]

Cartels, in whatever variation, have been encouraged by the government and, at one time or another, have covered most of Taiwan's major exports: textiles, canned mushrooms and asparagus, rubber, steel, paper products, and cement.[44] The government has tried to get the marketing of all exports into Taiwanese hands because both bureaucrats and businesspersons alike are sensitive to the inroads in overseas marketing made by large Japanese trading companies; this is in spite of the efficacy of these trading companies and the lackluster track record of those of Taiwan.

At issue is not merely the quibble that the government of Taiwan has intervened far more in the Taiwan economy than liberal economists who champion export-led growth acknowledge. The point, rather, is that the government of Taiwan has never been guided by free-market principles as such; so to attribute Taiwan's success to a commitment to such principles, whether in theory or in practice, is misleading. What has obsessed the Guomindang state since its defeat in China is economic stability. In the words of K. T. Li, one of the chief architects of government policy, "During the 1950s . . . the overriding economic consideration was stability."[45] And in the 1970s:

Everything possible is done to maintain price stability, even if it requires being less mindful of the growth rate. Our large governmental sector employs numerous military personnel, civil servants, and teachers, and any price increase affects these persons with particular severity[46]

And again:

I wish to emphasize . . . that we do not seek unduly rapid growth, but prefer a steady, moderate expansion in directions which will be of greatest benefit to our nation.[47]

To achieve stability, the government of Taiwan appears to have thought it prudent sometimes to shield the economy as much as possible from market forces and at other times to use them, but never to embrace them as a rule of thumb out of conviction.

Foreign Aid, Foreign Capital, and State Enterprises

Flows of U.S. aid in the 1950s and 1960s and, more recently, flows of foreign direct investment played a critical role in capital formation in Taiwan. These flows, particularly the initial deluge of U.S. aid, obviously had implications for policies and politics in addition to providing capital. The magnitude of the aid cannot be denied. In 1955, when aid reached its peak, it amounted to over half of gross investment, and it was not until 1964 that it fell below 20%.[48] Politically, aid was critically important: It kept the state in power by helping to bring inflation down from 3400% in 1949 to 9% in 1953[49] by means of the arrival of large quanties of both consumer goods and producer goods at a desperate moment.

In terms of long-run economic growth, the impact of aid was minor.[50] Most aid went for military purposes and the remainder for infrastructure broadly defined. (From this perspective, aid to Taiwan was a success by U.S. standards, for the goals of providing aid tend to be the buildup of infrastructure and the buttress of political stability.) Thus, the effects of aid may be said to have been felt in perpetuity only in terms of a multiplication of civil engineering projects and know-how and improvements in the administrative capability of the Taiwan technocracy. The extent to which Taiwan's turn to export-led growth can be attributed to U.S. pressures is difficult to say: Now, all parties concerned are eager to take credit for it. All that is certain is that freer trade and freer enterprise (including freer foreign enterprise) were preached by the American Aid Mission. In view of the preferences of its major benefactor, the extent to which the Guomindang government persisted in its "etatisme" is all the more impressive. To appreciate this fully, we must focus on public sector production as well as on policy making.

In 1952, as much as 57% of total industrial production (value added at 1966 prices) and 56.7% of manufacturing output were accounted for by public corporations (Table 3.2). Since then, the government has repeatedly been under pressure either to freeze or to reduce the size of its holdings. Partly under the persuasion of U.S. Agency for International Development, majority or 100% equity in four public corporations (one highly profitable, two others distinctly less so) was transferred to landlords in 1954 as partial compensation for confiscations carried out under the 1953 land reform. There has also been sporadic pressure for denationalization from local capitalists, who want less crowding out in credit markets or who want a greater share of the action in lucrative state enterprises (in 1982, however, fourteen of fifteen state enterprises were in the red).[51] Finally, there has been pressure from what may be termed the liberalization lobby to reduce both tariff protection and the scope of public corporations.

Yet the government has resisted divestment, in the tenacious tradition of Sun Yat Sen, whose criticisms of monopoly capitalism became integral to Guomindang ideology.[52] By the early 1980s, the share of the public sector in manufacturing production had fallen to less than 20%. Nevertheless, the government remains dominant in such fields as heavy machinery, steel, aluminum, shipbuilding, petroleum, synthetics, fertilizers, engineering, and, recently, semiconductors. Almost every bank in Taiwan is also wholly or partially owned by the state (foreign banks were not allowed to establish operations until 1969). The lending activities of all financial institutions have

Table 3.2. *Selected Indicators in Taiwan's Industrial Sector, 1952–80*

Indicator	1952	1962	1975	1980
Industrial output index (1952 = 100)	100	303	2,010	4,108
Share of industry in NDP[a]	18	26	39	46
Share of industry in total employment[b]	9	(25)	36	42
Share of public ownership in total industrial production	57	46	19	18
Share of industrial products in total exports	8	51	84	91
		1951	**1971**	**1980**
Selected shares in industrial production				
Mining		10.2	3.5	1.9
Food processing		18.4	7.2	10.1
Textiles		18.4	20.8	11.2
Chemicals, petroleum, rubber, and nonmetallic products		10.4	22.3	19.1
Metal products, machinery, and electrical machinery		5.6	17.3	20.1

Note: Industry includes mining, manufacturing, construction, and utilities.
[a] Net domestic product; all shares are expressed as percentages.
[b] The figure for 1952 is from Gustav Ranis (see note 49); the figure in parentheses is for 1967. Beginning with 1967, figures are averages per 1,000 workers.
Source: Taiwan Statistical Data Book (Taibei: Council for Economic Planning and Development, 1981); *National Income of the Republic of China* (Taibei: Directorate General of Budgets, Accounts, and Statistics, 1981).

been under strict state supervision.[53] Thus, if the government in Taiwan does not quite "control the commanding heights," it goes a long way toward doing so.

The government has been slow to divest itself of its holdings for two basic reasons. From the beginning, public enterprise has served to consolidate the power of the Mainlander bureaucracy. In recent years, public enterprise has also allowed the Guomindang to buttress its own power vis-à-vis foreign capital. One of the fundamental consequences of public enterprise has been the control by the state rather than by multinationals of key sectors in the economy. This is not to belittle the power of the multinations, nor to suggest the absence of an organic solidarity between the productive activities of the state and foreign investors. Recently, in the case of automobiles, they have tried to ally to form a nucleus of expansion. But the state has held its own in several crucial respects. The government did not abandon its traditionally conservative attitude toward foreign investment until the export boom of the late 1960s had gotten underway. Only then did foreign firms begin arriving in Taiwan in significant numbers.

By 1971, overseas Chinese and other foreign investments amounted to roughly one-seventh of total registered capital (about the same as in Brazil), although statistics on foreign investment are problematic.[54] Foreign investments, however, have been concentrated in electronics, chemicals, and textiles destined for export. Foreign investments have not mushroomed with the government's turn to heavy industry. According to one account, between 1973 and 1980, foreign firms were responsible for as much as half of total investment and as much as 20% of total exports in the electronics sector, but they were responsible for only 10% of total investment in manufacturing.[55] Finally, Taiwan has not become highly indebted to international banks to finance its heavy industry. As discussed shortly, a relatively low reliance on foreign credit is due to a high domestic propensity to save. Moreover, although Taiwan has been a sizable international borrower by the standards of less developed countries, its international debt service/export ratio is very low – ranging between 5 and 10% – as a consequence of its very rapid growth of exports.[56]

The Jiang Jie-Shi government, therefore, cannot be said to have delivered Taiwan into foreign hands, either by letting foreign banks dominate credit or by letting foreign firms dominate manufacturing. Nor can the government be said to have been overwhelmed by its own technocracy (mostly American-educated), which has lobbied for lower tariffs and a privatization of state enterprises. The voice of the military has remained audible even as its visibility within the state apparatus has diminished (e.g., in the 1950s, an army general served as economics minister). The voice has remained audible to the extent that it appears to speak for continued state control of the economy for purposes of defense and social order, much as in the old Guomindang tradition.

This contrasts with the behavior of another military in another small developing country with a highly educated population: Chile. Here, the military did buy the economic liberalism of its technocracy, closed the doors to state enterprise and opened them to foreign imports and investments – with disastrous effect.[57] The point is that there is no necessary association between militarism and economic nationalism, although in Taiwan, the relationship is positive.

The public sector in Taiwan is also still very important as far as capital formation is concerned. Although the state's share of gross domestic investment has fallen from a high of 62% in 1958, it still amounted in 1980 to as much as 50%.[58] State spending has gone largely to finance ten major development projects in infrastructure, integrated steel, shipbuilding, and petrochemicals, which contributes to the fact that manufacturing in Taiwan has progressed in breadth (the percentage of manufacturing in GDP) and in depth (the percentage of "sophisticated" products and processes in total manufacturing output). Whereas in 1952 agriculture accounted for 36% of net total domestic product and manufacturing for only a tenth, agriculture now accounts for only 9% and manufacturing for more than a third.[59] By 1980, 42% of all workers (15 and over) were engaged in the industrial sector

(Table 3.2). There has also been a decline in the absolute number of workers in the agricultural labor force since the early 1970s. In historical perspective, this is highly significant. In the United States, absolute declines in the farm population did not begin until the 1930s.[60]

Nor has manufacturing been confined to "wigs and wallets," as myth once held. In the course of six "plan periods," which incidentally can be described, at most, only as "indicative," important structural changes have occurred within manufacturing. Textiles and food processing were the leading sectors during the first two plan periods (1953–56 and 1957–60).[61] During the second plan period, however, the relative contribution of nondurable consumer goods, particularly food processing, declined, whereas that of intermediate goods (cement and paper) expanded. Chemicals (fertilizer, soda ash, plastics, and pharmaceuticals) assumed major importance during the third plan period (1961–64). Capital and the production of durable goods (electrical and nonelectrical machinery, such as radios and sewing machines, and transport equipment, such as bicycles and ships) as well as petroleum products grew enormously during the fourth and fifth plan periods (1965–68 and 1969–72). The seventh plan period (1976–81) saw large increases in heavy industry. These structural shifts are evident in Table 3.2, although they are not to be exaggerated. The percentage of so-called light industry in manufacturing output was still 48% in 1977, down, however, from 54% in 1970 and 60% in 1960.[62]

Exploiting the World Market

The nineteen-point reform program introduced by the government between 1956 and 1961 made exporting highly profitable. Not only were exporters wined on tax and credit subsidies; they were also dined on tariff reductions from prewar China heights. This allowed them to take advantage simultaneously of advanced levels of world productivity for their inputs and exotic Taiwan wage levels for their outputs. In what follows, we discuss the supply-side factors that permitted Taiwan to profit from the world market, directing attention to the role of the state.

Taiwan exports (90% of them manufactures) are highly competitive in world markets for reasons of low costs and rising productivity. There appears to have been a substantial fall in Taiwan's wage costs per unit of output relative to those of competitors in the period spanning 1954–71, although there is a great deal of uncertainty about the figures.[63] After the energy crisis in 1973, when the dust had settled, Taiwan could still be seen to have a cost advantage due to lower wage rates, by comparison not only with Japan, but also with South Korea, Hong Kong, and Singapore. International wage comparisons are difficult to make because of exchange-rate distortions and international variations in data collection. Nevertheless, estimates of industrywide trade associations tend to corroborate the information contained in Table 3.3; to wit, wages in Taiwan are a good deal lower in all job categories than wages in competitor countries.

Table 3.3. *Comparative Wages and Salaries, Midyear 1978 (Mean Monthly Salary[a] in U.S. Dollars)*

Professional group	Taiwan	South Korea	Hong Kong	Singapore	Philippines	Thailand	Indonesia	Malaysia	Japan	Federal Republic of Germany
Industrial engineer	358	639	618	821	190	437	752	552	1,587	2,884
Mechanical engineer	407	587	627	710	191	460	786	677	1,244	2,884
Electrical engineer	322	509	590	803	203	492	299	762	1,025	2,884
Accountant	482	930	904	923	189	498	733	949	1,521	1,923
General manager	1,051	1,192	2,389	2,097	809	1,784	1,513	2,672	3,413	5,495
Production manager	729	1,049	1,203	1,215	498	669	851	1,050	2,488	3,745
Section chief	461	889	1,015	518	219	392	439	786	1,587	3,222
Executive secretary	435	590	729	503	175	425	496	404	1,360	1,465
Typist	184	318	245	211	73	153	214	133	756	1,099
Junior clerk	150	344	258	198	114	135	173	180	785	1,190
Foreman	369	493	425	413	198	203	241	390	1,500	1,328
Skilled worker	167	318	255	206	81	86	137	181	1,161	1,282
Semiskilled worker	115	311	189	133	70	76	96	129	942	1,145
Unskilled worker	93	146	158	102	52	51	65	84	698	915
Tool maker	245	330	303	210	64	135	482	304	665	1,465
Cleaning worker	120	208	170	108	59	77	53	82	550	824

[a]In addition to the monthly base salary, most companies pay regular bonuses ranging from 1 to 12 months of the salary, varying by company and by country. In order to make the monthly base salary information meaningful in terms of actual cost, this survey has increased the monthly base salary to include any bonuses paid. However, extraordinary bonuses, commission payments, etc., have not been included.

Source: International Business Review, Hong Kong as cited and adapted by Anton Galli, *Economic Facts and Trends* (London: Verlag Weltforum for the Institut für Wirtschaftsforschung, 1980).

Table 3.4. *Long-Run Changes in Industrial Wages, Productivity, and Labor Costs (Annual Rate of Change)*

	1954–61	1961–73	1973–75
Real wages	2.5	6.3	5.2
Money wages	11.4	9.7	29.5
Labor productivity[a]	4.2	10.8	6.0
Unit labor cost	7.2	−1.2	23.5

Note: Data are expressed as percentages.
[a]The first column is for the years 1953–61.
Source: Adapted from Lundberg (note 64).

Apart from the noise of exchange-rate distortions, wage levels remain relatively low because the *rate of increase* in wages has been modest. What is more, the movement of wages in relation to labor productivity has been favorable for unit labor costs. In both regards, one detects the arm of the state. Labor unions are virtually nonexistent and strikes are prohibited, because Taiwan is still technically at war. One key to the advance in productivity is the enormous emphasis placed on public education, financed by a tax system that is highly regressive.

Table 3.4 presents data on changes in real and nominal wages, labor productivity, and unit labor costs, which constitute the most proximate causes of Taiwan's export success, as well as its extraordinary price stability.[64] By comparison with other countries, including South Korea, Taiwan's rate of real wage increase has been low, particularly if one juxtaposes it against the rate of change of per capita income, which may be taken as a proxy for demand conditions in the labor market.[65] Also striking is the rapid rise in labor productivity and the *fall* in unit labor costs in the critical period from 1961 to 1973.

The rapid rise in labor productivity has not been autonomous and may be understood as emerging out of the cumulative process of fast growth itself. As growth has accelerated, throughput time has decreased, profitability has risen, and investments have skyrocketed in foreign technology (both embodied in machinery imports and disembodied in the form of services). The scale of production has mounted and, with it, specialization and the division of labor; and, finally, the time required for the accumulation of experience has been telescoped, opportunities to use such experience to improve process and product have multiplied, and firm-level increments in productivity have been realized.[66]

That Taiwan has assimilated foreign technology as effectively as it has in no small part harks to its highly educated population. It was thought to be the most educated in all of Asia, with the exception of Japan, when the Japanese occupation of Taiwan ended after World War II. High investments in education continued thereafter, increasingly in the technical fields.

By the early 1970s, Taiwan had more engineers per 1,000 persons engaged in manufacturing than all other developing countries for which data are available, with the exception of Singapore.[67] Since then, investments in education have soared in tandem with the rate of growth of output; the number of engineering students studying abroad almost doubled between 1975 and 1976, and the number of engineering students studying in Taiwan doubled between 1968–69 and 1972–73 and then doubled again between 1973 and 1982–83.[68] Taiwan trains 50% more engineers in proportion to its population than the United States.[69]

Although there has been no shortage of profitable investment outlets for Taiwan firms to exploit, the opposite has been true of savings. Over the years, however, as a proportion of gross national product (GNP), savings have risen phenomenally. This has spared Taiwan the mutilation of over-extended international indebtedness, as discussed earlier. Savings as a percentage of national income were less than 5% in 1952, 6.5% in 1962, 26.8% in 1972, and almost one-third a decade later.[70] The composition of savings has also altered. The share of foreign savings has nose-dived, from around 40% in 1952–60, the heyday of U.S. aid, to a *negative* percentage in the period since 1972, whereas the shares of both public and private domestic savings have risen.[71]

According to Lundberg,[72] the phenomenal rise in the savings ratio can to a considerable extent be explained by the high and increasing share of gross profits in national income. As for the government, it has been able to save as much as it has, despite a fivefold increase in real expenditures, by holding back on certain allocations and by raising revenues. On the payments side, the proportion allocated to defense expenditures – the largest single item in the government budget – has been halved, and social, health, and pension payments have been kept remarkably low by Western standards. On the revenue side, the tax structure in Taiwan has remained regressive. Initially, agriculture provided a massive investment fund for industry. Now, tax receipts accrue largely from commodities; income and corporate taxation is either negligible or evaded. In short, a "favorable climate for capital formation exists in Taiwan, with a minimum concern for the distribution of income and wealth."[73]

A few remarks on the relationship between the Nationalist government and Taiwan firms are in order, lest it be thought that the interests of capital have been served by the state unstintingly. Taiwan's ability, by comparison with, say, a Latin American country, to situate its economy in the lap of the international market has rested in part on the clout that the state has used against private producers. Because the governance of private producers is nowhere clearly defined, capital everywhere imagines incursions into its domain by the state, but it is understandable why such complaints are so vocal in Taiwan.

We have already noted how "the arm of the state reaches down to virtually every farmer."[74] Similarly, "the government is deeply involved in all aspects of industry."[75] Even after most import and foreign exchange controls were lifted, the government exercised its will through the myriad licenses necessary for a firm to operate; the requirement of prior approval for foreign loans and technology agreements; public ownership of the banking system, which held interest rates much higher than in most Third World countries; vagueness in tax laws such that politically uncooperative firms could be threatened with audits; and so on. All businesspersons agree that they could be put out of business at the caprice of the state in a matter of months. Whereas a large percentage of output in, say, South Korea is realized by giant conglomerates, Taiwan is still a land of small farmers and firms.[76] Recently, government policy has shifted toward the encouragement of consolidation in agriculture and merger in industry. Not only has this policy met resistance by the parties concerned; one might also imagine the government's ambivalence toward it, for small entities tend to be less threatening and more tractable than large ones.

Rentiers and capitalists alike in Taiwan have, in the past, experienced the dismembering or disabling effects of state power: The former were expropriated by a land reform, and the latter succumbed to the liberalization reforms that ushered in export-led growth. When a government charts a new economic course, entrenched interests are threatened. In the case of a turn to export-led growth, class conflict is stirred up by devaluation and deflation. A liberalization of imports hurts import-substituting firms and the banks that are financing them. When these are foreign, they can bring extraeconomic power to bear against new policy directives. These consequences of the turn to export-led growth were relatively mild in Taiwan. For one thing, the economy was both far less industrialized and far less inflationary than, say, some of the Latin American economies, so that fewer entrenched interests were upset. The state also controlled many sectors that would otherwise have been hurt, and foreign firms and foreign banks were absent. Nevertheless, private domestic firms that were not satisfied with the sweeteners of export subsidies and protection for second-generation import substitutes were swept away. In short, Taiwan was better able to turn to the international market than other poor countries because the balance of power between the state and both labor and capital was weighted far more to the state's advantage.

To a certain degree Taiwan enjoyed an edge over other developing countries in its export effort because of historical and geopolitical specificities: Taiwan's careful study of its erstwhile colonizer enabled it to absorb the Japanese economic experience and to appreciate that export-led growth was a viable strategy. In addition, the way was paved for the acceptance of Taiwan products in the U.S. market first by Japanese exports and then by those of U.S. multinationals, which had chosen Taiwan as an export platform after U.S. aid had secured it for democracy. Clearly, however, these explanations of Taiwan's ability to exploit the international market – whereas most developing countries appear instead to have been exploited by it – are dwarfed by those explanations that focus on the forceful manipulation of Taiwan's political economy by the state.

Economic Growth and the Changing Nature of the State

The initial puzzle of the role of the Taiwan state was not just a question of magnitude. In terms of scope, Taiwan is simply a particularly striking example of the positive association between state intervention and the acceleration of economic growth that is now generally accepted to prevail in cases of Third World capitalist development.[77] What made Taiwan particularly interesting was that the state was so effective despite the clear priority the military placed on defense over development and the clear dominance of the military within the state apparatus. The discussion so far has not resolved this puzzle. On the contrary, the turn to export-led growth seems to make the relation between apparent military dominance of the state and successful economic policy even more perplexing.

The important role of public enterprises, like the early economic self-sufficiency promoted by the state, is quite consistent with what can be presumed to be the interests of the military. Import-substitution industrialization, low reliance on foreign investors, and a focus on greater output of basic foodstuffs would all square with the military's presumed preference for autarky. Export-led growth, on the other hand, appears to contradict the policies the military could be expected to favor. Why should a regime fanatically committed to national security tolerate a policy change that made the Taiwan economy highly vulnerable to foreign supply and demand as well as more dependent on foreign-owned firms?

The answer to this question is complex. First, it must be emphasized that the increased reliance on international markets and capital that characterized the civilian economy did not extend to defense production. The military ran its own production facilities, supplied with basic inputs by state enterprises. In addition to state enterprises, there are many special-status companies that obtain favors and/or incentives from the state. Among these are the enterprises owned or invested in by the Guomindang or by the Vocational Assistance Committee for Retired Soldiers, a complex of more than forty firms reputed to be the largest single enterprise on the island.[78] By the 1960s, military arsenals produced much of the equipment and less sophisticated weaponry and ammunition needed by the armed forces. In 1969, a loan was made to Taiwan to build a factory to co-produce military helicopters (with Bell Helicopter Co.). By that year, Taiwan was producing M-14 rifles, machine guns, artillery shells, mortars, and other defense materials.[79] Soon, another small step toward self-sufficiency was taken with the initiation of an agreement with Northrop Aircraft Co. to co-produce F-5E fighter planes.[80] This mushrooming military economy may have made the generals less concerned with the diminishing autarky of the civilian sector.

Export-led growth, then, was consistent with the maintenance, and even expansion, of previous levels of autarky in the sectors that were most critical for warfare. Nevertheless, there is abundant evidence, beginning at the time of Taiwan's turn to export-led growth, that the influence of the military over economic affairs began to wane. For instance, the government began to support family planning, whereas it was once deterred by the insistence of party elders that such a policy would reduce the number of soldiers available for retaking the Mainland.[81] Taiwan ceased being self-sufficient in basic foodstuffs because it was more profitable to specialize in cash crops for export. Defense spending as a percentage of GNP and of government expenditures also fell (until recently). In 1960, when export-led growth was just getting underway, military expenditure as a percentage of GNP was roughly 13% and, as a percentage of government expenditure, 65%.[82] By 1978, these figures had fallen to 8 and 34%, respectively.[83]

Part of the answer to the apparent contradiction between the turn to export-led growth and the military's interests is that these interests were no longer reflected in state policy as monolithically as they had been in the period immediately following the takeover of Taiwan. And even if the military had held complete sway, it would have had little option other than to turn to export-led growth. Given the exhaustion of import-substitution industrialization and foreign reserves, the continued pursuit of increased autarky would have been economically suicidal, although reliance should not be placed on the functionalist argument that because a decision was economically necessary the military would endorse it even at the expense of its own geopolitical ends.

More understanding is gained, however, by a closer examination of the changing relationship over time of economic and geopolitical factors. On the one hand, the dream of retaking the Mainland grew dimmer as the Communist regime there proved its durability. The repossession of China "had begun as a fierce resolve; it became an aspiration, then a myth, then a liturgy."[84] At the same time, it became less clear that Taiwan could rely simply on its anti-Communist credentials to ensure support from its major ally, the United States. From this perspective, increased reliance on foreign investment, which went along with export-led growth, might be seen to be as valuable in securing powerful political allies as in reaping economic benefits.[85]

The key to the changing logic of Taiwan's international position, however, was bread and butter. Taiwan, as well as Communist China, was proving itself to be a viable economic entity, as evidenced by its control over inflation and its fast growth. The economic viability of Taiwan meant that the population of Mainlanders as a social collectivity no longer needed to retake China to enrich itself. This was all the more true when it became clearer in the 1960s that economic gains in Taiwan were being realized not on the ephemeral basis of plunder, as they had been between 1945 and

1949, or of buying cheap and selling dear, as they had been to some extent during the earliest years of import-substitution industrialization, but rather on the sustained basis of capital accumulation. I think that this, more than anything else, is what underlay the military's acceptance of export-led growth and its exit from the center of the stage of Taiwan's political economy.

In the last analysis, despite the continued power of the military within the state, Taiwan provides an interesting commentary on Engels's classic dictum that when "the internal public force of a country stands in opposition to its economic development. . . . [i]nexorably and without exception, the economic evolution has forced its way through."[86] Engels's concern was with the open contest between an economically reactionary elite's attempt to maintain its rule by political means and the transformative power of economic change. Taiwan does not exactly fit this description, but one can observe in Taiwan the powerful effect of economic change on the orientation of political force. The military was not overcome by the emergence of successful capitalist development, but it does seem that it found the expanding opportunities such development offered to be more attractive then the shrinking ones that were promised by a continued fixation on geopolitical struggle.

Taiwan, then, is more than a case in which the essential contribution of state intervention to economic development can be observed. It is a case that demonstrates the reciprocal interaction between the structure of the state apparatus and the process of economic growth. The Taiwan state, which appeared on its arrival from the Mainland to be an unlikely instrument for the promotion of development, proved to be a most effective one. At the same time, changes in the nature of the state itself appear to have been an important by-product of economic development. The state, in short, can be said both to have transformed Taiwan's economic structure and to have been transformed by it.

Notes

1. By "developed" is meant a fully employed economy wherein output rises not merely because inputs of land, labor, and capital rise, but also because productivity rises.
2. Edwin A. Winckler, Remarks to a conference on Taiwan (Columbia University, 1982).
3. I. M. D. Little, "An Economic Reconnaissance," in *Economic Growth and Structural Change in Taiwan: The Postwar Experience of the ROC*, ed. Walter Galenson (Ithaca, N. Y.: Cornell University Press, 1979), pp. 448–507.
4. The sections of this chapter on Taiwan's colonial heritage and agriculture borrow heavily from Alice H. Amsden, "Taiwan's Economic History: A Case of Etatisme and a Challenge to Dependency Theory," *Modern China*, July 1979: 341–79.
5. A. Y. C. Koo, *The Role of Land Reform in Economic Development* (New York: Praeger, 1968).

6. H. Y. Chang and R. H. Myers, "Japanese Colonial Development Policy in Tai-wan, 1895–1906: A Case of Bureaucratic Entrepreneurship," *Journal of Asian Studies* 22 (1963): 433–49; S. P. S. Ho, "The Development of Japanese Colonial Government in Taiwan, 1895–1945," in *Government and Economic Development,* ed. Gustav Ranis (New Haven, Conn.: Yale University Press, 1971), pp. 287–327.

7. R. H. Myers, "The Commercialization of Agriculture in Modern China," in *Economic Organization in Chinese Society,* ed. W. E. Willmott (Stanford, Calif.: Stanford University Press, 1972), pp. 173–91.

8. A. J. Gradanzev, *Formosa Today* (New York: Institute for Pacific Relations, 1942).

9. S. P. S. Ho, "Agricultural Transformation under Colonialism: The Case of Tai-wan," *Journal of Economic History* 28 (1968): 313–40; R. H. Myers and A. Ching, "Agricultural Development in Taiwan under Japanese Colonial Rule," *Journal of Asian Studies* 23 (1964): 555–70; R. P. Christensen, *Taiwan's Agricultural Development,* prepared for the Department of Agriculture, Economic Research Studies, Foreign Agricultural Economic Report no. 39 (Washington, D.C.: U. S. Government Printing Office, 1968); S. C. Hsieh and T. H. Lee, *Agricultural Development and Its Contributions to Economic Growth in Taiwan: Input–Output and Productivity Analysis of Taiwan Agricultural Development,* Chinese–American Joint Commission on Rural Reconstruction, Economic Digest Series, no. 17, Taibei, 1966. Teng-Hui Lee, *Inter-sectional Capital Flows in the Development of Taiwan: 1895–1960* (Ithaca, N. Y.: Cornell University Press, 1971).

10. Myers and Ching, "Agricultural Development in Taiwan."

11. Ho, "Development of Japanese Colonial Government."

12. T. Ouchi, "Agricultural Depression and Japanese Villages," *The Developing Economies* 5 (1967): 597–627.

13. Edwin A. Winckler, "National, Regional, and Local Politics," in *The Anthropology of Taiwanese Society,* ed. Emily A. Ahern and Hill Gates (Stanford, Calif.: Stanford University Press, 1981), pp. 13–37.

14. Simon Kuznets, "Growth and Structural Shifts," in *Economic Growth and Structural Change in Taiwan,* ed. Galenson, pp. 15–131.

15. Barbara W. Tuchman, *Stilwell and the American Experience in China, 1911–1945* (New York: Bantam Books, 1974).

16. Ralph N. Clough, *Island China* (Cambridge: Harvard University Press, 1978).

17. N. Jacoby, *U.S. Aid to Taiwan* (New York: Praeger, 1966).

18. Clough, *Island China.*

19. See Christensen, *Taiwan's Agricultural Development.*

20. Koo, *Role of Land Reform.*

21. *Taiwan Agricultural Yearbook* (Taibei: Department of Agriculture and Forestry, Provincial Government, 1974).

22. Lee, *Inter-sectional Capital Flows.*

23. John C. H. Fei, Gustav Ranis, and Shirley W. Y. Kuo, *Growth with Equity: The Taiwan Case* (New York: Oxford University Press for the World Bank, 1979).

24. Lee, *Inter-sectional Capital Flows,* p. 28.

25. Sung Hsing Wang and R. Apthorpe, *Rice Farming in Taiwan: Three Village Studies,* monograph ser. B, no. 5 (Taibei: Academia Sinica, 1974), pp. 10–11.

26. Christensen, *Taiwan's Agricultural Development.*

27. A cruder form of state power with a purpose altogether unrelated to economic

planning was also remarked upon by Wang and Apthorpe (*Rice Farming in Taiwan*):

> At least for as long as relations between island and continental China continue in their present form, presumably a justification will be found for continuing a form of reliance on the kind of police methods which have now become part and parcel of everyday life. The Minister of the Interior in the Nationalist government used very often in 1971, for instance, to the astonishment of persons familiar with a very different tradition, to speak of the policeman as the most important resource person of all for community development in the island. Villagers, too, speak of the intimacy of police participation in parts of their daily life (p. 10).

28. W. P. Falcon, "Key Issues in Taiwan's Agricultural Development," *Industry of Free China* 41(4) (1974): 2–7.
29. Christensen, *Taiwan's Agricultural Development*.
30. Shirley W. Y. Kuo, "Income Distribution by Size in Taiwan Area: Changes and Causes," *Industry of Free China* 45, nos. 1–3 (1976): 9–38, 9–21, 20–34, respectively. It is interesting that, in spite of the high degree of commercialization of Taiwanese agriculture, the government placed minimal reliance on market forces to extract a surplus from the countryside. Rice collections were made in kind, and rice was bartered for fertilizer. Indicative of the government's avoidance of the market mechanism were its attempts (albeit unsuccessful) to barter rice not only for fertilizer but also for cotton cloth, bicycles, soybean cakes, and the like. See Kuo, "Income Distribution."
31. Hla Myint, *The Economics of the Developing Countries* (New York: Praeger, 1964), p. 48.
32. T. H. Shen, "A New Agricultural Policy," in *Agriculture's Place in the Strategy of Development: The Taiwan Experience*, ed. T. H. Shen (Taibei: Joint Commission on Rural Reconstruction, 1974), pp. 38–58.
33. Hsieh and Lee, "Agricultural Development."
34. Even after the export of labor-intensive manufactures got underway, Taiwan ran a trade deficit. The trade balance remained negative until 1969. It became negative again in 1974 and 1975 (*Taiwan Statistical Data Book* [Taibei: Council for Economic Planning and Development, 1981]). This is a consequence of the fact that per capita income has been growing rapidly and so, too, have imports, especially since 1973 (see Table 3.1). Much exporting also relies on imported inputs. Had Taiwan's agriculture not been so productive, the strain on the balance of payments would have been greater.
35. *Free China Review* (Taibei, March 1976).
36. I. M. D. Little, T. Scitovsky, and M. Scott, *Industry and Trade in Some Developing Countries* (London: Oxford University Press, 1970).
37. The OECD's study of industrialization in seven developing countries compared effective rates of protection and found them to be lowest in Mexico and next lowest in Taiwan (the effective rate of protection measures the percentage by which import restrictions make it possible for the price of the value added in production to exceed what it would be in their absence). The study cautions, however, that, although "the average levels of protection for all manufacturing industry . . . in Taiwan were moderate . . . these moderate levels were due to zero or negative protection for exporting, while protection given to production for sale on the home market was much higher than in Mexico" (Little, Scitovsky, and Scott, *Industry and Trade*).

38. Maurice Scott, "Foreign Trade," in *Economic Growth and Structural Change in Taiwan*, ed. Galenson, pp. 308–83.
39. Teng-Hui Lee and Kuo-shu Liang, "Taiwan," in *Development Strategies in Semi-industrial Economies*, ed. Bela Balassa (Baltimore, Md.: Johns Hopkins Press, 1982), pp. 310–50.
40. Balassa, ed., *Development Strategies*.
41. Robert Wade, "Dirigisme Taiwan-Style," *IDS Bulletin* 15 (2) (April 1984): 65–70 (Institute of Development Studies, Sussex, England).
42. Ching-Yuan Lin, *Industrialization in Taiwan, 1946–1972: Trade and Import Substitution Policies for Developing Countries* (New York: Praeger, 1973).
43. H. D. Fong, "Taiwan's Industry, with Special Reference to Policies and Control," *Journal of Nanyang University* 11 (1968).
44. Mo-Huan Hsing, *Taiwan and the Philippines: Industry and Trade Relations* (London: Oxford University Press, 1971).
45. K. T. Li, *My Views on Taiwan's Economic Development: A Collection of Essays from 1975–1980* (Taibei, 1980), p. 10.
46. Ibid., p. 15.
47. Ibid., p. 3.
48. See Little, "An Economic Reconnaissance."
49. Gustav Ranis, "Industrial Development," in *Economic Growth and Structural Change in Taiwan*, ed. Galenson, pp. 206–62.
50. Economists of various ideologies have debated the economic importance of U.S. aid. Economic nationalists, advocates of export-led growth, and advocates of Third World self-reliance all tend to disparage the consequences of aid, though their reasons are very different (see Scott, "Foreign Trade," for a discussion of different views, including his own). In contrast, Jacoby, *U.S. Aid to Taiwan*, author of the most thorough study of aid to Taiwan, argues that without it per capita income would have stagnated, assuming no cutback in military outlays. Sifting through these debates and with the hindsight of history, I tend to agree with the disparagers.
51. Specifics of the relationship between the Taiwan state and Taiwan business-persons are still something of a mystery, but see Robert Silin, *Leadership and Values: The Organization of Large-Scale Taiwanese Enterprises* (Cambridge: Harvard University Press, 1976), who also discusses managerial practices in Taiwan. There can be no doubt that these have also played an important role in the development process.
52. P. M. A. Linebarger, *The Political Doctrines of Sun Yat-Sen* (Baltimore, Md.: Johns Hopkins Press, 1937).
53. Hsing, *Taiwan and the Philippines*.
54. "Manufacturing (Taiwan Area)," in *Industrial and Commercial Census of Taiwan and Fukien*, vol. 3, Table 16 (Taibei, 1971). E. L. Bacha, "Issues and Evidence on Recent Brazilian Economic Growth," *World Development* 6 (1977): 46–47.
55. This information was compiled by Professor Chi Shive of Taiwan National University and cited by *The Economist*, July 31, 1982, pp. 1–14.
56. Morgan Guarantee Trust, *World Financial Markets* (New York, June 1982).
57. Alejandro Foxley, *Neoliberal Experiments in Latin America* (Berkeley: University of California Press, 1983); see also Alfred Stepan, Chapter 10, this volume.
58. *Taiwan Statistical Data Book* (1981).
59. Ibid.
60. S. Lebergott, "Labor Force and Employment, 1800–1960," in *Output, Employ-*

ment and Productivity in the U.S. after 1800, vol. 30 of *Studies in Income and Wealth* (National Bureau of Economic Research, Conference on Research on Income and Wealth, New York, 1966), pp. 126–31.

61. The analysis of early industrialization that follows is based on Teng-Hui Lee, "Development of Industry," in *Agriculture's Place in the Strategy of Development*, ed. Shen, pp. 66–70, and on *Industrial and Commercial Census of Taiwan and Fukien* (1971).

62. Li, *My Views on Taiwan's Economic Development*.

63. Scott, "Foreign Trade."

64. The rate of inflation in Taiwan was 12.3% between 1952 and 1961 and an unbelievable 2.9% between 1962 and 1972. This compares with 33.9 and 13.6%, respectively, for Korea in the same periods; see Erik Lundberg, "Fiscal and Monetary Policies," in *Economic Growth and Structural Change in Taiwan*, Galenson, pp. 263–307. Taiwan's price performance, however, has deteriorated since the energy crisis. The GNP deflator was 32.3% in 1974 alone and averaged 10.4% for the period 1971–81. Economists have been unable to explain this deterioration except as a general consequence of both demand pull and cost push factors (Shirley W. Y. Kuo, *The Taiwan Economy in Transition* [Boulder, Colo.: Westview Press, 1983]).

65. Richard Webb, "Wage Policy and Income Distribution in Developing Countries," in *Income Distribution in the Less-Developed Countries*, ed. by Charles R. Frank, Jr., and Richard C. Webb (Washington, D.C.: Brookings Institution, 1977), pp. 215–58.

66. Alice H. Amsden, "The Division of Labor Is Limited by the *Rate of Growth* of the Market: The Taiwan Machine Tool Industry Revisited" (Harvard University, Graduate School of Business Administration, 1983, Mimeographed).

67. Manuel Zymelman, *Occupational Structures of Industries* (Washington, D.C.: International Bank for Reconstruction and Development, 1980).

68. *Taiwan Statistical Data Book* (1983).

69. *The Economist*, July 31, 1982, pp. 1–14.

70. Gross capital formation has also risen, from 15.4% of GDP in 1952 to 36.3% in 1980. The last figure is something of a world record; see Council for Economic Planning and Development, *Taiwan Statistical Data Book* (1981).

71. *Taiwan Statistical Data Book* (1982).

72. Lundberg, "Fiscal and Monetary Policies."

73. Ibid., p. 300.

74. Wang and Apthorpe, *Rice Farming in Taiwan*, pp. 10–11.

75. Silin, *Leadership and Values*, p. 18.

76. For information on the structure of Korean industry, see L. P. Jones and Il. SaKong, *Government, Business, and Entrepreneurship in Economic Development: The Korean Case* (Cambridge: Council on East Asian Studies, Harvard University Press, 1980); for information on both Korea and Taiwan, see S. P. S. Ho, "Small-Scale Enterprise in Taiwan," Staff Working Paper no. 384 (Washington, D.C.: World Bank, 1980).

77. See Rueschemeyer and Evans, Chapter 2, this volume.

78. Silin, *Leadership and Values*.

79. Clough, *Island China*.

80. Stockholm International Peace Research Institute, *World Armaments and Disarmament Yearbook* (London: Taylor & Frances, various years).

81. Clough, *Island China*.

82. Ho, "Development of Japanese Colonial Government."
83. United States Arms Control and Disarmament Agency, *World Military Expenditures and Arms Transfers, 1969–78* (Washington, D.C.: U.S. Government Printing Office, 1980).
84. Brian Crozier, *The Man Who Lost China* (New York: Scribner, 1976).
85. Denis Fred Simon, "Taiwan, Technology Transfer and Trans-Nationalism: The Political Management of Dependency" (Ph.D. diss., University of California, Berkeley, 1980).
86. Frederick Engels, *Anti-Duhring* (New York: International Publishers, 1939), pp. 202–203.

4. State Structures and the Possibilities for "Keynesian" Responses to the Great Depression in Sweden, Britain, and the United States

Margaret Weir
and Theda Skocpol

When the Great Depression of the 1930s swept across the Western industrial democracies, it undermined classical liberal orthodoxies of public finance. Economic crisis called into question the predominant conviction that government should balance its budget, maintain the gold standard, and let business reequilibrate of its own accord during economic downturns. Demands were voiced for extraordinary government actions on behalf of industrial workers, farmers, and other distressed groups. Established political coalitions came unraveled, and new opportunities opened for politicians and parties that could devise appealing responses to the exigencies of the decade. One of the greatest dilemmas was how to cope with an unprecedented volume of unemployment in suddenly and severely contracted economies.

Out of the traumas of the 1930s came new political and theoretical understandings of the much more active roles that states might henceforth play in maintaining growth and employment in advanced industrial-capitalist democracies. Thus was born the "Keynesian era," as it would retrospectively come to be called in honor of the breakthrough in economic theory embodied in John Maynard Keynes's 1936 book, *The General Theory of Employment, Interest, and Money*.

National reactions to the crisis of the depression varied widely, however.[1] In many cases either conservative stasis or a turn toward authoritarianism prevailed. Among the countries that avoided the breakdown of democratic institutions, Sweden and the United States were the sites of the boldest responses to the crisis by reformist political leaderships. Supported electorally by industrial workers and farmers, America's New Deal and Sweden's "new deal" (as Bjarne Braatoy called it in 1939) both embarked on programs of deficit government spending to provide emergency relief, to create jobs on public works projects, and to enhance popular social security.[2]

In both Sweden and the United States, moreover, coherent economic arguments were developed to justify government spending not merely (in timeworn fashion) as a humanitarian response to emergency, but also as a proper strategy of national macroeconomic management in advanced capitalism. At first these arguments were not fully or explicitly "Keynesian," but they did focus on ways in which government deficit spending could stimulate consumer demand, private investments, and reemployment.[3] Such economic arguments were much more promptly and thoroughly adopted as a national political strategy for coping with the depression in Sweden. In the United States, a deliberate recovery strategy of deficit spending was devised only in the late 1930s, and it was not fully implemented during the New Deal.[4]

Indeed, the kinds of Keynesian economic breakthroughs ultimately institutionalized in these two nations were quite different. From 1936 onward, Sweden aimed to become – and very largely succeeded in achieving – a full-employment economy with high levels of public income allocation for social welfare purposes. Sweden also synthesized Keynesian macroeconomic management and welfare spending with labor market interventions designed to facilitate labor mobility.[5] Meanwhile, from 1938 through 1946, the United States came to practice, not Swedish-style "social Keynesianism," but what has aptly been called "commercial Keynesianism."[6] This meant that the federal government used tax cuts and "automatic" (rather than discretionary) adjustments of public spending to manage the economy, with more emphasis on controlling inflation than on eliminating unemployment.[7] To be sure, the role of the federal government in the U.S. economy and society became much greater than it had been before the 1930s, but U.S. domestic public spending was kept at modest levels, and neither social welfare nor industrial interventions by the federal government were effectively coordinated with macroeconomic management.[8]

Despite the eventually different outcomes, both Sweden and the United States did experience remarkably similar reformist responses to the Great Depression itself. Surprisingly, events proceeded very differently in Great Britain. Britain might well have been the earliest and most successful nation to launch a "new deal," using Keynesian economic strategies to consolidate a full-employment welfare state. After all, Britain was the pioneer among liberal capitalist countries in establishing comprehensive public social protections for its working class. Before World War I, British leaders instituted workers' compensation, old-age pensions, health insurance, and, most extraordinary of all, the world's first compulsory unemployment insurance program, which was extended to virtually the entire industrial working class at the close of the war.[9]

Persistent, large-scale unemployment was a publicly recognized problem in Britain throughout the 1920s, and the Labour, Conservative, and Liberal parties alike contested the 1929 election on platforms promising to cope with unemployment.[10] The Liberal platform, eloquently championed by Keynes himself, called for a large-scale program of loan-financed public works. "We Can Conquer Unemployment," the Liberals declared. After Labour won the 1929 election and formed a minority government just as the Great Depression was starting, the Liberals and Keynes offered the party of the industrial working class parliamentary and intellectual backing for such a program. This was just the kind of response to unemployment and the national economic depression that would, only a few years later, in 1932–34, launch Sweden toward a full-employment welfare state and bring long-lasting political hegemony to the Swedish Social Democrats.

Nothing so innovative happened in Britain. The 1929 Labour government vacillated for two excruciating years, until it bowed out in August of 1931, after trying and failing to impose cuts in social spending on its own political base. Thereafter, the Labour party split apart and declined precipitously, and the Liberals further contracted into insignificance. A multiparty "national government" came to power in 1931 – in effect dominated by Conservatives. It took Britain off the gold standard, erected some tariffs, and sat complacently atop the national polity in the 1930s, as Britain gradually attained a strong aggregate economic recovery, but with unemployment remaining high.[11] Britain would not adopt Keynesian macroeconomic strategies before the coming of World War II, and it would not reform and extend its public social benefits into a comprehensive "welfare state" until after the close of that massive war.[12]

Explaining the Variation in National Responses to the Depression

Why did Sweden and the United States devise broadly similar political responses to the economic crisis of the Great Depression? Why, despite the similarities in their reformist responses, did Sweden end up with social Keynesianism, whereas the United States institutionalized commercial Keynesianism? And why did Britain fail to deal with the depression in innovative ways comparable to the Swedish and U.S. "new deals"?

These historical questions are addressed in this essay. Yet our argument also has a broader theoretical purpose. It aims to demonstrate the fruitfulness of a distinctive kind of explanatory approach, highlighting the structural features of states and the preexisting legacies of public policies. In particular, we shall analyze the ways in which various state structures and policy legacies in Sweden, Britain, and the United States (a) influenced the political orientations and capacities of groups and parties active in political struggles over the ways in which governments should cope with the circumstances of the depression and (b) affected the processes of intellectual innovation and expert access to policy-making centers through which new economic ideas did (or did not) enter into the formulation of governmental strategies for coping with the economic crisis.

Before we proceed, however, let us introduce various analytical perspectives that have been used to explain Swedish, British, and U.S. patterns.[13]

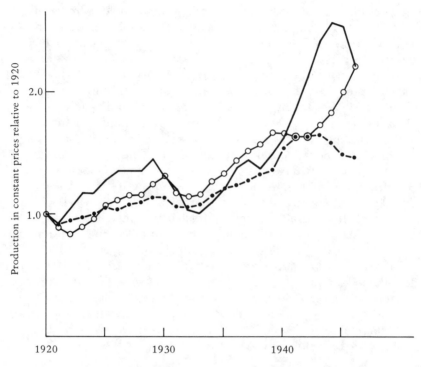

Figure 4.1. National production in Sweden, Britain, and the United States, 1920–1946. Sweden: Gross Domestic Product, o-o-o; Britain: Gross National Product, ●-●-●; the United States, Gross National Product, ———. (Sources: U.S. Department of Commerce, *Historical Statistics of the United States: Colonial Times to 1970, Part I*, Washington, D.C., 1975, p. 224; B. R. Mitchell, *European Historical Statistics, 1750–1970*, New York: Columbia University Press, 1976, pp. 789–90.)

After explaining why we find these perspectives inadequate, we shall outline the theoretical frame of reference for our own subsequent comparative-historical analysis.

Economic Conditions and National Responses

At the start, we can set aside a sort of "economic-determinist" argument that might, at first glance, seem to provide a common-sense explanation for political happenings in the 1930s. A purely functionalist and materialist perspective might try to derive the extent of reformist politics in the 1930s from the severity with which the depression hit individual countries, suggesting that more innovative responses developed to cope with more severe dislocations. As Figs. 4.1 and 4.2 reveal, however, among our three

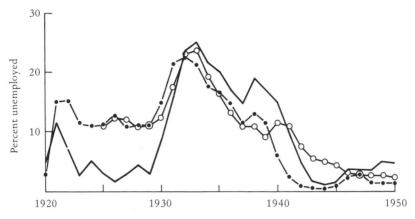

Figure 4.2. Percent unemployed in Sweden, Britain, and the United States, 1920–1950. Sweden: members of trade union benefit funds unemployed, o-o-o; Britain: 1920–23 unemployment in trade unions; 1924–50 averages of monthly numbers of registered insured wholly unemployed, ●-●-●; the United States: percent of civilian labor force fourteen years and over unemployed, annual averages, ———. (Sources: U.S. Department of Commerce, *Historical Statistics of the United States;* p. 224; B. R. Mitchell, *European Historical Statistics 1750–1970,* pp. 789–90.)

cases the United States was the hardest hit by the depression, whereas both Sweden and Britain, despite their contrasting political responses, experienced earlier and more stable recoveries than the United States. Sweden's recovery was *sustained* into the later 1930s more smoothly than the British and (especially) the American recoveries.

For all three countries, it is difficult to attribute phases of economic recovery or setback directly to the effects of governmental actions (or nonactions). We make no claims whatsoever about the actual efficacy of deficit-spending policies compared with other economic policies or circumstances.[14] Economic historians do not agree about these issues for our national cases or others in the 1930s. Moreover, much contemporary and historical evidence suggests that government policies need not be economically efficacious to be successful politically. During the 1930s, the governments and policies in power when each nation began, for whatever reasons, to recover from the depths of economic decline benefited politically, especially if those governments and policies *appeared* to have been actively grappling with the economic difficulties. But this only places a premium on understanding why the British Labour government vacillated until it reached the impasse that forced it to resign prematurely, before the British recovery commenced in 1932.

The "Working-Class-Strength" Approach to Modern Welfare States

Perhaps the most influential arguments today about policy variations among advanced industrial-capitalist democracies emphasize the strength of working-class organizations in political class struggles. Variations in the growth of public socioeconomic interventions throughout the twentieth century are explained in terms of the capacities of industrial working classes to struggle for their interests in opposition to capitalist classes.[15] In a bold version of this argument put forward by John Stephens, the agents of the origins and continuing development of the welfare state (ultimately the Keynesian full-employment welfare state) are said to be centrally coordinated industrial unions working through a working-class-based political party.[16] The party comes to power through electoral politics and then uses governmental authority to implement welfare-oriented policies. Business interests may be "brought along" to support these policies, but fundamentally – so the argument goes – the policies are the product of a working class that is politically stronger than the capitalist class, specifically because the workers are better organized and mobilized to take full advantage of electoral democracy.

Apparently, this model accounts well for the Swedish Social Democratic breakthroughs of the 1930s, which led to the use of high levels of public spending to promote social welfare and full employment.[17] Apparently, too, it can account for the failure of the American New Deal to result in a full social Keynesian breakthrough – by pointing to the long-term weakness of U.S. industrial unions in contrast to Swedish unions and by pointing to the resilient and enduring political strength of American business.[18] In our view, however, contrasts between Sweden and the United States can be attributed to the strength of labor versus business only if one is prepared to take an excessively zero-sum and highly teleological view of the fluid events of the 1930s. And once British developments in the 1930s are introduced into the comparative picture, the argument falls down altogether.

For the United States considered in comparison with Sweden, a working-class-strength approach reads eventual historical outcomes back into original causes. Although Swedish industrial workers were much more highly organized – into industrial unions and a political party – than were American workers at the start of the 1930s, U.S. workers made momentous organizational gains during the 1930s and 1940s. Industrial unions mushroomed, and organized labor's influence in the Democratic party became important.[19] The momentum was subsequently stalled in both areas of labor power; yet this was surely a result, as well as a cause, of the conservative turns in U.S. public policy as the reformism of the New Deal came to an end. Nor can the eventual failure of social democratic Keynesian tendencies emerging from the New Deal be directly attributed to the political preeminence of American capitalists. From the middle to the later 1930s, the political influence of U.S. business groups was at an all-time nadir.[20] Thus, the recovery of business influence over public policy making, including applications of Keynesian ideas, must be attributed as much to the faltering of alternative political forces as to the strength and initiatives of the business actors themselves.

In any event, it would be very wrong to suppose that well-organized and politically influential business groups are inherently opposed to Keynesian programs that embody high levels of public spending for social welfare purposes. All types of Keynesian strategies are oriented to the national economy as a whole and aim to defuse conflicts among groups and classes by expanding the economy to everyone's absolute benefit.[21] In fact, Swedish capitalists have long been well organized on a nationally centralized basis and, though they did not originate Sweden's full-employment welfare state, they were part of the political bargaining processes that securely institutionalized it from the late 1930s onward.[22]

Depression-era public policies in Sweden did greatly enhance the organizational power and solidarity of labor, thus increasing the strength of unions and the Social Democratic party,[23] but again it is important not to read results back into causes. Coming into the 1930s, it was not at all certain that the Swedish Social Democratic party would do as well as it did. Had other parties taken the initiative or had a political stalemate occurred around more conservative policies, as in Britain, the organizational strength of Swedish industrial workers and the electoral strength of the Social Democratic party almost certainly would have been sapped rather than strengthened by the depression crisis and its political accompaniments.

There was something very special about the ability and willingness of the Swedish Social Democratic leadership to formulate a reformist public spending strategy in the early 1930s.[24] That this special something was not a result of the party's class basis alone is made strikingly apparent by the contrasting behavior of the British Labour party.[25] A comparison between these two parties around 1930 is certainly appropriate. Although their fortunes were destined to diverge rather sharply after 1930, during the 1920s the two parties experienced parallel situations in key respects and, where their circumstances differed, had offsetting balances of advantages and disadvantages.[26] Both the British Labour party and the Swedish Social Democrats were rooted in moderately strong union movements and enjoyed comparable (primarily working-class) electoral support.[27] To be sure, the Social Democratic party was the first parliamentary party to emerge in Sweden and was the strongest of the four Swedish parties during the 1920s, whereas the British Labour party, a late entrant to parliamentary politics, lagged behind the Conservatives in parliament until 1929.[28] Nevertheless, neither social democratic party could form majority governments, and both faced determined opposition from more conservative political forces throughout the 1920s and into the early 1930s.

In parliamentary terms, moreover, the British Labour party enjoyed *greater* maneuvering room for launching a deficit-spending economic recovery strategy immediately after it came to power in 1929. Both parties, of course, were urged by union leaders and working-class electoral supporters to take bold steps against unemployment. But, after forming a minority government in 1932, the Swedish Social Democrats had to negotiate a delicate (and, from their point of view, imperfect) compromise with the Agrarian party representing farmers before they could proceed with their public works initiatives to address unemployment.[29] In contrast, the British Labour party in 1929 (and after) might have enjoyed full support from the Liberals for attacking unemployment through loan-financed public works.[30] The Labour party did not have to make concessions to agrarian concerns because farmers were but a tiny social and political presence in highly industrialized and urbanized Britain.[31] Indeed, given the unusually heavy weight of the industrial working class in the British social structure, as well as the prior development of the world's most extensive public social benefits in Britain before the 1930s, one would have to predict from the premises of working-class-strength models that Britain, not Sweden, should have been the site of the earliest and fullest social Keynesian response to the Great Depression. The first full-employment welfare state should have been launched in Britain, if these models adequately explain public policy development.

Sectoral Coalitions and Links to the International Economy

Recently, dissatisfaction with the broad categories of class-based models has prompted more sophisticated (and more determined!) efforts to tie political outcomes to the interests of socioeconomic actors. Analysts who pursue what we shall call the "economic coalition" approach look for interest-based alliances led by sectors within business, perhaps tied to sectors within agriculture, and perhaps willing to ally with organized industrial labor.[32] Interests are posited by identifying the positions of industries and firms in relation to labor costs and technology and, more importantly, in relation to domestic or international markets. Cross-sector alliances are said to favor and support alternative government economic policies according to the orientations of industries and firms toward open international trade and also according to the tolerance that different factions of business may have for wage and public benefit concessions to labor.

The coalitional approach has been applied to developments in the 1930s by Peter Gourevitch and Thomas Ferguson. Ferguson, unmistakably a writer in the peculiarly American "Beardsian" tradition of attributing political events to behind-the-scenes business influence, places great stress in explaining the "second" U.S. New Deal on the influence of leaders from the internationalist, low-labor-cost sectors of business.[33] Gourevitch ranges much more widely and attributes fewer magical powers to business leaders. He attempts to find similar business–farmer–labor coalitions across nations –

Sweden, the United States, and Germany.[34] Regardless of the very different contexts involved in the weakness of Weimar democracy and the triumph of Nazi authoritarianism in Germany versus the continuity of liberal democracy in Sweden and America, Gourevitch seems to argue that similar socioeconomic coalitions brought about and supported deficit-spending policies in all three nations. For the contrasting case of Britain, he stresses that many economic sectors had an interest in maintaining the gold standard and an open international economy. Above all, he argues that London financiers were hegemonic in British politics.

Coalitional approaches improve on class struggle models by highlighting the positive-sum character of many modern social policies. What is more, by permitting more fine-grained distinctions to be made among social groups, the coalitional approach can pinpoint socioeconomic influences on public policy making that may escape theorists who place such great stress on the organizational leverage of industrial labor. Nevertheless, the coalitional approach has important lacunae. For one thing, it cannot easily account for variations over time in the political efficacy of given sectoral interests: Why, for example, were the financial interests of "the City" in Britain unable to prevent social welfare innovations before World War I, yet able to cut social spending and block deficit-financed public works in 1929–30? The answer cannot lie simply in the internationalist orientation of the British economy, which was equally strong in the two periods. We shall argue that the shifting strength of Treasury controls over British social policies stemmed from changes within the structure of the British civil service itself, not from changing economic circumstances outside the state.

Coalitional analysts may also underestimate the political mutability of interests and group alliances. Alternative alliances are almost always possible for given groups, and their very "interests" can be redefined depending on the unfolding politics of the situation. Existing patterns of state intervention and the initiatives of political leaders often activate particular interests and coalitions within a range of alternative possibilities. And the institutional structures of states play a critical role in determining the access and weight of various interests and coalitions. We shall demonstrate these points in our discussion of the divergent influences that farm interests ended up having in the Swedish and U.S. "new deals."

The Role of Keynes's General Theory

A final line of argument about the politics of national recovery strategies in the 1930s takes us in the opposite direction from the social-group analyses just discussed. An intellectually determinist perspective maintains that deficit spending strategies could be devised by governments only after John Maynard Keynes published the appropriate new economic theory in his 1936 book, *The General Theory of Employment, Interest, and Money*. This sort of argument has sometimes been invoked to explain why federal executive policy makers in the United States deliberately planned deficits as a recovery strategy only in the later 1930s and not during the "first" New Deal of 1933–35. The preface and the closing pages of Keynes's *General Theory* provide the model of the processes by which theorists might influence policy innovations. The "power of vested interests," Keynes wrote, "is vastly exaggerated compared with the gradual encroachment of ideas. . . . The ideas of economists and political philosophers, both when they are right and when they are wrong, are more powerful than is commonly understood. Indeed the world is ruled by little else."[35]

Keynes was certainly right about the exaggerated influence all too often attributed to "vested interests"; yet to assert that ideas are powerful is not to reveal how policy-relevant ideas emerge and how they may be variously influential. In Keynes's own experience, the workings of intellectual influence on public policy came to be understood as roundabout, routed through the prior achievement of academic credibility. Before writing *The General Theory*, Keynes spent many years trying, with little success, to press new practical programs on British politicians.[36] The book itself represented a new tack for Keynes the public actor: First a new, highly abstract theory would have to persuade academic economists, overcoming their "deep divergences of opinion . . . which have for the time being almost destroyed the practical influence of economic theory, and will, until they are resolved, continue to do so." Then, "after a certain interval" the new, academically accepted theory would powerfully influence the initiatives of politicians, civil servants, "and even agitators." In normal times, Keynes felt, such a process of roundabout intellectual influence might take twenty-five or thirty years, but in the midst of a crisis it might work more quickly.[37]

As Kerry Schott has written: "In scenarios of this type, practical economic policy simply follows theoretical developments with a time lag. The underlying premise . . . is the . . . notion that the state is little more than an active respondent to the advice of its economists."[38] Another equally important premise is that economic theories develop on their own in academic circles and then exert influence on policy making. Yet beguiling as this model might seem, especially to university-based scholars, it cannot account for British, Swedish, or American patterns in the 1930s.[39]

In Britain, no Keynesian response to the Great Depression was launched by British governments either before or after *The General Theory*. Neither the presence of Keynes the publicist and policy adviser, nor the achievement of Keynes the grand academic theorist was enough to persuade his homeland to use his ideas to devise a recovery strategy. In the United States, the influence of a certain academic interpretation of the principles of *The General Theory* did percolate into national policy making from the late 1930s onward, carried especially by Harvard-trained economists recruited into government service or public advisory bodies. Yet, as we shall see, the first rationales for deficit-spending recovery policies came neither from Keynes nor from academic circles. And, subsequently, the policy prescriptions of the version of Keynesianism that initially gained prestigious academic backing in the United States were not the prescriptions that became the most politically successful. In Sweden, finally, economists and their ideas were crucial to the Social Democratic reforms of the 1930s, but Keynes's *General Theory* was certainly not the inspiration for Swedish policies in 1932–34. The processes of intellectual influence that did underpin those reforms were complex and did not run simply from an "academic establishment" to governmental and party leaders.

The issues raised by Keynes's brief excursus in *The General Theory* into the sociology of politically influential knowledge are indeed important, but they must be addressed with an analysis that pays more attention (than Keynes, or many others since, have paid) to the structures within and surrounding the state that pattern the mutually influential interactions of experts and politicians. We are going to keep a close eye on such structures as we examine intellectual and policy developments in Sweden, Britain, and the United States.

States Structures and Policy Developments

Of the perspectives on the politics of the 1930s that we have just reviewed, two – the working-class-strength approach and the coalitional approach – view politics as a process by which policy outcomes are determined by relatively immediate expressions of socially rooted demands:

Socially rooted ⟶ What groups or ⟶ Government
demands   parties propose   policies

Politics in these perspectives becomes an arena of struggles among class or group interests, and government is the agent of the consensus, compromise, or balance of power that emerges from such socially rooted political struggle. New policy departures, especially in a period of economic crisis or structural transformation, are thus to be understood as the result of changing balances of class power or changing coalitions of socioeconomic interests.

The final approach we discussed in the previous section also roots policy outcomes in the nonstate environment, here understood in a more idealistic fashion:

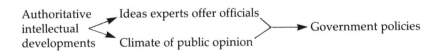

Authoritative   Ideas experts offer officials
intellectual   <   > ⟶ Government policies
developments   Climate of public opinion

Despite their very considerable differences, both of these perspectives fail to give any significant weight to states as sites of potentially autonomous official action or as complexes of preexisting policies and institutional arrangements. Politics is seen either as an arena of socioeconomic interest struggles or as an intellectual conversation among people trying to understand the situation and decide what conceivably might (or should) be done about it. Each of these ways of thinking about politics has much to recommend it. Yet both can be analytically enriched by taking states seriously as actors and structures.

States affect the possibilities for policy outcomes in two major ways. First, states may be sites of autonomous official action, not reducible to any social-group pressures or preferences. This is true because both appointed and elected officials have organizational and career interests of their own, and they devise and work for policies that will further those interests, or at least not harm them. Of course, elected or appointed officials will be sensitive in various ways to social preferences and to the economic environment in which the state must operate. Yet politicians and officials are also engaged in struggles among themselves, and they must pursue these struggles, along with any initiatives they take in relation to the economy or the mobilization of social support, by using – or taking into account – the coercive, fiscal, judicial, and administrative capacities of the state structure within which they are located. If a given state structure provides no existing, or readily foreseeable, "policy instruments" for implementing a given line of action, government officials are not likely to pursue it, and politicians aspiring to office are not likely to propose it. Conversely, government officials (or aspiring politicians) are quite likely to take new initiatives, conceivably well ahead of social demands, if existing state capacities can be readily adapted or reworked to do things that will bring advantages to them in their struggles with competitive political forces.

Equally important for the historical issues tackled in this essay, the organizational structures of states indirectly influence politics for *all* groups in society. This happens in various ways. It is already well known by political scientists that the organizations and tactics through which variously situated social groups can (or cannot) influence policy processes are partially shaped by the structures of government within which groups must operate. More than this, the administrative, fiscal, coercive, and judicial arrangements of given states, as well as the policies that states are already pursuing, influence the conceptions that groups or their representatives are likely to develop about what is desirable, or possible at all, in the realm of governmental action. Thus, state structures help to inspire the very demands that are pursued through politics.

For intellectuals puzzling about potentially policy-relevant phenomena, the structures of states are just as important as for classes and interest groups. Modern states and the social sciences have grown up together, not only because states themselves monitor social realities and devise theories about them, but also because the growth of state interventions for economic and social welfare purposes has directly and indirectly stimulated research and theorizing in the social sciences. Given these realities, we may assume that the various specific structures of states pattern the ways in which experts and their ideas enter into public policy making at given times. In turn, the access to centers of policy making and implementation enjoyed by experts, or the lack of such access, influences the development of social theories and research in their own right.

The complex relationships sketched in the previous paragraphs can be summed up in a model of causal interrelationships that, in an overall analysis, would have to be explored along with the relationships indicated in the two diagrams offered earlier.

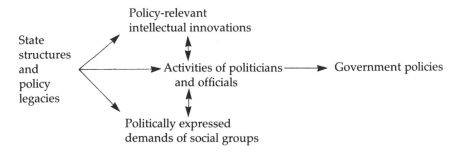

Inevitably, diagrams such as this have a static, ahistorical quality. Let us underline, therefore, that we take from Hugh Heclo the fundamental insight that policy making is inherently a historical – that is, over time – process in which all actors consciously build on and/or react against previous governmental efforts for dealing with the same (or similar) problems.[40] This means that the goals of politically active groups, policy intellectuals, and politicians can never simply be "read off" their current structural positions (no matter how "structures" are defined). Instead, the investigator must take into account meaningful reactions to previous policies. Such reactions color the very interests and ideals that politically engaged actors define for themselves at any given point.

For the remainder of this essay, we turn to events in and surrounding the depression decade of the 1930s, using comparisons among Sweden, Britain, and the United States to develop an explanation for the variation in policy responses the national governments devised to cope with economic crisis. Our explanation focuses on the ways in which the Swedish, British, and U.S. state structures and policy legacies affected the possibilities for new economic ideas to be formulated and applied to innovative government policies and influenced the political orientations and capacities of conflicting parties and coalitions of social groups. We proceed in two steps. First, we analyze the divergent initial responses of Sweden and Britain to the depression crisis. Then we bring the United States into the picture, examining relevant features of the entire New Deal and its aftermath, with special emphasis on comparisons with Swedish developments.

Sweden and Britain in the Early Depression Years: Labor Governments Confront the Dilemmas of Mass Unemployment

Why were the Swedish Social Democrats, after they came to governmental power in 1932, prepared to launch deficit-financed public works as an explicit strategy for both national economic recovery and unemployment relief, whereas the British Labour party refused to take this road during its abbreviated period in governmental power between 1929 and 1931?

Of the existing approaches we surveyed earlier, only the coalitional approach, with its stress on international economic ties, pointed to a causal factor that could be sufficient to answer this straightforward question. By the time the Swedish Social Democrats came to national power in 1932, their country, normally highly involved in international trade, had abandoned the gold standard, thus opening the way for an active domestic macroeconomic strategy. But Britain did not depart from gold until late 1931, and the Labour government of 1929–31 could not enjoy the room for manuever available to the Swedish Social Democrats – unless Labour itself was prepared to take Britain off the gold standard. The fact remains that it could have done so. Some voices of all political persuasions were advocating this step in 1930 and 1931 as a prelude either to protectionism or to fiscal activism, and the Liberals were willing to support the Labour government in any measures necessary to institute loan-financed public works.[41] Moreover, to say that the Swedish Social Democrats benefited by the fact that their nation had already been taken off the gold standard and temporarily weaned from international trade is hardly to explain how and why they took new macroeconomic initiatives.

It makes no sense to reduce political choices to the dictates of economic circumstances, for economic circumstances do not command so unambiguously, not even at moments of extraordinary crisis. Our approach to explaining the contrasting choices of the British Labour government and its Swedish Social Democratic counterpart focuses on two features of the respective national states: (a) their established policy approaches for addressing problems of unemployment and (b) the institutional mechanisms they provided for allowing economic experts to participate in public policy making. As we are about to see, clear contrasts between Britain and Sweden appear on each dimension, and by considering these contrasts together we can make sense of why governments similarly run by programmatic parties based on working-class support took such different steps in the face of deepening economic crisis in the early depression.

Social Policy Legacies and Party Orientations

Even when a major disruption such as the Great Depression creates new political demands and opens possibilities for policy innovations, political responses continue to be powerfully influenced by earlier patterns of government activity. Existing policies influence the political demands of contending groups and parties, who define their options in response to current practices. Previous interventions also shape the notions held by administrators and politicians about what is feasible, for administrative capacity built up in one area cannot easily be altered to implement a new set of policies. The resources and time required to create new capacities discourage radical policy changes, perhaps especially so in an economic emergency, when a premium is placed on quick results. In this section, we shall see that British Labour politicians, long locked into struggles over unemployment benefits, continued to center their attention on that form of government activity, whereas the Swedish Social Democrats formulated their responses to the depression in the context of ongoing struggles over public works nationally supervised by a conservative Unemployment Commission.

The introduction of unemployment insurance in Britain in 1911 was due above all to efforts by Liberal reform politicians and by civil servants at the Board of Trade, and immediate postwar extensions of the program to cover most of the industrial working class stemmed from the initiatives of the new Ministry of Labour.[42] In 1911, trade unions were coaxed into support of unemployment insurance, and their primary efforts thereafter continued to be (unsuccessfully) directed toward abolishing required contributory payments by employed workers. Yet the British Labour party grew rapidly with the democratization of the suffrage after World War I, and it soon took to heart the unemployment benefits that the organized working class had originally greeted with at best wary support.[43] During the 1920s, Labour became the chief proponent of extending and liberalizing unemployment benefits, as well as the main parliamentary bulwark against Conservative efforts to limit eligibility and trim payments to the unemployed.

All British parties, including the Labour party, worried about Britain's persistently high unemployment throughout the 1920s.[44] During the electoral campaign of 1924, the leaders of what would become the first Labour government promised a sweeping program of public works to alleviate unemployment. But, once in power, the minority Labour government concentrated on liberalizing unemployment benefits and proposed only a minor public works effort (though it also introduced a program of housing subsidies with implications for both welfare and employment).[45] This government fell only nine months after its formation, and thereafter the Labour party advocated liberalizations in the terms and extent of unemployment coverage. William Beveridge's warning that unemployment insurance might "demoralize the government of the day and cause them to give up the search for remedies" was insightful for the Labour party out of power as well.[46]

After the second Labour government came to power in 1929, it again focused its reformist energies on unemployment benefits rather than on introducing public works.[47] The unemployment issue dominated the May 1929 election, and soon after the depression crisis took hold with what Bentley Gilbert has aptly called an "explosion of unemployment."[48] Faced with an unemployment rate in late 1930 amounting to 19.6 percent of all insured persons,[49] the new Labour government found the extension of unemployment benefits a more obvious way to cushion workers against distress than striking out in new directions for which there was no support within the government bureaucracy. In the absence of extensive experience with large-scale or centrally managed public works expenditures, the administrative difficulties of launching any such new endeavor appeared to be formidable. Labour government leaders argued with Liberal spokesmen about the feasibility of undertaking new public works swiftly enough to have any impact on unemployment, and they repeatedly rejected Liberal overtures for cooperation on an overall program that would include this approach to combating unemployment and economic decline.

The public works route not having been chosen, benefits from unemployment insurance and the supplementary "dole" provided British workers with their only bulwark against the ravages of depression. Yet unconnected to any plausible program for economic recovery, these benefits proved a fragile defense – if not for those workers who happened to be eligible for the greatest relief, then certainly for the Labour party itself, for the Labour government was caught in the contradictions inherent in a "self-financing" unemployment insurance scheme in depression times.[50] On the one side, party backbenchers and the Trades Union Congress pressed government leaders to extend and liberalize unemployment coverage to meet human needs in the economic crisis. On the other side, Treasury officials issued dire warnings about the disastrous consequences for the soundness of the pound of unrestrained government borrowing to replendish the depleted "insurance" fund. Reluctant to cut benefits, Prime Minister Ramsey MacDonald nonetheless felt he had no economic justification for repeated borrowing by the government.

The prime minister's decision in August 1931 to cut unemployment benefits in deference to the dire warnings about budget deficits in the May Commission Report tore apart the Labour party and precipitated the Labour government's resignation. This paved the way for the Conservative-dominated "National" government that remained in power for the rest of the 1930s and benefited from the economic recovery that commenced after Britain departed from the gold standard. Of course, in devaluing the pound and erecting tariffs, the National government strayed from laissez faire orthodoxies in its recovery strategies, but its policies were not those of innovative economic theorists such as Keynes. In fact, the National government's most distinctive feature was its avoidance after 1931 of any further bold policy initiatives during the nine years that (in C. W. Mowat's words) "it shambled its unimaginative way to its fall in 1940."[51]

Looking back over the entire British experience with the birth and early growth of a modern welfare state, we can see that Britain's early steps made more difficult subsequent progress toward combining "social" and "economic" interventions in the form of deficit-financed public works. Before the Great Depression, Britain's pioneering adoption of unemployment insurance and the expansion of this program into a massive relief system for most of the working class put the country at the forefront worldwide in providing state aid to the unemployed. Yet this prior achievement also channeled the efforts of the Labour party away from alternative efforts to provide employment as such, a dilemma amusingly echoed in a 1929 political cartoon (Fig. 4.3).

Apparently, developments toward full-employment welfare states are not so smoothly evolutionary as many social scientific theories imply. The nations that start first or fastest may not be the ones that arrive soonest. This conclusion is reinforced as we now turn to the history of Swedish efforts to cope with unemployment from World War I through the early 1930s.

During the 1920s, Swedish Social Democrats did not find themselves engaged in political struggles over unemployment benefits. Before they fell from power in 1914, Swedish Liberals had come close, but failed to parallel the achievement of their British counterparts by launching unemployment insurance.[52] Thus, when the end of the war brought soaring unemployment, just as it did in Britain, Sweden had no established unemployment insurance program to extend. As in Britain, the Swedish state's approach to postwar unemployment followed existing administrative and policy grooves, but in the Swedish case this meant relief works administered by a national Unemployment Commission.[53]

First set up in 1914 as an investigatory and advisory board, the Unemployment Commission soon became involved in granting relief to the victims of wartime economic dislocations. Because such relief was not tied to any insurance principle, localities were encouraged to require work in exchange for relief, and in areas of concentrated unemployment, the commission itself operated special employment programs. Paying well below the market rate, the Unemployment Commission's work programs provided the framework for dealing with Sweden's chronic unemployment during the 1920s. Step by step, the commission expanded its activities, tightened its control over local projects, and, like many Swedish administrative bodies, set day-to-day policy quite independently of the many governments that came and went during the politically unstable 1920s.

Understandably, the Swedish Social Democrats formulated many of their own demands and ideas about how to cope with unemployment in reaction to the activities of the Unemployment Commission. Like the British Labour party, the Swedish Social Democrats were buoyed into serious national political contention by the institution of mass suffrage around World War I. Also like their British counterparts, they worried about unemployment – and found it more practical to try to modify existing state programs than to initiate alternative approaches. Thus, although the Swedish Social Democrats unsuccessfully lobbied for state subsidies to union-administered unemployment funds, when they found themselves in office they spent much of their energy responding to unions' complaints about the Unemployment Commission. They were not, however, initially able to

Cart before the Horse

Figure 4.3. From *The London Express*. (Source: Robert Skidelsky, *Politicians and the Slump: The Labour Government of 1929–1931*. London: Macmillan, 1967.)

modify the commission's practices. In 1923 and again in 1926, Social Democratic minority governments fell over disputes with the commission.[54]

With persistent unemployment a continuing concern for Swedish workers and unions throughout the 1920s, the Social Democrats had to keep facing the challenge of how to deal with a national state already active on this issue in what the party and its supporters considered inadequate ways. After defeat in 1928 on a platform that espoused a radical inheritance tax, the Social Democrats began to draft a new political program designed to boost their electoral appeal and free them from the impotence that plagued the earlier Social Democratic governments.[55] During this process, a key party leader, Ernst Wigforss, successfully advocated plans for public works at prevailing wages. Such plans directly responded to the concerns of the unions about below-market wage rates on existing relief projects. The frustrations the Social Democrats had faced during their brief periods of government power would be addressed through replacement of the Unemployment Commission by a new, permanent agency to plan local and national public works.

Thus, the proposals that would in due course become central to the Social Democratic strategy for coping with the depression *emerged before the major crisis itself* through critical dialogue with the Swedish state's existing means for addressing the needs of the unemployed. The parallels to, and differences from, the British case are striking. In the British case, the Labour party focused throughout the 1920s on struggles over unemployment benefits, whereas in the Swedish case, frustrated Social Democrats focused on a national body administering public works for the unemployed. Both parties simply reacted to the existing means their national state had for coping with unemployment and its effects.

Yet labor party struggles over public works offered a better bridge to proto-Keynesian macroeconomic strategies than did prior struggles over the terms on which individuals would receive unemployment benefits. This was so not only because it was easier for public works to be conceptualized and justified in collective national terms. Equally important, it was also easier, in Sweden, as in many other countries, for politically active people to arrive at rationales for financing "useful" public works through government deficits during a national economic crisis. Thus, it mattered greatly that the Swedish Social Democrats, operating in a polity without unemployment insurance, were much more open to public works as a way to cope with unemployment than were their British Labour counterparts.

State Structures, Economic Experts, and Policy Innovations

If the Swedish Social Democrats were prepared to reform public works when they came to power, it nevertheless remains to be seen why they could build reformed public works into a combined strategy for national economic recovery and unemployment relief. After all, government deficits to finance expanded public works were just as anathema to conservative opinion leaders in early-depression Sweden as in Britain, so we must probe further than we have so far to explain why the Social Democrats chose to follow this path.

Certain liberal tenets about the proper role of the government in capitalism remained politically influential throughout the West in the 1920s. Predominant views were that governments should do little to modify the "self-equilibrating" workings of domestic markets and that open international trade should be supported through "sound" currencies based on the gold standard. Regardless of such political orthodoxies, however, important new ideas germinated during the 1920s in intellectual circles of economists.[56] Students of business cycles argued that public spending could play a positive role in smoothing economic fluctuations, or even speeding recoveries from economic downturns. And new views emerged about active governmental roles in managing currencies and interest rates. By the later 1920s, proto-Keynesian suggestions about the economic functions of national governments – ideas as yet unsystematized into any coherent theory – were being developed by quite a few respectable Western economists, including, of course, John Maynard Keynes himself.

In order to assess why and how new, proto-Keynesian economic ideas became, or failed to become, credible with governmental and political leaders in a position to act on them, we must ask not about the presence of individual persons or ideas in the abstract, but whether key state agencies were open or closed to the development or use of innovative perspectives. In effect, we must investigate how the normal mechanisms used by states to incorporate educated expertise served to facilitate or hamper innovations in economic policy.

If new and politically visible economic ideas could have been decisive in their own right, then Britain would have been the first nation to adopt new macroeconomic strategies to deal with unemployment. As early as 1924, Keynes began making arguments about unemployment that pointed away from traditional remedies involving wage deflation and government economies.[57] Four years later, Keynes's ideas took center stage in political debates with the publication of the Liberal "Yellow Book" entitled *Britain's Industrial Future*. Adopted by Lloyd George as his 1929 campaign program, Keynes's unorthodox ideas were again featured in the Liberal pamplet *We Can Conquer Unemployment*, which aroused quite a public stir.[58] Not only did arguments for using government spending to combat unemployment enjoy a most eloquent proponent and the early support of a political party in Britain; they also eventually attracted support from some Labour politicians. The most notable of these was Oswald Mosely, who, as a member of the Labour government's Unemployment Committee of 1929–30, penned a memorandum to Prime Minister MacDonald endorsing a program of spending to combat unemployment, along with a long-term program of industrial rationalization.[59]

Despite all of this, the weight and unanimity of bureaucratic opposition to innovative economic ideas were a prime factor, along with the Labour party's fixation on unemployment benefits, in discouraging bold initiatives by the Labour government to cope with the depression. The key to bureaucratic intertia in the 1920s and 1930s can be found in the organizational and intellectual stranglehold that one ministry, the Treasury, had gained over all other government departments inside the British civil service.

Before World War I, the Labour Department of the Board of Trade functioned as a center of policy innovation in matters relating to labor, including wage regulations and social insurance.[60] Especially between 1906 and 1911, Labour Department officials were able to gain the ear of the Liberal cabinet, countering the Treasury's perpetual calls for restrictions on new measures that would require government expenditures or administrative expansions. Well-developed statistical capacities and newly expanded field organizations of labor inspectors figured in this remarkable department's ability to pioneer much of the British welfare state. Even more important, perhaps, the Labour Department repeatedly took advantage of a special loophole in the British civil service regulations to recruit laterally to its top official ranks professional experts and other people experienced in dealing with labor problems. The fresh perspectives on social issues that such top-level recruits brought with them into government service gave the Labour Department a dynamism on policy matters that contrasted sharply with the stodgy conservatism of the older domestic departments, such as the Local Government Board, that relied on recruiting officials directly out of Cambridge and Oxford and promoting them by seniority over the years.

The autonomy and status of the Labour Department were apparently enhanced when an independent Ministry of Labour was established in December 1916. But, in fact, postwar administrative reorganization affecting the civil service as a whole fundamentally undermined the earlier conditions favoring policy innovations and thus negated any advantages the new ministry might have gained over the earlier department.[61] In 1919, the permanent secretary of the Treasury became the head of the entire civil service, being thus placed in a position to control career advancement for senior officials in all departments of government. The special regulations allowing lateral recruitment to top official ranks were also eliminated in 1919, ensuring that official mindsets would henceforth change much more slowly. Treasury controls over administrative and staff expenditures in all other departments were tightened, and after 1924 any departmental policy proposal calling for increased government expenditures had to pass Treasury scrutiny before it could go to the cabinet of the day. With these organizational changes in place, tentative official proposals for new uses of government administistative powers or expenditures to address social and economic problems were choked off in early stages of formulation and tended not to be raised repeatedly by officials who knew that their career prospects depended on currying favor with Treasury.[62] A profound bias against policy innovations contravening economic orthodoxy spread throughout the entire British state apparatus.

When the Labour government came to power in 1919, therefore, its prime minister and cabinet officials, all relatively new to government office, heard nothing but unanimous bureaucratic advice against unbalanced budgets, new social expenditures, and innovative schemes for national economic recovery. During the Labour government's brief time in office, the only likely route for the injection of alternative policy ideas into the strategic thinking of the Labour leaders was via the Economic Advisory Council that Prime Minister MacDonald established in January 1930. This body was, of course, entirely ad hoc and started its deliberations very late in the game for the troubled Labour government. Moreover, the council as a whole was very unwieldy. Following twentieth-century patterns for British public commissions, it included ministers along with a range of extragovernmental figures: industrialists, trade unionists, and professional economists. Civil servants, however, were not included.[63]

Coherent advice was unlikely to emerge from such a contentious blend of viewpoints, and this prompted the subsequent appointment (at Keynes's urging) of a smaller committee of economists. Keynes and A. C. Pigou were the leading members. During the 1930s, members of the group would make headway at gradually modifying Treasury's views of possible economic policies for Britain,[64] but in 1930–31, even this more manageable set of economic experts could do little to overcome quickly the practical impotence of ad hoc public commissions within the British policy-making system. Nor could it immediately establish the idea that "outside" economic experts should be taken seriously by officials and politicians. The Economic Advisory Council and its committee of economists remained isolated from the governmental machineries responsible for dealing with unemployment and were viewed by Chancellor of the Exchequer Philip Snowden as a potential threat to his control over financial policy.[65] Thus, cautious recommendations for a modest program including domestic public investment, reform of unemployment insurance, and a general tariff found no sympathetic agency to serve as a point of entry into British government.[66] Ironically, it seems to have been after this frustrating experience that Keynes decided that a new, grand theoretical synthesis would be needed to overthrow the hold of "economic orthodoxy." Without the impermeability of the British polity to specific new economic policy recommendations, *The General Theory* might not have been written![67]

In sum, stifled from within the state by Treasury control and parried from without by the normal, self-enclosed functioning of British government, new economic ideas about feasible public policies, especially those calling for public works and budget deficits, could not find their way into officially sponsored programs. Only a Labour party determined and clearsighted about *its own political need* for bold, state-sponsored initiatives against unemployment and domestic economic decline could have bypassed the British state apparatus and the cacophony of publicly debated views to take up Keynes's new ideas. But we have already seen why the Labour party's orientations toward the problems of the unemployed were set in an alternative political frame of reference. Together, the social policy legacies that the British state brought into the depression and the imperviousness of the state apparatus to innovative ideas in the later 1920s and early 1930s seem explanation enough for why the hapless Labour government of 1929–31 missed a major opportunity to combine social progress and a strategy for national economic recovery in depression-era Britain.

As we turn back again to Sweden, we can begin to grasp some important points about the Swedish state and its relation to economic experts by looking briefly through the eyes of Brinley Thomas, an assistant lecturer in the Commerce Department of the London School of Economics, who visited Sweden between 1933 and 1935 and talked extensively with economists, officials, and political leaders. In 1936, Thomas published *Monetary Policy and Crises: A Study of Swedish Experience*. By now Thomas's economic analysis has been superseded, but some of his more sociological observations remain acute. Thomas emphasized that the Swedish state had a special capacity to pursue coordinated monetary and budgetary policies because the "Bank of Sweden is publicly owned and is responsible to the Banking Committee of the Riksdag."[68] He was especially impressed that

in Sweden great respect is paid to the professional economist. He commands an honoured place in the scheme of things in marked contrast to the scepticism or the polite indifference with which he is regarded in this country [i.e., Britain] or the United States. . . . The curious thing is that though [Swedish economists] . . . often take part in the hurly-burly of politics, the authority attaching to their pronouncements is not thereby weakened.[69]

In his preface to the Thomas book, Professor Hugh Dalton of the London School of Economics pointed to an explanation for this: "Economists in that country [Sweden] are, and have long been, in closer touch with practical affairs than in some others, with benefit both to themselves and to public policy."[70] Indeed, much of the answer to why the Swedish Social Democrats launched a deficit-financed recovery strategy in 1932–34 lies in the history of the Swedish state from preindustrial times and its long-established mechanisms for bringing experts, bureaucrats, and political representatives together for sustained planning of public policies.

Apart from brief interludes when parliaments checked royal power, Sweden, from the seventeenth century to the early twentieth, was a bureaucratically centered monarchical regime.[71] Central administrative boards charged with overseeing governance through royally appointed regional officials were established in the seventeenth century by King Gustavus Adolphus II and his chancellor Axel Oxenstierna. Henceforth, policy formation was strongly influenced by the dominance of central administrative boards.[72] These boards were separate from departments engaged in policy implementation and thus could take a strong role in longer-term policy planning. Moreover, royal investigatory commissions recurrently deliberated new national policies, and these included state officials as well as representatives of major social groups. Standing parliamentary committees – with representatives from all estates, or from both houses of the Riksdag after a two-house national representative system replaced the four estates in 1866 – also regularly cooperated with the king's officials to frame compromises and pass proposed measures.

Very rapidly, between the 1880s and 1920s, Sweden was transformed from an agrarian monarchical bureaucracy into an industrial-capitalist parliamentary democracy.[73] In the years surrounding World War I, sharp but nonrevolutionary political struggles, centered in a working alliance between the Social Democrats and the Liberals, led step by step to a universal franchise and to fully responsible parliamentary government. Despite these fundamental changes, initiative in the realm of public policy making did not simply devolve into parliamentary bargaining. Instead, Liberal and Social Democratic party leaders, especially those elected to the Riksdag, were absorbed along with economic interest-group leaders into modernized versions of Sweden's deeply rooted system of deliberative, consultative, and state-centered policy making.[74] Investigatory commissions and parliamentary standing committees guided by administrative officials carried on in the new democratic polity. Such bodies increasingly mobilized the expertise of the modern social sciences through the direct participation of professors, graduate students, and other researchers in their policy investigations.

Against this background, we can understand how a key Social Democratic politician, Ernst Wigforss, along with some young Swedish economists, carried out policy-relevant deliberations on issues of unemployment in the later 1920s. During one of their brief interludes in power, in 1926, the Social Democrats appointed a Committee of Inquiry into Unemployment to investigate the causes of unemployment and conceivable remedies for it.[75] Ernst Wigforss served on this investigatory commission, along with the prominent conservative economist Gosta Bagge. During the years of the commission's typically unhurried operation, Wigforss formulated the new Social Democratic proposals for public works at prevailing wages. Meanwhile, the commission "engaged the research energies of practically all of Sweden's handful of young economists," including Dag Hammarskjöld, Alf Johansson, Gunnar Myrdal, and Bertil Ohlin.[76] A series of important research monographs was completed under the auspices of the official investigation, and the younger economists associated with it would later come to be known as the "Stockholm school."[77]

The origins of breaks with orthodox neoclassical economics in Sweden have been the subject of vigorous debate among historians of economic thought.[78] One position is that the Swedish economists arrived at new analytical understanding about possibilities for activist financial measures and the use of government deficits as a recovery tool by building on the indigenous Swedish theoretical tradition established by Knut Wicksell. This argument suggests that the young economists influenced the thinking of Ernst Wigforss. An alternative interpretation is that Wigforss was inspired primarily by the English Liberals and Keynes and that he in turn influenced the theorizing of the emerging economists of the Stockholm school. Whatever the precise lines of influence, however, it is obvious that, under the aegis of investigations and discussions conducted by the committee established in 1926, important policy-relevant economic ideas were developed. Quite likely, both Wigforss and the young economists were affected by participation in the public investigatory effort.

The worldwide depression engulfed Sweden in 1930–31, and the electoral victory of the Social Democrats the following year provided the ideal context for the continuance and practical culmination of the ongoing cooperation between party leaders and innovative Swedish economists. The international financial collapse opened the way for new Central Bank policies to cushion domestic deflation.[79] With nearly one-fourth of the unionized labor force out of work,[80] unemployment was a more pressing issue than ever for the Social Democrats; so the Riksdag appointed a new Commission on Unemployment, with the leading figures of the emerging Stockholm school – Myrdal, Ohlin, and Hammarskjöld – as the directors. Drawing on accumulated studies and ideas, this team of economists cooperated closely with Wigforss, now finance minister, in formulating the Social Democrats' strategy for economic recovery.[81] At the heart of the Social Democratic strategy were proposals, rationalized simultaneously in humanitarian and in demand-stimulus economic terms, calling for loan-financed public works that would employ workers at union wage rates. The party's long-standing concern with reforming public works projects in the interest of unemployed workers was fused with the economists' ideas about fiscal measures likely to stimulate national recovery from depression.

After six months of negotiations in the Riksdag, a version of the Social Democrats' proposed program was enacted. The compromise ultimately struck was known as the "Cow Deal" between the Social Democrats and the Agrarian party. (Later we shall discuss how the Swedish state structure facilitated this and subsequent worker–farmer compromises.) To help farmers, the Cow Deal called for $10 million in agricultural loans along with agricultural price supports.[82] To address industrial unemployment, large grants for public works were approved.[83] The old Unemployment Commission was left in operation for the time being, but wages on its projects were raised to the prevailing market rate for unskilled labor.[84] Separately administered new public projects were to pay union rates. Ironically, a prolonged strike by construction workers in 1933–34 delayed the full implementation of the public works proposal, but after 1934 greater emphasis was placed on new public works, which were more generously financed than the activities of the Unemployment Commission.[85]

Today, most analysts agree that the early revival of Swedish exports in the 1930s, rather than the Social Democratic program of deficit spending for public works, was the primary cause of the country's relatively rapid recovery from the depression.[86] Arguably, however, the Social Democratic program did ensure the domestic conditions needed to sustain an export-led recovery.[87] Swedish national production regained predepression levels by 1935–36, and growth continued apace after that (although residual unemployment lingered in Sweden as elsewhere).[88] In any event, the primary significance of the Social Democratic recovery strategy of the early 1930s lay not in its difficult to pinpoint economic results, but in the stable basis it laid for continuing Social Democratic governance. Moreover, the Social Democratic alliance with experts, who continued to be drawn into government-appointed commissions, would therafter regularly expand the economic and welfare functions of the Swedish state.[89]

In sum, the Swedish state's policies and structure in the 1920s provide the key to the Social Democrats' remarkable proto-Keynesian recovery strategy of 1933. Reacting to the state's established means for handling problems of unemployment, the Social Democratic party continually looked for ways to reform the implementation of public works. And the unique institutional mechanism of the state-sponsored investigatory commission allowed economic experts, Social Democratic politicians, and officials to ponder togehter – for several years *before* the depression crisis – how it might be politically and administratively feasible and intellectually justifiable to devise public policies to combat mass unemployment. Of course, irreducible elements of individual creativity were involved in the answers they devised, but it is difficult to imagine a better structural matrix for the crystallization of "Keynesian" macroeconomic strategies several years before the appearance of *The General Theory* itself.

The U.S. State Structure and the Limits of America's New Deal

Just as the Swedish Social Democrats benefited electorally from the onslaught of the Great Depression, so did the Democratic party in the United States and the "New Deal" wing within it led by Franklin Delano Roosevelt of New York. As Roosevelt and the Democrats came to national power in 1932–33, an especially devastating economic crisis by international standards pushed them toward bold national state actions – including public spending on an unprecedented scale – to aid farmers, relieve the unemployed, and promote national economic recovery.

In response to the severe and prolonged economic crisis and the pressing political demands it repeatedly engendered, the New Deal moved through major phases, each of which will be analyzed in subsections to follow.[90] The early New Deal pursued a de facto policy of running federal deficits to finance public works and emergency relief but did *not* launch an explicit program of national economic recovery along these lines. Only quite late in the 1930s, in 1938–39, did Roosevelt finally accept Keynesian-style economic reasoning to justify public expenditures for social purposes. At this point, the liberal New Deal was reconceptualized in social Keynesian terms that resembled the goals of Swedish social democracy. Nevertheless, despite many conditions that favored such a culmination of New Deal reforms, the United States ended up instead with commercial Keynesianism.

As we analyze these successive phases of the U.S. New Deal, we must keep in mind that the depression era in the United States not only engendered a series of debates over how to use the existing capacities of the national government to deal with social and economic problems, but also unleashed struggles over unprecedented initiatives by the federal government and the executive branch. A state structure previously quite decentralized, with national policy making coordinated more through congressional brokering than through presidential initiatives, was itself undergoing basic changes during the New Deal. Whatever the (considerable) remaining roles for local administration in Britain and Sweden, truly "national" states and polities had already been established well before the 1930s in both countries. But the American New Deal was a period of central state building and the nationalization of politics – and a time of conflicts over just how far those wrenching processes might go.[91]

The Two-Track Strategy of the Early New Deal

The early New Deal in the United States brought to power an activist president and a Democratic party anxious to expand federal initiatives to cope with a depression already of unprecedented scope, depth, and duration by 1932–33. The situation faced by the U.S. New Dealers had closer resemblances to Swedish than to British circumstances. As in Sweden, agriculture remained economically important, and workers and farmers alike supported the forces of political reform in 1932.[92] Also as in Sweden, the United States lacked established public benefits to cushion the unemployed or preoccupy the Democratic party, and public works were a recognized means of coping with rising unemployment.

Indeed, from the 1920s, both popularizing economic writers and a whole array of academic economists urged that the federal government use increased spending on public works as a method to combat unemployment and counter business downturns. In 1928, two popularizers, William Trufant Foster and Waddill Catchings, published a widely read book, *The Road to Plenty*, in which they argued that government spending on public works was needed to regulate the balance between savings and investment.[93] Foster himself testified before the Senate in 1932, urging that spending be boosted for all kinds of public works and that the national debt be increased "as far as is necessary to restore employment and production."[94] Nor were academic economists, as is often supposed, unanimously urging the "orthodox" course of wage cuts and governmental budget balancing. As the research of J. Ronnie Davis has amply demonstrated, there were dozens of respectable academic economists, especially from Chicago, Columbia, and many state universities, who urged deficit-financed public works expenditures upon Congress, President Hoover, and President Roosevelt.[95] This was not surprising, because research on business cycles had, by the 1920s, made the notion of timing public works expenditures for countercyclical or pump-priming purposes a well-known possibility, and intellectual departures from neoclassical equilibrium assumptions were underway on a variety of empirical and theoretical fronts.[96]

To be sure, public works in the United States before the 1930s had been primarily a local and state responsibility, as were welfare for the impoverished and relief for the unemployed.[97] Nevertheless, by 1932, local and state governments were begging the federal government to take over the burden of dealing with the problems of their distressed constituents. Democratic party politicians were similarly disposed. With local finances at the breaking point and the party holding national power for the first time in twelve years, federal money and patronage had great appeal.[98] The unusual docility of locally based political power that prevailed in the United States in 1932–34 thus offered the national government the chance to forge a fundamentally expanded and new role for itself.

Roosevelt did not, however, choose to implement a national recovery strategy based on public deficit spending during his "first" New Deal (or even during the "second" New Deal of 1935–36). Instead, for many years the New Deal proceeded along two tracks not explicitly coordinated with one another. On one track, the officially most visible one, regulatory efforts and self-financing interventions were featured in the New Deal's first national recovery strategy and also in the first steps it took to create a permanent federal welfare state in America. The National Recovery Administration (NRA) of 1933–35 emphasized business regulation.[99] The first Agricultural Adjustment Administration (AAA) of 1933–35 was "self-financing" through a tax on agricultural processers.[100] And the Social Security Act was formulated and passed in 1934–35 strictly on what Roosevelt called a "sound" fiscal basis, mandating the collection of taxes from workers well in advance of their eligibility for benefits from unemployment or old-age insurance.[101]

Meanwhile, federal deficits were run up right from the start of the New Deal to pay for public works and relief efforts on an unprecedented scale.[102] But these expenditures were strictly for humanitarian purposes and were carefully segregated into an "emergency budget," while Roosevelt and his financial advisers endeavored to keep the "regular" budget in balance. Moreover, the goal of the "balanced budget" was held up as the measure of New Deal success. As soon as the economic emergency let up, Roosevelt repeatedly promised, all federal expenditures would be balanced against tax income.[103]

To explain why the New Deal so doggedly avoided a recovery strategy of deficit spending, we need to examine the historical formation of the U.S. state structure. In the nineteenth century, the United States had a "state of courts and parties." This form of political organization flourished in the absence of both public bureaucracy and programmatic political parties, and its legacies limited the capacities of the federal government in the 1930s.[104]

In contrast to Britain, Sweden, and most other European nations, the United States experienced the early establishment of (white) manhood suffrage – before any national bureaucratic state was formed.[105] Despite the fact that American workers voted sooner and more universally than European workers – in fact, in significant part *because* they did – their collective interests as a class did not come to be directly represented in national politics. Because there was no bureaucratic state in place at the time of the accomplishment of popular democracy for white men in the 1820s to 1840s, patronage-oriented political parties (along with courts) dominated much of the polity from the very start of industrialization. Competing parties vied for workers' votes within local residence communities, on the basis of the patchwork of ethnoreligious identities that divided workers among themselves, yet tied subsets of them to sets of farmers and businessmen. To be sure, there were many benefits for workers, especially in local jurisdictions where they were the solid majority, but no major labor or socialist political party emerged in the United States to pursue pro–trade union or specifically worker interests through programmatic national appeals.

The nineteenth-century U.S. state structure changed in some important ways before the coming of the New Deal. Progressive reformers in the early twentieth century sought to undercut the hold of patronage-oriented political parties on public policy making and to carve out room for expert-dominated administrative agencies within urban, state, and federal governments.[106] However, the Progressive reformers did not typically try to create national bureaucracies with authority penetrating into localities, and they were largely opposed to any great expansion of the spending powers of government. An essential part of their struggle was directed against the free-spending "corruption" that they thought to be characteristic of the patronage-oriented political parties, whose hold over public policy making they were trying to break.[107] Moreover, the successes of the Progressive administrative reformers were scattered and incomplete, and their partial successes combined with the weakening of party competition in the early twentieth-century United States to exacerbate tendencies toward dispersion of political authority within the American state structure as a whole. Conflicts increased among presidents and congressional coalitions, and the various levels of government in the federal system became more decoupled from one another.[108]

Conflicts of sovereignty, fragmentary administrative reforms, and federal decentralization all, in turn, affected the relationships of emerging social science professionals to public policy making in the United States. To be sure, significant "expert" access to public policy making was first achieved by the reformers of the Progressive Era, many of whom were social scientists, and then enhanced by the wartime mobilization of academic experts into federal service.[109] Herbert Hoover also had a penchant for organizing expert-dominated conferences and advisory commissions during the 1920s.[110] The elaborate reports and policy recommendations of such conferences and commissions were frequently ignored, however, especially when they called for federal spending.[111] Congressional brokering remained preeminent in the 1920s, and Herbert Hoover did not advocate direct federal government interventions.[112]

In the absence of access to national centers of policy making and implementation such as the Swedish economists enjoyed through participation on that country's administratively anchored investigatory commissions, U.S. economists could hardly lay the strategic groundwork for coherent macroeconomic inventions in response to the depression. Nor could academic economists, often isolated from practical policy making and inevitably scattered across the country's large and competitive system of universities, easily assemble a unified school of thought to challenge orthodox assumptions with well-reasoned and mutually reinforcing alternative ideas, as did the young economists in Sweden. Only two groups of U.S. economists seem to have managed during the 1920s to fuse practical politicoadminstrative considerations with theoretical innovations in the style of the emerging Stockholm school. These groups were the "Commons school" of institutional economists in Wisconsin and a network of agricultural economists oriented to the activities of the U.S. Department of Agriculture (USDA) and its Extension Service. In the early to middle 1930s, each of these groups would forge a particularly successful program within the New Deal as a whole. Wisconsin people would shape the Social Security Act,[113] and the USDA economists would shape the New Deal's agricultural price supports and subsequent efforts at agricultural planning.[114] But there was no counterpart group in a position to shape national economic recovery strategies as such.

Given this background on the historical formation of the state structure – of America's distinctive complex of weak national administration, divided and fragmentary public authority, and nonprogrammatic political parties – it is easy to understand why the early New Deal of 1932–34 produced a welter of federal initiatives in response to the troubles of the depression, yet put the NRA and the AAA rather than a coherent strategy of public deficit spending at the center of its efforts. In contrast to the situation in Sweden, there could be no synthesis of initiatives from a centralized administrative state and from a national parliamentary party devoted to pursuing a collective working-class interest in full employment. Neither the administrative state nor the programmatic party existed. Instead, the early New Dealers married wide popular support – achieved by channeling "temporary" spending for relief and public works through locally rooted congressmen and Democratic politicians – with low-cost, Progressive-style extensions of federal regulation in the national interest. Without having to fashion any political program explicitly recognizing class interests, the New

Dealers could offer something to individuals or groups in all classes. They put the federal government in the role of an active umpire ensuring common efforts for national recovery by regulating against "uncooperative" elements in all groups.

All of this could be done, moreover, without explicitly planning *permanently* to expand federal spending, let alone budget deficits. For Roosevelt and the other reform politicians who launched the New Deal, it seemed not merely economically wise, but also morally important to avoid permanent fiscal expansions. To understand why, we must recall that Roosevelt himself, along with most of the key officials he brought with him to Washington (especially from the states of New York and Wisconsin), had originally "come of age" politically during the Progressive Era. For these veterans of fights against "political corruption," "balanced government budgets" symbolized honest government itself.[115] Thus, the earlier history of efforts to overcome patronage democracy and create a certain kind of regulatory – but not free-spending – state in America made it very unlikely that the mature reform politicians who came to Washington to cope with the depression would find notions of *deliberate* deficit spending very appealing.

Possibilities for Social Keynesianism in the Later New Deal

In contrast to the British Labour party, America's New Deal Democrats remained in power and enjoyed continued room for maneuver throughout the 1930s. The activist humanitarian reforms of the early New Deal allowed Democratic majorities to grow in 1934 and 1936. Unlike the Social Democratic strategy in Sweden, however, the New Deal's initial program for national economic recovery was not confirmed by a rapid recovery of economic production or employment to predepression levels. The recovery strategy centered on the NRA collapsed even before it was declared unconstitutional in 1935. Without pausing to discuss all of the developments of 1934–36, we turn to the later New Deal, when changes came together in a way that might have facilitated a U.S. breakthrough to social Keynesianism.

Indeed, the last part of the New Deal provides a more telling comparison with Swedish social democracy than does the early New Deal. Between 1936 and 1939, class-oriented politics was at an all-time high in the United States. The organizational power of industrial labor expanded to an unprecedented degree, and programmatic alliances of unions and liberal Democrats took shape.[116] Within this general context, a number of elements pointed very specifically toward the adoption of a social Keynesian program for national economic recovery, to be followed by a more long term marriage of public social spending and macroeconomic management.

For one thing, by 1937 a variety of federal programs and agencies existed through which increases in spending could be readily effected.[117] Moreover, the Works Progress Administration (WPA) in particular had established a national program of public works that could serve as a basis for further federal interventions. Although WPA projects were initiated locally, Washington approved all proposals. The central administration set employment quotas and monthly program budgets for each state. Regional offices reporting back to the chief administrator, Harry Hopkins, monitored and advised state and district administrations to ensure that federal guidelines and intentions were followed.[118] The movement toward greater central control grew in each year of the program's existence, from 1935 onward.

Although the WPA provided a framework through which flexible central spending policies could be implemented, neither it nor other federal spending programs were originally conceived as part of an explicitly countercyclical strategy. Yet support for exactly such a strategy had been growing for some years inside the federal executive. It is interesting that the key architect of the original proto-Keynesian policy thrust from within the U.S. state was not a university-trained economist. He was Marriner Eccles, a Utah businessman-banker whose formal eduction was only to the high school level.[119]

Early in the 1930s, Eccles became convinced that deficit government spending could produce recovery from the depression, and he carried his idiosyncratic views into the Federal Reserve Board when he became its chairman in 1934. As his assistant, Eccles recruited a former Harvard instructor, Lauchlin Currie, whose diplomatic skills smoothed Eccles's relations with other officials and whose technical skills led in 1935 to the development of crucial new techniques for calculating on a monthly basis the "net income-producing expenditures of the federal government."[120] Together, Eccles and Currie built up, step by step, a like-minded network of allies prepared to lobby the president on both economic and humanitarian grounds for expanded social spending.[121] The network included some cabinet-level officials, especially Harry Hopkins at WPA and Henry Wallace at Agriculture, along with various young academically trained economists in executive-branch staff positions. Working from within the New Deal executive establishment, in short, Eccles and Currie gradually accomplished for the United States something akin to the fusion of new economic thought with concretely feasible policies that those involved in investigatory commissions accomplished in Sweden in the late 1920s and early 1930s.

Along with these administrative and intellectual developments, the configuration of power in Congress suggested that those working for the interests of farmers and industrial labor might cooperate over sustained public spending. Before the first AAA was declared unconstitutional in 1936, farm subsidies had been paid by a tax on processors. Once that tax became illegal, farmers were dependent on congressional trade-offs to secure annual appropriations for the parity payments to which they were now accustomed. No liberal on most matters, American Farm Bureau leader Edward O'Neal urged workers and farmers to stick together in the face of "economy boys" who threatened programs desired by each group.[122]

The Sour Note

Figure 4.4. A cartoon by C. K. Berryman in the *Washington Star*, December 4, 1938. (Source: Dean L. May, *From New Deal to New Economics: The American Liberal Response to the Recession of 1937*. New York: Garland Publishing, 1981.)

Finally, at a critical conjuncture, the budget-minded Franklin Roosevelt was converted to deficit spending as a solution to the continued depression in the American economy. When the sharp economic downturn in 1937 cut industrial production by one-third, the New Deal was thrown into an acute political and intellectual crisis.[123] Executive-branch advocates of deficit-spending remedies urged the president to disregard the budget-minded advice of Treasury Secretary Henry Morgenthau. The *Washington Star* cartoon in Fig. 4.4 shows who won this crucial argument. After prolonged indecision, Roosevelt heeded the advice of the spenders and in April 1938 announced a program for releasing some $6.5 billion in federal funds, through over $2 billion in monetary measures, $1.5 billion in Reconstruction Finance Corporation loans, and about $3 billion in congressional appropriations, mostly for the WPA and the Public Works Administration. Although there were some congressional attempts to place restrictions on such funds, these objections were overridden in the face of the economic downturn. In fact, with congressional elections only seven months away, the final bill actually allocated more funds than Roosevelt had requested, thanks to rural representatives who tacked on a parity payment.[124]

In the aftermath of this policy watershed in 1938, Roosevelt and liberal New Dealers remained believers in government spending as a way to combine economic and social policies, fusing, in short, what had been the two separate tracks of the earlier New Deal.[125] Roosevelt's 1939 budget and annual messages attributed the 1938 recovery to planned increases in federal spending and argued for the continued use of fiscal stimuli to increase national income. Then the Roosevelt administration proposed a hefty Works Financing Bill to Congress, justified as a needed boost for the economy, which had leveled off after recovery from the 1937 recession. This "spend–lend bill" called for the establishment of a $3.06 billion revolving fund for self-liquidating public projects.[126]

These developments in the New Deal's official orientation occurred, moreover, just as Keynes's new economic theory found a prestigious university home among American academic economists. It is interesting that, in its U.S. interpretation, Keynesian economics initially took on a distinctly more social democratic guise than one could find in Keynes's own writings. What is more, American Keynesians in the late 1930s were often openly critical of the prerogatives of private business, and, ironically, this happened even as the politically well-established Swedish Social Democrats were moving toward a rapprochement with Swedish capitalists.[127]

As John Kenneth Galbraith aptly put it, "The trumpet . . . that was sounded in Cambridge, England, was heard most clearly in Cambridge, Massachusetts. Harvard was the principal avenue by which Keynes's ideas passed into the United States."[128] Alvin Hansen moved to Harvard in 1938 from the University of Minnesota, arriving just as he converted intellectually from a skeptic to a disciple of Keynes's 1936 theory.[129] Once at Harvard, Hansen galvanized a preexisting group of graduate students and young academics into what became for a time the "stagnationist school" of Keynesian thought. This orientation held that private investment in the United States would probably not be able to attain and sustain a full-employment, growth economy without permanent infusions of public spending.[130] In the 1938 pamphlet *An Economic Program for American Democracy*, a popularized version of such ideas was deployed by a group of young Harvard and Tufts economists to celebrate the liberal New Deal and its response to the 1937 recession.[131] An unmistakable antibusiness tone suffused this tract, which called for increased public spending in combination with structural reforms in the U.S. economy and redistributions in the income structure.

Hansen was more cautious, as his December 1938 presidential address to the American Economic Association reveals.[132] Nevertheless, his theoretical and humanitarian commitment to heightened levels of public social spending was clear and became sharper as his and his students' ties to liberals in the Roosevelt adminstration grew,[133] for stagnationist Keynesianism in the United States was no mere "ivory tower" phenomenon. Hansen taught in Harvard's new Littauer School of Public Administration as well as in the Department of Economics, and from 1939 onward, his students and followers moved in considerable numbers into important executive-branch posts.[134] Hansen himself gave celebrated testimony before Congress in 1939 and served in important advisory posts.

By 1939, therefore, two streams of "new economics" had come together in the United States: The Eccles–Currie deficit spenders, who had labored for years within the federal executive, were emboldened and inspired by the new stagnationist Keynesianism of the Cambridge academics.[135] The academics, in turn, had discovered in the New Deal's course, from the early 1930s through the spending response to the 1937 recession, a real-world justification for their distinctive reading of Keynes and the policy conclusions they wanted to draw from it.[136]

The Obstacles to Social Keynesianism in the United States

Propitious as the post-1938 situation looked, however, it would take more than particular congressional votes and the conversion of Roosevelt administration officials – even more than a social democratic reading of Keynes by prestigious U.S. economists – to institutionalize Keynesian macroeconomic management combined with high levels of social spending in the United States. Some contrasts to the ways in which social Keynesian policies were institutionalized in Sweden during the 1930s can help us to understand the obstacles to a comparable accomplishment in the United States.

In Sweden, the long tradition of central administrative guidance and the programmatic discipline of national parliamentary parties allowed the Social Democrats to implement and build on their social-spending strategy with little controversy once the Cow Deal of 1933 was struck. Public works programs in Sweden could be centrally planned yet locally implemented, because local governments were accustomed to working with national administrative boards. With remarkable ease, the Swedish state was able to centralize formerly local functions in the course of the 1930s. For example, Social Democratic reforms in 1934 undertook to reorient local labor exchanges to the national labor market by increasing central control, boosting state subsidies, and expanding the scope of operations.[137] Moreover, in a context in which the Riksdag was attuned to working cooperatively with government leaders and administrators, it proved relatively easy to reorganize Swedish budget planning in 1936–38. And the timeworn device of the public commission could be used again and again by the Social Democrats to plan new forms of social spending, labor–market interventions, and macroeconomic planning.[138]

The ready adaptability of Swedish administrative and party arrangements to the implementation of public works and the relative ease with which further modifications of government operations could be made compatible with enlarged welfare-state efforts contrast sharply with the major, and politically controversial, changes in the federal administration and the role of the executive that were needed for comparable policy purposes to be consistently pursued in the United States. Because the rapid growth of the federal government during the New Deal had occurred in a disparate and unchecked fashion, a profusion of agencies carried on more or less independently of one another. Better control and coordination were needed before any coherent macroeconomic strategy based on public spending could be put into place. Proponents of a sweeping program of executive reorganization that Roosevelt tried to get through Congress in 1937–38 understood this. They aimed to create a powerful presidency "equipped with the personnel, planning, and fiscal control necessary to implement [its] . . . social program."[139]

In the light of the long-standing twentieth-century rivalry between presidents and Congresses for control over expanding realms of federal administration, it was hardly surprising that Roosevelt's proposals for reorganizing the executive were interpreted, even by many of his regular liberal supporters, as a power grab that could strip Congress of its authority and disrupt carefully cultivated relationships among congressional committees, interest groups, and federal administrative agencies.[140] Thus, the reorganization proposals were eviscerated by Congress. The defeat of the boldest features of executive reorganization boded ill for efforts, from the late 1930s through the 1940s, to carry out policy planning or exert fiscal coordination in ways that would have facilitated Keynesian macroeconomic management and made more credible sustained programs of public spending for full employment and social welfare. The defeat made quite clear that, despite all the forces apparently pushing the United States toward social Keynesianism in the later New Deal, established institutional channels of policy making centered in Congress were proving to be immovable obstacles to prerequisite administrative reforms.

Contrasts in state capacities for introducing and controlling social-spending programs were not the only factors pushing the Swedish and U.S. new deals toward different outcomes. There were also important contrasts in the interests and political capacities of the sectors of agriculture drawn into policy coalitions during the 1930s in the two nations. These contrasts were closely bound up with the ways in which state structures and initial depression-era policies strengthened alternative possible political alliances involving farmers in Sweden and the United States.

In Sweden, the alliance between the Social Democrats and the Agrarian party embodied in the Cow Deal of 1933 was essential for the initial introduction of the deficit-financed strategy for coping with the depression. This alliance was quite a new departure in Swedish political history. In part, prior social changes in the base of the Agrarian party made it possible, as did the depression crisis itself, yet the alliance was also crystallized and solidified by the workings of the Swedish state structure and party system.

Since its formation in 1917, the Agrarian party had aligned with parties of the Right, because it opposed the free-market, proconsumer stance of the Social Democrats and feared that they might bring higher wages to the countryside.[141] Obstacles to a new alliance were relieved by the late 1920s through the ascendance of leaders oriented to the interests of a growing number of smaller farmers in the Agrarian party and through the movement of large grain farmers into the Conservative party.[142] When the collapse of British and German markets in 1932 spelled disaster for Swedish small producers, they turned to government for an active program of price supports (without production controls), which the bourgeois parties were reluctant to provide.[143] At that point, the Agrarians were still worried about rural wages, and the Social Democrats, for their part, were reluctant to back policies that would raise the cost of living for workers.[144] Thus, there was nothing economically inevitable about the Cow Deal. It was politically and economically *possible*, however. The Social Democrats could not pass their program without additional parliamentary support, and beleaguered Swedish farmers found expanded consumption and government subsidies attractive.

The centralized structure of Swedish policy bargaining – involving representatives of social groups and economic experts, all arguing from what might be called the point of view of the state – helped turn the potential farmer alliance with labor into an actual and enduring agreement. The arguments of the officially influential economists about the beneficial effects of public spending facilitated the initial 1933 agreement by underscoring the common, non-zero-sum interest that workers and farmers might have in a government-stimulated economy. And because parliamentary parties and politics in Sweden were nationally organized, striking a programmatic political bargain within the central government arena was the only meaningful channel open to farmers looking for relief from the depression. It was, likewise, the only way for the Agrarian party to expand its influence.

That continued to be true after 1933, especially as the alliance gained political momentum from the success of its policies. Although the Social Democratic government fell briefly in 1936 in a dispute with the Agrarians over defense and pensions, the Social Democratic party scored a substantial victory in the election that year, and the coalition with the Agrarians was reformed (and endured thereafter through various permutations for decades).[145] The Social Democrats continued to support farmers along the lines of the 1933 agreement, and between 1937 and 1939, the coalition "enacted a broad program of social legislation," including improvements in old-age and disability benefits, stronger labor laws, free maternity care, rent allowances for large families, and subsidized dental care for all Swedes.[146]

Cooperation between political representatives of industrial labor and agricultural interests proved much less durable in the American Democratic party, even though it, like the Social Democratic party, gained electoral ground by 1936. The trouble lay in the group alliances that the New Deal's policies eventually strengthened. Rather than enduringly uniting labor with those farmers who would benefit most from increased domestic consumption and state interventions in agriculture, the New Deal ended up joining together larger, commercially well-established, export-oriented southern cotton producers with better-off midwestern corn and wheat farmers oriented to domestic as well as international markets. This cross-regional alliance, which took shape from the middle 1930s, was embodied in the American Farm Bureau Federation (AFBF), an organization that became very influential in Congress owing to its presence in many local districts.[147] The AFBF increasingly opposed federal government reforms that might in any way compromise the interests of established agricultural producers and concentrated instead on securing price subsidies tied to production controls favorable to all of its larger-farmer constituents regardless of their international or domestic market orientations. By the later 1930s and the 1940s, the AFBF frequently cooperated with the conservative alliance of southern Democrats and Republicans in Congress to oppose many urban liberal Democratic initiatives.

In the early stages of the New Deal, it was not at all foreordained that this particular coalition involving farmers would emerge as dominant. An alternative coalition might have brought together labor and consumers with dairy farmers, smaller midwestern grain producers, and southern farm tenants. The National Farmers' Union did, in fact, embody a weak version of this alliance, and its policies consistently demonstrated sympathy with continuing federal reforms and a domestic spending strategy.[148] Ironically, however, the initial New Deal agricultural program, in particular the production controls implemented through the first AAA and the federal Extension Service, had the unforeseen and unintended effect of organizationally strengthening the AFBF's ties to larger southern and midwestern farmers. The most significant consequence of the links between the AFBF and the Extension Service was the expansion of the AFBF in the South, traditionally its weakest area of operations.[149] By encouraging AFBF membership in the South in order to facilitate the administration of federal production controls, the AAA cemented ties among large commercial farmers in the United States through a lobbying organization that would, after 1935, work to stymie many AAA-initiated programs of agricultural planning as well as liberal New Deal efforts to help poorer farmers and tenants.

Although the cotton–grain alliance embodied in the AFBF was less sympathetic to increases in public social spending in the United States than an alternative alliance involving farmers might have been, its opposition to liberal New Deal initiatives after the mid-1930s (by which time commercial farmers had recovered from the depression) did not stem from any unwillingness to take federal subsidies as such. It was, rather, the governmental controls that might accompany federal expenditures that provoked the stiffest farm opposition, especially from southern landlords. Many of the New Deal programs introduced after 1935, especially the WPA and the Farm Security Administration, entailed the intrusion of the federal government into jealously guarded local terrain. In the South the stakes were particularly high. Many southern representatives in Congress had strong ties to landlords who had dominated the region's political and economic life for over half a century. Proposals to expand the purview of central government or to transfer local functions to Washington were staunchly resisted by these people.[150] Especially as the national upheaval in industrial relations spread, southern elites sought to protect themselves from the Roosevelt administration, which they held responsible for the growth of union power. Likewise, the few overtures toward blacks made by the Roosevelt administration threatened to disrupt the caste system of race relations so fundamental both to modes of labor control and to nondemocratic electoral politics in the South.

Even though representatives of farm districts were not a majority in Congress, the processes of legislation and the control that the seniority system gave rural and southern committee chairmen allowed the best-organized agricultural interests sufficient leverage to resist any permanent compromise with the liberal wing of the Democratic party.[151] Swedish farmers had little choice but to enter right at the start of the 1930s into a centrally negotiated compromise with industrial labor and the Social Democrats, or else be excluded from power altogether. In the United States, however, farmers, especially the richer ones who consolidated their alliance through the AFBF, benefited economically from the special farm programs of the early New Deal and thereafter had no incentive to reach a lasting agreement with labor and urban liberals in Congress. This was true despite the fact that the 1936 Supreme Court invalidation of the processing tax that had financed the first AAA made farmers dependent on congressional votes for recurrent crop subsidies. Even with this heightened potential for urban–rural trade-offs in Congress, no enduring programmatic alliance resulted. Representatives concerned with agricultural interests could strike ad hoc deals with liberals over particular packages of legislation, yet oppose them on others and all the while continue to look for bases of cooperation with other interests.

Congressional conservatives initially did not oppose federal spending packages as such, but instead worked to earmark funds and to attach other restrictions reducing federal discretion. After the 1938 election had diminished Roosevelt's support in Congress, however, his 1939 "Spend–Lend bill" was defeated.[152] This defeat marked the first occasion on which Congress rejected a major New Deal spending package strongly backed by the president. Keynesians had considered this measure barely adequate, and their hopes for continuing the spending approach to economic recovery begun in 1938 were thwarted by this setback.

In sum, the strength of local bases of power and congressional determination to block the institutionalization of stronger federal executive controls were the essential barriers to constructing a permanent, nationally coordinated system of social spending in the late 1930s. The upshot was that potential contributions by the increasing number of Keynesian experts were deflected. Although Keynesian advocates were scattered throughout the federal executive after 1938, their effectiveness depended on capturing Roosevelt's support in competition with other executive officials, and they had little leverage with many congressional centers of legislative power. Without programmatic political parties and without a strong administrative state capable of bringing spending coalitions together for planning and compromise, American Keynesians of the late 1930s could not parallel the public policy achievements of the Swedish economists, even though the programmatic hopes of many of them were quite similar.

Mobilization for World War II put an end to the political quarrels that stalemated the later New Deal, yet the conflicts were only temporarily postponed. Support persisted in Congress for national social spending and federally sponsored reforms, but so did growing conservative opposition to any further government expansion. During the war, the National Resources Planning Board (NRPB), established under the auspices of the watered-down version of the Reorganization Act passed in 1939, became something of a magnet for planners and social Keynesians.[153] The NRPB's major report, *Security, Work and Relief Policies,* published in 1942, presented a comprehensive survey of all relief policies and argued for greater coordination and advance planning of federal social spending. Congressional treatment of the board previewed the struggle over full employment that would be fought three years later. In each year of NRPB's existence, Congress attached increasingly restrictive provisions on its operations, and finally, after its major report was issued, Congress cut off appropriations for the NRPB, ensuring the agency's demise.[154]

Despite the lack of support for Keynesian social planning in Congress, discussion of measures to ensure adequate employment opportunities after the war absorbed professional economists and the general public, reflecting the widespread fear of a major postwar recession. In early 1945, the Full Employment bill was introduced in Congress.[155] Based on stagnationist Keynesian theory and expectations, the bill proposed that government spending make up any shortfall between private investment and full employment. It envisaged a substantial and permanent role for the federal government in the economy and received strong support from liberal representatives in Congress and from the labor movement and its allies. Its fate was to presage the shape of federal involvement in the economy for much of the postwar period.

As in the later New Deal and in the struggle over the NRPB, southern and rural conservatives held the balance of power in Congress. Opposition to the bill by the AFBF and by the U.S. Chamber of Commerce and other business organizations stressed the shared interest of farmers and business in curbing the growth of federal government. Strategically placed conservatives in the House, especially Representative William Whittington of Mississippi, who worked closely with Chamber of Commerce economists, were instrumental in substituting and passing a greatly watered down version of the employment bill.[156] The new Employment Act of 1946 did not commit the federal government to spending to ensure full employment. It merely authorized the president to monitor the economy and to submit economic projections to Congress. The new mechanism it established was the Council of Economic Advisors, whose authority was simply to advise the president, not to prepare anything so comprehensive as the annual National Production and Employment Budget proposed by the original Full Employment bill.[157]

In the United States, the battle during 1945–46 over the Full Employment bill marked the denouement of the drama that had begun when Roosevelt assumed office in 1932. Tendencies similar to those that had produced Sweden's social Keynesian response to the depression gathered force during the 1930s in the United States, but the structure of the American state prevented them from producing a comparable synthesis of social spending and macroeconomic management. In turn, the differing fates of the new deals in Sweden and America had major and enduring consequences for the way in which business was reintegrated into public policy making once the depression was over.

In Sweden, the political dominance of the Social Democrats, reconfirmed by electoral victory in 1936, induced business to come to terms with Swedish labor unions and with the emerging Swedish welfare state. Reconciled to the continuation of the Social Democrats in office, the Swedish Confederation of Employers' Organizations concluded a pact with the unions designed to ensure increased stability in industrial relations and to shield wage negotiations from direct state regulation.[158] Although this "private" corporatist system of centralized wage negotiations sanctioned in the Saltsjobaden Agreement of 1938 limited the direct reach of the Swedish state, it was established in the context of high levels of public spending and it eased future public policymaking for an internationally efficient economy and for generous social welfare by establishing uniform and regular procedures for negotiating nationally standardized wage increases. Swedish business, in short, made peace with social Keynesianism – from which, indeed, larger and more efficient enterprises would benefit considerably in the postwar period.[159]

In the United States, by contrast, *after* the supporters of the Full Employment bill of 1945 had been blocked by the congressionally centered alliance of AFBF farmers and Chamber of Commerce businessmen, advocates of commercial Keynesianism in the big-business-affiliated Committee for Economic Development (CED) were able to pick up the pieces.[160] The CED cooperated with moderate economists on the new Council of Economic Advisors, and its economic thinking drew on long-standing work by University of Chicago–based economists who had anticipated some of Keynes's policy prescriptions before *The General Theory* and who had never converted to the Harvard-led stagnationist understanding of the U.S. economy and the role that public spending should play in it.[161] By accepting the least objectionable feature of Keynesianism – balancing budgets over a period of years, rather than annually – the CED and its moderate economist allies were able to institutionalize countercyclical policies that relied on automatic stabilizers, not on increased government spending and the discretionary power and stronger welfare state that would have accompanied it.

Consumer purchasing power in the postwar United States was partially sustained by such federal automatic stabilizers but also depended strongly on recurrent union gains in private wage negotiations.[162] These gains were achieved through much more industrial conflict than occurred in Sweden.[163] National military outlays in the Korean War and its aftermath became another important prop for the economy, which also benefited from America's international economic leadership while Europe and Japan rebuilt from the devastations of war. Meanwhile, authority over diverse and uncoordinated programs of federal domestic spending in the United States continued to be centered in Congress, the many local and interest-group constituencies of which could enjoy public resources without federal control. At the national level, macroeconomic management remained divorced from public social welfare efforts, and the wholehearted pursuit of full employment – defined as jobs for everyone willing to work – remained beyond the purview of public policy in the United States.

Conclusion

The Great Depression of the 1930s undermined previous tenets of public finance and opened new possibilities for the state in capitalist liberal democracies to become the active agent of societal welfare through a synthesis of social spending and macroeconomic management. The realization of such possibilities depended on the emergence of new ideas about the management of national economies, on shifts in political power that strengthened organized labor, and on socially rooted coalitions politically willing and able to support deficit-spending policies. Yet such factors, we have maintained, were not sufficient to account for various national policy choices. Instead, we have analyzed the social policy legacies and the structures of states in order to account for the recovery strategies pursued by Sweden, Britain, and the United States in response to the depression crisis.

Our emphasis has not been primarily on states as sites of direct official action. Rather we have probed more subtle, often overlooked relationships between states and societies – relationships that profoundly affected the capacities of states and political leaders in Sweden, Britain, and America to conceive and implement public strategies. We have discovered that political parties, even those historically formed as programmatic agents for working-class interests, defined their goals in the 1930s in close relationship to existing policies and capacities of the states with which they were dealing. We have found, too, that political coalitions of social groups willing to support deficit-spending programs gained leverage only through state structures and came together – or broke apart – partially in response to the sequence and effects of state policies themselves. We have also examined ways in which the Swedish, British, and U.S. state structures patterned the formulation and successful application of new, policy-relevant economic ideas, and here we may point, not so much to firm conclusions, as to several comparative observations worth turning into questions for further exploration.

The Swedish "new" economists achieved the earliest and fullest "Keynesian" policy successes and subsequently reaped rich rewards through their academic and public careers and international intellectual reputations. Yet the Swedish economists achieved their policy impact *without* first forging a strikingly new grand theory, as Keynes did in Britain, and without clothing their economic prescriptions in politically partisan and conflictual prescriptions, as the stagnationists did in the United States. Our analysis has suggested that early and sustained access to administratively strategic centers of public policy made it possible for the Swedish economists to produce effective intellectual justifications for state-sponsored reforms in this relatively atheoretical and nonconflictual mode. Do analogous conditions regularly lie behind successful social-scientific contributions to public reforms in capitalist democracies (and other kinds of polities)? Under what alternative conditions do grand academic theories or conflictual presentations of theories prove more effective, directly or indirectly, in the complex processes that lead to transformations in public policies?

Still more intriguing, What effects on processes of intellectual innovation, and on intellectual reflection itself, are exerted by the policy successes and setbacks of experts? Would John Maynard Keynes have bothered to fashion the grand theory that gave his name to an epoch – and that inspired such an array of followers and policies ranging across intellectual and political spectra – if he had enjoyed immediate access to centers of public policy making in interwar Britain? If Keynesianism, in turn, had not been born, would the Swedish economists ever have bothered to declare themselves members of the Stockholm school? What difference would it have made for economic theorizing and research, and for public policies and political debates in the postwar period, if these paradigms and schools had not been created? And if Keynesianism had not been fashioned as a transnational language of discourse on public economics, how would we and the comparative political sociologists with whom we debate have conceptualized our guiding questions about Sweden, Britain, the United States, and other advanced nations from the 1930s to the present? Perhaps, in fact, we all owe more than we can even imagine to the organizational structure of the British state in the 1920s!

Notes

This chapter grew out of an earlier paper on Sweden and the United States published in the *International Journal of Comparative Sociology* 24(1–2) (1983): 4–29. We benefited from reactions to that paper and to the first draft of this essay, presented in the session entitled "Comparative Social and Economic Policy" at the annual meeting of the American Political Science Association, Chicago, September 2, 1983. Helpful comments and criticisms came especially from Douglas Ashford, Barry Eichengreen, Peter Gourevitch, Barbara Haskel, Hugh Heclo, Albert Hirschman, Peter Lange, Axel Leijhonufvud, Stephen Krasner, Charles Sabel, Philippe Schmitter, Bill Skocpol, and David Stark. We also benefited from stimulating discussions when these ideas were presented at the University of Chicago's Center for the Study of Industrial Societies, in a Social Science Luncheon Seminar at the Institute for Advanced Study in Princeton, and in a lecture at Duke University.

1. For some overviews of national variations, see H. W. Arndt, *The Economic Lessons of the 1930s* (London: Oxford University Press, 1944); W. Arthur Lewis, *Economic Survey* (London: Allen & Unwin, 1960); and Bradford Lee, "Budget Balancing in an Historical Perspective: National Priorities in Britain, France, and the United States" (Paper presented at the Woodrow Wilson Center, Washington, D.C., June 1981).

2. The "new deal" label for Swedish reforms in the 1930s comes from Bjarne Braatoy, *The New Sweden* (London: Nelson, 1939), chap. 1. for overviews of Swedish and U.S. policies in the 1930s, see especially Arndt, *Economic Lessons*, chap. 2 and 8; Bertil Ohlin, ed., "Social Problems and Policies in Sweden," a collection of articles in *Annals of the American Academy of Political and Social Sciences* 197 (May 1938); Harrison Clark, *Swedish Unemployment Policy: 1914 to 1940* (Washington D.C.: American Council on Public Affairs, 1941), chaps. 5–12; Herbert Stein, *The Fiscal Revolution in America* (Chicago: University of Chicago Press, 1969), chaps. 3–7; and Albert U. Romasco, *The Politics of Recovery: Roosevelt's New Deal* (New York: Oxford University Press, 1983).

3. There are major and continuing controversies over what should count as a truly "Keynesian" argument, either in theoretical or in policy-oriented terms. Here, we are inclined to accept Don Patinkin's point that the *theoretical* "central message" of Keynesian economics did not appear until Keynes's 1936 book *The General Theory of Employment, Interest, and Money*. See Don Patinkin's "Multiple Discoveries and the Central Message," *American Journal of Sociology* 89(2) (1983): 306–23; and also his *Anticipations of the General Theory?* (Chicago: University of Chicago Press, 1982). Nevertheless, well before 1936, Keynes himself in Britain and various other economists there and in other nations anticipated parts of the Keynesian theoretical message and, especially, many of its policy-relevant implications. We shall discuss relevant instances later. For now, let us simply point out that, failing a better terminology, we shall use "proto-Keynesian" to refer to such pre-1936 anticipations. After 1936, the term "Keynesian" becomes appropriate even for theoretical and policy ideas that might have been developed parallel to, or separate from, Keynes's writings, precisely because his "central message" did quickly come to dramatize and symbolize a transnational revolution in economic thinking.

4. See Stein, *Fiscal Revolution*, chaps. 5–7; and Dean L. May, *From New Deal to New*

Economics: The American Liberal Response to the Recession of 1937 (New York: Garland, 1981), chaps. 6 and 7.

5. On Swedish policies from the 1930s, see Gösta Esping-Andersen and Roger Friedland, "Class Coalitions in the Making of West European Economies," *Political Power and Social Theory* 3 (1982): 17–25; Assar Lindbeck, *Swedish Economic Policy* (Berkeley: University of California Press, 1974); Andrew Martin, "The Dynamics of Change in a Keynesian System," in *The State, Capital, and Liberal Democracy*, ed. Colin Crouch (New York: St. Martin's Press, 1979), pp. 88–121; and William Snavely, "Macroeconomic Institutional Innovation: Some Observations from the Swedish Experience," *Journal of Economic Issues* 6 (1972): 27–60.

6. "Social Keynesianism" is our own phrase. "Commercial Keynesianism" comes from Robert Lekachman, *The Ages of Keynes* (New York: McGraw-Hill, 1966), p. 287.

7. On U.S. macroeconomic policies since World War II, see Lekachman, *Age of Keynes*, chaps. 8–11; Robert M. Collins, *The Business Response to Keynes, 1929–1964* (New York: Columbia University Press, 1981), chaps. 6 and 7; and Stein, *Fiscal Revolution*, chaps. 9–17. In the postwar period, the United States and Sweden gravitated toward opposite poles both in terms of levels of public spending and in terms of the trade-off between unemployment and inflation. See Andrew Martin, *The Politics of Economic Policy in the United States: A Tentative View from a Comparative Perspective* (Beverly Hills, Calif.: Sage, 1973), pp. 5–20; and Douglas Hibbs, "Political Parties and Macroeconomic Policy," *American Political Science Review* 71 (1977): 1472.

8. On the specific difficulties of coordinating Keynesian economic intervention with unemployment insurance in the United States, see Edward J. Harpham, "Federalism, Keynesianism and the Transformation of Unemployment Insurance in the United States," in *Nationalizing Social Security*, ed. Douglas E. Ashford and E. W. Kelley (Greenwich, Conn.: JAI Press, forthcoming).

9. On Britain's pre-1930s social policies, see especially Bentley V. Gilbert, *The Evolution of National Insurance in Great Britain: The Origins of the Welfare State* (London: Michael Joseph, 1966); Bentley V. Gilbert, *British Social Policy, 1914–1939* (London: Batsford, 1970), chaps. 1–3; and Peter Flora and Jens Alber, "Modernization, Democratization, and the Development of Welfare States in Western Europe," in *The Development of Welfare States in Europe and America*, ed. Peter Flora and Arnold J. Heidenheimer (New Brunswick, N.J.: Transaction Books, 1981), especially Figure 2.4, p. 55, which summarizes the programmatic and labor-force coverage of British social policies compared with those of other European nations.

10. The following account relies especially on Robert Skidelsky, *Politicians and the Slump: The Labour Government of 1929–1931* (London: Macmillan, 1967).

11. On Britain's recovery in the 1930s, see Arndt, *Economic Lessons*, chap. 4, which presents a quite optimistic picture.

12. There is disagreement about whether Britain ever fully implemented Keynesian macroeconomic policies, although much of what is at issue depends on how "Keynesian" policies are defined. See Jim Tomlinson, "Why Was There Never a 'Keynesian Revolution' in Economic Policy?" *Economy and Society* 10(1) (1981): 72–87; and Kerry Schott, "The Rise of Keynesian Economics: Britain 1940–64,"

Economy and Society 11(3) (1982): 292–316. On the "Beveridge" reforms in the British welfare state after World War II, see Norman Furniss and Timothy Tilton, *The Case for the Welfare State* (Bloomington: Indiana University Press, 1979), pp. 104–109.

13. We deal only with explicitly *comparative* arguments, direct competitors of our own. In the historical literatures on each individual country, however, the personalities and outlooks of key national leaders are often emphasized. Comparative analysts may fall back on ad hoc explanations along these lines, when economic-determinist or "rational-choice" arguments fail. See, for example, Peter Gourevitch's treatment of the British case in "Breaking with Orthodoxy: The Politics of Economic Policy Responses to the Depression of the 1930s," *International Organization* 38(1) (1984): 121–22; and Dennis Kavanagh, "Crisis Management and Incremental Adaptation in British Politics: The 1932 Crisis of the British Party System," in *Crisis, Choice, and Change: Historical Studies of Political Development*, ed. Gabriel A. Almond, Scott C. Flanagan, and Robert J. Mundt (Boston: Little, Brown, 1973), pp. 194–95.

Ironically, *similar* leadership personalities and outlooks have been invoked to explain *different* outcomes across our three cases. In particular, British Labour leaders of 1929–31 have been criticized for excessive willingness to compromise in the name of national unity and for combining idealism with pragmatism, whereas Swedish Social Democratic leaders and American New Dealers have been praised for similar qualities, which supposedly explain their reformist initiatives! In our view, the actual goals, outlooks, and normative ideals of leaders and groups must be seriously considered, but in a historically grounded way. They should not be treated as fixed essences built into personalities or party ideologies, but rather analyzed in close relationship to the overall institutional contexts, patterns of political culture, and conjunctures of political conflict within which leaders and groups operated over time.

14. For example, international monetary and trade fluctuations, the precise effects of which in relation to national policies and domestic economic circumstances are difficult to assess, exerted powerful influences on the course of national economic recessions and recoveries in the Great Depression. See Arndt, *Economic Lessons*, and the arguments about Sweden cited in note 86.

15. Proponents of various kinds of working-class-strength arguments include Francis G. Castles, ed., *The Impact of Parties* (Beverly Hills, Calif.: Sage, 1982); Esping-Andersen and Friedland, "Class Coalitions"; Walter Korpi, *The Working Class in Welfare Capitalism* (London: Routledge & Kegan Paul, 1978); Walter Korpi, *The Democratic Class Struggle* (London: Routledge & Kegan Paul, 1983); Martin, *Politics of Economic Policy*; and John Stephens, *The Transition from Capitalism to Socialism* (London: Macmillan, 1979). An excellent review of this approach to the development of Western welfare states is to be found in Michael Shalev, "The Social Democratic Model and Beyond: Two Generations of Comparative Research on the Welfare State," *Comparative Social Research* 6 (1983): 87–148.

16. Stephens, *Transition to Socialism*.

17. Every one of the works cited in note 15 dwells on the Swedish case, especially since the 1930s. The working-class-strength model is, in effect, an attempt to derive a cross-nationally relevant theory from a certain understanding of the rise of Swedish social democracy.

18. Martin, *Economic Policy in the United States*, and Stephens, *Transition to Socialism*, pp. 149–56, discuss U.S. developments in these terms.

19. David Brody, "The Emergence of Mass Production Unionism," in *Change and Continuity in Twentieth Century America*, ed. J. Braeman, R. Bremner, and E. Walters (Columbus: Ohio State University Press, 1964), pp. 221–62; Milton Derber, "Growth and Expansion," in *Labor and the New Deal*, ed. M. Derber and E. Young (New York: DaCapo Press, 1972), pp. 1–44; and J. David Greenstone, *Labor in American Politics* (New York: Knopf, 1969), chap. 2.

20. Collins, *Business Response to Keynes*, chap. 2.

21. This point has been especially emphasized by Adam Przeworski. See his "Social Democracy as a Historical Phenomenon," *New Left Review*, no. 122 (July–August 1980): 27–58.

22. Stephens, *Transition to Socialism*, pp. 130–31; Korpi, *Working Class in Welfare Capitalism*, p. 86; and Sven Anders Soderpalm, "The Crisis Agreement and the Social Democratic Road to Power," in *Sweden's Development from Poverty to Affluence, 1750–1970*, ed. Steven Koblick (Minneapolis: University of Minnesota Press, 1975), p. 277.

23. See especially Korpi, *Working Class in Welfare Capitalism*. Also, John Stephens discusses the "feedback effects" of Social Democratic incumbency on Swedish union strength in "Class Formation and Class Consciousness: A Theoretical and Empirical Analysis with Reference to Britain and Sweden," *British Journal of Sociology* 30(4) (1979): 389–414, especially pp. 406–407.

24. Strictly speaking, three Scandinavian Social Democratic parties pursued reformist public-spending strategies in the 1930s: the Danish (from 1929), Norwegian (from 1935), and Swedish (from 1932). Swedish Social Democrats and economic experts played the leading role in fashioning an economically rationalized recovery strategy, but the Danish Social Democrats were the first to attain power and implement such a strategy. During the 1920s, the Danish Social Democrats formed an alliance with the Radical party representing small farmers in an agrarian sector that was more socioeconomically differentiated than in Sweden or Norway. See Francis G. Castles, *The Social Democratic Image of Society* (London: Routledge & Kegan Paul, 1978), pp. 22–23, 113. Moreover, the Danish state, like the British, was an early pioneer among liberal countries in launching social benefits programs. However, Danish unemployment insurance was in the form of public subsidies to voluntary union-run plans, not compulsory (contributory and publically funded) benefits for virtually the entire industrial working class, as in Britain.

25. Like the British Labour party, the German Social Democratic party also failed to launch innovative policies against unemployment, despite support from key union leaders for demand-stimulus ideas. See the discussions in Gourevitch, "Breaking with Orthodoxy," p. 108; Martin, *Economic Policy in the United States*, pp. 45–46; and Vladimir Woytinski, *Stormy Passage* (New York: Vanguard, 1961), pp. 458–72.

26. As we read him, Stephens, *Transition to Socialism*, p. 145, agrees with this point, but he does not seem to realize that the comparability of British and Swedish working-class organizational strength in the 1920s raises basic questions about using such strength to explain the sharply contrasting Labour versus Social Democratic responses to the depression crisis. Those divergent responses, in

turn (as Stephens agrees), were a primary reason for the divergent fates of the two social democratic labor movements after the early 1930s.

27. Stephens, *Transition to Socialism,* pp. 115–16, provides interesting figures on Swedish and British unionization. The post–World War I peak of union membership was far higher in Britain than in Sweden; thereafter, the trends favored Sweden, although sharp divergence came only *after* the early 1930s. In 1930, union members were 23 percent of the total labor force in Britain and 20 percent in Sweden. For 1930–31, if only nonagricultural wage and salary workers are used as the base, Sweden had 35 percent unionized compared with 31 percent for Britain. According to Castles, *Social Democratic Image,* Table 1.1, p. 6, the British Labour party averaged 33 percent of the vote during the 1920s, whereas the Swedish Social Democrats averaged 36 percent. Obviously, all of these percentages are quite close to one another.

28. Hugh Heclo, *Modern Social Politics in Britain and Sweden* (New Haven, Conn.: Yale University Press, 1974), pp. 38–41.

29. Soderpalm, "Crisis Agreement."

30. Skidelsky, *Politicians and the Slump.*

31. Heclo, *Modern Social Politics,* Fig. 3, p. 23, shows the contrasting balances between manufacturing and agriculture in the British versus Swedish national economies. In 1930 those employed in agriculture (including forestry and fishing) constituted 36 percent of the Swedish labor force, but only 6 percent of the British labor force. The source is B. R. Mitchell, *European Historical Statistics, 1750–1970* (New York: Columbia University Press, 1976), pp. 162–63.

32. Aside from those cited and discussed later, important works using the "economic coalition" approach to explain public policies include Alexander Gerschenkron, *Bread and Democracy in Germany* (New York: Howard Fertig, 1966; originally 1943); James Kurth, "The Political Consequences of the Product Cycle: Industrial History and Political Outcomes," *International Organization 33* (1979): 1–34; and Peter Gourevitch, "International Trade, Domestic Coalitions and Liberty: Comparative Responses to the Crisis of 1873–95," *Journal of Interdisciplinary History* 8 (1977): 281–313. In *The Collapse of the Weimar Republic* (Princeton, N. J.: Princeton University Press, 1981), David Abraham uses this approach to illuminate a regime change as well as shifting policy patterns.

33. Thomas Ferguson, "From Normalcy to New Deal: Industrial Structure, Party Competition, and American Public Policy in the Great Depression," *International Organization* 38(1) (1984): 41–93. Despite the title, Ferguson does not really say much about which policies were adopted and exactly how, especially after the "first" New Deal of 1932–34. Apparently, he mistakenly conflates the labor regulation and social insurance reforms of 1935–36 with Keynesianism. He also seems to make strong assumptions, not empirically demonstrated in this article, about the role of the Democratic party as such in shaping policy choices.

34. Peter Gourevitch, "Breaking with Orthodoxy: The Politics of Economic Policy Responses to the Depression of the 1930s," *International Organization* 38(1) (1984): 95–129.

35. John Maynard Keynes, *The General Theory of Employment, Interest, and Money* (New York: Harcourt Brace Jovanovich, 1964; originally 1936), p. 383.

36. Some useful reflections on Keynes's lack of short-term successes as a policy adviser in the interwar years appear in Professor Donald Muggeridge's discussion of Lord Kaldor's "Keynes as an Economic Advisor," in *Keynes as a Policy*

Advisor, ed. A. P. Thirwall (London: Macmillan, 1982), pp. 28–33. Other insights about Keynes's distinctive blend of scientific and political concerns appear in Elizabeth S. Johnson and Harry G. Johnson, *The Shadow of Keynes* (Chicago: University of Chicago Press, 1978), chaps. 2 and 6; and in John Vaizy, "Keynes and Cambridge," in *The End of the Keynesian Era*, ed. Robert Skidelsky (London: Macmillan, 1977), pp. 10–24.

37. Keynes, *General Theory*, pp. vi, 383–84.

38. Schott, "Rise of Keynesian Economics," p. 292.

39. The assertions of the following paragraph are elaborated and documented later at appropriate points in our comparative-historical analysis.

40. Heclo, *Modern Social Politics*, especially chap. 6.

41. Skidelsky, *Politicians and the Slump, passim*.

42. Heclo, *Modern Social Politics*, pp. 78–90, 105–110; see also Jose Harris, *Unemployment and Politics: A Study in English Social Policy, 1886–1914* (Oxford: Oxford University Press, 1972).

43. Kavanagh, "Crisis Managment and Incremental Adaptation," pp. 175, 181–83; and Skidelsky, *Politicians and the Slump*, chap. 2.

44. See Fig. 4.2 for British rates of unemployment in the 1920s.

45. On Labour's election promises, see Heclo, *Modern Social Politics*, p. 114. On the Labour government's record, see C. L. Mowat, *Britain between the Wars, 1918–1940* (Chicago: University of Chicago Press, 1955), pp. 174–78.

46. Quoted in Heclo, *Modern Social Politics*, p. 115.

47. This paragraph draws broadly from Skidelsky, *Politicians and the Slump*, chaps. 3–7.

48. Bentley V. Gilbert, *British Social Policy, 1914–1939* (London: Bratsford, 1970), p. 162.

49. Ibid.

50. Ibid, pp. 162–75; and Skidelsky, *Politicians and the Slump*, chaps. 11–13.

51. Mowat, *Britain between the Wars*, p. 413.

52. This paragraph draws from Heclo, *Modern Social Politics*, pp. 74–78, 92–97. See also Douglas Verney, "The Foundations of Modern Sweden: The Swift Rise and Fall of Swedish Liberalism," *Political Studies* 22(1) (1972): 42–59.

53. On the Unemployment Commission, see Harrison Clark, *Swedish Unemployment Policy* (Washington D.C.: American Council on Public Affairs, 1941), chaps. 2 and 3; and Gustav Moller, "The Unemployment Policy," *Annals* 197 (1938): 47–48.

54. Clark, *Swedish Unemployment Policy*, pp. 49–50; and Herbert Tingsten, *The Swedish Social Democrats* (Totowa, N. J.: Bedminster Press, 1973; originally 1941), pp. 261, 430.

55. Castles, *Social Democratic Image*, pp. 24–25; Donald Winch, "The Keynesian Revolution in Sweden," *Journal of Political Economy* 74(2) (1966): pp. 170–71; Timothy Tilton, "A Swedish Road to Socialism: Ernst Wigforss and the Ideological Foundations of Swedish Social Democracy," *American Political Science Review* 73 (1979): 508; and C. G. Uhr, "Economists and Policymaking 1930–1936: Sweden's Experience," *History of Political Economy* 9(1) (1977): 91, note 4.

56. Some relevant treatments of trends in policy-relevant economic thought in the 1920s and early 1930s include Stein, *Fiscal Revolution*, pp. 131–62; J. Ronnie Davis, *The New Economics and the Old Economists* (Ames: Iowa State University Press, 1971); Keith Hancock, "Unemployment and the Economists in the 1920s,"

Economica, new ser., 27 (1960): 305–21; Brinley Thomas, "Swedish Monetary Policy since Wicksell," in *Monetary Policy and Crises: A Study of Swedish Experience* (London: Routledge, 1936), chap. 3; and Everett J. Burtt, Jr., *Social Perspectives in the History of Economic Theory* (New York: St. Martin's Press, 1972), pp. 233–37 (on Keynes's own evolution from 1924 to 1933). All of these works emphasize ways in which modifications of neoclassical economic ideas were pushing toward fully "Keynesian" models and policy prescriptions. For a fuller understanding of the disputes in intellectual history to which these works contribute, see also the works cited in notes 3, 77, and 78.

57. Roy Harrod, *The Life of John Maynard Keynes* (New York: Norton, 1951), pp. 345–86. The first important statement by Keynes about deficit-financed public works was "Does Unemployment Need a Drastic Remedy?" which appeared in *The Nation* on May 24, 1924. Further articles and public lectures regularly ensued.

58. Skidelsky, *Politicians and the Slump*, pp. 51–57.

59. Ibid., chap. 8.

60. This paragraph draws on Roger Davidson, "Llewellen Smith and the Labour Department," in *Studies in the Growth of Nineteenth Century Government*, ed. Gillian Sutherland (London: Routledge & Kegan Paul, 1972), pp. 227–62; Roger Davidson, "Board of Trade and Industrial Relations," *Historical Journal* 21(3) (1978): 571–91; J. A. M. Caldwell, "The Genesis of the Ministry of Labour," *Public Administration* 37(4) (1959): 367–91; and especially R. Davidson and R. Lowe, "Bureaucracy and Innovation in British Welfare Policy, 1870–1945," in *The Emergence of the Welfare State in Britain and Germany*, ed. W. J. Mommsen (London: Croom Helm, 1981), pp. 264–77 (on the pre-1916 period).

61. See Davidson and Lowe, "Bureaucracy and Innovation," especially pp. 277–91; Rodney Lowe, "The Ministry of Labour, 1916–24: A Graveyard of Social Reform?" *Public Administration* 52 (1974): 415–38; and Rodney Lowe, "The Erosion of State Intervention in Britain, 1917–24," *Economic History Review*, 2nd ser., 31(2) (1978): 270–86.

62. Davidson and Lowe, "Bureaucracy and Innovation," pp. 283–84, and Lowe, "Erosion of State Intervention," pp. 279–82, discuss telling examples of individual officials within the Labour Ministry who came up with proto-Keynesian proposals or ideas, only to have them deflected in ways traceable to Treasury's organizational controls.

63. Skidelsky, *Politicians and the Slump*, pp. 134–36, 142–45. See Heclo's useful comments on British commissions, especially in comparison with Swedish commissions, in *Modern Social Politics*, pp. 44–46.

64. Skidelsky, *Politicians and the Slump*, pp. 202–15. The longer-run impact of this body (which became the Committee on Economic Information in 1932) is traced in Susan Howson and Donald Winch, *The Economic Advisory Council 1930–1939: A Study in Economic Advice during Depression and Recovery* (Cambridge: Cambridge University Press, 1977). In "Keynes and the Treasury View: The Case for and against Unemployment Policy," in *The Emergence of the Modern Welfare State in Britain and Germany*, ed. W. J. Mommsen (London: Croom Helm, 1982), pp. 184–87, Skidelsky introduces notes of caution about some of Howson and Winch's conclusions concerning Keynes's influence on Treasury thinking in the middle 1930s.

65. Skidelsky, *Politicians and the Slump*, pp. 145, 204.

66. Ibid., p. 215.

67. The "orthodoxy" that Keynes (rather unfairly) attributed to his fellow economist A. C. Pigou is better understood as the "Treasury view," with which Keynes had long been in political contention.

68. Brinley Thomas, *Monetary Policy and Crises: A Study of Swedish Experience* (London: Routledge, 1936), p. xviii.

69. Ibid., pp. xix–xx.

70. Ibid., p. ix.

71. For historical overviews revealing how the Swedish monarchy strengthened itself along with independent peasants at the expense of a feudal landed aristocracy, see Perry Anderson, *Lineages of the Absolutist State* (London: New Left Books, 1974), chap. 7; Hans Brems, "Sweden: From Great Power to Welfare State," *Journal of Economic Issues* 4(2–3) (1970): 1–17; Eli F. Heckscher, *An Economic History of Sweden* (Cambridge: Harvard University Press, 1954), pp. 117–28; Nils Herlitz, *Sweden: A Modern Democracy on Ancient Foundations* (Minneapolis: University of Minnesota Press, 1939), pp. 3–21; and Stephen Kelman, *Regulating America, Regulating Sweden* (Cambridge: MIT Press, 1981), pp. 119–20.

72. Heclo, *Modern Social Politics*, pp. 41–43; and Hans Meijer, "Bureaucracy and Policy Formulation in Sweden," *Scandinavian Political Studies* 4 (1969): 103–16.

73. Timothy Tilton, "The Social Origins of Liberal Democracy: The Swedish Case," *American Political Science Review* 68(2) (1974): 561–71; and Dankwart Rustow, *The Politics of Compromise: A Study of Parties and Cabinet Government in Sweden* (Princeton, N. J.: Princeton University Press, 1955), chap. 2.

74. Meijer, "Bureaucracy and Policy Formulation," and Thomas J. Anton, "Policy-Making and Political Culture in Sweden," *Scandinavian Political Studies* 4 (1969): 88–102.

75. C. G. Uhr, "Economists and Policymaking 1930–1936: Sweden's Experience," *History of Political Economy* 9(1) (1977): 92; Thomas, *Monetary Policy and Crises*, pp. xv–xvi.

76. Uhr, "Economists and Policymaking," p. 92.

77. According to Donald Winch, "The Keynesian Revolution in Sweden," *Journal of Political Economy* 74(2) (1966): 169, the appellation "Stockholm school" was not coined until 1937, when Bertil Ohlin "attempted to explain the differentiating characteristics of Swedish and Keynesian macroeconomic analysis." See Ohlin's "Some Notes on the Stockholm Theory of Savings and Investment," *Economic Journal* 47 (March/June 1937): 53–69, 221–50. Uhr, "Economists and Policymaking," p. 89, note 1, provides a cohort-based definition of the "Stockholm school" in the making during the late 1920s and early 1930s.

78. This debate, which is primarily about questions of theoretical priority rather than the broader issues about politically influential intellectual innovations that more directly concern us here, is ably summarized in Winch, "Keynesian Revolution in Sweden," and in Bo Gustafsson, "Review Article – A Perennial of Doctrinal History: Keynes and 'The Stockholm School,' " *Economy and History* 16 (1973): 114–28. The most important contribution is Karl-Gustav Landgren's *Den 'nya economien' i Sveriege: J. M. Keynes, E. Wigforss, B. Ohlin och utvecklinger 1927–39* (Stockholm: Almqvist & Wiksell, 1960), which was debated in a special issue entitled "The Stockholm School: Ideas, Origin, and Development – A Symposium," *Economisk Tidskrift* 42 (September 1960). More recently, conclusions different from Landgren's are drawn in Otto Steiger, *Studien zur Entstehung der Nuen Wirtschaftslehre in Schweden – Ein Anti-Kritik* (Berlin: Duncker &

Humblot, 1971). Steiger's argument is sympathetically discussed in C. G. Uhr, "The Emergence of the 'New Economics' in Sweden: A Review of a Study by Otto Steiger," *History of Political Economy* 5 (1973): 243–60. See also the citations by Don Patinkin in note 3.

79. Thomas, *Monetary Policy and Crises,* pp. 178–205.
80. The unemployment figure comes from the Swedish Board of Trade, *Swedish Economic Review,* no. 1 (1936): 14.
81. Uhr, "Emergence of the 'New Economics,' " pp. 249–50.
82. Soderpalm, "Crisis Agreement," p. 270.
83. Moller, "Unemployment Policy," p. 51.
84. Clark, *Swedish Unemployment Policy,* chap. 6.
85. Ibid., pp. 95, 154.
86. Assar Lindbeck, *Swedish Economic Policy* (Berkeley: University of California Press, 1974), p. 23; Gustaffson, "Perennial of Doctrinal History," p. 128; Uhr, "Economists and Policymaking," pp. 116–19.
87. Moller, "Unemployment Policy," pp. 57–62.
88. Uhr, "Economists and Policymaking," pp. 110–15.
89. Ibid., p. 119; see also note 138.
90. It has been standard in the historical literature to divide the New Deal around 1935 into "first" and "second" stages. Here we will not dwell much on this division, because (even after the turn to prolabor regulations and social insurance in 1935) aspirations for a balanced federal budget remained characteristic of the Roosevelt administration's thinking about the role of government in national economic recovery – until the 1937 "Roosevelt recession" and its aftermath created apparent possibilities for a turn to Keynesianism combined with increased social spending. Periodizations of the New Deal should obviously not be reified, but devised for analytically useful purposes in various ways from study to study.
91. On the nationalizing significance of the New Deal, see Samuel H. Beer, "Liberalism and the National Idea," in *Left, Right and Center: Essays on Liberalism and Conservatism in the United States,* ed. Robert A. Goldwin (Chicago: Rand McNally, 1965), pp. 142–69.
92. Those employed in agriculture (including fishing, but not forestry) remained 21.8 percent of the labor force in the United States in 1930 (U.S. Department of Commerce, *Historical Statistics of the United States: Colonial Times to 1970* [Washington D.C.: Government Printing Office, 1975], p. 139), part 1. This figure can be juxtaposed to those given in note 31. In 1932, Roosevelt pitched his reformist campaign appeals to farm interests more than to urban workers. Southern and western support were critical in his bid for the Democratic nomination, and in the general election he received strong electoral support from farm areas, especially from the South and from other areas with poorer farmers or tenants. As the 1930s progressed, Roosevelt and the Democrats gained urban and industrial worker support and lost ground among better-off farmers. See John M. Allswang, *The New Deal and American Politics* (New York: Wiley, 1978), chap. 2.
93. William T. Foster and Waddill Catchings, *The Road to Plenty* (Cambridge, Mass.: Riverside Press, 1928).
94. Quoted in Arthur M. Schlesinger, Jr., *The Crisis of the Old Order, 1919–1933* (Boston: Houghton Mifflin, 1957), p. 187.

95. Davis, *The New Economics.*
96. Ibid., chaps. 3 and 4; and Dean L. May, *From New Deal to New Economics: The American Liberal Response to the Recession of 1937* (New York: Garland, 1981), pp. 67–76. Many relevant technical and theoretical innovations both built on and reacted critically to the pioneering macroeconomic work on business cycles of Wesley Clair Mitchell and the National Bureau of Economic Research. See John Maurice Clark, "Contribution to the Theory of Business Cycles" and other essays in *Wesley Clair Mitchell: The Economic Scientist* (New York: National Bureau of Economic Research, 1952). Davis's discussion (pp. 47–60) of Chicago economist Paul Douglas's important 1935 book, *Controlling Depressions,* emphasizes its critical dialogue with Mitchell's 1913 *Business Cycles.*
97. See Stein, *Fiscal Revolution,* pp. 12–14; Leah Hannah Feder, *Unemployment Relief in Periods of Depression: A Study of Measures Adopted in Certain American Cities, 1857 through 1922* (New York: Russell Sage Foundation, 1936); and Lester V. Chandler, *America's Greatest Depression, 1929–1941* (New York: Harper & Row, 1970), pp. 31–33.
98. Chandler, *America's Greatest Depression,* pp. 48–51; and James T. Patterson, *Congressional Conservatism and the New Deal* (Lexington: University of Kentucky Press, 1967), pp. 10–11.
99. Ellis W. Hawley, *The New Deal and the Problem of Monopoly* (Princeton, N. J.: Princeton University Press, 1966), part 1.
100. Chandler, *America's Greatest Depression,* p. 216.
101. Theda Skocpol and John Ikenberry, "The Political Formation of the American Welfare State in Historical and Comparative Perspective," *Comparative Social Research* 6 (1983): 124–25; and Mark H. Leff, "Taxing the 'Forgotten Man': The Politics of Social Security Finance in the New Deal," *Journal of American History* 70(2) (1983): 359–81.
102. Chandler, *America's Greatest Depression,* pp. 136–38, 189–207.
103. Stein, *Fiscal Revolution,* pp. 49–73.
104. The "courts and parties" label is from Stephen Skowronek, *Building a New American State: The Expansion of National Administrative Capacities, 1877–1920* (Cambridge: Cambridge University Press, 1982), chap. 2. See also Morton Keller, *Affairs of State: Public Life in Late Nineteenth Century America* (Cambridge: Harvard University Press, 1977), chaps. 7, 8, and 14; and Richard L. McCormick, "The Party Period and Public Policy: An Exploratory Hypothesis," *Journal of American History* 66 (1979): 279–98.
105. For the British and Swedish patterns in overall European context, see Reinhard Bendix, *Nation-Building and Citizenship* (New York: Wiley, 1964), chap. 3; Ira Katznelson, Chapter 8, this volume; and Donald J. Blake, "Swedish Trade Unions and the Social Democratic Party: The Formative Years," *Scandinavian Economic History Review* 8(1) (1960): 19–44. The discussion of the U.S. case in the remainder of this paragraph draws on Ira Katznelson, *City Trenches: Urban Politics and the Patterning of Class in the United States* (New York: Pantheon Press 1981), chaps. 1–4; and Martin Shefter, "Trades Unions and Political Machines: The Organization and Disorganization of the American Working Class in the Late Nineteenth Century," in *Working Class Formation: Nineteenth Century Patterns in Western Europe and the United States,* ed. Ira Katznelson and Aristide Zolberg (Princeton, N. J.: Princeton University Press, forthcoming).
106. Skowronek, *Building a New American State;* and Martin J. Schiesl, *The Politics of*

Efficiency: Municipal Administration and Reform in America: 1880–1920 (Berkeley: University of California Press, 1977).

107. Skocpol and Ikenberry, "Political Formation of the American Welfare State," pp. 98–119.
108. Skowronek, *Building a New American State*, part 2.
109. Carol S. Gruber, *Mars and Minerva: World War I and the Uses of Higher Learning in America* (Baton Rouge: Louisiana State University Press, 1975).
110. Carolyn Grin, "The Unemployment Conference of 1921: An Experiment in National Cooperative Planning," *Mid-America* 55 (1973): 83–107; and Barry D. Karl, "Presidential Planning and Social Science Research: Mr. Hoover's Experts," *Perspectives in American History* 3 (1969): 347–409.
111. See, for example, Grin, "Unemployment Conference"; and William Chenery, "Unemployment at Washington," *Survey* 37 (1921): 42.
112. Ellis W. Hawley, "Herbert Hoover, the Commerce Secretariat, and the Vision of an "Associative State,' " *Journal of American History* 61 (1974): 116–40; and Joan Hoff Wilson, *Herbert Hoover: Forgotten Progressive* (Boston: Little, Brown, 1975).
113. On the "Commons school" in relation to the Social Security Act, see Layfayette G. Harter, *John R. Commons: His Assault on Laissez-Faire* (Corvallis: Oregon State University Press, 1962); Daniel Nelson, *Unemployment Insurance: The American Experience, 1915–1935* (Madison: University of Wisconsin Press, 1969), chaps. 6 and 9; Theron F. Schlabach, *Edwin E. Witte: Cautious Reformer* (Madison: State Historical Society of Wisconsin, 1969).
114. Theda Skocpol and Kenneth Finegold, "State Capacity and Economic Intervention in the Early New Deal," *Political Science Quarterly* 97 (1982): 268–78; and Richard S. Kirkendall, *Social Scientists and Farm Politics in the Age of Roosevelt* (Columbia: University of Missouri Press, 1966).
115. May, *From New Deal to New Economics*, chap. 2, is especially insightful on the politicomoral basis of Roosevelt's and Treasury Secretary Henry Morgenthau, Jr.'s views about budget balancing.
116. See note 19.
117. Stein, *Fiscal Revolution*, p. 106.
118. Arthur W. MacMahon, John D. Millet, and Gladys Ogden, *The Administration of Federal Work Relief* (Chicago: Public Administration Service, 1941), pp. 200–20.
119. May, *From New Deal to New Economics*, pp. 40–52, sketches Eccles's biography. See also Sidney Hyman, *Marriner S. Eccles: Private Entrepreneur and Public Servant* (Stanford, Calif.: Graduate School of Business, Stanford University, 1976).
120. On Currie, see Stein, *Fiscal Revolution*, pp. 165–67; Alan Sweezy, "The Keynesians and Government Policy, 1933–1939," *American Economic Review* 62 (1972): 117–118; and John Kenneth Galbraith, "How Keynes Came to America," in *Economics, Peace and Laughter*, ed. Andrea D. Williams (Boston: Houghton Mifflin, 1971), pp. 47–48.
121. Eccles's economic ideas and the contacts he built up before 1937 are described in May, *From New Deal to New Economics*, pp. 53–66. Both May and Stein, *Fiscal Policy*, chap. 7, stress that Keynes (whether in person or through his writings) had little direct influence on the president or administration officials before 1937.

122. Christiana McFadyen Campbell, *The Farm Bureau and the New Deal: A Study of the Making of National Farm Policy, 1933–40* (Urbana: University of Illinois Press, 1962), pp. 190–91.

123. Chandler, *America's Greatest Depression*, p. 130; and May, *From New Deal to New Economics*, chap. 1.

124. Patterson, *Congressional Conservatism*, pp. 234–41,

125. May, *From New Deal to New Economics*, pp. 152–56. May notes more of a post-1937 recession shift toward Keynesian views on Roosevelt's part than does Stein.

126. Robert Collins, *The Business Response to Keynes, 1929–1964* (New York: Columbia University Press, 1981), p. 46.

127. See note 22.

128. Galbraith, "How Keynes Came to America," p. 48.

129. Our information on Alvin Hansen and his influence comes from Galbraith, "How Keynes Came to America"; Stein, *Fiscal Revolution*, pp. 163–68; and especially the collection of articles on Alvin H. Hansen in *Quarterly Journal of Economics* 90 (1976): 1–37. Hansen was initially very skeptical about Keynes's *General Theory*. In "Alvin Hansen as a Creative Economic Theorist," *Quarterly Journal of Economics* 90 (1976), p. 29, Paul Samuelson has wryly "hazarded the guess that Hansen received his call to Harvard by miscalculation. They did not know what they were getting. And neither did he." The last observation refers to the fact that Hansen was a creative, involved teacher, who was influenced by the youthful Keynesians already in Cambridge, just as he subsequently influenced and sponsored them.

130. A good discussion of "stagnationist" views appears in Collins, *Business Response to Keynes*, pp. 10–11, 51. "From the outset," Collins writes "the stagnationist analysis comprised a complex mixture of economic ideas and political preferences. It simultaneously explained the nature of modern American capitalism and yielded a set of programs for altering that system. But also, just as importantly, it became an emphasis, a collection of attitudes, a vision of the future which assumed that economic progress and sweeping social change were not antithetical" (p. 11).

131. Richard V. Gilbert, George H. Hildebrand, Jr., Arthur W. Stuart, Maxine Yaple Sweezy, Paul M. Sweezy, Lorie Tarshis, and John D. Wilson, *An Economic Program for American Democracy* (New York: Vanguard Press, 1938).

132. Alvin H. Hansen, "Economic Progress and Declining Population Growth," *American Economic Review* 29 (1939): 1–15.

133. By 1941, Hansen was "calling for 'a really positive expansionist policy' to replace the New Deal's tepid 'salvaging program.' " Here Collins, *Business Response to Keynes*, p. 11, is quoting from Hansen's *Fiscal Policy and Business Cycles* (New York: Norton, 1941), p. 84. See also Hansen's "Social Planning for Tomorrow," in *The United States After the War*, ed. Alvin H. Hansen, F. F. Hill, Louis Hollander, Walter D. Fuller, Herbert W. Briggs, and George O. Stoddard (Ithaca, N.Y.: Cornell University Press, 1945), pp. 15–34; and *After the War – Full Employment*, National Resources Planning Board (Washington, D. C.: Government Printing Office, 1942).

134. Stein, *Fiscal Revolution*, p. 168; James Tobin, "Hansen and Public Policy," *Quarterly Journal of Economics* 90 (1976): 32–37; Walter S. Salant, "Alvin Hansen

and the Fiscal Policy Seminar," *Quarterly Journal of Economics* 90 (1976), pp. 21–22; and Byrd L. Jones, "The Role of Keynesians in Wartime Policy and Postwar Planning, 1940–1946," *American Economic Review* 62 (1972): 125–33.

135. May, *From New Deal to New Economics*, pp. 146–50; and Stein, *Fiscal Revolution*, pp. 165–68.

136. The grounding of the stagnationists' theoretical arguments in interpretations of the concrete history of the New Deal is apparent both in Gilbert et al., *An Economic Program for American Democracy*, and in Alvin Hansen's first full Keynesian statement, *Full Recovery or Stagnation?* (New York: Norton, 1938).

137. Harrison Clark, *Swedish Unemployment Policy* (Washington, D.C.: American Council on Public Affairs, 1941), p. 118.

138. Hans Meijer, "Bureaucracy and Policy Formation in Sweden," *Scandinavian Political Studies* 4 (1969): 109, presents statistics showing that about 750 commissions per decade were at work during the Social Democrats' first three decades in power in Sweden, up from about 450 per decade earlier in the century.

139. Richard Polenberg, *Reorganizing Roosevelt's Government: The Controversy over Executive Reorganization* (Cambridge: Harvard University Press, 1966), p. 26.

140. Ibid.; Patterson, *Congressional Conservatism*, pp. 214–29; and J. Joseph Huthmacher, *Senator Robert E. Wagner and the Rise of Urban Liberalism* (New York: Atheneum, 1968), pp. 243–45.

141. Sven Anders Soderpalm, "The Crisis Agreement and the Social Democratic Road to Power," in *Sweden's Development from Poverty to Affluence, 1750–1970*, ed. Steven Koblik (Minneapolis: University of Minnesota Press, 1975), p. 262.

142. Svenska Handelsbanken, "Government Measures for the Relief of Agriculture in Sweden since 1930," suppl. to Svenska Handelbanken's *Index* 14 (March 1939), p. 5; and Kurt Samuelsson, *Sweden: From Great Power to Welfare State* (London: Allen & Unwin, 1968), pp. 140–41.

143. Jean Jusissant, *La Structure Economique de la Suede et de la Belgique*, (Brussels: Collection de l'Ecole des Sciences Politiques et Sociales de l'Université de Louvain, 1938) and Svenska Handelsbanken, "Government Measures," pp. 24–25.

144. Ernst Wigforss, "The Financial Policy during Depression and Boom," *Annals* 197 (1938): 31.

145. Soderpalm, "Crisis Agreement," pp. 275–77.

146. Dankwart Rustow, *The Politics of Compromise: A Study of Parties and Cabinet Government in Sweden* (Princeton, N.J.: Princeton University Press, 1955), p. 109.

147. See Richard S. Kirkendall, "The New Deal and Agriculture," in *The New Deal: The National Level*, ed. John Braeman, Robert H. Bremner, and David Brody (Columbus: Ohio State University Press, 1975), pp. 83–109; Grant McConnell, *The Decline of Agrarian Democracy* (New York: Atheneum, 1969), chaps. 7–16; and Campbell, *Farm Bureau and the New Deal*, chaps. 8 and 9.

148. On the National Farmers' Union and its policies, see McConnell, *Decline of Agrarian Democracy*, pp. 37–39, 68–69, 108, 137, 146; and Campbell, *Farm Bureau and the New Deal*, pp. 169–71. On related, radical reformist agrarian organizations, see also John L. Shover, *Cornbelt Rebellion: The Farmers' Holiday Association* (Urbana: University of Illinois Press, 1965); and Donald H. Grubbs,

Cry from the Cotton: The Southern Tenant Farmers' Union and the New Deal (Chapel Hill: University of North Carolina Press, 1971).

149. Campbell, *Farm Bureau and the New Deal*, chap. 6.

150. McConnell, *Decline of Agrarian Democracy*, chaps. 8–10; Sidney Baldwin, *Poverty and Politics: The Rise and Decline of the Farm Security Administration* (Chapel Hill: University of North Carolina Press, 1968); and Paul E. Mertz, *New Deal Policy and Southern Rural Poverty* (Baton Rouge: Louisiana State University Press, 1978).

151. Murray Edelman, "New Deal Sensitivity to Labor Interests," in *Labor and the New Deal*, ed. Milton Derber and Edwin Young (New York: DaCapo Press, 1972), pp. 185–86; and Patterson, *Congressional Conservatism*, pp. 334–35 and *passim*.

152. Patterson, *Congressional Conservatism*, pp. 318–22; and Collins, *Business Response to Keynes*, pp. 46–47.

153. Collins, *Business Response to Keynes*, pp. 13–14.

154. Marion Clawson, *New Deal Planning: The National Resources Planning Board* (Baltimore, Md.: Johns Hopkins University Press, 1981), pp. 225–32.

155. Stephen Kemp Bailey, *Congress Makes a Law: The Story Behind the Employment Act of 1946* (New York: Columbia University Press, 1950), chaps. 1–3.

156. Ibid., pp. 150–78, 202–205; and Collins, *Business Response to Keynes*, pp. 102–109.

157. Bailey, *Congress Makes a Law*, pp. 220–34, 243–48.

158. See note 22.

159. Esping-Andersen and Friedland, "Class Coalitions," p. 20.

160. Collins, *Business Response to Keynes*, chaps. 5 and 6; Stein, *Fiscal Revolution*, chaps. 8 and 9.

161. On the Chicago economists in relation to the Council for Economic Development and the fashioning of commercial Keynesian ideas, see Collins, *Business Response to Keynes*, pp. 71–72, 83–84; and Davis, *New Economics and Old Economists*, chap. 3 on the Chicago school. Clearly, the fact that the U.S. university system is large and multiply centered made it more possible than it would have been in a centralized, European-style academic establishment for separate strands of macroeconomic thinking to develop parallel to the stagnationist Keynesian school centered at Harvard.

162. See the useful discussion of postwar U.S. "macroeconomic stabilization" in Michael J. Piore and Charles Sabel, *The Industrial Divide* (New York: Basic Books, 1984), chap. 4.

163. Walter Korpi and Michael Shalev, "Strikes, Power, and Conflict in the Western Nations, 1900–1976," *Political Power and Social Theory* 1 (1980): 309–16.

Part II

States and Transnational Relations

Individual states as actors and institutions have always been embedded in political and economic relations that move beyond the territories and people they directly govern. Indeed, in the "modern world system," which emerged out of the fragmented sovereignties of European feudalism in the context of commercial relations linking Northeastern Europe to Eastern Europe and Latin America, transnational economic flows and international geopolitical competition have been especially intense. Such relations have directly constituted the boundaries and identities of the modern national states that now monopolize coercive sovereignty across the globe. Looking at the behavior of states in relation to political and economic activities that cross their borders is therefore an essential part of any attempt to understand the modern state. The three essays in this section demonstrate diverse and mutually complementary ways in which this analytical task may be pursued.

At first glance, the heterogeneity of the essays in this part is striking, for they focus on quite different problems, times, and places. Charles Tilly's "War Making and State Making" juxtaposes examples from fourteenth- to seventeenth-century European history with provocative economic models of states as predators. Peter Katzenstein's contribution offers a carefully crafted comparison of domestic political arrangements as they relate to international economic openness for Switzerland and Austria, two of the least predatory nations of post–World War II Europe. And Peter Evans offers a general argument in "Transnational Linkages and the Economic Role of the State" that focuses principally on the domestic economic policies of contemporary Third World countries. Yet, in the end, the heterogeneity of topics and settings encompassed by these essays coexists with some intriguing commonalities of substantive concern and analytical strategy.

A central theme brings the essays of this part together: All of them are principally concerned with how states acquire specific capacities to act and, more precisely, how the process of constructing such capacities is affected by transnational flows and challenges. None of the essays treats states as epiphenomena serving simply to formalize relations among powerful social actors at home and abroad. More significantly, none of them goes to the opposite extreme of taking for granted that the states with which they deal are unified, purposeful actors. Rather, all three essays are interested in the emergence of particular kinds of organizational substructures within state apparatuses and in the influence these have on the subsequent capacities of states. Moreover, the emergence of such substructures is seen to be simultaneously rooted in relations between state authorities and domestic constituencies, on the one hand, and in relations between state authorities and transnational contexts, on the other.

Tilly, Katzenstein, and Evans also share a common commitment to considering both geopolitical and economic aspects of the linkages of states into transnational structures. All three authors consider, at least to some degree, the interactions of geopolitical and transnational economic processes. Each author necessarily attacks this task in his own way, however.

The integration is most subtle in Katzenstein's analysis, perhaps because the geopolitical goals of Austria and Switzerland are so limited and taken for granted in the international setting within which they have recently found themselves. For Austria and Switzerland, the primary goal with regard to the international system is not predation, but preservation of political integrity, along with neutrality in relation to larger powers and unimpeded access to international markets. To preserve political integrity, these states must simultaneously avoid internal political schisms and carefully manage transnational economic participation. The main thrust of Katzenstein's essay is to lay bare the complex workings of the contrastingly structured, but similarly functioning corporatist political arrangements of Switzerland and Austria, arrangements that bind together state apparatuses and domestic social groups in ways that maintain internal political consensus without threatening the international economic adaptability that has become essential to the standard of living that both small nations enjoy.

Tilly's states are above all geopolitical actors, built on foundations of recurrent warfare and the construction of state capacities to mobilize social resources for war; yet his analysis weaves war making together with interesting economic undercurrents throughout. The theoretical models from which Tilly starts are "economistic" in the sense of focusing on the profits that accrue to states – like organized criminals – as a result of effective predation and "protection rackets." More critical are the connections he draws between war making and the elaboration of the fiscal aspects of state apparatuses. More than any other state activity, Tilly points out, war making requires the development of fiscal and extractive capacities. For this reason, success in war depends on the state's ability not only to tax its subject population, but also to persuade transnational finance capitalists to make some of their resources available, for a fee of course.

Evans is principally concerned with the capacities of states to intervene in their national economies and with the ways these capacities are affected by transnational economic relationships, but he is careful to acknowledge that both the development of transnational economic linkages and the responses of variously situated states to them must be placed in the context of geopolitical aims and relationships. More specifically, Evans agrees with Stephen Krasner and others that the preeminence of geopolitical goals among U.S. state officials concerned with international relations tends to affect American official attitudes toward the possible expansion of the economic interventions of Third World states, as well as to affect stances toward the domestic economic role of the U.S. government itself. American policies, in turn, have a crucial influence on the aims and capacities of Third World state managers.

Like the essays in the preceding part, each of those found here opens up questions and offers fruitful hypotheses for future research. Taken together, moreover, the three pieces especially point toward the intellectual returns that might be gained from a more systematic integration of comparative work on states in developing regions with scholarship on the history and contemporary situations of states in the now advanced industrial parts of the world. Normally, theorizing and empirical research on these two categories of countries tend to proceed in mutual isolation, but intriguing possibilities emerge when unusual juxtapositions are made across the divide between "First World" and Third World studies.

Tilly's closing paragraphs, for example, brim with suggestive ideas about how military officials and organizations might relate to the rest of the state apparatuses in contemporary "new nations." Tilly draws on his analyses of war making and state building in European history to hypothesize how relationships might be similar and different in today's Third World, and his hunches point to the need for further analysis and careful research on key cases. Evans makes the relationship between transnational economic elites and state managers in core countries problematic in a way that clearly stems from his familiarity with Third World cases. Even Katzenstein's essay, so thoroughly grounded in two First World cases, suggests the benefits of a more wide-ranging attack on the same set of issues. Reaching the end of his essay, one cannot help but wonder whether the logic that connects tightly knit corporatist political arrangements with international economic openness ought not to hold as well for many developing nations outside Western Europe – and if not, why.

An emphasis on the future research directions opened up by the essays in this section must not distract us from the important analytical contributions made by each in its own right. Tilly provides one of the most succinct and powerful formulations available of the theoretical advantages that accrue from viewing the formation of national states in terms of relatively autonomous geopolitical dynamics and not simply as a reflection of the expansion of markets or the growth of new production relations. Katzenstein's discussion of European corporatism elaborates the logic of his distinctive dual vision of the state as an actor and as part of a "policy network" encompassing state and society alike. Thus, his empirical essay fleshes out and further demonstrates the value of his general approach, to which we were first introduced in the opening essay of this volume. Evans, finally, offers a frame of reference that moves well beyond any understanding of the state previously offered in the "dependency" literature. His essay provides provocative starting points for future debates on relations between states and transnational corporations. In sum, these essays make wide-ranging and original contributions to the enduringly essential task of analyzing state goals and capacities in the context of transnational relations.

5.   War Making and State Making as Organized Crime

Charles Tilly

Warning

If protection rackets represent organized crime at its smoothest, then war making and state making – quintessential protection rackets with the advantage of legitimacy – qualify as our largest examples of organized crime. Without branding all generals and statesmen as murderers or thieves, I want to urge the value of that analogy. At least for the European experience of the past few centuries, a portrait of war makers and state makers as coercive and self-seeking entrepreneurs bears a far greater resemblance to the facts than do its chief alternatives: the idea of a social contract, the idea of an open market in which operators of armies and states offer services to willing consumers, the idea of a society whose shared norms and expectations call forth a certain kind of government.

The reflections that follow merely illustrate the analogy of war making and state making with organized crime from a few hundred years of European experience and offer tentative arguments concerning principles of change and variation underlying the experience. My reflections grow from contemporary concerns: worries about the increasing destructiveness of war, the expanding role of great powers as suppliers of arms and military organization to poor countries, and the growing importance of military rule in those same countries. They spring from the hope that the European experience, properly understood, will help us to grasp what is happening today, perhaps even to do something about it.

The Third World of the twentieth century does not greatly resemble Europe of the sixteenth or seventeenth century. In no simple sense can we read the future of Third World countries from the pasts of European countries. Yet a thoughtful exploration of European experience will serve us well. It will show us that coercive exploitation played a large part in the creation of the European states. It will show us that popular resistance to coercive exploitation forced would-be power holders to concede protection and constraints on their own action. It will therefore help us to eliminate faulty implicit comparisons between today's Third World and yesterday's Europe. That clarification will make it easier to understand exactly how today's world is different and what we therefore have to explain. It may even help us to explain the current looming presence of military organization and action throughout the world. Although that result would delight me, I do not promise anything so grand.

This essay, then, concerns the place of organized means of violence in the growth and change of those peculiar forms of government we call national states: relatively centralized, differentiated organizations the officials of which more or less successfully claim control over the chief concentrated means of violence within a population inhabiting a large, contiguous territory. The argument grows from historical work on the formation of national states in Western Europe, especially on the growth of the French state from 1600 onward. But it takes several deliberate steps away from that work, wheels, and stares hard at it from theoretical ground. The argument brings with it few illustrations and no evidence worthy of the name.

Just as one repacks a hastily filled rucksack after a few days on the trail – throwing out the waste, putting things in order of importance, and balancing the load – I have repacked my theoretical baggage for the climb to come; the real test of the new packing arrives only with the next stretch of the trail. The trimmed-down argument stresses the interdependence of war making and state making and the analogy between both of those processes and what, when less successful and smaller in scale, we call organized crime. War makes states, I shall claim. Banditry, piracy, gangland rivalry, policing, and war making all belong on the same continuum – that I shall claim as well. For the historically limited period in which national states were becoming the dominant organizations in Western countries, I shall also claim that mercantile capitalism and state making reinforced each other.

Double-Edged Protection

In contemporary American parlance, the word "protection" sounds two contrasting tones. One is comforting, the other ominous. With one tone, "protection" calls up images of the shelter against danger provided by a powerful friend, a large insurance policy, or a sturdy roof. With the other, it evokes the racket in which a local strong man forces merchants to pay tribute in order to avoid damage – damage the strong man himself threatens to deliver. The difference, to be sure, is a matter of degree: A hell-and-damnation priest is likely to collect contributions from his parishioners only to the extent that they believe his predictions of brimstone for infidels; our neighborhood mobster may actually be, as he claims to be, a brothel's best guarantee of operation free of police interference.

Which image the word "protection" brings to mind depends mainly on our assessment of the reality and externality of the threat. Someone who produces both the danger and, at a price, the shield against it is a racketeer. Someone who provides a needed shield but has little control over the danger's appearance qualifies as a legitimate protector, especially if his price is no higher than his competitors'. Someone who supplies reliable, low-priced shielding both from local racketeers and from outside marauders makes the best offer of all.

Apologists for particular governments and for government in general commonly argue, precisely, that they offer protection from local and external violence. They claim that the prices they charge barely cover the costs of protection. They call people who complain about the price of protection "anarchists," "subversives," or both at once. But consider the definition of a racketeer as someone who creates a threat and then charges for its reduction. Governments' provision of protection, by this standard, often qualifies as racketeering. To the extent that the threats against which a given government protects its citizens are imaginary or are consequences of its own activities, the government has organized a protection racket. Since governments themselves commonly simulate, stimulate, or even fabricate threats of external war and since the repressive and extractive activities of governments often constitute the largest current threats to the livelihoods of their own citizens, many governments operate in essentially the same ways as racketeers. There is, of course, a difference: Racketeers, by the conventional definition, operate without the sanctity of governments.

How do racketeer governments themselves acquire authority? As a question of fact and of ethics, that is one of the oldest conundrums of political analysis. Back to Machiavelli and Hobbes, nevertheless, political observers have recognized that, whatever else they do, governments organize and, wherever possible, monopolize violence. It matters little whether we take violence in a narrow sense, such as damage to persons and objects, or in a broad sense, such as violation of people's desires and interests; by either criterion, governments stand out from other organizations by their tendency to monopolize the concentrated means of violence. The distinction between "legitimate" and "illegitimate" force, furthermore, makes no difference to the fact. If we take legitimacy to depend on conformity to an abstract principle or on the assent of the governed (or both at once), these conditions may serve to justify, perhaps even to explain, the tendency to monopolize force; they do not contradict the fact.

In any case, Arthur Stinchcombe's agreeably cynical treatment of legitimacy serves the purposes of political analysis much more efficiently. Legitimacy, according to Stinchcombe, depends rather little on abstract principle or assent of the governed: "The person *over whom power is exercised* is not usually as important as *other power-holders.*"[1] Legitimacy is the probability that other authorities will act to confirm the decisions of a given authority. Other authorities, I would add, are much more likely to confirm the decisions of a challenged authority that controls substantial force; not only fear of retaliation, but also desire to maintain a stable environment recommend that general rule. The rule underscores the importance of the authority's monopoly of force. A tendency to monopolize the means of violence makes a government's claim to provide protection, in either the comforting or the ominous sense of the word, more credible and more difficult to resist.

Frank recognition of the central place of force in governmental activity does not require us to believe that governmental authority rests "only" or "ultimately" on the threat of violence. Nor does it entail the assumption that a government's only service is protection. Even when a government's use of force imposes a large cost, some people may well decide that the government's other services outbalance the costs of acceding to its monopoly of violence. Recognition of the centrality of force opens the way to an understanding of the growth and change of governmental forms.

Here is a preview of the most general argument: Power holders' pursuit of war involved them willy-nilly in the extraction of resources for war making from the populations over which they had control and in the promotion of capital accumulation by those who could help them borrow and buy. War making, extraction, and capital accumulation interacted to shape European state making. Power holders did not undertake those three momentous activities with the intention of creating national states – centralized, differentiated, autonomous, extensive political organizations. Nor did they ordinarily foresee that national states would emerge from war making, extraction, and capital accumulation.

Instead, the people who controlled European states and states in the making warred in order to check or overcome their competitors and thus to enjoy the advantages of power within a secure or expanding territory. To make more effective war, they attempted to locate more capital. In the short run, they might acquire that capital by conquest, by selling off their assets, or by coercing or dispossessing accumulators of capital. In the long run, the quest inevitably involved them in establishing regular access to capitalists who could supply and arrange credit and in imposing one form of regular taxation or another on the people and activities within their spheres of control.

As the process continued, state makers developed a durable interest in promoting the accumulation of capital, sometimes in the guise of direct return to their own enterprises. Variations in the difficulty of collecting taxes, in the expense of the particular kind of armed force adopted, in the amount of war making required to hold off competitors, and so on resulted in the principal variations in the forms of European states. It all began with the effort to monopolize the means of violence within a delimited territory adjacent to a power holder's base.

Violence and Government

What distinguished the violence produced by states from the violence delivered by anyone else? In the long run, enough to make the division between "legitimate" and "illegitimate" force credible. Eventually, the personnel of states purveyed violence on a larger scale, more effectively, more efficiently, with wider assent from their subject populations, and with readier collaboration from neighboring authorities than did the personnel of other organizations. But it took a long time for that series of distinctions to become established. Early in the state-making process, many parties shared the right to use violence, the practice of using it routinely to accomplish their ends, or both at once. The continuum ran from bandits and pirates to kings via tax collectors, regional power holders, and professional soldiers.

The uncertain, elastic line between "legitimate" and "illegitimate" violence appeared in the upper reaches of power. Early in the state-making process, many parties shared the right to use violence, its actual employment, or both at once. The long love–hate affair between aspiring state makers and pirates or bandits illustrates the division. "Behind piracy on the seas acted cities and city-states," writes Fernand Braudel of the sixteenth century. "Behind banditry, that terrestrial piracy, appeared the continual aid of lords."[2] In times of war, indeed, the managers of full-fledged states often commissioned privateers, hired sometime bandits to raid their enemies, and encouraged their regular troops to take booty. In royal service, soldiers and sailors were often expected to provide for themselves by preying on the civilian population: commandeering, raping, looting, taking prizes. When demobilized, they commonly continued the same practices, but without the same royal protection; demobilized ships became pirate vessels, demobilized troops bandits.

It also worked the other way: A king's best source of armed supporters was sometimes the world of outlaws. Robin Hood's conversion to royal archer may be a myth, but the myth records a practice. The distinctions between "legitimate" and "illegitimate" users of violence came clear only very slowly, in the process during which the state's armed forces became relatively unified and permanent.

Up to that point, as Braudel says, maritime cities and terrestrial lords commonly offered protection, or even sponsorship, to freebooters. Many lords who did not pretend to be kings, furthermore, successfully claimed the right to levy troops and maintain their own armed retainers. Without calling on some of those lords to bring their armies with them, no king could fight a war; yet the same armed lords constituted the king's rivals and opponents, his enemies' potential allies. For that reason, before the seventeenth century, regencies for child sovereigns reliably produced civil wars. For the same reason, disarming the great stood high on the agenda of every would-be state maker.

The Tudors, for example, accomplished that agenda through most of England. "The greatest triumph of the Tudors," writes Lawrence Stone,

was the ultimately successful assertion of a royal monopoly of violence both public and private, an achievement which profoundly altered not only the nature of politics but also the quality of daily life. There occurred a change in English habits that can only be compared with the further step taken in the nineteenth century, when the growth of a police force finally consolidated the monopoly and made it effective in the greatest cities and the smallest villages.[3]

Tudor demilitarization of the great lords entailed four complementary campaigns: eliminating their great personal bands of armed retainers, razing their fortresses, taming their habitual resort to violence for the settlement of disputes, and discouraging the cooperation of their dependents and tenants. In the Marches of England and Scotland, the task was more delicate, for the Percys and Dacres, who kept armies and castles along the border, threatened the Crown but also provided a buffer against Scottish invaders. Yet they, too, eventually fell into line.

In France, Richelieu began the great disarmament in the 1620s. With Richelieu's advice, Louis XIII systematically destroyed the castles of the great rebel lords, Protestant and Catholic, against whom his forces battled incessantly. He began to condemn dueling, the carrying of lethal weapons, and the maintenance of private armies. By the later 1620s, Richelieu was declaring the royal monopoly of force as doctrine. The doctrine took another half-century to become effective:

Once more the conflicts of the Fronde had witnessed armies assembled by the "grands." Only the last of the regencies, the one after the death of Louis XIV, did not lead to armed uprisings. By that time Richelieu's principle had become a reality. Likewise in the Empire after the Thirty Years' War only the territorial princes had the right of levying troops and of maintaining fortresses. . . . Everywhere the razing of castles, the high cost of artillery, the attraction of court life, and the ensuing domestication of the nobility had its share in this development.[4]

By the later eighteenth century, through most of Europe, monarchs controlled permanent, professional military forces that rivaled those of their neighbors and far exceeded any other organized armed force within their own territories. The state's monopoly of large-scale violence was turning from theory to reality.

The elimination of local rivals, however, posed a serious problem. Beyond the scale of a small city-state, no monarch could govern a population with his armed force alone, nor could any monarch afford to create a professional staff large and strong enough to reach from him to the ordinary citizen. Before quite recently, no European government approached the completeness of articulation from top to bottom achieved by imperial China. Even the Roman Empire did not come close. In one way or another, every European government before the French Revolution relied on indirect rule via local magnates. The magnates collaborated with the government without becoming officials in any strong sense of the term, had some access to government-backed force, and exercised wide discretion within their own territories: junkers, justices of the peace, lords. Yet the same magnates were potential rivals, possible allies of a rebellious people.

Eventually, European governments reduced their reliance on indirect rule by means of two expensive but effective strategies: (a) extending their officialdom to the local community and (b) encouraging the creation of police forces that were subordinate to the government rather than to individual patrons, distinct from war-making forces, and therefore less useful as the tools of dissident magnates. In between, however, the builders of national power all played a mixed strategy: eliminating, subjugating, dividing, conquering, cajoling, buying as the occasions presented themselves. The buying manifested itself in exemptions from taxation, creations of honorific offices, the establishment of claims on the national treasury, and a variety of other devices that made a magnate's welfare dependent on the maintenance of the existing structure of power. In the long run, it all came down to massive pacification and monopolization of the means of coercion.

Protection as Business

In retrospect, the pacification, cooptation, or elimination of fractious rivals to the sovereign seems an awesome, noble, prescient enterprise, destined to bring peace to a people; yet it followed almost ineluctably from the logic of expanding power. If a power holder was to gain from the provision of protection, his competitors had to yield. As economic historian Frederic Lane put it twenty-five years ago, governments are in the business of selling protection . . . whether people want it or not. Lane argued that the very activity of producing and controlling violence favored monopoly, because competition within that realm generally raised costs, instead of lowering them. The production of violence, he suggested, enjoyed large economies of scale.

Working from there, Lane distinguished between (a) the monopoly profit, or *tribute*, coming to owners of the means of producing violence as a result of the difference between production costs and the price exacted from "customers" and (b) the *protection rent* accruing to those customers – for example, merchants – who drew effective protection against outside competitors. Lane, a superbly attentive historian of Venice, allowed specifically for the case of a government that generates protection rents for its merchants by deliberately attacking their competitors. In their adaptation of Lane's scheme, furthermore, Edward Ames and Richard Rapp substitute the apt word "extortion" for Lane's "tribute." In this model, predation, coercion, piracy, banditry, and racketeering share a home with their upright cousins in responsible government.

This is how Lane's model worked: If a prince could create a sufficient armed force to hold off his and his subjects' external enemies and to keep the subjects in line for 50 megapounds but was able to extract 75 megapounds in taxes from those subjects for that purpose, he gained a tribute of $(75 - 50 =) 25$ megapounds. If the 10-pound share of those taxes paid by one of the prince's merchant-subjects gave him assured access to world markets at less than the 15-pound shares paid by the merchant's foreign competitors to *their* princes, the merchant also gained a protection rent of $(15 - 10 =)$ 5 pounds by virtue of his prince's greater efficiency. That reasoning differs only in degree and in scale from the reasoning of violence-wielding criminals and their clients. Labor racketeering (in which, for example, a ship owner holds off trouble from longshoremen by means of a timely payment to the local union boss) works on exactly the same principle: The union boss receives tribute for his no-strike pressure on the longshoremen, while the ship owner avoids the strikes and slowdowns longshoremen impose on his competitors.

Lane pointed out the different behavior we might expect of the managers of a protection-providing government owned by

1. Citizens in general
2. A single self-interested monarch
3. The managers themselves

If citizens in general exercised effective ownership of the government – O distant ideal! – we might expect the managers to minimize protection costs and tribute, thus maximizing protection rent. A single self-interested monarch, in contrast, would maximize tribute, set costs so as to accomplish that maximization of tribute, and be indifferent to the level of protection rent. If the managers owned the government, they would tend to keep costs high by maximizing their own wages, to maximize tribute over and above those costs by exacting a high price from their subjects, and likewise to be indifferent to the level of protection rent. The first model approximates a Jeffersonian democracy, the second a petty despotism, and the third a military junta.

Lane did not discuss the obvious fourth category of owner: a dominant class. If he had, his scheme would have yielded interesting empirical criteria for evaluating claims that a given government was "relatively autonomous" or strictly subordinate to the interests of a dominant class. Presumably, a subordinate government would tend to maximize monopoly profits – returns to the dominant class resulting from the difference between the costs of protection and the price received for it – as well as tuning protection rents nicely to the economic interests of the dominant class. An autonomous government, in contrast, would tend to maximize managers' wages and its own size as well and would be indifferent to protection rents. Lane's analysis immediately suggests fresh propositions and ways of testing them.

Lane also speculated that the logic of the situation produced four successive stages in the general history of capitalism:

1. A period of anarchy and plunder
2. A stage in which tribute takers attracted customers and established their monopolies by struggling to create exclusive, substantial states

3. A stage in which merchants and landlords began to gain more from protection rents than governors did from tribute
4. A period (fairly recent) in which technological changes surpassed protection rents as sources of profit for entrepreneurs

In their new economic history of the Western world, Douglass North and Robert Paul Thomas make stages 2 and 3 – those in which state makers created their monopolies of force and established property rights that permitted individuals to capture much of the return from their own growth-generating innovations – the pivotal moment for sustained economic growth. Protection, at this point, overwhelms tribute. If we recognize that the protected property rights were mainly those of capital and that the development of capitalism also facilitated the accumulation of the wherewithal to operate massive states, that extension of Lane's analysis provides a good deal of insight into the coincidence of war making, state making, and capital accumulation.

Unfortunately, Lane did not take full advantage of his own insight. Wanting to contain his analysis neatly within the neoclassical theory of industrial organization, Lane cramped his treatment of protection: treating all taxpayers as "customers" for the "service" provided by protection-manufacturing governments, brushing aside the objections to the idea of a forced sale by insisting that the "customer" always had the choice of not paying and taking the consequences of nonpayment, minimizing the problems of divisibility created by the public-goods character of protection, and deliberately neglecting the distinction between the costs of producing the means of violence in general and the costs of giving "customers" protection by means of that violence. Lane's ideas suffocate inside the neoclassical box and breathe easily outside it. Nevertheless, inside or outside, they properly draw the economic analysis of government back to the chief activities that real governments have carried on historically: war, repression, protection, adjudication.

More recently, Richard Bean has applied a similar logic to the rise of European national states between 1400 and 1600. He appeals to economies of scale in the production of effective force, counteracted by diseconomies of scale in command and control. He then claims that the improvement of artillery in the fifteenth century (cannon made small medieval forts much more vulnerable to an organized force) shifted the curve of economies and diseconomies to make larger armies, standing armies, and centralized governments advantageous to their masters. Hence, according to Bean, military innovation promoted the creation of large, expensive, well-armed national states.

History Talks

Bean's summary does not stand up to historical scrutiny. As a matter of practice, the shift to infantry-backed artillery sieges of fortified cities occurred only during the sixteenth and seventeenth centuries. Artillery did improve during the fifteenth century, but the invention of new fortifications, especially the *trace italienne,* rapidly countered the advantage of artillery. The arrival of effective artillery came too late to have *caused* the increase in the viable size of states. (However, the increased cost of fortifications to defend against artillery did give an advantage to states enjoying larger fiscal bases.)

Nor is it obvious that changes in land war had the sweeping influence Bean attributes to them. The increasing decisiveness of naval warfare, which occurred simultaneously, could well have shifted the military advantage to small maritime powers such as the Dutch Republic. Furthermore, although many city-states and other microscopic entities disappeared into larger political units before 1600, such events as the fractionation of the Habsburg Empire and such facts as the persistence of large but loosely knit Poland and Russia render ambiguous the claim of a significant increase in geographic scale. In short, both Bean's proposed explanation and his statement of what must be explained raise historical doubts.

Stripped of its technological determinism, nevertheless, Bean's logic provides a useful complement to Lane's, for different military formats do cost substantially different amounts to produce and do provide substantially different ranges of control over opponents, domestic and foreign. After 1400 the European pursuit of larger, more permanent, and more costly varieties of military organization did, in fact, drive spectacular increases in princely budgets, taxes, and staffs. After 1500 or so, princes who managed to create the costly varieties of military organization were, indeed, able to conquer new chunks of territory.

The word "territory" should not mislead us. Until the eighteenth century, the greatest powers were maritime states, and naval warfare remained crucial to international position. Consider Fernand Braudel's roll call of successive hegemonic powers within the capitalist world: Venice and its empire, Genoa and its empire, Antwerp–Spain, Amsterdam–Holland, London–England, New York–the United States. Although Brandenburg–Prussia offers a partial exception, only in our own time have such essentially landbound states as Russia and China achieved preponderant positions in the world's system of states. Naval warfare was by no means the only reason for that bias toward the sea. Before the later nineteenth century, land transportation was so expensive everywhere in Europe that no country could afford to supply a large army or a big city with grain and other heavy goods without having efficient water transport. Rulers fed major inland centers such as Berlin and Madrid only at great effort and at considerable cost to their hinterlands. The exceptional efficiency of waterways in the Netherlands undoubtedly gave the Dutch great advantages at peace and at war.

Access to water mattered in another important way. Those metropolises on Braudel's list were all major ports, great centers of commerce, and outstanding mobilizers of capital. Both the trade and the capital served the purposes of ambitious rulers. By a circuitous route, that observation brings us back to the arguments of Lane and Bean. Considering that both of them wrote as economic historians, the greatest weakness in their analyses comes as a surprise: Both of them understate the importance of capital accumulation to military expansion. As Jan de Vries says of the period after 1600:

Looking back, one cannot help but be struck by the seemingly symbiotic relationship existing between the state, military power, and the private economy's efficiency in the age of absolutism. Behind every successful dynasty stood an array of opulent banking families. Access to such bourgeois resources proved crucial to the princes' state-building and centralizing policies. Princes also needed direct access to agricultural resources, which could be mobilized only when agricultural productivity grew *and* an effective administrative and military power existed to enforce the princes' claims. But the lines of causation also ran in the opposite direction. Successful state-building and empire-building activities plus the associated tendency toward concentration of urban population and government expenditure, offered the private economy unique and invaluable opportunities to capture economies of scale. These economies of scale occasionally affected industrial production but were most significant in the development of trade and finance. In addition, the sheer pressure of cental government taxation did as much as any other economic force to channel peasant production into the market and thereby augment the opportunities for trade creation and economic specialization.[5]

Nor does the "symbiotic relationship" hold only for the period after 1600. For the precocious case of France, we need only consider the increase in royal expenditures and revenues from 1515 to 1785. Although the rates of growth in both regards accelerated appropriately after 1600, they also rose substantially during the sixteenth century. After 1550, the internal Wars of Religion checked the work of international expansion that Francis I had begun earlier in the century, but from the 1620s onward Louis XIII and Louis XIV (aided and abetted, to be sure, by Richelieu, Mazarin, Colbert, and other state-making wizards) resumed the task with a vengeance. "As always," comments V. G. Kiernan, "war had every political recommendation and every financial drawback."[6]

Borrowing and then paying interest on the debt accounts for much of the discrepancy between the two curves. Great capitalists played crucial parts on both sides of the transaction: as the principal sources of royal credit, especially in the short term, and as the most important contractors in the risky but lucrative business of collecting royal taxes. For this reason, it is worth noticing that

for practical purposes the national debt began in the reign of Francis I. Following the loss of Milan, the key to northern Italy, on September 15, 1522, Francis I borrowed 200,000 francs . . . at 12.5 percent from the merchants of Paris, to intensify the war against Charles V. Administered by the city government, this loan inaugurated the famous series of bonds based on revenues from the capital and known as *rentes sur l'Hôtel de Ville*.[7]

(The government's failure to pay those *rentes*, incidentally, helped align the Parisian bourgeoisie against the Crown during the Fronde, some twelve decades later.) By 1595, the national debt had risen to 300 million francs; despite governmental bankruptcies, currency manipulations, and the monumental rise in taxes, by Louis XIV's death in 1715 war-induced borrowing had inflated the total to about 3 billion francs, the equivalent of about eighteen years in royal revenues.[8] War, state apparatus, taxation, and borrowing advanced in tight cadence.

Although France was precocious, it was by no means alone. "Even more than in the case of France," reports the ever-useful Earl J. Hamilton,

the national debt of England originated and has grown during major wars. Except for an insignificant carry-over from the Stuarts, the debt began in 1689 with the reign of William and Mary. In the words of Adam Smith, "it was in the war which began in 1688, and was concluded by the treaty of Ryswick in 1697, that the foundation of the present enormous debt of Great Britain was first laid."[9]

Hamilton, it is true, goes on to quote the mercantilist Charles Davenant, who complained in 1698 that the high interest rates promoted by government borrowing were cramping English trade. Davenant's complaint suggests, however, that England was already entering Frederic Lane's third stage of state–capital relations, when merchants and landowners receive more of the surplus than do the suppliers of protection.

Until the sixteenth century, the English expected their kings to live on revenues from their own property and to levy taxes only for war. G. R. Elton marks the great innovation at Thomas Cromwell's drafting of Henry VIII's subsidy bills for 1534 and 1540: "1540 was very careful to continue the real innovation of 1534, namely that extraordinary contributions could be levied for reasons other than war."[10] After that point as before, however, war making provided the main stimulus to increases in the level of taxation as well as of debt. Rarely did debt and taxes recede. What A. T. Peacock and J. Wiseman call a "displacement effect" (and others sometimes call a "ratchet effect") occurred: When public revenues and expenditures rose abruptly during war, they set a new, higher floor beneath which peacetime revenues and expenditures did not sink. During the Napoleonic Wars, British taxes rose from 15 to 24 percent of national income and to almost three times the French level of taxation.[11]

True, Britain had the double advantage of relying less on expensive land forces than its Continental rivals and of drawing more of its tax revenues from customs and excise – taxes that were, despite evasion, significantly cheaper to collect than land taxes, property taxes, and poll taxes. Nevertheless, in England as well as elsewhere, both debt and taxes rose enormously from the seventeenth century onward. They rose mainly as a function of the increasing cost of war making.

What Do States Do?

As should now be clear, Lane's analysis of protection fails to distinguish among several different uses of state-controlled violence. Under the general heading of organized violence, the agents of states characteristically carry on four different activities:

1. War making: Eliminating or neutralizing their own rivals outside the territories in which they have clear and continuous priority as wielders of force
2. State making: Eliminating or neutralizing their rivals inside those territories
3. Protection: Eliminating or neutralizing the enemies of their clients
4. Extraction: Acquiring the means of carrying out the first three activities – war making, state making, and protection

The third item corresponds to protection as analyzed by Lane, but the other three also involve the application of force. They overlap incompletely and to various degrees; for example, war making against the commercial rivals of the local bourgeoisie delivers protection to that bourgeoisie. To the extent that a population is divided into enemy classes and the state extends its favors partially to one class or another, state making actually reduces the protection given some classes.

War making, state making, protection, and extraction each take a number of forms. Extraction, for instance, ranges from outright plunder to regular tribute to bureaucratized taxation. Yet all four depend on the state's tendency to monopolize the concentrated means of coercion. From the perspectives of those who dominate the state, each of them – if carried on effectively – generally reinforces the others. Thus, a state that successfully eradicates its internal rivals strengthens its ability to extract resources, to wage war, and to protect its chief supporters. In the earlier European experience, broadly speaking, those supporters were typically landlords, armed retainers of the monarch, and churchmen.

Each of the major uses of violence produced characteristic forms of organization. War making yielded armies, navies, and supporting services. State making produced durable instruments of surveillance and control within the territory. Protection relied on the organization of war making and state making but added to it an apparatus by which the protected called forth the protection that was their due, notably through courts and representative assemblies. Extraction brought fiscal and accounting structures into being. The organization and deployment of violence themselves account for much of the characteristic structure of European states.

The general rule seems to have operated like this: The more costly the activity, all other things being equal, the greater was the organizational residue. To the extent, for example, that a given government invested in large standing armies – a very costly, if effective, means of war making –

the bureaucracy created to service the army was likely to become bulky. Furthermore, a government building a standing army while controlling a small population was likely to incur greater costs, and therefore to build a bulkier structure, than a government within a populous country. Branden-burg–Prussia was the classic case of high cost for available resources. The Prussian effort to build an army matching those of its larger Continental neighbors created an immense structure; it militarized and bureaucratized much of German social life.

In the case of extraction, the smaller the pool of resources and the less commercialized the economy, other things being equal, the more difficult was the work of extracting resources to sustain war and other governmental activities; hence, the more extensive was the fiscal apparatus. England illustrated the corollary of that proposition, with a relatively large and commercialized pool of resources drawn on by a relatively small fiscal apparatus. As Gabriel Ardant has argued, the choice of fiscal strategy probably made an additional difference. On the whole, taxes on land were expensive to collect as compared with taxes on trade, especially large flows of trade past easily controlled checkpoints. Its position astride the entrance to the Baltic gave Denmark an extraordinary opportunity to profit from customs revenues.

With respect to state making (in the narrow sense of eliminating or neutralizing the local rivals of the people who controlled the state), a territory populated by great landlords or by distinct religious groups generally imposed larger costs on a conqueror than one of fragmented power or homogeneous culture. This time, fragmented and homogeneous Sweden, with its relatively small but effective apparatus of control, illustrates the corollary.

Finally, the cost of protection (in the sense of eliminating or neutralizing the enemies of the state makers' clients) mounted with the range over which that protection extended. Portugal's effort to bar the Mediterranean to its merchants' competitors in the spice trade provides a textbook case of an unsuccessful protection effort that nonetheless built up a massive structure.

Thus, the sheer size of the government varied directly with the effort devoted to extraction, state making, protection, and, especially, war making but inversely with the commercialization of the economy and the extent of the resource base. What is more, the relative bulk of different features of the government varied with the cost/resource ratios of extraction, state making, protection, and war making. In Spain we see hypertrophy of Court and courts as the outcome of centuries of effort at subduing internal enemies, whereas in Holland we are amazed to see how small a fiscal apparatus grows up with high taxes within a rich, commercialized economy.

Clearly, war making, extraction, state making, and protection were interdependent. Speaking very, very generally, the classic European state-making experience followed this causal pattern:

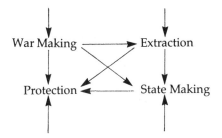

In an idealized sequence, a great lord made war so effectively as to become dominant in a substantial territory, but that war making led to increased extraction of the means of war – men, arms, food, lodging, transportation, supplies, and/or the money to buy them – from the population within that territory. The building up of war-making capacity likewise increased the capacity to extract. The very activity of extraction, if successful, entailed the elimination, neutralization, or cooptation of the great lord's local rivals; thus, it led to state making. As a by-product, it created organization in the form of tax-collection agencies, police forces, courts, exchequers, account keepers; thus it again led to state making. To a lesser extent, war making likewise led to state making through the expansion of military organization itself, as a standing army, war industries, supporting bureaucracies, and (rather later) schools grew up within the state apparatus. All of these structures checked potential rivals and opponents. In the course of making war, extracting resources, and building up the state apparatus, the managers of states formed alliances with specific social classes. The members of those classes loaned resources, provided technical services, or helped ensure the compliance of the rest of the population, all in return for a measure of protection against their own rivals and enemies. As a result of these multiple strategic choices, a distinctive state apparatus grew up within each major section of Europe.

How States Formed

This analysis, if correct, has two strong implications for the development of national states. First, popular resistance to war making and state making made a difference. When ordinary people resisted vigorously, authorities made concessions: guarantees of rights, representative institutions, courts of appeal. Those concessions, in their turn, constrained the later paths of war making and state making. To be sure, alliances with fragments of the ruling class greatly increased the effects of popular action; the broad mobilization of gentry against Charles I helped give the English Revolution of 1640 a far greater impact on political institutions than did any of the multiple rebellions during the Tudor era.

Second, the relative balance among war making, protection, extraction, and state making significantly affected the organization of the states that emerged from the four activities. To the extent that war making went on with relatively little extraction, protection, and state making, for example, military forces ended up playing a larger and more autonomous part in national politics. Spain is perhaps the best European example. To the extent that protection, as in Venice or Holland, prevailed over war making, extraction, and state making, oligarchies of the protected classes tended to dominate subsequent national politics. From the relative predominance of state making sprang the disproportionate elaboration of policing and surveillance; the Papal States illustrate that extreme. Before the twentieth century, the range of viable imbalances was fairly small. Any state that failed to put considerable effort into war making was likely to disappear. As the twentieth century wore on, however, it became increasingly common for one state to lend, give, or sell war-making means to another; in those cases, the recipient state could put a disproportionate effort into extraction, protection, and/or state making and yet survive. In our own time, clients of the United States and the Soviet Union provide numerous examples.

This simplified model, however, neglects the external relations that shaped every national state. Early in the process, the distinction between "internal" and "external" remained as unclear as the distinction between state power and the power accruing to lords allied with the state. Later, three interlocking influences connected any given national state to the European network of states. First, there were the flows of resources in the form of loans and supplies, especially loans and supplies devoted to war making. Second, there was the competition among states for hegemony in disputed territories, which stimulated war making and temporarily erased the distinctions among war making, state making, and extraction. Third, there was the intermittent creation of coalitions of states that temporarily combined their efforts to force a given state into a certain form and position within the international network. The war-making coalition is one example, but the peace-making coalition played an even more crucial part: From 1648, if not before, at the ends of wars all effective European states coalesced temporarily to bargain over the boundaries and rulers of the recent belligerents. From that point on, periods of major reorganization of the European state system came in spurts, at the settlement of widespread wars. From each large war, in general, emerged fewer national states than had entered it.

War as International Relations

In these circumstances, war became the normal condition of the international system of states and the normal means of defending or enhancing a position within the system. Why war? No simple answer will do; war as a potent means served more than one end. But surely part of the answer goes back to the central mechanisms of state making: The very logic by which a local lord extended or defended the perimeter within which he monopolized the means of violence, and thereby increased his return from tribute, continued on a larger scale into the logic of war. Early in the process, external and internal rivals overlapped to a large degree. Only the establishment of large perimeters of control within which great lords had checked their rivals sharpened the line between internal and external. George Modelski sums up the competitive logic cogently:

Global power . . . strengthened those states that attained it relatively to all other political and other organizations. What is more, other states competing in the global power game developed similar organizational forms and similar hardiness: they too became nation-states – in a defensive reaction, because forced to take issue with or to confront a global power, as France confronted Spain and later Britain, or in imitation of its obvious success and effectiveness, as Germany followed the example of Britain in Weltmacht, or as earlier Peter the Great had rebuilt Russia on Dutch precepts and examples. Thus not only Portugal, the Netherlands, Britain and the United States became nation-states, but also Spain, France, Germany, Russia and Japan. The short, and the most parsimonious, answer to the question of why these succeeded where "most of the European efforts to build states failed" is that they were either global powers or successfully fought with or against them.[12]

This logic of international state making acts out on a large scale the logic of local aggrandizement. The external complements the internal.

If we allow that fragile distinction between "internal" and "external" state-making processes, then we might schematize the history of European state making as three stages: (a) The differential success of some power holders in "external" struggles establishes the difference between an "internal" and an "external" arena for the deployment of force; (b) "external" competition generates "internal" state making; (c) "external" compacts among states influence the form and locus of particular states ever more powerfully. In this perspective, state-certifying organizations such as the League of Nations and the United Nations simply extended the European-based process to the world as a whole. Whether forced or voluntary, bloody or peaceful, decolonization simply completed that process by which existing states leagued to create new ones.

The extension of the Europe-based state-making process to the rest of the world, however, did not result in the creation of states in the strict European image. Broadly speaking, internal struggles such as the checking of great regional lords and the imposition of taxation on peasant villages produced important organizational features of European states: the relative subordination of military power to civilian control, the extensive bureaucracy of fiscal surveillance, the representation of wronged interests via petition and parliament. On the whole, states elsewhere developed differently. The most telling feature of that difference appears in military organization. European states built up their military apparatuses through sustained struggles with their subject populations and by means of selective extension of protection to different classes within those populations. The agreements on protection constrained the rulers themselves, making them vulnerable to courts, to assemblies, to withdrawals of credit, services, and expertise.

To a larger degree, states that have come into being recently through decolonization or through reallocations of territory by dominant states have acquired their military organization from outside, without the same internal forging of mutual constraints between rulers and ruled. To the extent that outside states continue to supply military goods and expertise in return for commodities, military alliance or both, the new states harbor powerful, unconstrained organizations that easily overshadow all other organizations within their territories. To the extent that outside states guarantee their boundaries, the managers of those military organizations exercise extraordinary power within them. The advantages of military power become enormous, the incentives to seize power over the state as a whole by means of that advantage very strong. Despite the great place that war making occupied in the making of European states, the old national states of Europe almost never experienced the great disproportion between military organization and all other forms of organization that seems the fate of client states throughout the contemporary world. A century ago, Europeans might have congratulated themselves on the spread of civil government throughout the world. In our own time, the analogy between war making and state making, on the one hand, and organized crime, on the other, is becoming tragically apt.

Notes

1. Arthur L. Stinchcombe, *Constructing Social Theories* (New York: Harcourt, Brace & World, 1968), p. 150; italics in the original.
2. Fernand Braudel, *La Méditerranée et le monde méditerranéen à l'époque de Philippe II* (Paris: Armand Colin, 1966), vol. 2, pp. 88–89.
3. Lawrence Stone, *The Crisis of the Aristocracy* (Oxford: Clarendon Press, 1965), p. 200.
4. Dietrich Gerhard, *Old Europe: A Study of Continuity, 1000–1800* (New York: Academic Press, 1981), pp. 124–25.
5. Jan de Vries, *The Economy of Europe in an Age of Crisis, 1600–1750* (Cambridge: Cambridge University Press, 1976).
6. V. G. Kiernan, *State and Society in Europe, 1550–1650* (Oxford: Blackwell, 1980), p. 104. For French finances, see Alain Guery, "Les Finances de la Monarchie Française sous l'Ancien Regime," *Annales Economies, Sociétés, Civilisations* 33 (1978), p. 227.
7. Earl J. Hamilton, "Origin and Growth of the National Debt in France and England," in *Studi in onore di Gino Luzzato* (Milan: Giuffre, 1950), vol. 2, p. 254.
8. Ibid., pp. 247, 249.
9. Ibid., p. 254.
10. G. R. Elton, "Taxation for War and Peace in Early-Tudor England," in *War and Economic Development: Essays in Memory of David Joslin*, ed. J. M. Winter (Cambridge: Cambridge University Press, 1975), p. 42.

11. Peter Mathias, *The Transformation of England: Essays in the Economic and Social History of England in the Eighteenth Century* (New York: Oxford University Press, 1979), p. 122.
12. George Modelski, "The Long Cycle of Global Politics and the Nation State," *Comparative Studies in Society and History* 20 (1978): 231.

Bibliography

Ames, Edward, and Richard T. Rapp. "The Birth and Death of Taxes: A Hypothesis." *Journal of Economic History* 37 (1977): 161–78.

Ardent, Gabriel. "Financial Policy and Economic Infrastructure of Modern States and Nations." In *The Formation of National States in Western Europe,* edited by Charles Tilly. Princeton, N.J.: Princeton University Press, 1975.

Badie, Bertrand. *Le développement politique.* 2nd ed. Paris: Economica, 1980.

Badie, Bertrand, and Pierre Birnbaum. *Sociologie de l'Etat.* Paris: Bernard Grasset, 1979.

Bayard, Francoise. "Fermes et traités en France dans la premiere moitié du XVIIe siècle (premiere esquisse 1631–1653)." *Bulletin du Centre d'Histoire, Economique et Sociale de la Region Lyonnaise,* no. 1 (1976): 45–80.

Bean, Richard. "War and the Birth of the Nation State." *Journal of Economic History* 33 (1973): 203–21.

Blockmans, W. P. "A Typology of Representative Institutions in Late Medieval Europe." *Journal of Medieval History* 4 (1978): 189–215.

Blok, Anton. *The Mafia of a Sicilian Village, 1860–1960: A Study of Violent Peasant Entrepreneurs.* Oxford: Blackwell, 1974.

Booney, Richard. *Political Change under Richelieu and Mazarin, 1624–1661.* Oxford: Oxford University Press, 1978.

Braudel, Fernand. *La Méditerranée et le monde méditerranéen à l'époque de Philippe II.* 2d ed. 2 vols. Paris: Armand Colin, 1966.
Civilisation materielle, économie, et capitalisme, XVe–XVIIIe siècle. 3 vols. Paris: Armand Colin, 1979.

Braun, Rudolf. "Taxation, Sociopolitical Structure, and State-Building: Great Britain and Brandenburg-Prussia." In *The Formation of National States in Western Europe,* edited by Charles Tilly. Princeton, N.J.: Princeton University Press, 1975.
"Steuern und Staatsfinanzierung als Modernisierungsfaktoren: Ein deutsch-englischer Vergleich." In *Studien zum Beginn der modernen Welt,* edited by Reinhard Koselleck. Stuttgart: Klett-Cotta, 1977.

Carneiro, Robert. "Political Expansion as an Expression of the Principle of Competitive Exclusion." In *Origins of the State,* edited by Ronald Cohen and Elman R. Service. Philadelphia: Institute for the Study of Human Issues, 1978.

Carsten, F. L. *The Origins of Prussia.* Oxford: Clarendon Press, 1954.

Chapman, Brian. *Police State.* London: Pall Mall, 1970.

Cipolla, Carlo M. *Guns, Sails, and Empires: Technological Innovation and the Early Phases of European Expansion 1400–1700.* New York: Pantheon Press, 1965.

Clark, Sir George. "The Social Foundations of States." In *The New Cambridge Modern History,* vol. 5, *The Ascendancy of France, 1648–88,* edited by F. L. Carsten. Cambridge: Cambridge University Press, 1969.

Cooper, J. P. "Differences between English and Continental Governments in the Early Seventeenth Century." In *Britain and the Netherlands,* edited by J. S. Bromley and E. H. Kossmann. London: Chatto & Windus, 1960.

"General Introduction." In *The New Cambridge Modern History*, vol. 4, *The Decline of Spain and Thirty Years War, 1609–58/59*, edited by J. P. Cooper. Cambridge: Cambridge University Press, 1970.

Davis, Lance E. "It's a Long, Long Road to Tipperary, or Reflections on Organized Violence, Protection Rates, and Related Topics: The New Political History." *Journal of Economic History* 40 (1980): 1–16.

Dent, Julian. *Crisis in Finance: Crown, Financiers, and Society in Seventeenth-Century France*. Newton Abbot, United Kingdom: David & Charles, 1973.

Dickson, P. G. M. *The Financial Revolution in England: A Study in the Development of Public Credit, 1688–1756*. London: St. Martin's Press, 1967.

Elton, G. R. "Taxation for War and Peace in Early-Tudor England." In *War and Economic Development: Essays in Memory of David Joslin*, edited by J. M. Winter. Cambridge: Cambridge University Press, 1975.

Finer, Samuel E. "State-building, State Boundaries, and Border Control." *Social Science Information* 13 (1974): 79–126.

"State- and Nation-Building in Europe: The Role of the Military." In *The Formation of National States in Western Europe*, edited by Charles Tilly. Princeton, N.J.: Princeton University Press, 1975.

Fueter, Edward. *Geschichte des europäischen Staatensystems von 1492–1559*. Munich: Oldenbourg, 1919.

Gerhard, Dietrich. *Old Europe: A Study of Continuity, 1000–1800*. New York: Academic Press, 1981.

Gooch, John, *Armies in Europe*. London: Routledge & Kegan Paul, 1980.

Guenee, Bernard. "Y a-t-il un Etat des XIVe et XVe siècles?" *Annales Economies, Societes, Civilisations* 36 (1981): 399–406.

Guery, Alain. "Les finances de la monarchie francaise sous l'Ancien Regime, *Annales Economies, Sociétés, Civilisations* 33 (1978), 216–39.

Hale, J. R. "Armies, Navies, and the Art of War." In *The New Cambridge Modern History, vol. 2, The Reformation 1520–1559*, edited by G. R. Elton. Cambridge: Cambridge University Press, 1968.

"Armies, Navies, and the Art of War" (sic). In *The New Cambridge Modern History, vol. 3, The Counter-Reformation and Price Revolution, 1559–1610*, edited by R. B. Wernham. Cambridge: Cambridge University Press, 1968.

Hamilton, Earl J. "Origin and Growth of the National Debt in France and England." In *Studi in onore di Gino Luzzato*, vol. 2. Milan: Giuffre, 1950.

Harding, Robert R. *Anatomy of a Power Elite: The Provincial Governors of Early Modern France*. New Haven, Conn.: Yale University Press, 1978.

Hechter, Michael, and William Brustein. "Regional Modes of Production and Patterns of State Formation in Western Europe." *American Journal of Sociology* 85 (1980): 1061–94.

Hintze, Otto. *Staat and Verfassung: Gesammelte Abhandlungen zur allgemeinen Verfassungsgeschichte*. Edited by Gerhard Oestreich. Gottingen:Vandenhoeck & Ruprecht, 1962; originally 1910.

Howard, Michael. *War in European History*. Oxford: Oxford University Press, 1976.

James, M. E. *Change and Continuity in the Tudor North: The Rise of Thomas First Lord Wharton*. Borthwick Papers no. 27. York: St. Anthony's Press, 1965.

"The First Earl of Cumberland (1493–1542) and the Decline of Northern Feudalism." *Northern History* 1 (1966): 43–69.

"The Concept of Order and the Northern Rising, 1569." *Past and Present* 60 (1973): 49–83.

John, A. H. "Wars and the British Economy, 1700–1763." *Economic History Review,* 2d ser., 7 (1955): 329–44.

Kiernan, V. G. "Conscription and Society in Europe before the War of 1914–18." In *War and Society: Historical Essays in Honour and Memory of J. R. Western, 1928–1971,* edited by M. R. D. Foot. London: Elek Books, 1973.

State and Society in Europe, 1550–1650. Oxford: Blackwell, 1980.

van Klaveren, Jacob. "Die historische Erscheinung der Korruption." *Vierteljahrschrift für Sozial- und Wirtschaftsgeschichte* 44 (1957): 289–324.

"Fiskalismus – Merkantilismus – Korruption: Drei Aspekte der Finanz- und Wirtschaftspolitik während des Ancien Regime." *Vierteljahrschrift für Sozial- und Wirtschaftsgeschichte* 47 (1960): 333–53.

Ladero Quesado, Miguel Angel. "Les finances royales de Castille a la veille des temps modernes." *Annales Economies, Sociétés, Civilisations* 25 (1970): 775–88.

Lane, Frederic C. "Force and Enterprise in the Creation of Oceanic Commerce." In *The Tasks of Economic History* (Supplemental issue of the *Journal of Economic History* 10 [1950]), pp. 19–31.

"Economic Consequences of Organized Violence." *Journal of Economic History* 18 (1958): 401–17.

"The Economic Meaning of War and Protection." In *Venice and History: The Collected Papers of Frederic C. Lane.* Baltimore, Md.: Johns Hopkins University Press, 1966; originally 1942.

"The Role of Government in Economic Growth in Early Modern Times." *Journal of Economic History* 35 (1975): 8–17; with comment by Douglass C. North and Robert Paul Thomas, pp. 18–19.

Levi, Margaret. "The Predatory Theory of Rule." In *The Microfoundations of Macrosociology,* edited by Michael Hechter. Philadelphia: Temple University Press, 1983.

Ludtke, Alf. "Genesis und Durchsetzung des modernen Staates: Zur Analyse von Herrschaft und Verwaltung." *Archiv für Sozialgeschichte* 20 (1980): 470–91.

Lyons, G. M. "Exigences militaires et budgets militaires aux U.S.A." *Revue Francaise de Sociologie* 2 (1961): 66–74.

Mathias, Peter. "Taxation and Industrialization in Britain, 1700–1870." In *The Transformation of England: Essays in the Economic and Social History of England in the Eighteenth Century,* edited by Peter Mathias. New York: Oxford University Press, 1979.

Michaud, Claude. "Finances et guerres de religion en France." *Revue d'Histoire Moderne et Contemporaine* 28 (1981): 572–96.

Modelski, George. "The Long Cycle of Global Politics and the Nation-State." *Comparative Studies in Society and History* 20 (1978): 214–35.

Nef, John U. *War and Human Progress: An Essay on the Rise of Industrial Civilization.* Cambridge: Harvard University Press, 1952.

Industry and Government in France and England, 1540–1640. Ithaca, N.Y.: Cornell University Press, 1965; originally 1940.

North, Douglass C., and Robert Paul Thomas, *The Rise of the Western World: A New Economic History.* Cambridge: Cambridge University Press, 1973.

O'Donnell, Guillermo. "Comparative Historical Formations of the State Apparatus and Socio-economic Change in the Third World." *International Social Science Journal* 32 (1980): 717–29.

Parker, Geoffrey. *The Army of Flanders and the Spanish Road 1567–1659*. Cambridge: Cambridge University Press, 1972.

Peacock, Alan T., and Jack Wiseman. *The Growth of Public Expenditure in the United Kingdom*. Princeton, N.J.: Princeton University Press, 1961.

Poggi, Gianfranco. *The Development of the Modern State: A Sociological Introduction*. Stanford, Calif.: Stanford University Press, 1978.

Polisensky, Josef V. *War and Society in Europe, 1618–1648*. Cambridge: Cambridge University Press, 1978.

Pounds, Norman J. G., and Sue Simons Ball. "Core-Areas and the Development of the European States System." *Annals of the Association of American Geographers* 54 (1964): 24–40.

Ramsey, G. D. *The City of London in International Politics at the Accession of Elizabeth Tudor*. Manchester: Manchester University Press, 1975.

Redlich, Fritz. *The German Military Enterpriser and His Work Force*. 2 vols. Wiesbaden: Steiner, 1964–65. *Vierteljahrschrift für Sozial- und Wirtschaftsgeschichte*, Beiheften 47, 48.

Riemersma, Jelle C. "Government Influence on Company Organization in Holland and England (1550–1650)." *The Tasks of Economic History* (Supplemental issue of the *Journal of Economic History* 10 [1950]), pp. 31–39.

Romano, Salvatore Francesco. *Storia della mafia*. Milan: Sugar, 1963.

Rosenberg, Hans. *Bureaucracy, Aristocracy and Autocracy: The Prussian Experience, 1660–1815*. Cambridge: Harvard University Press, 1958.

Russett, Bruce M. *What Price Vigilance? The Burdens of National Defense*. New Haven, Conn.: Yale University Press, 1970.

Schelling, Thomas C. "Economics and Criminal Enterprise." *The Public Interest* 7 (1967): 61–78.

Steensgaard, Niels. *The Asian Trade Revolution of the Seventeenth Century: The East India Companies and the Decline of the Caravan Trades*. Chicago: University of Chicago Press, 1974.

Stein, Arthur A., and Bruce M. Russett. "Evaluating War: Outcomes and Consequences." In *Handbook of Political Conflict: Theory and Research*, edited by Ted Robert Gurr. New York: Free Press, 1980.

Stinchcombe, Arthur L. *Constructing Social Theories*. New York: Harcourt, Brace & World, 1968.

Stone, Lawrence. "State Control in Sixteenth-Century England." *Economic History Review* 17 (1947): 103–20.

The Crisis of the Aristocracy, 1558–1641. Oxford: Clarendon Press, 1965.

Tenenti, Alberto. *Piracy and the Decline of Venice, 1580–1615*. Berkeley: University of California Press, 1967.

Torsvik, Per, ed. *Mobilization, Center-Periphery Structures and Nation-Building: A Volume in Commemoration of Stein Rokkan*. Bergen: Universitetsforlaget, 1981.

de Vries, Jan. "On the Modernity of the Dutch Republic." *Journal of Economic History* 33 (1973): 191–202.

The Economy of Europe in an Age of Crisis, 1600–1750. Cambridge: Cambridge University Press, 1976.

"Barges and Capitalism: Passenger Transportation in the Dutch Economy, 1632–1839," *A.A.G. Bifdragen* 21 (1978): 33–398.

Wijn, J. W. "Military Forces and Warfare 1610–48." In *The New Cambridge Modern History*, vol. 4, *The Decline of Spain and the Thirty Years War 1609–58/59*, edited by J. P. Cooper. Cambridge: Cambridge University Press, 1970.

Williams, Penry. "Rebellion and Revolution in Early Modern England." In *War and Society: Historical Essays in Honour and Memory of J. R. Western, 1928–1971*, edited by M. R. D. Foot. London: Elek Books, 1973.

Wolfe, Martin. *The Fiscal System of Renaissance France.* New Haven, Conn.: Yale University Press, 1972.

Zolberg, Aristide R. "Strategic Interactions and the Formation of Modern States: France and England." *International Social Science Journal* 32 (1980): 687–716.

6. Transnational Linkages and the Economic Role of the State: An Analysis of Developing and Industrialized Nations in the Post–World War II Period

Peter B. Evans

As J. P. Nettl reminded us in his pioneering essay on the state, regulating relations with the external world is the classic locus of state power.[1] States as institutions have always had to look outward as well as inward, not just because success in political and military competition with other states has been a prime requisite of survival, but also because markets have always been transnational. In the contemporary period the transnational character of economic activity has become much more pervasive.

The increasing role of transnational flows of goods and capital has been a universal feature of postwar economic growth for all countries that participate in the capitalist world system. In the poorest countries, development has meant shifting from relatively autarkic subsistence production to the export of primary commodities into international markets. For industrializing Third World countries, the achievement of an increasingly differentiated domestic economy has meant, first, the increasing domination of leading industrial sectors by transnational corporations (TNCs) and, more recently, an ever-heavier reliance on international finance capital. In center countries, such as the United States, leading industrial and financial corporations derive an increasing proportion of their profits from foreign activities, and the productive investment undertaken by these corporations is increasingly foreign rather than domestic.

Over the past twenty years, all categories of countries have seen an increase in the share of production and consumption that is devoted to international trade. Trade as a percentage of gross domestic product (GDP) increased 50 percent for industrial market economies and for the poorest Third World countries. For the United States it almost doubled.[2] International flows of capital also increased relative to the growth of production within nation states. In the case of the United States, for example, outflows of direct investment increased their share of GDP by two-thirds, while inflows of direct investment from other countries quadrupled as a percentage of GDP.[3] Flows of loan capital increased most rapidly of all, outpacing trade and direct foreign investment. This was especially true of the most transnational of all capital markets, the Eurocurrency markets.

As markets become increasingly transnational, how does this affect the economic role of the state? The obvious hypothesis is that the state as an economic actor becomes an anachronism. As the scope and importance of private transnational actors grow, state apparatuses, the legitimate jurisdictions of which are geographically limited, are correspondingly weakened. Adherents of this view can be found both among proponents of transnational corporate power, such as George Ball,[4] and among critics of the transnationals, such as Barnet and Müller.[5]

For those whose vantage on the transnational economy comes via the dependency approach or a world system perspective, a different hypothesis is likely to seem more plausible. The consequences of intensified transnational interchange depend on a state's position in the world system. The power of transnational actors based in core states enhances the power of those states. Increased transnational flows weaken peripheral states while simultaneously strengthening core states. Both trade relations and capital flows are asymmetrical, shifting surplus to the core and undermining the resource base of peripheral states. Both favor peripheral elites whose interests lie with weak rather than strong state bureaucracies.

A third possibility, that the growing importance of transnational flows might somehow increase the salience of state apparatuses as economic actors in both center and periphery, lacks the same prominence as the others in the literature; yet there is some basis for arguing that recent decades have been characterized, not just by an increase in the importance of transnational economic flows, but also by a simultaneous increase in the role of state machineries. During the post–World War II period, the share of government revenues in national incomes has grown, not just in the center, as a dependency or world system perspective might predict, but in both center and periphery.[6] Transnationalization and the growth of state machineries might be, of course, concomitant but independent trends. Nonetheless, such concomitant development suggests the possibility of a direct rather than an inverse relation between the expansion of the state's economic role and the increasing pervasiveness of transnational linkages.

In this essay, a fourth, even more extreme logical possibility will be the focus. I shall argue that an intensification of transnational economic linkages tends to be associated with an expansion of the state's role in a range of developing countries (though emphatically not all) and that such intensification has a dampening effect on the expansion of the state's role in those core countries that become major capital exporters (especially centers of international finance capital). This position is not taken simply for purposes of provocation; considerable evidence can be marshaled in its support. More important, its exploration will provide an opportunity for concrete consideration of the blend of positive and negative effects that transnational linkages have had on the expansion of the state's role in developing and advanced industrial countries.

The expansion of the state's economic role will be considered primarily in terms of increasing capacity to exert control over local economic resources. This means that organizational capacity and the relative power of the state vis-à-vis private domestic elites is the focus rather than the state's overall ability to realize its economic goals. Nonetheless, disjunctions between state capacity in the larger sense of ability to realize goals and the expansion of the state's economic role will be a recurring theme.

Working from the literature on transnational linkages and the state forces a separate treatment of peripheral- and core-country states, at least initially. There is a strong tradition of research on Third World states and the consequences of dependency in the periphery, and there is a substantial amount of literature on the consequences of international economic ties for advanced capitalist states, but the two literatures remain distinct. Highlighting some of the parallels between them and thereby pointing to the possibility of their integration should be one of the by-products of this chapter, but they must be dealt with in their own terms first.

In the discussion of peripheral states the effects of trade, direct investments in extractive ventures, manufacturing investments, and foreign debt will be examined in turn. In the treatment of core countries, the distinction between capital exporters and nations for which trade and inflows of capital were the most important kinds of transnational linkages is primary. Although the discussion is predominantly "economistic" throughout, it will require at various points consideration of the interaction between transnational economic interests and geopolitical goals, especially the geopolitical goals of core states.

Transnational Linkages and Third World States

Transnational factors have always been central to arguments about the nature and capacity of Third World states. Once drawn into the world capitalist system, countries of the periphery were forced by the rudimentary development of their internal productive apparatuses into positions of acute dependence on internationalized markets. External economic dependency was reinforced by the cultural and political impact of colonialism and by the military inferiority of peripheral states relative to core states. Along with foreign owners of mines and plantations, the dominant elites that controlled or confronted the state apparatuses of Third World countries included compradore merchants and agrarian exporters. Their economic fortunes depended primarily on preserving open channels to international markets, not in transforming the structure of the local economy. Once Third World economies achieve a measure of industrialization, the most dynamic sectors of industry are dominated by TNCs, the interests in global profitability of which must often run counter to the logic of local accumulation.

That state apparatuses in Third World countries are constrained by transnational linkages in ways that undermine their ability to promote domestic accumulation is incontrovertible. Nonetheless, the challenges of dealing with transnational linkages in general and contests with transnational capital in particular may, under certain circumstances, stimulate the development of new state capacities and may legitimate the expansion of the state's role into areas that would otherwise be the preserve of private capital. Furthermore, transnational capital may, under certain circumstances, prefer dealing with a "stronger," more bureaucratically capable state apparatus.

Dealing seriously with the expansionary effects of transnational linkages on the economic role of the state in a way that clarifies rather than denies the fact that the transnationalization of local economic activities constrains the ability of the state to realize its economic objectives is the aim. Achieving it requires a careful look at the effects of different kinds of linkages in different times and countries.

Effects of Trade

Heavy reliance on trade, whatever the economic gains from trade may be, leaves a society vulnerable to the vicissitudes of economic interactions that lie outside the jurisdiction of the state and are therefore in principle beyond its capacity to control. In this rudimentary sense, reliance on trade will always place limits on the state's capacity to effect economic outcomes. Analysts of peripheral states, at least since the pioneering work of Prebisch, have considered the problem to be compounded by the nature of the goods these states import and export. Somewhat independent of the question of the economic costs of unequal exchange, however, is the issue of how the capacity of the state is affected. The evidence here is ambiguous.

Trade concentrated on a particular partner does appear to be associated with a lack of ability to extract revenues on the part of the state apparatus.[7] When monopolistic trade patterns come together with political control, formal or informal, by the dominant trading partner, the possibilities of effective state action grow even dimmer. The classic cases of developmentally ineffectual colonial administrations fall into this category, as do the more flagrant examples of U.S. neocolonialism in Latin America.[8] Hirschman's account of Nazi attempts to use monopolistic trading patterns as a means of generating neocolonial relations with the smaller states of Southern and Eastern Europe points to the same sort of relation.[9] The relative weight of trade in itself, however, does not seem to have any clear-cut negative effects on state capacity. Crude tests such as correlating trade as a proportion of gross national product (GNP) with state capacity as measured by government revenues in relation to GDP fail to reveal any consistent negative effects.[10]

A systematic analysis of the consequences of trade for Third World states

would require examining a diversity of cases: primary products and manufactured products, states with high and low partner and commodity concentration, and so on. I shall offer here only a single illustration designed
to undercut the assumption that heavy reliance on a single product, sold
in large part to a single customer, will work in the direction of producing
or sustaining a supine compradore state.

Stephen Krasner's study of the role of the Brazilian state in regulating
the coffee trade during the first half of the century provides the illustration.[11] Krasner shows that, despite a combination of partner and commodity concentration, Brazil was able to manipulate the world coffee market in
such a way as to increase export earnings and diminish their fluctuation.
The ability of the state to intervene in this market internationally stood in
contrast to its inability to control the behavior of local producers and had
important Keynesian consequences for the maintenance of aggregate demand during the 1930s.[12]

The reliance of local agrarian elites on an international market the vagaries of which they could not control forced them to recognize the importance of having a state apparatus willing and able to deal with the problem
of regulating prices. Thus, Brazilian coffee planters accepted state support early in the twentieth century and abandoned a classically liberal,
noninterventionist regime at a critical juncture (the revolution of 1930)
in large part because they did not consider this regime to be willing and
able to defend their economic interests.[13] Such support for a more active
state apparatus depends somewhat on the particularities of the crop and
nature of the international market, but it still stands in contrast to
the behavior of more domestically oriented agrarian elites in relation to the
state.[14]

The ability of the Brazilian state to intervene in the coffee trade depended in part, of course, on the politically motivated willingness of the
U.S. state to collaborate at the expense of American consumers. Had the
price of coffee domestically been of greater political importance to the U.S.
government or had the United States been less inclined for geopolitical
reasons to support Brazilian efforts, the international coffee agreements
that were the keystone of attempts to regulate international prices would
not have been possible. More important, Brazil's ability to circumvent the
logic of the international market was strictly limited. The precipitous fall of
the price of coffee at the beginning of the Great Depression, the stagnation
of demand throughout the twentieth century, and the gradual encroachment of other countries into a market that had been a Brazilian preserve
are all reminders of the limits imposed on the state's capacity in the area of
trade.

Coffee is a useful case for examining the effects of trade because it does
not involve foreign ownership of local productive facilities. For most products and countries, the effects of reliance on international markets must be
treated jointly with the effects of reliance on foreign capital. Indeed, it is in
relation to the consequences of transnational extractive investments that

the most extensive literature on transnational linkages and the state has been produced.

Transnational Corporations and the State in Extractive Industries

Foreign direct investment in extractive industries is the archetypal basis for classic dependence of the type described by Paul Baran. Operating in an enclave, affected by development of the local market only insofar as development makes local labor more expensive, the extractive investor would seem to have every reason to prefer a state with capacities that are limited to the ability to maintain law and order. Yet quantitative cross-national data suggest a positive relationship between the share of government revenues in the national income and the share of the extractive sector.[15] Historical case studies suggest the same relationship. In country after country, intensive penetration of local economies by such transnational actors has, with increasingly shorter lags, been followed by the rise of state apparatuses that not only gain control over local extractive activities, but in certain cases become the dominant actors in the local economy overall.

The sequence is familiar and does not need to be reiterated in detail. The bargain over the appropriate distribution of the returns from an extractive investment tends to "obsolesce" once the initial capital has been invested. Given the relatively stable technology in most extractive industries, local production operations have a diminishing need for the inputs of the transnational firm once the initial costs are sunk. Thus, the state is in a position to increase its share of the resources generated and demand a greater share of control over the local operation.[16] Hirschman has been sufficiently impressed by the differential ability of Third World states to tax foreign-owned export enclaves to suggest that such industries create a "fiscal linkage" analogous to the "backward" and "forward" linkages created by other industries.[17] In addition, having transnational actors sitting astride key sources of government revenue and foreign exchange also has an organizational impact on the state apparatus. Even the least aggressive regimes cannot avoid the need to set up bureaucracies that at least monitor the activities of transnational firms.

The experience of peripheral countries engaged in the most transnational of all extractive industries, oil, is strongly suggestive. Tugwell documents well for Venezuela the way in which the unvoidable necessity of monitoring the activities of the international oil companies gradually produced a state apparatus with the bureaucratic capacity to operate the petroleum industry for itself, albeit with the continued profitable collaboration of the TNCs.[18] A similar progression from state passivity and transnational appropriation of the surplus, through rising state shares in the returns, to nationalization and state ownership has repeated itself in the Middle East and North Africa.[19] Where the sequence was more abrupt, as in Mexico, the resulting juridical and organizational control of local production by the state was even more clear-cut.[20]

The sequence is best documented in mining. Moran's classic study of copper in Chile is a fine example. It shows how organizational development may occur even in the context of politics oriented almost completely toward accommodating the TNCs. Chile's 1955 "Nuevo Trato" legislation, otherwise a model of state passivity in the face of transnational economic power, contained provision for the establishment of a Copper Department to monitor the activities of industry.[21] This, in turn, became the training ground for the state managers who would eventually make it feasible for Chile to take over ownership of the industry.

More recently, Becker has provided an excellent study of a variation on the sequence in Peruvian copper mining.[22] Here, the Peruvians avoided nationalization in the case of one major TNC (ASARCO), but the overall outcome was still expansion of the state's role. Giant state-owned enterprises became major actors in the industry. Substantial technocratic capacity in the mining industry was incorporated into the state apparatus, and instead of being the "great absent member" of the industry the state became a central participant.

Involvement in extractive activities leads in turn to state involvement in other activities. Just as the development of bureaucratic monitoring agencies within the state apparatus prepares the way for the creation of state-owned enterprises, these enterprises once created in the extractive sector tend to move with an entrepreneurial logic of their own into industrial activities. In states where ideological and domestic political constraints are also lacking, extractive activities may provide the basis for a fully "statist" economy. In Algeria, for example, the state makes over 90 percent of the country's industrial investments and controls almost as large a proportion of the country's industrial assets.[23] Even where the ideological predilections of dominant political elites are less oriented toward intervention, there is an organizational logic that pushes the effects of extractive initiatives in the direction of industrial activity.

Forward linkages are the first and most obvious target of the state's industrial initiative, as, for example, in MineroPeru's highly profitable copper refining project.[24] In many instances, however, forward integration goes far beyond the requirements of refining the locally extracted raw materials. The highly developed petrochemical empires of Brazil and Mexico's state-owned oil companies (Petrobras and PEMEX) are an example.[25] The recent petrochemical initiatives of state-owned oil producers in the Middle East confirms the generality of the trend.[26] Eventually, the entrepreneurial endeavors of extractive state enterprises may even go beyond the elaboration of downstream products. Brazil's iron mining giant, the Companhia Vale do Rio Doce, for example, has become involved in other extractive industries (e.g., paper products) and in a range of diversified manufacturing and service activities, including fertilizer production, railway construction, consulting, and engineering.[27]

The rise of state-owned enterprises in extractive industries is an incontrovertible fact. In Raymond Vernon's succinct summary,

In the past thirty years, state-owned enterprises have taken a commanding position in the international oil industry, as well as in all the major branches of mining, including bauxite, iron ore, copper and the lesser ores.[28]

The question is not whether the state's role has expanded; it is whether this expansion can be attributed to the prior presence of transnational linkages. Obviously, there are technical and economic characteristics of extractive industries that facilitate and encourage state intervention.[29] At the same time, there are at least three reasons for arguing that prior transnational corporate control increases the probability of state entry.

First, there is the obvious fact that nationalism may provide the only effective counterargument to accusations of "statism." State takeovers of TNCs must be, and have been repeatedly, supported by groups strongly in favor of "private enterprise." In Chile, for example, the conservative Nationalist party backed the takeover of Anaconda while at the same time strongly affirming its opposition to *estatismo*.[30] In Jamaica, the Manley regime's moves against the bauxite TNCs were its most successful initiatives, in part because there was strong private sector support for the project.[31] The Peruvian military regime not only refrained completely from entering those sectors of mining in which local capital was strong, but also undertook to strengthen private local capital in the sector.[32]

Second, "nationalism" is more than an ideological gloss that serves to draw conservative support for state expansion. On certain important issues the structurally defined interests of the TNCs conflict with those of a "developmentalist" state in ways that those of a local capitalist would not. The behavior of TNCs stands in the way of developmentalist goals, not always and everywhere, but in certain key instances that provide critical ammunition for those arguing that the state must move in. The most common examples are failure to pursue aggressively possibilities for forward integration locally and using returns generated locally for expansion elsewhere. Kennecott's utilization of profits generated in part by Chile's generous tax provisions to construct a refinery in Maryland that could be used for refining Chilean copper is only the most blatant example.[33] Even more cooperative TNCs have proved resistant to forward integration.[34] Thus, extractive TNCs may force a "developmentalist" elite to become "statist" in order to pursue its developmental goals.

A third, more paradoxical connection between transnational linkages and state entry into extractive industries is fostered by a different set of transnational corporate preferences. Given a global political climate in which unencumbered control over Third World resources in not attainable, TNCs may, Baran's arguments notwithstanding, actually develop a vested interest in the emergence of a more bureaucratically capable, entrepreneurially oriented state apparatus. Becker argues, for example, that modern resource TNCs prefer "a more knowledgeable and competent host state –

one administered by persons who understand the national interest in resource exploitation, write it into access agreements, and see to it that those agreements are observed over time."[35] Both conflicts with TNCs and alliances with them create a connection between transnational control of extractive resources and subsequent state participation in the sector.

The outcome and even the possibility of both conflicts and alliances depend, of course, on the character of the state itself. The nature of the state's political base, for example, is fundamental in determining when a given transnational intrusion will become the occasion for expansion of the state's role. Although even the most conservative regimes (e.g., Saudi Arabia) may be eventually stimulated to take over transnationally controlled extractive industires, the fact remains that, from Cardenas in Mexico to Mossadegh in Iran to Vellasco in Peru and Manley in Jamaica, regimes that have some degree of autonomy from dominant local classes are more likely to take initiatives.[36]

Expansion of the state's role is not synonymous with enhanced capacity. Ineffective intervention, corruption, and capture by other social actors are all possible results of the expansion of the state's role. Nonetheless, there are also plausible links between the challenge of extractive TNCs and the enhancement of state capacity. First of all, it should be clear that there is a positive interaction between state capacity in the sense of the construction of a competent bureaucratic apparatus and the expansion of the state's role. An initial level of bureaucratic competence is a prerequisite of successful negotiation with TNCs, and the challenges of negotiating and later managing extractive industries in turn stimulate further expansion of the state's capacity as a bureaucratic apparatus.

There is also a clear connection between the extractive sequence we have described and the power of the state vis-à-vis the local bourgeoisie. Initial transnational control of primary production increases the likelihood that national control, to the degree that it is achieved, will gravitate into the hands of the state apparatus, bypassing dispersion of control into the hands of private national owners. Insofar as this primary production is central to the overall process of local accumulation, the local bourgeoisie must therefore work through and with the state in order to attain its ends. In short, contests with transnational capital are likely to leave the state with enhanced capacity to shape the conditions under which local capital makes its profits.

Capacity in the sense of increased power vis-à-vis the TNCs themselves is more difficult to judge. In some respects the leverage of the state apparatus is obvious. Third World states have won a share of juridical control and rights to equity returns of property that were previously the exclusive domain of transnational capital, but the expansion of the state's role has not meant the exclusion of transnational capital. At the local level TNCs remain involved as joint-venture partners or retain effective managerial control on the basis of management contracts. If their freedom of action and share of the returns have been reduced, their risks have been even more substantially reduced. Internationally, their power remains largely unchallenged. If Third World states have increased their power, the extent to which this increase has been at the expense of the TNCs remains ambiguous at best.

Still more problematic is the connection between the expansion of the state's role and increased capacity in the sense of increased ability to realize national economic goals. There is some evidence that speaks for a positive answer. At least some of the states that have become more directly involved in extractive industries have, in addition to expanding their own revenues, succeeded in expanding local output.[37] Likewise, as has already been noted, state initiatives have been crucial in promoting forward integration. But state intervention has not necessarily enhanced the ability of Third World exporters to maximize returns from participation in global markets.

In 1974 Moran warned that state-owned mineral exporters ran the risk of becoming marginalized producers in an international oligopoly that was weaker and more unstable precisely because of their presence.[38] More recent analyses suggest that this is precisely what has happened.[39] State-owned enterprises are almost by definition less vertically integrated internationally than TNCs. It is also more difficult for them to restrict output, either individually or in concert. In the extreme, it might be argued that Third World states are even farther from achieving the goal of stable international markets for their mineral markets than they were when TNCs dominated local production.

This last thesis should not be overstated. Much of the negative assessment of the ability of state-owned producers to deal with international markets is based on observations of very difficult current internationnal economic situations. There is good reason to believe that state-owned producers would benefit disproportionately from tighter minerals markets. In addition, not all state-owned mineral exporters are in the dire straits of state-owned copper mines in Zambia and Zaire (the most common examples). Finally, some of the apparent disadvantages of state actors may be overcome by further organizational learning rather than being inherent in state ownership.[40]

Qualifications aside, the expansion of state control over local production has not produced a clear increase in the ability to realize national aims in international markets. The state's expanded control over extractive industries has made it a powerful economic actor locally but has also put it more squarely in the difficult position of mediating the relation between the local economy and international markets that it cannot control. Thus, although there are clear connections between transnational presence and an expansion of the state's role, on the one hand, and capacity defined narrowly in terms of organization building and power relative to local private actors, on the other hand, the constraints imposed on the state by the necessity of relying on global markets remain no less powerful.

Effects of Manufacturing Investment

Arguments for a connection between foreign direct investment and state intervention are less clear-cut in manufacturing than in raw materials. The more rapid evolution of technology in these industries makes it easier for TNCs to keep their bargains from obsolescing. Since no single manufacturing industry is likely to play the kind of central role in a peripheral economy that is often played by extractive industries, it is much more difficult to convince domestic elites that returns from a manufacturing industry should be appropriated by the state in order to defend national sovereignty. Finally, manufacturing industries, even if controlled by transnational elites, are likely to have closer, more intricate ties to domestic economic actors. Consequently, it is difficult to convince local capital that increasing state power over manufacturing TNCs has no implications for the domestic bourgeoisie's own freedom from control by the state.

For all these reasons, a sequence running from increasing appropriation of the returns to eventual juridical ownership is as uncommon in manufacturing as it is common in extractive industries. Yet even in manufacturing, the presence of powerful transnational actors has still served on occasion to induce an expansion of state involvement.

The evolution of bargaining between the Mexican state and the major automobile TNCs, as chronicled by Bennett and Sharpe, provides a good illustration.[41] Bennett and Sharpe set out the gradual evolution of the capacity of the Mexican state bureaucracy from the early 1960s, when, lacking technical expertise and divided among themselves, state managers were ineffective in their attempts to shape the behavior of the TNCs that dominated the local auto industry, to the late 1970s, by which time the state apparatus had achieved the unity and expertise necessary to break the united front of the auto companies and secure an agreement that was favorable both to Mexico's balance of payments and to nationally owned auto parts companies. In manufacturing as in extractive industries, the challenge of dealing with TNCs can move the state bureaucracy along a "learning curve" in the direction of increased bureaucratic capacity.

Transnational involvement in manufacturing may also present a "challenge to national sovereignty" that is as ideologically compelling as that generated by transnational control of mineral resources and thereby legitimate the expansion of the state's role. Recent struggles in the Brazilian computer industry offer a good example. The overwhelming technological superiority of the TNCs pointed in the direction of unqualified foreign domination, but the importance of the industry to "national security" made such an outcome unacceptable to the military. Under state sponsorship, a set of local producers was created with strong organizational ties to the state apparatus in general and the navy in particular.[42] State participation was supported by local capital both because of the weight of the ideological rationale and because it was the only strategy likely to produce significant local participation in the industry.

As in the extractive sector, the expansion of the state's role in manufacturing may be stimulated by alliances, as well as by contests, with TNCs. For TNCs interested in expanding into areas that are either politically uncertain or risky in economic terms, bringing the state in as a partner may be a very attractive proposition. A state enterprise is likely to offer greater financial resources, stability, and even technical expertise than most available local partners, as well as to provide a political insurance policy against nationalist attacks from other quarters. For early U.S. arrivals on Taiwan, the logic of alliance with the state was compelling. According to Gold, "American investments in the fifties were generally joint ventures with the only enterprises that could offer the large markets and production scale to justify the effort, the state corporations."[43] For TNCs interested in becoming involved in basic petrochemical production in Brazil in the early 1970s, the attractions of an alliance with the state were equally compelling.[44]

At this point it is appropriate to raise the same question that was raised in relation to the expansion of the state's role in the extractive sector: Are the effects of contest and the possibilities of alliance really peculiar to the state's relations with transnational capital, or might the same arguments be made in relation to any kind of powerful private economic actor? The answer proposed is obviously no, and a number of the arguments in favor of that response have already been given. In the case of manufacturing investment, there is also a rather impressive two-case comparison in support of the argument.

Haggard and Cheng, in their analysis of the "Gang of Four," point out an interesting pair of contrasts between Hong Kong and Singapore. Singapore stands out among the Gang of Four as having a manufacturing sector most thoroughly dominated by TNCs. At the same time its state apparatus is, like those of Taiwan and South Korea, "characterized by 'strong' dirigiste bureaucracies capable of extracting and channeling resources."[45] Hong Kong, in contrast, inherited Shanghai's sophisticated bourgeoisie. There [multinational corporations] came to occupy a small but not insignificant position in an economy largely dominated by local firms." The state apparatus of Hong Kong, unlike that of Singapore, Taiwan, or South Korea, is exceptional in its lack of intervention. The Hong Kong government takes a "pure laissez faire approach," and there are not parastatals involved in manufacturing.[46]

There are, of course, other explanations for the restricted role of the state in Hong Kong, most notably its colonial character. Nonetheless, this pair suggests not only that, under certain historical conditions, there may be a positive relation between transnational dominance in manufacturing and a dirigiste state apparatus, but also that powerful local bourgeoisies may find affinities with a state apparatus the role of which is highly restricted, especially if they do not feel that they require protection against transnational competitors.

What about manufacturing-related expansion of the state's role and its capacity, organizationally, in relation to other social actors or in terms of its ability to realize goals? In terms of organizational capacity, the consequences of the expansion of the state's role are the same as in the extractive sector. A stronger, more technically competent administrative apparatus is the likely result. In terms of power vis-à-vis the local bourgeoisie, the results are less obvious. In manufacturing, both contests with the multinationals and alliances with them are likely to produce returns for the local bourgeoisie as well as the state. Mexican auto parts producers, local petrochemical firms in Brazil and Taiwan, and local entrants in the computer industry in Brazil have all benefited from the expansion of the state's role. More than power over the local bourgeoisie, expansion of the state's role in manufacturing is likely to imply greater exercise of power over labor. In Singapore the state's alliance with the TNCs in manufacturing went hand in hand with the destruction of the labor movement.[47] Labor repression is also a feature of other states that have expanded into manufacturing (e.g., Brazil, Taiwan, and South Korea).

As in extractive industries, the implications of the state's expanded role for its power vis-à-vis TNCs and international markets are ambiguous at best. In manufacturing, even more clearly than in extractive investments, expansion of the state's role has the effect of involving the state more closely with the TNCs rather than excluding them. In manufacturing, there can be even less pretense of controlling international markets. Gereffi's analysis of the attempts of the Mexican state to stem the adverse movement in the international market for steroid hormones is an excellent example. State initiatives, including the formation of a state-owned firm, were impotent in the face of the TNCs desire to manufacture steroids elsewhere. Mexico, which had supplied 75 percent of the raw materials for steroid hormones in 1963, had only 10 percent of the market by 1980.[48] State intervention in manufacturing has generally been associated with local accumulation of capital and internalization of manufacturing value-added, but it has in equal measure been associated with increased reliance on international markets and on transnational marketing channels.[49]

Despite the very different technological and economic characteristics of manufacturing, the effects of transnational penetration in manufacturing on state activities seem quite congruent with those in extraction. Although the case is not quite as strong, the presence of TNCs seems more associated with an expansion of the state's role than with its contraction. Again the state's capacity increases in organizational terms and in terms of power relative to local actors (in this case labor more than local capital). Again, exclusion of the TNCs and even more clearly control over international markets lie well beyond the state's grasp.

Effects of Transnational Loan Capital

In the 1970s, flows of transnational loan capital replaced direct investment, both extractive and industrial, as the most rapidly expanding form of transnational capital. There are a number of compelling case studies demonstrating how foreign creditors can use the leverage they have acquired, usually concretized in the form of negotiations with the International Monetary Fund (IMF), to constrict the actions of Third World states and effectively exclude a range of policy options.[50] Generally, the external constraints associated with debt not only are extremely negative in their distributional and welfare consequences, but also limit the developmentalist aspirations of Third World nations.

It is not surprising that transnational loan capital is thought to undermine the autonomy of Third World state managers and undercut the possibility of a more activist state role. It unquestionably has this effect, but even more than the other two kinds of capital that have been examined here, transnational loan capital has doubled-edged consequences for the role of the state. Without denying the eventual problems created for the state, it is also necessary to examine the ways in which a flood of foreign loans in the 1970s underwrote or reinforced an expansion of the state's role to an extent unlikely to be reversed by the hard times of the 1980s.

The growing importance of private loans to Third World countries made state managers ever more crucial intermediaries between private bankers in the core and productive investments in the periphery. According to Frieden, 80 to 90 percent of commercial bank Eurocurrency lending to Third World countries consisted of loans to various public sector entities: central governments themselves, central banks, state-owned enterprises, national development banks, and state-owned public utilities.[51] The rest were likely to carry state guarantees. Burgeoning flows of transnational loan capital propelled state apparatuses in major borrowing countries into "the central roles of overseer of industrial growth and intermediary between foreign financiers and domestic productive investment."[52]

Foreign loans substantially increase the power of the state vis-à-vis the local bourgeoisie, first of all because the state is not forced to rely on private domestic elites as its sole source of resources. This is especially important for regimes with a transformative project that involves displacement of some segment of the domestic elite (e.g., the Peruvian military in the Vellasco period).[53] In addition to enabling the state to pursue its own projects with fewer constraints imposed by the local bourgeoisie, the state's control over foreign loans makes it an important source of capital for local industrialists attempting to implement their own private projects. The regime of Park Chung-hee offers one of the best illustrations of this possibility.

In the late 1960s, the role of foreign debt in South Korea's industrialization was of a magnitude almost unprecedented in the Third World. According to Haggard and Cheng, foreign capital accounted for almost 40 percent of total savings, and loan capital accounted for more than 90 percent of foreign capital.[54] This pattern continued, though in slightly less extreme form, into the 1970s. In the view of most analysts, one of the primary motivations for Korea's exceptional preference for debt was the leverage that it gave the state over local industrialists. Foreign loans required government approval and repayment guarantees, and so local capitalists needed the favor of the state apparatus in order to obtain them. Since the cost of foreign loans was substantially less than the cost of domestic loans, access to them was a critical competitive advantage. Haggard and Cheng assert that "the preference for foreign borrowing had a political motivation" and go on to say, "Foreign loans provided an additional instrument of control to the government, while allowing it to extend greater assistance to local enterprises,"[55] In Lim's view, "The most potent instrument for influencing local capitalists, particularly those engaged in large scale enterprises, was control of bank credit and foreign borrowing."[56]

Under certain historical circumstances, reliance on loan capital, like flows of extractive and manufacturing direct investment, not only is compatible with an expansion of the state's economic role, but may even enhance the possibility of such expansion. It should be underlined once more, however, that the expansion of the state's role is not necessarily synonymous with either the ability to realize national goals in the face of adverse trends in international markets or the achievement of distributional or welfare goals internally. The current agonies of major Third World borrowers that must be considered a direct result of "debt-led industrialization" are a dramatic reminder that loans, even loans acquired during the halcyon days when real interest rates were barely positive, still reinforce external dependency and carry with them the problems that dependency entails.

Rather than simply undercutting the state's role in the Third World, trade, extractive investments, manufacturing investments, and loan capital may serve, in parallel ways, to stimulate and facilitate the expansion of the state's role. The evidence examined suggests that the challenges of transnational economic linkages, whether flows of goods or capital, may lead the state to expand the scope of its economic role, generating new organizational capacity within the state bureaucracy and placing the state in a more powerful strategic position vis-à-vis private domestic actors. At the same time, it is clear that the frustration and sense of powerlessness that lead Third World scholars to describe the relation of their nations to the global economy as one of "dependence" is not misplaced. In no case did the enhanced bureaucratic capacity or domestic power of the state convey a means of escaping the power of international markets or, for that matter, of negating the power that accrues to TNCs on the basis of their symbiotic relation to international markets.

The simplistic hypothesis that increasing transnationalization of economic relations has a generally debilitating effect on the Third World state as an institution and social actor can safely be abandoned, provided that some caveats are kept in mind. First, the discussion has been limited to the postwar period. An earlier historical focus might well have produced results more consonant with the hypothesis of negative effects. Likewise, the focus here has been on states that are more properly labeled "semiperipheral" rather than "peripheral." Had we focused on smaller, weaker nations in which the primary tasks of defending territorial integrity and constructing a state apparatus capable of maintaining domestic order were still problematic, we might have found that the effects of transnational challenges were indeed to undermine the state's fragile institutional capacities. Across the gamut of peripheral states, Delacroix and Ragin's finding of an overall negative relation between transnational linkages and state capacities is not unreasonable.[57] The more complicated and partially positive relation postulated here applies mainly to the more advanced Third World states and the postwar period. The principal condition of its applicability elsewhere would be the prior development of a state apparatus with some degree of bureaucratic institutionalization and with some "relative autonomy."

The scope claimed for this reinterpretation of the relation between transnational linkages and the expansion of the state's role in the Third World having been clarified, the way is now clear to broaden the focus of the inquiry to include advanced industrial countries on the way to some eventual comments on transnational linkages and the state in the world system as a whole.

Transnational Linkages and Advanced Industrial States

Some of the predicaments created for Third World states by transnational linkages find strong echoes in the advanced industrial countries. Germany and Japan are much more dependent on trade than Brazil or India, and the small industrialized democracies depend even more on international markets. With the exception of the United States, most industrial countries entered the postwar period confronting externally based TNCs with economic power that was vastly superior to that of local firms. There is no obvious reason, if such challenges have resulted in an expansion of the state's role in the Third World, that they should not also be associated with a more ample definition of legitimate state activity in the First World.

The parallelism breaks down insofar as advanced industrial countries are the cradle and home base for TNCs. In this case the transnational challenge is much more subtle if it is perceived at all. The economic power of "home" transnationals may even be seen to be an extension of national sovereignty rather than a challenge to it. In cases in which a nation's primary relation to transnational capital is one of managing exports of capital or serving as a home base, the arguments that have been used so far to connect transnational linkages and the expansion of the state's role do not apply. Indeed, our fourth hypothesis predicts that, in these core countries, transnational economic relations will inhibit rather than facilitate the expansion of the state's role.

Effects of Trade and Transnational Penetration

Impressionistic observations of the consequences of trade for states in developed capitalist countries fit well with the expected pattern. At one extreme, the United States, the exports of which are equal to less than 10 percent of its GDP, has a state apparatus with a highly restricted economic role. At the other, the smaller countries of Europe, the exports plus imports of which may be larger than their entire GDPs, have developed extensive and intricate mechanisms for state intervention. Available research is also supportive. Cameron's cross-national data analysis is a good example. Cameron found that openness to trade not only was positively associated with the expansion of the state in his sample of eighteen developed countries, but predicted this expansion better than any other variable.[58] He concluded, "Among the nations considered here, the expansion of the public economy was most closely associated with a relatively high exposure to, and dependence upon, external producers and consumers."[59] Katzenstein also noted the connection between the expansion of the state in smaller European countries and the exigencies of facing an increasingly "transnationalized" economy, citing the opinion that in small European states "all governments – whether formed by leftists or nonleftist parties – have been impelled by the exigencies of the open economy to expand the role of the state."[60]

The positive effects of dependence on trade on the expansion of the state's economic role are also well illustrated by Japan. It is symptomatic that the central bureaucratic locus of Japanese industrial policy is called the Ministry of International Trade and Industry (MITI), not simply the Ministry of Industry. The rationale for state-sponsored structural change in Japanese industry has always been set out in terms of the requisites of competing for a share of international markets. Forced to import virtually the gamut of industrial raw materials and therefore dependent on the competitiveness of manufactured exports in order to maintain the momentum of domestic accumulation, Japan was able to define the cost competitiveness of its industry as a "national interest" issue rather than a private one. Consequently, the development of an elaborate set of mechanisms for state economic intervention appeared as a natural part of the state's prerogative to defend national sovereignty. As Borrus puts it, "The Japanese have actively pursued international competitiveness as a tenet of national security."[61]

Steel provides a useful illustration of the links between dependence on trade and the expansion of the state's role. From the beginning of the postwar period, Japan set out to construct a steel industry that would be cost competitive internationally despite its reliance on imported inputs, thereby transforming a natural comparative advantage. During the same period in which the U.S. share of world steel production was being cut in half, Japanese production was increasing tenfold in what "must be seen as the fruit of state intervention to secure international competitiveness."[62]

The connection between trade dependence and state intervention derives not only from the fact that the Japanese saw the possibility of steel exports being in the "national interest." The very fact that the steel industry depended on imported inputs played an important part in facilitating state intervention. As Borrus puts it, "The most important features of the state's repertoire of policy instruments were control over credit and control over imported materials."[63] Precisely because 90 percent of Japan's iron ore and 84 percent of its coal were imported, controls over importation allowed the state effectively to shape the growth of the industry.

Penetration or the threat of penetration by transnational corporations, like reliance on trade, has consequences in developed countries that parallel those in the Third World. Japan is again a prime case in point. Since its first contact with the West, the Japanese state has played an active role in limiting direct investment by transnational capital. Until the early 1970s, Japan's restrictions were much more stringent than those of most Third World states.[64] Protecting Japanese industry from penetration by transnational capital was, like the promotion of international competitiveness, defined as a national interest question and was presided over by MITI.

An even more interesting case of the interaction between penetration by transnational capital and the development of state capacities for economic intervention is France. Through the end of the 1970s, France was the only major industrial power in which the inflow of transnational capital based in other countries exceeded the outflow of transnational locally based capital.[65] Competition simply according to market rules put French capital in general (with some obvious exceptions, such as Michelin and Rhone-Poulenc) at a disadvantage in relation to TNCs based elsewhere.

Political intervention by the state was an obvious response. Thus, faced in the 1920s with the fact that all of its crude oil was supplied by TNCs based in Britain or the United States, the French state helped to create the Compagnie Française Pétrole (CFP). The same motivations led more recently to interventions in electronics and steel.[66] To be sure France, like Third World countries, has discovered that the structure of international markets is relatively impervious to modification, as its difficulties in the electronics industry illustrate. Nonetheless, the threat that the local economy might come under the domination of transnational capital of foreign origins is an important element in legitimating the development of an extensive array of mechanisms for state economic intervention, including state-owned industrial enterprises. Like Third World states, advanced industrial states with local economies that are vulnerable to the vagaries of transnational markets and susceptible to domination by TNCs based elsewhere tend to take on an expanded role – both because the "foreign" character of the threat legitimates state intervention and because the self-interest of local capital in protection from economically superior adversaries reduces resistance to the expansion of the state's role. The same logic does not apply to states that are "homes" rather than "hosts" to TNCs.

Capital Exports and the State's Role

States for which the expansion of "home" TNCs is the most significant form of transnational linkages are few. If only industrial capital is considered, the United States stands practically in a class by itself. As late as 1971, all of Japan's foreign direct investment had a book value of less than half of U.S. investment in West Germany alone.[67] Even as late as 1979, following a long period of dramatic expansion in the overseas activities by German and Japanese TNCs, the net outflow of direct private investment from the United States easily exceeded that of all other OECD (Organization for Economic Cooperation and Development) countries combined.[68]

North American TNCs have little reason in their "home" economy to support the kinds of state intervention that we have seen in Third World and developed "host" states. The argument that the state must develop its capacity for economic intervention in order to protect the national economy from the detrimental effects of external economic forces is hardly compelling from the point of view of TNCs. They, after all, are among the external economic forces from which the domestic economy might be protected. To use the most obvious example, protection of the domestic economy from low-wage electronic assembly plants in the Far East would destroy the profits of U.S. electronics companies, which depend on a geographic division of labor within the firm.

Even if the economic interests of TNCs were not affected directly by state economic intervention in the domestic economy, setting of precedents that might be followed by other countries would make it undesirable. A proposal to allow TNCs based elsewhere to set up subsidiaries in the United States only if 50 percent of the equity were sold to U.S. citizens might be quite interesting to U.S. TNCs in itself (since they would be the most likely co-owners), but it would also have the effect of legitimating similar measures in other countries and would therefore be strongly opposed.

As long as the U.S. domestic economy was characterized by rapid growth, generally full employment, and technological dominance in leading industries, there was no need to invoke the special predilections of transnational capital to help explain the restricted domestic role of the U.S. state. American capital in general seemed to lack the motivations that might lead capital in nonhegemonic states to admit to an expansion of the state's role. By the late 1970s, lagging growth, rising unemployment, and declining technological leadership made the divergence between the role of the state in the United States and its role in competing states more striking. American

TNCs continued to do well, but it seemed plausible that important segments of domestic capital would have benefited from an expansion of the
state's role.

The contrast between the effective intervention of the Japanese state on
behalf of its steel industry and the continued passivity of the U.S. state in
the face of the undeniable decline of an industry that was basic not only in
the sense of being a major employer, but also in the sense of determining
the raw materials cost of a range of metal fabricating industries is a case in
point. The "Solomon Plan," which was touted as a major governmental
response to the problems of the steel industry, continued to be based on
the premise that any plan "must avoid any direct government involvement
in the industry's decisions."[69]

The point is not that the preferences of transnational capital explain the
restricted economic role of the U.S. state. The argument is rather that insofar as the preferences of transnational capital shape state policy, TNCs
are less likely than domestic companies to have an interest in the expansion of the state's role in relation to the domestic economy. It may be argued that in compensation TNCs are more likely to support expansion of
the state's economic role internationally, but if one uses the U.S. state as
an example, there is an odd asymmetry between the consequences of the
kind of state intervention desired by TNCs internationally and the kinds of
state intervention that characterize host (as opposed to home) states. The
primary interest of TNCs is in the preservation of a "liberal" international
economic order that allows them freedom of action. Insofar as the U.S.
state acts in behalf of this interest, benefits accrue not just to U.S.-based
transnational capital but to competitors as well. German, French, and Japanese TNCs are "free riders" ·in relation to U.S. state efforts to maintain
global political and economic conditions amenable to the free flow of transnational capital. Even when interventions are more specific, their consequences for the U.S. state and the U.S. economy are often ambiguous at
best.

When the U.S. State Department renegotiated the tax status of Middle
East oil TNCs, the consequence for the U.S. state was essentially a loss of
revenue, precisely the reverse, as far as the state apparatus itself is concerned, of the consequences of negotiations between host countries and
extractive TNCs.[70] In the Mexican auto case as analyzed by Bennett and
Sharpe, U.S. TNCs opposed State Department attempts at intervention so
that they could arrive at a bargain with the Mexican state without having
to take its implications for nontransnational actors in the U.S. auto industry too heavily into account. According to Krasner's analysis of the Brazilian coffee trade, the U.S. acted to preserve its positive relation with an
important South American ally at the expense of U.S. coffee consumers.
Overall, divergence between the interests of U.S. TNCs and U.S. domestic
economic interests is not confined to transnational attitudes toward expan-

sion of the state's domestic economic role, but can be seen in the international arena as well.

The U.S. case certainly undercuts any model of the global economy founded on the assumption that TNCs are simply instruments of the national interests of their homes states and lends support to the idea that having a bourgeoisie in which locally based transnational capital is the dominant fraction may inhibit the expansion of the state's role. Nor is the U.S. a unique example. Britain also serves as a good illustration. Although Britain does not rival the U.S. in terms of export of industrial capital, it has retained a central role in the provision of transnational finance. Even at the end of the 1970s, with the British industrial economy in shambles, the foreign asset deposits of British banks were twice those of other major financial centers, including New York.[71] The financial institutions of the City of London have been remarkably successful at insulating themselves from Britain's decline.

British financial capital has survived so well in part because of its own orientation toward transnational rather than domestic finance and in part because British state managers have consistently favored economic policies compatible with the City's orientation. Stephen Blank summarizes the correspondence as follows:

Clearly the interests of the British financial community were far more closely identified with postwar economic policies than the interests either of British industry or labor. The British financial community tended to be far more interested and involved in external relations and dealings than with domestic industries, and thus strongly supported all efforts to defend sterling.[72]

Even after it became impossible to defend the role of sterling as the principal international reserve currency, British state policy was critical to the maintenance of the role of the city. Zysman comments that the Eurocurrency market

emerged not as a product of irresistible economic forces but as a part of a Bank of England policy to maintain England as an international financial center despite the decline of Sterling as an international reserve currency. Such a policy required that London-based banks be free to conduct their operations in the new international money, dollars.[73]

The domestic consequences of the British state's focus on attempting to maintain the conditions for the City's preeminence in international finance during the 1950s were labeled "tragic and absurd" by one of Britain's more farsighted economists.[74] Considering devaluation and direct controls on capital flows beyond the pale, the government responded to balance of payments crises and pressure on the pound by severely restricting the growth of the domestic economy in an attempt to slow inflation. In effect, British workers had to "learn to live within their means" so that the City could continue to be a center of international finance.

Under both Labour and Conservative governments, British state policy continued to focus on external economic parameters and failed to develop new policy instruments for intervention in the domestic economy. When the French and British governments both attempted to promote industrial reorganization in the 1960s, the French had "a well-stocked armory of instruments for direct and specific intervention in the economy and industry," whereas the British had to rely on voluntary cooperation.[75] The French had a "power of disposition over investment capital not possessed by the British treasury," whereas the British state had to work through a financial system more adapted to serving as "an institutional support for world commerce" than as an organizing force for domestic industrial growth.[76]

Switzerland offers a third variation on the same theme. It is often noted that, for a small, economically open country, Switzerland has a remarkably small public sector and a surprisingly "antistatist" political orientation. As Katzenstein puts it, "In Switzerland the state is relatively weak and decentralized and enjoys only a narrow scope of action."[77] In terms of the argument advanced here, Switzerland is not such an anomalous case. Since it is a country for which the overseas activities of locally based transnational capital are exceptionally important in relation to the size of the domestic economy, relatively less state intervention would be expected. At the same time, its heavy dependence on trade puts it under cross-pressure and occasionally produces uncharacteristically intrusive state initiatives, as in the case of the agricultural sector.[78]

To reiterate, the argument is not that capital exports (industrial or financial) *explain* the restricted role of the state. It is simply that the influence of capital exports is in the direction of inhibiting the expansion of the state's role. While all three of the states considered here have long traditions of noninterventionist policies,[79] it does seem reasonable to suggest that the influence of transnational capital may have contributed (in combination with the other effects of transnational linkages discussed earlier) to the widening of the differences in the scope of public sector activities among developed countries over the past thirty years.[80] For Britain and the United States, however, an additional argument must be considered. Preferences of transnational capital with respect to the evolution of "home" states must be understood in interaction with geopolitical strategies of state officials.

Geopolitical Aims and Transnational Interests

Central to understanding the behavior of the state apparatus in the two principal capital exporters – Britain and the United States – are their pretensions to political and ideological hegemony internationally. In the case of Britain, despite the historical distance that separated it from realistic aspirations to hegemony, the commitment of politicians and higher civil servants to the maintenance of the imperial legacy should not be underestimated.[81] In the case of the United States, political and military hegemony persist despite economic decline, and the attempt to preserve them is central to the behavior of the state apparatus. Explicit recognition of the importance of political motivations in these cases is necessary in order to make the arguments that have been raised so far more realistic.

The principal issue here is the restriction of the domestic economic role of transnational capital and those of geopolitically oriented state officials. For state officials whose primary orientation is geopolitical, expansion of the state's economic role domestically is likely to have costs both in terms of resources required and in terms of enmeshing the state more deeply in domestic social conflicts. As long as domestic economic policy produces the required revenues and as long as its performance provides an adequate base from a "national security" point of view, minimal intervention goes well with geopolitical preoccupations.

In the international arena, the relationship between geopolitical goals and the interests of transnational capital is more complicated. At the most abstract level, there is again correspondence. Transnational corporations and transnational bankers prefer a world in which private enterprise is not restricted and the "free world" of U.S. foreign policy is such a world. When concrete policies are in question, however, the correspondence is far from automatic. Franz Schurmann has argued persuasively that the internationalism of transnational capital must be distinguished analytically from the ideologically expansionist policies favored by politicians at the apex of the state apparatus.[82] Krasner provides concrete examples of cases in which the immediate interests of extractive TNCs were neglected in pursuit of geopolitical goals.[83] Geopolitically oriented state officials and transnationally oriented capitalists are likely to agree on the desirability of a state that is strong abroad and weak domestically, but they may very well disagree on what the policy content of external strength should be.

An obvious area of disagreement has already been noted. When TNCs are forced by more aggressive Third World states to make bargains that prejudice U.S. domestic interests and when the state attempts to protect those interests, as in the Mexican auto case (see the discussion of Bennett and Sharpe cited earlier), TNCs cease being interested in having an externally strong state. A second, more theoretically critical area of potential conflict involves the state's capacity to regulate international economic trends. One of the best examples is the conflict between transnational bankers and the U.S. state that emerged in the late 1960s, especially as viewed through the suggestive interpretations of James Hawley.[84]

With the development of the Eurocurrency market and even more so with the emergence of paper subsidiaries in such places as the Bahamas, Bahrain, and the Cayman Islands, transnational banks (TNBs) have come ever closer to approximating the ideal typical "statelessness" of transnational capital. As Hawley puts it, "Never before has the ability to create money and credit been located to such a degree outside the territory of a core state, nominally the issuer of the reserve and transaction currency of an international monetary system."[85] At the same time, TNBs depend, perhaps more than any other form of transnational capital, on the ability of states to guarantee the value of the commodity in which they deal.

Without a currency of reasonably predictable future value in which to undertake transactions, international finance becomes an extremely risky endeavor, and at least since the demise of the gold standard, the creation of such a currency has depended directly on the fiscal and monetary policies of core states. This contradictory situation of remarkable independence from state control and ultimate reliance on the regulatory capacities of the state makes the relation between TNBs and state managers a particularly charged one, especially in the case of the United States, which is responsible for the maintenance of the primary international currency.

Conflicts between transnational capital and state policy makers came to the fore in the early 1960s over the issue of capital controls.[86] Faced with chronic balance of payments deficits and a glut of dollars abroad, U.S. state managers became convinced that the flows of capital abroad had to be curbed if devaluation was to be avoided. As a result, a series of restrictions on capital flows, first voluntary and then mandatory, were instituted. Transnational corporations countered by arguing that the proper state response to balance of payments problems was to act against inflation by slowing the growth of the domestic economy.[87] In addition, transnational corporate leadership began to suggest that, if it came to a choice between the free movement of capital and the military and foreign aid commitments on which the state had embarked, the latter should be cut back.[88] Finally, and most crucially, TNBs increased their participation in the Eurodollar market, which was beyond the power of the U.S. state to regulate.

At the end of the 1970s, having been forced, in part by the growth of Eurocurrency markets, to abandon the Bretton Woods system, the United States again found the dollar under pressure. The immediate response was to restrict supplies of credit in the domestic market, following the British pattern of sacrificing domestic accumulation in order to maintain international financial credibility. At the same time, various proposals were advanced that would have moved in the direction of attempted regulation of Eurocurrency markets.[89] These were strongly and successfully opposed by transnational bankers. The U.S. state could not, on its own, impose regulations on the Eurocurrency markets, and there was insufficient consensus among the various states in which Eurocurrency transactions were taking place to support any common movement toward regulation. The end result was not regulation of the Eurocurrency markets, but rather deregulation of important aspects of domestic banking activities as exemplified by the creation of international banking facilities that were allowed to engage in Eurocurrency transactions on shore without Federal Reserve oversight.

This result should not be seen simply as a victory of transnational finance capital over the state apparatus. Just as increases in the capacity of Third World states to deal with industrial TNCs do not necessarily indicate losses for TNCs, likewise diminished core-state capacity to regulate trans-national financial transactions is not necessarily a gain from the point of view of transnational capital. To begin with, transnational bankers were sorely disappointed at the ineffectiveness of the state in dealing with the domestic money supply, despite the fact that their own success in devel-oping unregulated mechanisms for credit creation helped undercut the ability of state managers to deliver the kind of fiscal and monetary policy the bankers demanded.[90]

Potentially even more serious in the long run are the risks to transna-tional finance capital itself inherent in the lack of regulation. Uncontrolled Eurocurrency markets make it extremely difficult to avoid instability in ex-change rates. Without compulsory reserve requirements or liquidity ratios, the risk of overextension in search of profit expansion becomes much greater. In short, by undercutting core states' capacities to regulate financial mar-kets, transnational capital may have robbed the state of its ability to, in Hawley's words, "protect capital from itself."[91]

Despite the correspondence between geopolitical goals and transna-tional interests in terms of the inhibition of the state's domestic economic role, there is no basis for hypothesizing that the state's role is defined by means of a smoothly functioning consensus concerning policies generated by geopolitically oriented state managers but consistent with the interests of U.S. TNCs. In core countries, as in the Third World, transnational link-ages make certain outcomes more likely, but transnational capital contin-ues to deal with the state on the basis of a contradictory relationship that contains bases for conflict as well as common interests.

Transnational Linkages, State Capacities, and the World System

Two arguments have been set out. The first is that, in the Third World, trade and capital flows are associated, not with supine and inhibited state apparatuses, but with an expansion of the domestic role of the state. The argument is not that we are witnessing the "ascendance of the host coun-tries."[92] On the contrary, the expansion of the state's role has, in some instances, particularly in the extractive sector, revealed even more clearly the disadvantageous position of Third World states in relation to interna-tional markets. Nonetheless, the challenge of dealing with transnational linkages has, in more advanced Third World states, led to the expansion and strengthening of the economic side of the state bureaucracy. In addi-tion, both conflicts with TNCs and alliances with them have increasingly left the state apparatus in the crucial position of mediating relations be-tween local private capital and the international economy. In a similar way, the challenge generated by increasing involvement in the transnational economy has been associated with the expansion of the state's role in ad-vanced industrial countries that are not primarily "homes bases" for TNCs.

The second argument is the inverse of the first. Presiding over an econ-omy in which transnational capital is the dominant fraction of the "local" bourgeoisie inhibits the expansion of the state's domestic economic role in capital exporting countries. The interests of transnational capital coalesce with the geopolitical concerns of state elites around an "externally strong, internally weak" state apparatus. The United States is the prime example, Britain and Switzerland provide supporting evidence.

Neither argument represents some inescapable universal logic of the capitalist world system. Rather, the relationships discovered are assumed to be conditioned by the historical conjuncture of the postwar period. The tremendous expansion of transnational capital, industrial and financial, and the impressive growth of international trade are basic facts of the postwar conjuncture. Equally important is the expansion of the number of independent Third World states[93] and the increased organizational capacity of previously independent states.[94] Finally, the political–military hegemony of the United States in the context of increasing economic competition among capital core countries and sharp political and military struggle between capitalist and socialist camps is fundamental. The implications of this last feature for the interaction of transnational capital and the state in the Third World must be made more explicit.

Although the hegemonic international position of the United States has clearly served to inhibit aggressive Third World attempts to restructure its relations with U.S. TNCs (and, by extension, transnational capital in general), it is the other side of the coin that should be emphasized at this point. In a number of key instances, U.S. geopolitical concerns have led the U.S. state to strengthen the position of Third World state apparatuses, sometimes even facilitating the expansion of their economic role vis-à-vis transnational capital. State Department support for increased royalty payments to Middle Eastern oil producers is a classic example. More diffuse, but probably more important in the long run, massive, geopolitically motivated U.S. assistance has been critical to the emergence of the bureaucratic authoritarian industrializing regimes[95] of East Asia. Despite the strong "pro-free-enterprise" bent of U.S. assistance, the principal goal was "stemming the tide of communism." Client states were allowed to expand their roles far beyond the Anglo-American ideal as long as they remained dedicated to the pursuit of this goal.[96]

If U.S. pursuit of geopolitical goals has created space for the expansion of the state's role in certain instances, it has had a negative effect on expansion in the direction of traditional welfare-state activities. From Mossadegh to Manley (without even considering more explicitly socialist regimes, such as those of Allende and the Sandinistas), U.S. concern with "stemming the tide" has consistently contributed to the destruction of regimes that attempted to expand their domestic economic role along social democratic lines. In short, U.S. geopolitical preoccupations can be added to the political and economic forces that make it easier for Third World states to expand their domestic economic role insofar as they demonstrate a thorough ideological commitment to capitalist principles.

If we were to assume a dramatically different context, then the relations that have been described here might not hold.[97] Rather than speculating in this direction, however, it seems more worthwhile to consider the implications of the two arguments that have been set out, first for the evolution of the international system as a whole and then for future research on transnational linkages and the state.

In the Third World, the expansion of the state's economic role, in combination with the extreme rarity with which TNCs are actually expelled, has left Third World states increasingly enmeshed in the transnational system of production organized in the first instance by the TNCs themselves. At the same time, the internationalization of production has increased the need of the TNCs themselves for strong, predictable Third World partners. The era in which supine, compradore "nonstates" were an option, even from the point of view of the TNCs themselves, is gone. The result is analogous to what Stanley Davis has called a "matrix" organization.[98] An increasing amount of production takes place under the joint partial control of two very different kinds of organizations. Transnational corporations concerned primarily with maximizing returns from a given product line organized globally and states concerned with maximizing returns within a particular geographic area organize production jointly. The question is whether such an arrangement can provide a stable basis for an international system of production.

One might choose to view the expanded economic role of the Third World state as a victory for transnational capital. Capital needs a local political infrastructure to ensure the continued accumulation of capital. Previous structures proved inadequate and increased state involvement offers a new alternative. No matter how thoroughly capitalist the states we have been discussing may be, however, this view overlooks the fact that Third World state managers preside over volatile, class-divided societies and also, like state managers in core countries, have geopolitical as well as economic concerns. Even if states were interested only in maximizing profits, the combination of "area" and "product" interests implied by the matrix organization would not be easy to sustain. Davis characterizes matrix organizations in normal corporations as "structurally unstable" because "conflict is inherent in the design."[99] Yet at the same time both state officials and transnational managers know that their survival (in their current roles at least) depends on their ability to achieve mutually acceptable accommodations.

The obvious prediction is that, in spite of the best efforts of the actors involved, the intermeshing of state and transnational control will produce a much more unstable international economy. Indeed, one could argue that the prediction has already been confirmed by the behavior of international mineral markets. Perhaps of more immediate interest than general predictions, however, are the research implications of this vision of international production.

To understand the matrix organization that has emerged (and even to verify that this is a useful conceptualization to begin with), we need more "postbargaining" studies, that is, studies of the interaction of states and TNCs in an industry, taking the participation of states as a starting point and not as the outcome to be explained. Unlike bargaining studies, these could not be national case studies; rather, they would have to look at the whole matrix of state and transnational actors in an industry. They would have to take state actors seriously, not assuming that they were simply a new set of firms, but looking carefully at the way in which domestic political pressures and geopolitical goals shaped their behavior as transnational actors. Furthermore, the behavior of state actors would have to be understood as a response to and as shaping in turn the decisions of the entire set of nonstate actors in the industry. To date, there have been a few excursions in this direction in minerals but nothing with pretensions of being a full analysis and hardly anything at all outside of the extractive sector.[100] An adequate study of an entire matrix of state–TNC interactions, even in one industry, is obviously an imposing order, but it would seem to be a necessary one if the analysis of transnational linkages and the state is to move forward.

The argument that capital exports tend to reinforce a restricted definition of the economic role of the state has complementary implications for the evolution of the international system, but rather different research implications. If we can assume that failure to expand the role of the state has eventual negative implications for domestic capital accumulation, which seems a reasonable assumption given either general theoretical arguments[101] or the example of Britain's economic decline during the postwar period, then we have a state-centric analogue of Hobson's argument for the negative economic effects of imperialism on the core.[102]

Semiperipheral countries and advanced industrial states that are hosts more than homes for transnational capital develop extensive bureaucratic machineries aimed at constructing more economically powerful bases of comparative advantage and promoting the domestic accumulation of capital, whereas economically hegemonic states remain passive in this area and gradually lose their competitive advantage. The result is not only the relative decline of the hegemonic state, but also movement in the direction of a more polycentric international economy, which is to say a more unstable one.[103]

At this point, serious questions have to be raised and addressed with some concrete research. It is all very well to predict the economic decline of a core power. In fact, the postwar experience of Britain is only the most recent in a series of such declines. But the argument used here to make the prediction in the case of the United States depends on the continued neglect by both U.S. TNCs and geopolitically oriented state officials of opportunities for effective state intervention in the U.S. domestic economy, even in the face of relative decline.

One might argue that state managers and finance capitalists in Britain have behaved in precisely this manner, but the analogy with Britain is misleading for two reasons. First, Britain's decline had only minimal geopolitical implications for the transnational system as a whole since Britain's role as the international defender of free trade and free investment could be assumed by the United States. Second, since Britain's role as a center of transnational capital is much more predominantly financial than that of the United States, decoupling the fortunes of transnational capital from those of the domestic economy was much easier.

In contrast to British banks, U.S. TNCs still depend on their core economy for activities that are central to the competitive position of their operations elsewhere in the world. Research and development is only one example of this. Can U.S. TCNs really afford to be indifferent to lagging growth in the United States, turning perhaps, like British capitalists before them, more to the financial area or perhaps creating partnerships with capital from other industrial economies to ensure continued technological superiority (e.g., with Japanese capital)? Or are U.S. TNCs likely to move in the direction of supporting increased state intervention in the hope of protecting their economic base? Similar questions might be asked of geopolitically oriented state actors. Beyond the obvious usefulness of a strong domestic economy in exerting geopolitical leverage, the economic underpinnings of military superiority require more than simply sustaining defense contractors. Here again, one might expect a movement in the direction of supporting increased state intervention. Taking the two sets of actors jointly, it becomes interesting to consider which is most likely to overcome its ideological aversion to state intervention and what implications it would have for policy outcomes if either one were to develop different attitudes without a complementary change in the attitudes of the other.

The attitudes of transnationally oriented actors, both economic and political, toward the expansion of the state's domestic economic role in the core have been set out in this chapter largely on the basis of theoretical argument bolstered by examples. Yet the arguments themselves suggest the emergence of a conjuncture in which the interests of those actors must become more ambivalent and therefore predictable only on the basis of thoroughly grounded research. Researching the orientations of transnationally oriented U.S. elites toward state intervention in the domestic economy is at least as challenging as the matrix research suggested earlier, but it is equally crucial if we are to gain a better sense of how transnational linkages affect the most important actor in the international system.

Both suggestions for future research reflect back on the initial set of hypotheses that formed the point of departure for this essay. Underlying these hypotheses was the assumption that the evolution of transnational linkages constituted the dynamic element in the world system, whereas states were victims (especially in the periphery) or passive beneficiaries (perhaps in the core). The reformulations offered here suggest that the state should have been included as an active element with a dynamic of its own in earlier analyses. Even more strongly, they suggest that state action (and inaction) during the first decades of the postwar period have made it impossible for anyone aspiring to understand the international system in the 1980s and 1990s to neglect the state in the same way.

Notes

1. J. P. Nettl, "The State as a Conceptual Variable," *World Politics* 20 (1968): 559–92.
2. World Bank, *World Development Report* (New York: Oxford University Press, 1981), pp. 142–43.
3. H. Peter Gray, T. Pugel, and I. Walter, "International Trade, Employment and Structural Adjustment: The Case of the United States," World Employment Programme Research Working Paper (Geneva: ILO, 1982).
4. George Ball, "The Promise of the Multinational Corporation," *Fortune* 75(6) (1967): 80.
5. R. Barnet and R. Müller, *Global Reach* (New York: Simon & Schuster, 1974).
6. John Boli-Bennett, "Global Integration and the Universal Increase of State Dominance, 1910–1970," in *Studies of the Modern World System*, ed. Albert Bergesen (New York: Academic Press, 1980), pp. 77–107.
7. Richard Rubinson, "Dependence, Government Revenue and Economic Growth 1955–1970," in *National Development and the World System: Educational, Economic and Political Change, 1950–1970*, ed. J. Meyer and M. Hannan (Chicago: University of Chicago Press, 1979), pp. 207–21; J. Delacroix and C. Ragin, "Structural Blockage: A Cross-National Study of Economic Dependence, State Efficacy, and Underdevelopment," *American Journal of Sociology* 86 (1981): 1311–47.
8. Paul Baran, *The Political Economy of Growth* (New York: Monthly Review Press, 1957); Leroy Vail, "Railway Development and Colonial Underdevelopment: The Nyasaland Case," in *The Roots of Rural Poverty in Central and Southern Africa*, ed. R. Palmer and N. Parsons (Berkeley: University of California Press, 1977), pp. 365–95; see, for example, Jeffery Paige, "Cotton and Revolution in Nicaragua." In *States versus Markets in the World System*, ed. P. Evans, D. Rueschemeyer, and E. Stephens (Beverly Hills, Calif.: Sage, forthcoming).
9. Albert Hirschman, *National Power and the Structure of Foreign Trade* (Berkeley: University of California Press, 1945).
10. Rubinson, "Dependence, Government Revenue and Economic Growth," pp. 212–17.
11. Stephen Krasner, "Manipulating International Commodity Markets: Brazilian Coffee Policy 1906–1962," *Public Policy* 21 (1973): 493–523.
12. The efforts of the Brazilian state to maintain international prices by purchasing excess production and keeping it off the market had the effect of maintaining aggregate demand domestically and thereby reducing the decline in GNP; see also Furtado, *The Economic Growth of Brazil* (Berkeley: University of California Press, 1963).
13. Peter Flynn, *Brazil: A Political Analysis* (Boulder, Colo.: Westview Press, 1978).
14. See Pranab Bardhan's discussion of the role of agrarian elites in relation to the Indian state for an interesting contrasting example: *The Political Economy of Development in India* (Oxford: Basil Blackwell, 1945).

15. Rubinson, "Dependence, Government Revenue and Economic Growth," p. 213.
16. See Raymond Vernon, *Sovereignty at Bay: The Multinational Spread of U.S. Enter-prises* (New York: Basic Books, 1971); T. H. Moran, *Multinational Corporations and the Politics of Dependence: Copper in Chile* (Princeton, N.J.: Princeton University Press, 1974); Fred C. Bergsten, Ted Moran, and Tom Horst, *American Multinationals and American Interests* (Washington, D.C.: Brookings Institution, 1978).
17. Albert Hirschman, "A Generalized Linkage Approach to Development, with Special Reference to Staples," *Economic Development and Cultural Change,* suppl. (1977): 67–98; reprinted in *Essays in Trespassing: Economics to Politics and Beyond* (New York: Cambridge University Press, 1981), chap. 4.
18. Frank Tugwell, *The Politics of Oil in Venezuela* (Stanford, Calif.: Stanford University Press, 1975).
19. John Blair, *The Control of Oil* (New York: Pantheon Press, 1976); Stephen Schneider, *The Oil Price Revolution* (Baltimore, Md.: Johns Hopkins University Press, 1983).
20. See Nora Hamilton, *The Limits of State Autonomy: Post-Revolutionary Mexico* (Princeton, N.J.: Princeton University Press, 1983).
21. Moran, *Multinational Corporations,* pp. 123–25.
22. David G. Becker, *The New Bourgeoisie and the Limits of Dependency: Mining Class and Power in "Revolutionary" Peru* (Princeton, N.J.: Princeton University Press, 1983).
23. Jeff Frieden, "Third World Indebted Industrialization: International Finance and State Capitalism in Mexico, Brazil, Algeria and South Korea," *International Organization* 35 (1981): 407–31.
24. Becker, "The New Bourgeoisie," pp. 216–18.
25. See Peter B. Evans, *Dependent Development: The Alliance of Multinational, State and Local Capital in Brazil* (Princeton, N.J.: Princeton University Press, 1979); P. Evans, "Collectivized Capitalism: Integrated Petrochemical Complexes and Capital Accumulation in Brazil," in *Authoritarian Capitalism: The Contemporary Economic and Political Development of Brazil,* ed. T. C. Burneau and P. Faucher (Boulder, Colo.: Westview Press, 1981), pp. 85–125; P. Evans, "Reinventing the Bourgeoisie: State Entrepreneurship and Class Formation in Dependent Capitalist Development," *American Journal of Sociology* 88 (supplement) (1982): 210–47.
26. See David T. Isaak, "Basic Petrochemicals in the 1980s: Mideast Expansions and the Global Industry," Working Paper WP-82-3 (Honolulu: Resource Systems Institute East–West Center, 1982).
27. See Evans, *Dependent Development,* pp. 249–54; Silvia Raw, "The Companhia Vale do Rio Doce: Goals and Financing Patterns" (Paper presented at the Conference on "Problemas de Gestión de las Empresas Publicas en America Latina" in Caracas, Venezuela, November 1983).
28. Raymond Vernon, "Uncertainty in the Resource Industries: The Special Role of State-owned Enterprises" (Unpublished manuscript, 1982), p. 10.
29. L. P. Jones and E. M. Mason, "The Role of Economic Factors in Determining the Size and Structure of the Public Enterprise Sector in Mixed Economy LDCs" (Paper presented at the Second Annual Boston Area Public Enterprise Group Conference, Boston, 1980).
30. Moran, *Multinational Corporations,* p. 212.
31. Evelyne Stephens and John D. Stephens, "Democratic Socialism in Dependent

Capitalism: An Analysis of the Manley Government in Jamaica," *Politics and Society* (Winter 1983): 373–411; E. Stephens and J. Stephens, "Renegotiating Dependency: The Bauxite Policy of the PNP Government in Jamaica" (Paper presented at the annual meeting of the American Sociological Association, Detroit, September 2, 1983).

32. Becker, "The New Bourgeoisie," pp. 221–22, 230.
33. Moran, *Multinational Corporations*, pp. 102–103.
34. See Becker, "The New Bourgeoisie, p. 102.
35. Ibid., p. 325.
36. See Peter B. Evans, "Foreign Capital and the Role of the State in the Third World" (Paper presented at the Joint Harvard–MIT Seminar on Political Development, Cambridge, February 29, 1984), p. 10. Another factor affecting the propensity of state intervention is the prevailing set of international norms. Expertise in negotiating with TNCs and managing extractive industries diffuses among Third World states, making it possible for newer states to move up the "learning curve" on the basis of the experience of others. Questions of the consequences of the transnational diffusion of policy-relevant knowledge for state capacity must, however, remain outside the scope of the present discussion.
37. Moran, *Multinational Corporations*, p. 133; Becker, "The New Bourgeoisie," pp. 97–131.
38. Moran, *Multinational Corporations*, p. 241.
39. See Michael Shafer, "Capturing the Mineral Multinationals: Advantage or Disadvantage," *International Organization* 37 (1982): 93–119; Vernon, "Uncertainty in the Resource Industries."
40. See Evans, "Foreign Capital and the Role of the State," pp. 13–14.
41. Douglas Bennett and Kenneth Sharpe, "Transnational Corporations and the Political Economy of Export Promotion: The Case of the Mexican Automobile Industry," *International Organization* 33 (179): 177–201; D. Bennett and K. Sharpe, "Transnational Corporations, Export Promotion Policies and U.S.–Mexican Automotive Trade" (Colloquium paper presented at the Woodrow Wilson International Center for Scholars, Washington, DC, September 1982).
42. Immanuel Adler, "A Cultural Theory of Change in International Political Economy: Science, Technology, and Computer Policies in Argentina and Brazil" (Ph.D. diss., University of California, Berkeley, 1982).
43. Thomas B. Gold, "Dependent Development in Taiwan" (Ph.D. diss., Harvard University, 1981), p. 192.
44. See Evans's *Dependent Development*, "Collectivized Capitalism," and "Reinventing the Bourgeoisie."
45. Stephan Haggard and Tun-jeng Cheng, "State Strategies, Local and Foreign Capital in the Gang of Four" (Paper presented at the annual meeting of the American Political Science Association, Chicago, September 2, 1983), p. 36.
46. Ibid., pp. 51, 37, 45.
47. Haggard and Cheng, "State Strategies," p. 43; see also Fred Deyo, *Dependent Development and Industrial Order: An Asian Case Study* (New York: Praeger, 1981).
48. Gary Gereffi and Peter B. Evans, "Transnational Corporations, Dependent Development, and State Policy in the Semiperiphery: A Comparison of Brazil and Mexico," *Latin American Research Review* 16 (1981): 31–64.
49. Ibid.

50. Cheryl Payer, *The Debt Trap* (New York: Monthly Review Press, 1975); Barbara Stallings, "Peru and the U.S. Banks: Privatization of Financial Relations," and Roberto Frenkel and Guillermo O'Donnell, "The 'Stabilization' Programs of the IMF and their Internal Impact," both in *Capitalism and the State in U.S.–Latin American Relations*, ed. R. Fagen (Stanford, Calif.: Stanford University Press, 1979), pp. 217–53 and 171–216, respectively; Stephens and Stephens, "Democratic Socialism in Dependent Capitalism."

51. Frieden, "Third World Indebted Industrialization," p. 411.

52. Ibid., p. 429.

53. See Stallings, "Peru and the U.S. Banks."

54. Haggard and Cheng, "State Strategies," p. 22.

55. Ibid., p. 58.

56. Hyun-Chin Lim, "Dependent Development in the World System: the Case of South Korea, 1963–1979" (Ph.D. diss., Harvard University, 1983), p. 147.

57. Delacroix and Ragin, "Structural Blockage."

58. It should be noted that the major differences in the size of the public sector are due primarily to welfare expenditures and transfer payments rather than to the consumption of the government itself. See Peter J. Katzenstein, "The Determinants of State Policy in Switzerland and Austria," (Paper presented at a conference, Research Implications of Current Theories of the State, Mt. Kisco, N.Y., February 1982), p. 51. Nonetheless, the size of the public sector provides an important source of leverage for the state apparatus both in terms of being better able to manage aggregate demand and in terms of being able to cushion the effects of necessary structural adjustments.

59. David Cameron, "The Expansion of the Public Economy: A Comparative Analysis," *American Political Science Review* (1978): 1243–61. A slightly different view of this connection, according to which the effects of openness on the expansion of the state are mediated through the concentration of industrial power, the concentration of the power of organized labor, and the development of power of social democratic parties, is found in John D. Stephens, *The Transition from Capitalism to Socialism* (London: Macmillan, 1979). In Cameron's later work, "Social Democracy, Corporatism, and Labor Quiescence: The Representation of Economic Interest in Advanced Capitalist Societies" (Paper presented at the Conference on Representation and the State, Stanford University, 1982), he seems closer to this view. Even in this more complex version of the hypothesis, however, the effects of trade dependence on the expansion of the state's role remain positive.

60. Cited in Peter J. Katzenstein, ed., *Small States in World Markets* (Ithaca, N.Y.: Cornell University Press, forthcoming).

61. Michael Borrus, "The Politics of Competitive Erosion in the U.S. Steel Industry," in *American Industry in International Competition*, ed. L. Tyson and J. Zysman (Ithaca, N.Y.: Cornell University Press, 1983), pp. 60–105.

62. Ibid., p. 72.

63. Ibid., p. 73.

64. Michael Yoshino, "Japan as Host to the International Corporation," in *The Japanese Economy in International Perspective*, ed. Isaiah Frank (Baltimore, Md.: Johns Hopkins Press, 1975), pp. 273–92.

65. World Bank, *World Development Report*, p. 161.

66. John Zysman, *Political Strategies for Industrial Order: State, Market, and Industry in France* (Berkeley: University of California Press, 1977).

67. Yoshino, "Japan as Host," p. 249.
68. World Bank, *World Development Report*, p. 161.
69. See Peter B. Evans, *The Changing International Position of the U.S. Manufacturing Sector and U.S. Industrial Policy: Implications for Latin American Industrialization* (Report submitted to UNIDO, Country and Regional Studies Branch, Vienna, Austria, 1983), p. 69; see also Borrus, "Politics of Competitive Erosion."
70. Blair, *Control of Oil*; Schneider, *Oil Price Revolution*.
71. U.S. Congress, Joint Economic Committee, *Special Study on Economic Change, vol. 9, The International Economy: U.S. Role in a World Market* (Washington, D.C.: U.S. Government Printing Office, 1980), p. 78.
72. Stephen Blank, "Britain: The Politics of Foreign Economic Policy, the Domestic Economy and the Problem of Pluralistic Stagnation," in *Between Power and Plenty: The Foreign Economic Policies of Advanced Industrial States*, ed. Peter J. Katzenstein (Special issue of *International Organization* 31 [1977]: 623–721.)
73. Zysman, *Political Strategies*, pp. 212.
74. Andrew Shonfield, *British Economic Policy since the War* (London: Penguin Books, 1958), p. 218.
75. Blank, "Politics of Foreign Economic Policy," p. 700.
76. Zysman, *Political Strategies*, p. 192. These differences might, of course, be attributed simply to historical continuity, given "statist" traditions in France that go back to the premodern era (see, for example, Robert Brenner, "Agrarian Class Structure and Economic Development in Pre-industrial Europe," *Past and Present* 70 [1976]: 30–75). The transnational orientation of the dominant segment of British capital supported continuity in the British case under conditions that would have led a more domestically oriented capitalist class to look for more help from the state.
77. Peter Katzenstein, Chapter 7, this volume.
78. Katzenstein, "Determinants of State Policy," p. 84.
79. On Britain and the United States see, among others, Nettl's, "The State as a Conceptual Variable," discussion of "low stateness"; on Switzerland, see Katzenstein, Chapter 7, this volume.
80. Katzenstein, 1982:51–52; Stephens, *Transition from Capitalism to Socialism*, p. 197.
81. See Blank, "Politics of Foreign Economic Policy."
82. Franz Schurmann, *The Logic of World Power* (New York: Pantheon Press, 1973).
83. Stephen D. Krasner, *Defending the National Interest: Raw Materials, Investments and U.S. Foreign Policy* (Princeton, N.J.: Princeton University Press, 1978).
84. James P. Hawley, "Interests, State Foreign Economic Policy and the World System: The Case of the U.S. Capital Control Programs, 1961–74," in *Foreign Policy and the Modern World System*, ed. P. McGowan and C. Kegley. Sage Yearbook of Foreign Policy Studies (Beverly Hills, Calif., Sage, 1983); J. Hawley, "Protecting Capital from Itself: Transnational Banks, Financial Innovation and U.S. State Regulation" (Paper presented at a meeting of the International Sociological Association, Mexico City, August 17, 1982).
85. Hawley, "Protecting Capital from Itself," p. 32.
86. Hawley, "State Foreign Economic Policy."
87. Ibid., p. 33.
88. Ibid., p. 29.
89. Ibid., pp. 25–31.
90. Hawley, "Protecting Capital from Itself," pp. 7–9.
91. Ibid.

92. Bergsten, Horst and Moran, *American Multinationals and American Interests*, set this argument out most effectively.

93. The multiplication of the number of independent states in itself may actually work against a positive association, because peripheral states that have not achieved the minimal state capacity necessary to respond to the challenge of transnational linkages may predominate numerically. In some cases, however, newly independent states inherited colonial state apparatuses of significant bureaucratic capacity, for example, Korea and Taiwan. In addition, the sheer increase in the number of independent states has been important in creating a "global learning curve" with respect to bargaining with TNCs (see note 36).

94. The prior development of the state apparatus in major Third World states is the key to understanding why the consequences of transnational linkages appeared so differently to those, like Baran, whose analysis was based essentially on evidence from the prewar period.

95. See Bruce Cumings, "The Origins of Development of the Northeast Asian Political Economy: Industrial Sectors, Product Cycles and Political Consequences, *International Organization* 38(1) (1984): 2–40.

96. See Alice H. Amsden, Chapter 3, this volume.

97. In particular, a dramatic retraction of international trade or international capital flows might change fundamentally the way in which states respond to transnational linkages.

98. S. M. Davis and P. R. Lawrence, *Matrix* (Reading, Mass.: Addison-Wesley, 1977).

99. S. M. Davis, *Managing and Organizing Multinational Corporations* (New York: Pergamon Press, 1979), pp. 246–47.

100. See, for example, Shafer, "Capturing the Mineral Multinationals." Richard Newfarmer, ed., *Profits, Progress and Poverty: Case Studies of International Industries in Latin America* (Notre Dame, Ind.: University of Notre Dame Press, 1984), could serve as a starting point here.

101. See Dietrich Rueschemeyer and Peter B. Evans, Chapter 2, this volume.

102. J. A. Hobson, *Imperialism: A Study* (London: George, Allen & Unwin, 1938; originally 1902).

103. See, for example, Peter J. Katzenstein, "Introduction: Domestic and International Forces and Strategies of Foreign Economic Policy," in *Between Power and Plenty*, ed. Katzenstein, pp. 593–95, for a discussion of the negative effects of the decline of British hegemony on the transnational system.

7. Small Nations in an Open International Economy: The Converging Balance of State and Society in Switzerland and Austria

Peter Katzenstein

Vulnerability in relation to the international economy is an inescapable fact of life for all of the small countries of Europe. Having chosen economic strategies that depend on international openness, they cannot shift the cost of economic change abroad. Because of the limitations imposed by the scale of their domestic economies, they cannot preempt change through ambitious attempts at industrial reorganization. None of this, however, has prevented them from developing political strategies for achieving national goals. The small European states have compensated for economic openness and dependence on world markets through political efforts at home, and by most indicators they have done so effectively. They have developed a variety of corporatist arrangements that combine support for international openness with domestic compensation and with flexible, reactive policies of industrial adjustment.

The strategies they have adopted, the state capacities they have developed, and the ways they have linked the state to other social actors all set the small European democracies apart from larger industrial countries. At the same time, however, these countries exhibit very different patterns of state structure and action among themselves. Nowhere is the combination of commonality and divergence more striking than in the Alps.

Because they seem to be so close together and yet so far apart, Austria and Switzerland offer an interesting subject for a comparative essay on the state. Austria exemplifies democratic socialism, Switzerland liberal capitalism. The strongest political force in Austria is the labor movement, in Switzerland the business community. The Swiss state enjoys restricted power in society, the Austrian state far-reaching ones. These differences notwithstanding, both countries are small and prosperous. Exposed to the vagaries of international politics and the pressures of the international economy, they have found benefit in military neutrality and strength in economic competitiveness. By most political and economic yardsticks, their consensual politics has been highly successful during the past three decades.

These contrasting images provide the organizing principle for this chapter. First, the chapter views the state as an actor characterized by its institutional structure, the scope of its jurisdiction, and its strength. Here the difference between Austria and Switzerland is very great. Second, the chapter views the state as part of a policy network linking state and society. That network affects state capacities in unexpected ways. Viewed as part of an encompassing system of collaborative political arrangements, state capacities appear to be enhanced in Switzerland and diminished in Austria. Finally, a brief summary of Swiss and Austrian policies lends support to both views.

Different strands in Austrian and Swiss history, I shall argue, explain this balance between difference and similarity. Austria's strong state was shaped by the political and military requirements of a vast empire, by belated industrialization, and by the nationalization of industry at the end of World War II. Switzerland's weak state emerged from the legacy of a federalist system removed from European power politics since the beginning of the nineteenth century, from the legacy of early industrialization, and from state involvement in the Swiss economy in the 1930s that stopped far short of outright nationalization. But there is a second strand of Austrian and Swiss history that also shapes the state. The experience of the 1930s and 1940s – depression, fascism, and war – prompted political leaders in both societies to develop far-reaching collaborative political arrangements involving the leaders of the major political parties and interest groups with the state bureaucracy. Since the late 1950s the pressing requirement to remain competitive in an increasingly liberal international economy has provided daily reinforcement for historical memories that otherwise might have faded. Austria's and Switzerland's collaborative political arrangements impose restraints on the unilateral exercise of power by strong actors – for example, the state in Austria – and they strengthen the political capacities of weak actors – such as the state in Switzerland.

The State as an Actor

Geography puts Austria and Switzerland close together; history sets them far apart. Business, labor, and the state are strikingly different in these two countries.

History explains why the Swiss and Austrian business communities differ greatly. These two countries have traveled different paths to industrial modernity. Since the late eighteenth century, Swiss business has cherished the principle of free trade and has expanded in foreign markets. As one of Europe's early industrializers, Switzerland suffered from a unique constellation of natural disadvantages: absence of essential raw materials, deficits in agricultural trade, lack of direct access to ocean transportation, and until the late nineteenth century relative isolation from Europe's system of railways and canals. These disadvantages were overcome successfully by the export of high-quality manufactured goods such as textiles and watches, which paid for the import of foodstuff and raw materials. Emigration reduced population pressure on limited resources at home and facilitated sales abroad. Entrepreneurial initiative rather than public action was the main force driving Switzerland's industrialization. When, in the late nineteenth century, the growth of protectionism threatened to close essential foreign markets, Swiss business moved from exports to foreign production. Its international market orientation has never wavered since.

Austria has traveled a different and bumpier road. By all accounts business matured in an economy that industrialized relatively late. Indeed, Alexander Gerschenkron argues that, when growth finally came at the beginning of the twentieth century, it was "a spurt that failed."[1] To be sure, the industrialization of the German and Czech provinces – Lower and Upper Austria, Bohemia, and Moravia – accelerated as early as the 1850s and 1860s, about two generations after Switzerland. But even in these decades of higher growth and lower tariffs, Austrian business never embraced a free-trade policy that looked to the conquest of world markets as the main stimulant for growth. Instead, Austrian business preferred to reap the benefits of empire behind high tariff walls. Eastern Europe offered a vast, sheltered market, which Austrian industry controlled. The loss of these markets at the end of World War I, made irrevocable by Soviet expansion at the end of World War II, stripped Austrian business of vast assets and left it without its traditional customers. As a result, business was greatly weakened. The capacity for regeneration, furthermore, was greatly impaired by the crushing burdens the 1920s imposed on Austria's middle class. The inflation of the early 1920s eliminated its monetary assets, and the strict rent-control legislation passed at the end of the war impeded the accumulation of new ones. Nationalization in the 1940s and 1950s, finally, was so extensive that today Austria's public economy is larger than that of any state in the Organization for Economic Cooperation and Development (OECD). Private business remained relatively fearful of competition well into the 1970s.

History has also left Austria and Switzerland with very different labor movements. As summarized by Klingman, Bull and Galenson have argued that the character of the labor movement – its degree of radicalization and centralization – is a function of the timing of industrialization.[2] Broadly speaking, Switzerland's decentralized and reformist labor movement fits this pattern. Swiss industry grew not in large urban areas but along the rivers and mountain brooks that provided cheap energy. The lack of industrial concentration impeded the organizing of workers. Furthermore, the incentives for radical political activity were relatively weak. Throughout the nineteenth century all Swiss men enjoyed the benefits of the franchise and participated in a system of direct democracy that afforded them an opportunity to shape the communities in which they lived. Finally, Swiss society is among the culturally most diverse in Europe. Switzerland's twenty-six cantons offer a veritable patchwork quilt of religions, languages, and traditions. For all these reasons, organizing Swiss workers into one radical labor movement proved to be an impossible task.

On this point the contrast with Austria could not be greater. Here most historical forces pushed in the opposite direction toward radicalism and centralization. Embedded in a society that industrialized relatively late, Austro-Marxism developed strong organizational cohesion and a well-developed body of radical political thought. Austria's working class was concentrated around the industrial sites in the German and Czech provinces and around Vienna. Politically excluded until the fall of the empire, the labor movement organized around the issue of achieving the franchise or of shifting the distribution of power through revolutionary action. Finally, the ethnic barriers that had splintered the labor movement in the polyglot Habsburg Empire were eliminated once that empire was reduced to its German core. During the First Republic the massive presence of Austria's Socialist camp, wavering between revolutionary talk and pragmatic action, provided a formidable opponent, which Austrian conservatism and fascism finally crushed in the civil war of 1934. Shorn of its revolutionary rhetoric, Austria's labor movement was finally accommodated fully in the commanding heights of the Second Republic and integrated into its nooks and crannies.

History, finally, has also given a very different shape to the Austrian and Swiss states. In the eighteenth and nineteenth centuries the Austrian bureaucracy administered from Vienna a vast empire. This prompted the emergence of a large and powerful state. Critics of the imperial bureaucracy charged (in the nineteenth century with increasing justification) that turning the wheels of this magnificent machine produced noise rather than movement. The fact remains, however, that the administration of a vast multiethnic empire established the Austrian state as a powerful institution. The military requirements of Europe's balance of power reinforced the development of a strong state.

Crossing the Swiss border, a nineteenth-century traveler found not an empire but a small state run by a weak central government in Berne. By 1850 it had been established once and for all that there would be one federal Switzerland rather than a multitude of cantons grouped in a loose confederation, but throughout the nineteenth century Switzerland was distinguished by what one might call central nongovernment. State power was exerted mostly at the local and cantonal level. Political developments in Berne were largely irrelevant. Switzerland's permanent neutrality and its citizen militia, furthermore, did not permit the growth of a large warmaking machine at the political center.

The difference in the power of the Austrian and Swiss states was probably greatest in 1914. But Austria lost World War I and its empire. It experienced a tumultuous interwar period that ended in civil war, fascism, another war, and foreign occupation until 1955. Both the painful shrinking of

Austria's oversized state bureaucracy in the 1920s and the delegitimation of the state's role in the subsequent two decades contributed toward narrowing the gap between the capacities of these two states. By Austrian standards twentieth-century Swiss history was uneventful. Whereas the Austrian state suffered from war, occupation, and poverty, the Swiss state lived in peace and enjoyed unimpaired sovereignty and prosperity. The depression of the 1930s involved the central bureaucracy directly in the organization of cartels and corporativist arrangements. It also prompted the executive in this bastion of democracy to rule by emergency decree more than by democratic legislation. Since the end of World War II, however, in both good times and bad, the Swiss government has increasingly extricated itself from any direct involvement in the economy, and, with the exception of Japan, more than all other industrial states Switzerland has resisted the building of a publicly funded welfare state.

In Austria, by way of contrast, the foundations of a welfare state – poured while the structure of the empire crumbled – were expanded at the end of World War I and administered by the Socialists in the city of Vienna in the 1920s. That experiment provided for both Conservatives and Socialists alike a model for building a modern social welfare state for all of Austria after 1945. This welfare state plays an exceptionally large role in the economy, for all of the industries seized first by Germany, and later the Soviet Union, had ended up in public ownership by 1955. There was no other institution in Austria that could have acquired or managed these vast properties. The dynastic empire that was the center of the Austrian state in the nineteenth century thus has been replaced by an industrial empire since 1945. The architecture of the sprawling Hofburg in Vienna and the unassuming Bundeshaus in Bern express today the different legacies that imperial and democratic politics have left for the state in Austria and in Switzerland.

These legacies account for the different roles the state plays in contemporary Swiss and Austrian politics. In their institutional structure, scope, and strength the Swiss and the Austrian states differ greatly. In Switzerland the state is decentralized, has a narrow scope for action, and is weak. In Austria the state is centralized, has a broad scope for action, and is strong.

The strict separation of powers stipulated in Switzerland's constitution is observed in practice; in a system distinguished by the role accumulation of its political elite, there is virtually no overlap in personnel between Parliament and the executive branch of government. In contrast to Austria, members of the Federal Council are forbidden to hold office simultaneously in major interest groups. The territorial decentralization of the Swiss state circumscribes its role in the formulation and implementation of policy. In policy matters, the government must take full account of the cantons and main interest groups; if it does not secure at least tacit support for its policies in these diverse quarters, state policy is always open to a possible challenge at the polls. Even if a controversial bill were to be passed in the Federal Assembly, often it could not be effectively implemented without the assistance of the centers of power outside the state. The economic resources and institutional capacities of the state bureaucracy are simply too small. In comparison with Austria, the decentralization and severely limited capacities of Switzerland's state institutions are striking. With some justification, therefore, Switzerland has been characterized as a "prescription for central non-government."[3]

The severe limitations that this weakness imposes on the Swiss government may explain why the Federal Council embodies the principles of administrative efficiency rather than partisan politics.[4] The seven counselors from whom the president of the Swiss Confederation is chosen on a rotating basis lack political visibility and charisma. Two institutional practices illustrate this depoliticization of the executive. First, the seven members of the government serve in a dual capacity as elected political heads of their departments and simultaneously as senior civil servants. Second, the federal counselors do not indicate in public the position they have chosen individually on political issues, and they refrain from criticizing openly decisions reached jointly. The British doctrine of the collective responsibility of the cabinet is stood on its head in Berne: Secrecy is the trademark of an administrative rather than a partisan type of executive politics. The encroachment of bureaucratic habits and norms into the arena of executive politics illustrates the neutralization of state power rather than the existence of a powerful civil service. The federal bureaucracy lacks officially sanctioned career patterns and the guarantee of lifetime employment, and it observes the dictates of a linguistic *Proporz*. Compared with Japan or Britain, the professional civil service (*Beamtenprofession*) is not as strongly united by common social background, training, or outlook. Because of the closely knit character of Switzerland's political elite in general, the absence of a cohesive state elite is particularly striking. In a country totally adverse to doctrines of etatisme, the civil service has very limited resources and information. Instead, it relies heavily on the cooperation of organized groups. With good reason, the Swiss insist that the peak association of business calls the main tune; the Swiss often remark that the "Vorort in Zurich sets the switches for the government in Berne" (Im Züricher Vorort werden die Weichen für Bern gestellt).

Switzerland's federal bureaucracy is relatively small (32,000), and the rate of increase since 1945 has been comparatively slow.[5] It compensates for its small size by a "militia" system of dispersed administration that relies for expertise and administrative capacity primarily on the major interest groups and prominent individuals. Because it leaves so many tasks, especially on questions of economic and social policy, to the major economic interest groups, it risks turning "into a series of guild-like fiefs."[6] In the 1970s, for example, for every one of the 4,000 higher or middle-level civil servants with academic training there existed a seat for an outside "expert" on one of the 334 "extraparliamentary" committees advising the state bureaucracy.[7]

The weakness of government and bureaucracy is reflected everywhere. The policy instruments of the federal government, few as they are, are restricted by the power of the populace. In 1977 and again in 1979, for example, the government's effort to adopt a value-added tax was defeated by a referendum. If compared with provincial or local authorities, Switzerland's federal government receives the lowest share of tax revenues among all the OECD countries, be they unitary or federal: 29 percent as compared with an OECD average of 58 percent. As a result, problems of policy implementation typically involve a process of complex bargaining among different levels of government.[8] This picture is consistent with the conclusions of a cross-national analysis of policy instruments that identified Switzerland as the only country in a sample of seventy-three still adhering to a minimum of intervention in the economy.[9]

The weakness of the Swiss state is reflected in its relations with the private banking system. Formal political supervision of Swiss banks is weak. The Swiss Banking Commission (Eidgenössische Bankenkommission) is independent of the government. Although the commission's position was strengthened somewhat in the 1970s, its ineffective supervision of Switzerland's 600 banks has been attested to, for example, by the scandal surrounding the Credit Suisse in 1977 and the closing of the Banque Leclerc in 1978. But even these spectacular episodes have left the banks' operations largely untouched politically. Musing about the political implications of somewhat stricter supervision, one Zurich official expressed a widespread opinion: "Well, it doesn't mean that banks are going to lose any of their freedom. It just puts a limit on how far they can go."[10] When the Banking Commission ruled in early 1982 that in the future Swiss banks would have to disclose in their balance sheets the extent to which they draw on their hidden reserves to absorb losses, another banking official viewed this as a typical Swiss compromise. "You still can have hidden reserves, but you no longer can have hidden losses."[11] In any case, whatever formal supervision may exist is much less important than the informal relations that tie the private banks to the National Bank. Private ownership of the National Bank makes it unique among the central banks of the advanced industrial states. The National Bank operates under some political controls and returns a part of its earning in the form of dividend payments to the cantons and to private shareholders. Its board of directors is under the supervision of the Banking Committee (Bankausschuss) composed of ten members, mostly Zurich bankers, which in turn reports to the Banking Council composed of forty members, twenty-five of whom are appointed by the government. This inner circle of power has been viewed by one observer "as a financial *Commune* where citizenship devolves on the managers of companies whose balance sheets are larger than SFr. 500 million."[12] The self-regulation of the Swiss banking community illustrates the weakness that characterizes the Swiss state generally.

The centralized structure of Austria's relatively strong state offers a striking contrast to Switzerland. The Second Republic's administrative tradition of a strong bureaucratic state dates back to the mercantilist unification of the German core of the Habsburg Empire under Maria Theresa and her son, Joseph II, in the eighteenth century. Furthermore, Austria's federal system is weak, and Vienna remains the undisputed center of the country's political life. Over the past three decades Austria's state bureaucracy has steadily expanded. If the size of Austria's welfare bureaucracy is measured by the number of officials per capita, it tops that of all other European bureaucracies. Civil service pensions as a share of earnings are the largest in Europe.[13] Austria's bureaucracy is intimately involved in the political relations between unions and business as well as in the formulation and implementation of a much broader range of public policies than can be found across the Swiss border. In the eyes of the public at least, the state bureaucracy is a very powerful institution indeed.

That power is illustrated very clearly by the prominent role the state plays in Austria's economic life. The Austrian state owns virtually all of the country's transportation, communication, and power industries, a number of state monopolies including tobacco, salt, the two largest commercial banks, and seven of the eight largest joint stock companies. Of all joint stock companies "in 1969, federal authorities accounted for 45 percent of total shares, regional authorities for 12 percent, and nationalized banks for 10 percent. Multinational corporations and Austrian private enterprise accounted for 13 percent each."[14] The state-owned enterprises employ 28 percent of Austria's industrial work force, the same proportion as for foreign firms; Austrian private firms account for the balance of 44 percent.[15] About one-sixth of the Austrian work force is employed in enterprises directly or indirectly owned by the federal government. Adding the employees in the public sector narrowly defined, such as civil servants, police, and teachers, the public sector accounts for close to one-third of Austria's national output.[16] Furthermore, the importance of public ownership in the economy is greatest among Austria's largest firms. Firms such as the Voest-Alpine steel combine play a critically important part in an economy otherwise characterized by relatively small private firms. It does not really matter whether one measures firm size by turnover, exports, or number of employees.[17] Among Austria's fifty largest corporations, nationalized firms account for more than two-thirds, private firms for little more than 10 percent, and foreign firms for about 15 percent of the total. Moreover, Austria's fifty largest firms account for more than half of Austria's total industrial production.

In addition to vast holdings in industry, the government also owns the four largest commercial banks, the two largest insurance companies, and a host of other financial institutions. Because of the banks' substantial direct ownership or indirect control over a large number of subsidiaries, the Austrian government could indirectly control an even larger part of Austrian industry. Calculating the extent of the banks' ownership and control of industry is a favorite pastime in Austria. By most accounts Austria's nationalized banks own about 10 percent of the nominal capital of all joint stock companies, and their subsidiaries have about 60,000 employees. In addition, the nationalized banks have at their disposal a variety of instruments falling short of ownership that, although defying all attempts at precise calculation, enhance the state's dominant position in Austria's economic life.[18]

The histories of Austria and Switzerland have given very different shapes to state, business, and labor. In Switzerland the state is relatively decentralized and weak, the business community is strong and thrives on international competition, and an acquiescent labor movement is fragmented and its power relatively circumscribed. In Austria the state is centralized and strong, the business community is relatively weak and has a national outlook, and an assertive labor movement is united and its power far reaching. As a result of these historical differences, the balance between public and private power tilts heavily toward the state in Austria and toward society in Switzerland.

The State as a Part of the Policy Network

History puts Austria and Switzerland close together; geography sets them far apart. Twentieth-century history has forced a partial political convergence that affects deeply the relation between state and society.

Austria and Switzerland have been transformed by the political experiences of the 1930s and 1940s: the depression, fascism, and World War II. Shared memories of German concentration camps, political exile, or life under foreign occupation prompted the Austrians to bury the conflicts that had exploded into civil war in 1934. Keenly aware of their exposed and vulnerable position in a hostile world, Austria's political leaders redefined narrowly conceived class interests into a broader conception of the national interest. The system of coalition governments that joined together Catholics and Socialists between 1945 and 1966 was both a symbol and a guarantor of political stability.

In Switzerland the risks of escalating industrial militance were effectively eliminated with the conclusion of the "peace agreement" that business, under pressure from the government, negotiated with the metalworkers' union in 1937. That agreement eventually became a model for Switzerland's industrial relations system generally. A constitutional amendment of 1948 mandated the consultation of interest groups by government, and the permanent inclusion of the Social Democratic party in Switzerland's executive branch, the Federal Council, in the 1950s completed the transformation of Switzerland's "voting democracy" to a "bargaining democracy."[19] As a result of these changes, during the postwar years consensus-style politics has prevailed in both countries. Indeed, both Austria and Switzerland describe their collaborative political arrangements as a system of social partnership, which contrasts with the politically organized class warfare that by now Austrian and Swiss political leaders remember only dimly.

Why did the system of social partnership in both countries regenerate itself as the memories of the 1930s and 1940s faded? Why did not the second generation of political leaders reject the lessons the first had learned? The reason, I argue elsewhere, lies in the pressure that an increasingly liberal international economy exerts on domestic political arrangements in small European democracies.[20]

In their openness to and dependence on the world economy, Switzerland and Austria resemble other small, rich European states. Small domestic markets lead to a dependence on market change, which for two reasons is much greater in the small European states than in the large industrial states. First, because they do not offer to a number of industries absolutely critical to the functioning of a modern economy the necessary economies of scale, the small European states must import a wide range of goods that the large industrial countries produce domestically. Secondly, small domestic markets lead Austria and Switzerland to seek their specialization and economies of scale in export markets. As a proportion of gross national product the export of goods and services was about twice as large in the small as in the large industrial states in the mid-1970s. Dependence on imports and the necessity to export make the transformation of the Swiss and Austrian economies the result of changes in international markets rather than of state action.[21]

The fragility of Austria's and Switzerland's positions in the international economy is reconfirmed by daily experience. International competition has intensified greatly and thus reinforces the enormous benefits that accrue from limiting domestic quarrels, especially quarrels over questions of economic and social policy. Annual strike statistics, for example, are counted in seconds in Austria and Switzerland. Everyone – business, unions, government, and consumers – agrees that strikes are simply too costly a method for settling domestic disputes. Because their economies are so open, elites in Austria and Switzerland have never lost the sense of being the object of developments that they cannot control fully. Their links to the international economy are thus of vital importance for the perpetuation of political collaboration in domestic politics.

That collaboration has led in both Austria and Switzerland to an unusually far-reaching interpenetration of state and society. The essence of collaboration is to entangle in a densely woven fabric political actors that elsewhere choose to walk their different ways. For the political fabric not to tear requires that great power inequalities between political actors be narrowed. This narrowing is not a natural process of adjustment. It resembles rather a deadlock. Fully cognizant of the external pressures acting on their societies, political leaders are able to compromise in a political environment they try hard to make predictable. This narrowing of power differences affects the relation between state and society, as I shall now argue, by diminishing state power in Austria and enlarging it in Switzerland.

Austria

The power of the Austrian state is circumscribed. The assertiveness of the political parties in Austria's corporatism contributes to the passivity of the bureaucracy and the partisan neutralization of state power. "Positions which involve major actors of economic decision-making are thought to entail ideological opportunities and power – therefore to be a vital matter for the parties and the people."[22] Yet Austria's Conservative People's party (OVP) and the Social Democratic party (SPO) have persistently disagreed on the role of the public sector in the economy; as a result, political control over the economy that potentially could be had by either the bureaucracy or the economic partners, simply because of the sheer size of Austria's public sector, has remained partly unrealized. The OVP has traditionally been interested in limiting the scope of the public sector and in having management conform to "economic" considerations. SPO leaders, on the other hand, have always argued that a planned and a market economy are mutually complementary; the nationalized sector in particular should therefore consider the effects of its strategy on the whole economy (and in particular on labor markets), rather than on company profits alone. Conflicting conceptions of the purpose of economic power to which Austria's two major parties have adhered have thus blunted both the potential for state intervention in the economy and the potential for invigorating competition in Austrian markets. The partisan penetration of Austria's nationalized industries and nationalized banks, as well as the institutional requirements of its industrial policy, illustrate how the political parties have neutralized state power.

Because of the enormous power base that they provide, the nationalized industries have been the source of intense partisan conflict in Austria's supposedly consensual political milieu. For the past thirty years the political control over Austria's public economy has been determined at the polls. Control was reflected before 1966 in the reorganization of ministerial responsibilities negotiated by the two main parties in their coalition agreements and, after 1966, in the administrative reorganization of public enterprises imposed after the OVP's and SPO's electoral victories, respectively, of 1966 and 1970. And throughout the postwar period, *Proporz* power was most immediately exercised in nationalized firms through the political staffing of top-level and middle-level management positions. In fact, for the nationalized sector the Proporz system was legally sanctioned in 1956. Different firms in the same economic sector tended to be either "black" or "'red." In the 1960s, for example, of the eighty-nine members of the board of directors and chairmen of the board surveyed in one study, only two were nonpartisan.[23] This clear partisan division of positions of economic power made it possible to calculate that, in the 1960s in Austria's nationalized industries, firms dominated by the OVP had 67,000 employees as comapred with 53,000 for those dominated by the SPO.[24] But political power is shared and thus neutralized not only between but within firms. In the mid-1960s the United Austrian Iron and Steel Works (Vereinigte Öster-reichische Eisen- und Stahlwerke) were often viewed as a citadel of "red" power; yet three of the six top management positions – the chairman of the board, the assistant general director, and one of the two assistant directors – were in fact staffed by the conservative OVP. The move to one-party government since 1966, the internal reorganization of the public enterprises in the late 1960s and early 1970s, as well as the SPO's gradual and successful implantation in power in the 1970s, have tended to diminish this explicit politicization of economic life. It is by no means clear, however, that an apparent depoliticization "really means kicking the other side out," as a leading bureaucrat predicted in 1966.[25] The holding company for Austria's nationalized firms, OIAG, set up by the Socialist party in the early 1970s, retains key elements of the *Proporz* legislated in 1956 even though these elements are not codified by the company law, which governs other parts of the OIAG's behavior. Its supervisory board, for example, is not elected at the annual shareholders meeting. Instead, fifteen members are nominated by the political parties according to their strength in Parliament, and three members are nominated by the government. This arrangement grants the OVP a very substantial representation of its interests while assuring the SPO of a working majority. In the 1970s the OVP dominated the appointees to 61 of 136 positions available on the supervisory boards of the nationalized firms under the control of the OIAG. Five of ten chairman-ships and 18 of 37 directorships are now held by managers with close ties to the OVP. The SPO controls virtually all of the other positions. "The allegiance of these politically appointed managers to their respective parties varies from case to case, even though practically all are members of party suborganizations that unite them within an informal club-like atmosphere."[26] Chancellor Kreisky and his successor have repeatedly reaffirmed the continued validity of this institutionalization of Austria's collaborative political arrangements.

The weakness of the state bureaucracy is thus very evident precisely in that area where the bureaucracy plays a very prominent role: in Austria's nationalized industry. Government intervention in Austrian industry is in fact remarkably restrained. Austria's nationalized firms make their contribution to the stabilization of employment and investment, but they resist vigorously direct forms of political intervention and conduct their business overwhelmingly along the lines of commercial profitability. The formal instruments of control that the government has at its disposal are quite limited. Since the Nationalization Acts of July 26, 1946, and March 26, 1947, transferred the shares of the affected firms to the Second Republic, normally "the only way the state is able to exert an influence on the enterprises is by exercising its rights as a shareholder."[27] As early as 1949 the Austrian government gave up all serious attempts at systematic economic planning policies. That year marked the beginning of the organizational fragmentation of the public sector. Nationalized industries and nationalized banks were put under the jurisdiction of different ministries, and the first Nationalization Act's mandate for a coordinated economic policy approach was repealed.[28] Subsequent developments reinforced the neutralization of state power. For example, for prolonged periods in the 1950s and 1960s, Austria's petroleum industry lacked vertical integration because of its organizational ties to different government agencies. Until recently, nationalized firms enjoyed substantial financial autonomy. Because Austria's nationalized firms have the same legal standing as the private firms, there exist neither special management associations nor different collective bargaining mechanisms. The management of nationalized firms, not the government, decides how much profit is to be reinvested in the firms and to be paid out to the government in the form of dividends. And countercyclical stabilization policies relying on the employment and investment decisions of nationalized firms cannot simply be achieved, as the programs of 1962 and the 1970s illustrate, by simple administrative decree and bureaucratic authority. Instead, these policies need the full prestige of the minister and the support of the political parties in the delicate negotiations the government conducts with public sector firms. The organizational fragmentation of the public enterprises and the relative lack of government control were clearly recognized by both the OVP and the SPO and were mirrored in the reorganization drives the two parties initiated when they seized full control of the government in 1966 and 1970, respectively. The organizational simplification that the OVP brought about through the establishment of a central, nationalized holding company in the late 1960s still left the Austrian Industrial Corporation with very little control over individual firms and enterprises. In the early 1970s the SPO converted the OIG from a trust company to a joint stock company, the OIAG, and increased slightly the power of central headquarters, but the SPO also refused to enlarge the government's limited formal control. Austria's nationalized industries display "the characteristics of nationalization and of state capitalism, but few of the characteristics of socialization. . . . For better or for worse, the role of the state as owner is largely passive."[29]

The partisan neutralization of the power of the state bureaucracy is evident also in the bureaucracy's relations with Austria's nationalized banks.[30] Throughout most of the postwar years, the banks succeeded in keeping government and bureaucracy at arm's length while running their industrial empires largely according to market criteria. The political autonomy of the banks benefited from their partial reprivatization between 1956 and 1959, the federal government's growing need for credit in the 1960s and 1970s, and the banks' comparatively strong capital base. Despite the formidable powers that legislation governing credit institutions gives to the Finance Ministry, in fact most of that power has been delegated by the government to the several associations of banking institutions. Furthermore, between 1949 and 1970 the Finance Ministry rested, without interruption, in the hands of the conservative OVP, which was not interested in further development of the government's instruments of financial intervention. Since 1970 the SPO government has continued to acknowledge the OVP's strong representation in top financial positions and has resisted the temptation to reduce sharply the OVP presence and influence in Austria's nationalized banks. "Austria's Socialists say comfortably that they need the conservative People's Party to run the state-owned banks."[31]

Despite their economic importance, Austria's nationalized banks have never become a political football to the extent that Austria's nationalized industries have. Nonetheless, the Austrian Proporz has ruled here as well. Throughout the postwar years the largest nationalized bank, the Creditanstalt, has been "black" and the second largest, the Länderbank, has been "red." Because of the mounting burden of bad debts, the board of managers of the Länderbank was summarily dismissed in the spring of 1981, but the principle of parity representation of business and unions, black and red, was strictly adhered to in its replacement. The appointment of the OVP's main parliamentary spokesperson on economic questions, Professor Stefan Koren, as the president of the National Bank in 1978 also illustrates that political power continued to be shared by both economic partners in the 1970s. One detailed study of the role of Austria's National Bank concluded in the mid-1960s that "in practice the National Bank in Austria does not depend as much on the government as on the two main political parties and the major interest groups."[32] Another analysis captures the spirit of Austria's democratic corporatism, which domesticates political conflict without abolishing it, by characterizing the situation in the following terms: "In principle the National Bank is independent. In practice it always acts in agreement with the Ministry of Finance. Some might even say that the Ministry of Finance always acts in agreement with the bank, but no one does, because the two appear to act as perfect partners, even though they disagree in public."[33]

Finally, the sharing of power and the partisan neutralization of state power are also illustrated in the SPO's attempt to establish the institutional machinery for an active industrial policy.[34] In the late 1960s Austria's bureaucracy suffered from numerous organizational weaknesses that impaired its ability to conduct a coherent policy. The Ministry of Industry and Trade was reorganized so as to include sections dealing with particular branches of industry, and some of its civil servants received additional training. Between 1968 and 1970 six different policy measures were initiated through which the Austrian government hoped to encourage innovation and reform in Austria's traditional industrial structure. But only two of these – the establishment of the Industrial Research Promotion Fund and the Working Group for the Promotion of Patents – were specific policy measures. New sectoral data were collected and published regularly from 1973 onward. Since the nationalized banks were very reluctant to go beyond their mostly limited financial rescue missions undertaken in the 1970s in defense of Austria's full employment, the Austrian government pressed ahead with the development of new institutions in preparation for an active industrial policy. But the limitations that impinged on that policy were very apparent. The new Commission for Industry, set up in 1976 and chaired by the chancellor, did not evolve, as the OVP had feared, into a centralized planning agency. Instead, it became still another body of consultation in charge of preparing detailed position papers on important industrial sectors. Nor did the commission push for a policy of concentration, as the business community had feared, but encouraged instead, in its early sessions, an enlargement of cooperative relations between Austria's medium-sized and small firms. Since the SPO's natural alliance partners are found in large-scale industry, this policy amounted to a strengthening of the political base of the OVP opposition, which typically favors small and medium-sized firms. In short, from the very outset the commission began to operate, not as a lever in the hands of government bureaucrats eager to alter Austria's industrial structure, but as another institutional pillar reinforcing Austria's collaborative structures.

Switzerland

In the case of Switzerland the narrowing of power differences enhances the power of the state in its relation to other political actors. It would be a mistake to view either the government or the state bureaucracy as impotent. The government provides information and direction to the work of the Federal Assembly, which by all accounts is its inferior in both power and status. Furthermore, the government's weakness vis-à-vis well-organized interest groups is also a source of strength. With so much power resting in the private sector, the inevitable divisions and conflicts among groups elevate the government frequently to the role of an arbiter that enjoys wide discretionary powers among plural conflicts. Through the adroit choice of institutional arenas for discussion and careful timing of the policy process, the government achieves an important impact on policy. And, at least in terms of numbers, the federal bureaucracy and the cantons dominate the early stages of the highly critical preparliamentary process of consultation.

State strength also manifests in other dimensions of Swiss life. Economic and security affairs are for the Swiss, as for the Japanese, intimately linked. In the area of agricultural policy, for example, this linkage has encouraged the adoption of policies that show the Swiss state to be in a position of unaccustomed strength and decisiveness.[35] The need to increase self-sufficiency in agriculture was one of the important lessons the Swiss learned from World War II. In 1939 Swiss agriculture covered only 30 percent of the Swiss consumption of bread cereals and produced virtually no fruit or vegetables. By 1975 more than 70 percent of bread and cereals and fruit and 40 percent of vegetables consumed in Switzerland were produced domestically. In addition, the Swiss are self-sufficient in meat and potatoes.

These dramatic changes in self-sufficiency resulted from a self-conscious and consistent policy. Every five years the Swiss formulate a plan in which they decide what Swiss agriculture should produce and in what quantities. The decision to increase self-sufficiency has also affected Switzerland's foreign trade policy in the area of agriculture. Switzerland decided in favor of joining the General Agreement on Tariffs and Trade (GATT) in 1966 only after it had been exempted from the principle of free trade in agriculture, a unique occurrence in the annals of GATT. Because the move to self-sufficiency brought with it a chronic oversupply of dairy products and the threat of long-term environmental deterioration (due to the intense application of fertilizers and the growing volume of untreated sewage), in the late 1970s Swiss policy began to impose limits on the number of cows permitted per acre. The move to self-sufficiency thus prompted further action by a strong Swiss state attempting to cope with the unintended consequences of its policy. "As liberal economic values with their emphasis on short-term factor costs erode the traditional ethic of stewardship of natural resources, an increasingly intrusive type of governmental intervention has been undertaken to protect the future . . . there were policy options open which enabled Switzerland to act and at a level of intrusion and coercion that the Swiss themselves profess to abhor."[36] Carried by a broad political consensus and embedded in an ideology that cherishes individual liberty as a component of rather than antidote to communal collectivism, the Swiss state, under conditions of crisis, can call upon residues of strength easily overlooked.[37]

Other policy arenas confirm this picture. For example, in contrast to Austria, a portion of Switzerland's low tariffs on imports are a levy imposed to help finance a vast program of economic preparedness in case of war. This is part of a larger program of civil defense that protects 90 percent of the Swiss population against nuclear attack. On questions, like those of defense or money, that touch the very core of Switzerland's security and vital interest, the laborious process of collaborative consultation, characteristic of almost all other economic and social issues, is less prominent. Switzerland's constant state of military preparedness is reflected by the fact that more than thirty years after the end of World War II about one-half of the total federal bureaucracy is employed by the defense department. A recent scandal in Switzerland's intelligence community revealed that in the latter part of the 1970s Switzerland's two top-secret government intelligence services were directed by the same official, who also headed a parallel private organization. When the Queen of England visited Switzerland in May 1981, British journalists were astonished by the extent of security precautions, which some likened to those of well-established dictatorships.[38]

The issue of foreign workers also enhances the role of state authority and reflects an underlying, forceful state presence often overlooked. The xenophobic streak in Switzerland resonates more deeply with the entrenched parochialism of the country's Alpine cantons than with its more cosmopolitan periphery. The intensification of the fear of foreign influences during the 1930s suggests historical and political parallels with Fascist movements that never won a wide following in Switzerland. The restrictive immigration legislation, which is still in force today, dates back to the 1930s. And Switzerland's Federal Aliens' Police is singularly efficient and omnipresent in identifying illegal immigrants. In close cooperation with the cantonal labor market authorities, it is a highly visible symbol of state power. Furthermore, the dramatic expansion in the number of foreign workers in the postwar years stands in sharp contrast to the restrictive naturalization policy that Switzerland has adhered to. In the late 1970s more than one-half of Switzerland's aliens possessed the formal qualifications of twelve years' residence for naturalization, but fewer than ten percent of those eligible have been extended citizenship since 1951. In 1975 the number of naturalized citizens was 10,000, or about 1 percent of the foreign work force. The strong role of the state is, finally, reinforced by the adoption of a highly restrictive immigration policy in the 1970s that relies on a quota system and is administered by the federal government rather than the cantons.[39]

In the area of foreign economic policy, close relations among business, the unions, and the government have also enhanced state power. Compared with the other small European states as well as the large, advanced industrial countries, the intimate connections between business and government, in particular, are unique. These connections consist of informal, personal consultation as well as institutionalized contacts. Parapublic institutions such as the Trade Development Office and the recent growth of "mixed" trade commissions organizing Switzerland's commercial relations with the Soviet Union, Iran, and Saudi Arabia provide arenas in which government officials and business cooperate in the implementation of commercial policy. It is standard practice for Swiss business to be directly represented in international trade negotiations. Furthermore, there exists a Consultative Commission for Foreign Trade Policy, which the Federal Council is obliged to consult on all important trade questions. Its thirty to forty members, drawn from the major interest groups, agree on the main policy questions, not through majority vote, but through prolonged discussions that lead to compromise solutions accepted by all. Owing to the difficulties that Swiss exports have encountered in world markets since 1973, this consultative commission was supplemented in 1975 by the Advisory Committee for Foreign Economic Policy. It draws on a more restricted circle of the Swiss elite and now serves as the major speaker for Switzerland's export industries. It, rather than the consultative commission, hammered out the series of policy decisions designed to strengthen the export sector in 1975 and 1976. The true center of power, the Permanent Economic Delegation for Economic Negotiations, is still more exclusive than either the consultative commission or the advisory committee. It lacks all legal foundation for its power. Its membership is not fixed but is normally restricted to top government officials, senior bureaucrats, the leaders of the big four interest groups, and a small and variable number of guests, who are invited on the basis of the subject matter under discussion. Invitations to attend particular sessions are extended to individuals rather than institutions, and the permanent delegation keeps no written records. Here all the threads run together, for under the auspices of the state one small group makes the fundamental decisions that Switzerland confronts in the international economy.[40]

It is not unheard of for the solutions to Switzerland's political problems fashioned in these exclusive circles to be challenged through the institutions of direct democracy. In 1976, for example, a coalition between voters of the traditional Right who distrusted Switzerland's increasing involvement in international organizations and voters of the new Left opposed to international financial institutions joined forces in a referendum. They managed to veto a bill, already passed by both houses of the Federal Assembly, which would have extended a loan to the International Development Agency. But in a broader perspective such incursions of the public into the interlocking corridors of power are very rare in the area of foreign economic policy. Between 1920 and 1974 seven of the eight foreign policy measures that the government had to subject to popular referendum passed; only one of the fourteen popular initiatives brought against government policy was accepted.[41] Normally, then, the close cooperation between peak associations, the state bureaucracy, and the government is not challenged by the public in the area of foreign economic policy. "In general, the decision-making in foreign economic policy is different from the decision-making on domestic issues. The efficiency, flexibility, and quickness of centralized oligarchic foreign economic policy is functional with regard to the rapid changes of the international economic regime. The rather conservative, pragmatic, and time-consuming consociational decision-making . . . is functional with regard to democracy and legitimacy."[42]

The strict limitations imposed on the power of the decentralized Swiss state are themselves, as in the United States, a source of fundamental political strength, especially in times of economic crisis. The Swiss constitution is a "kind of working brief, always redescribing and redefining its authority."[43] Since the last constitutional revision of 1874, ninety amendments have been passed by popular vote. Reliance on bypassing democratic practices in times of crisis has historical precedents. For example, between 1919 and 1939 one-half of all federal laws and decrees were issued under the constitution's emergency clause and were thus removed from all popular control. Sixty percent of these measures were passed between 1930 and 1938. In the 1950s and 1960s, by way of contrast, the political process was typically marked by a long process of complex bargaining and informal agreements. The antiinflation program of 1964, which, in an atmosphere of crisis, was drawn up, debated, and adopted within a week, was a notable exception.[44]

Since the early 1970s, however, that exception has almost become the norm. For example, with the advent of flexible exchange rates, the emergency decree for the Protection of the Currency of 1971 accords the Federal Council and the National Bank broad discretionary powers that have been in constant use throughout the 1970s. A more stringent antiinflation program (1972), regional planning policy (1972), fiscal policy (1975), and unemployment insurance scheme (1975–1976) are prominent examples of a growing reliance on rule by emergency decree. Between 1971 and 1976 the government issued nine extraconstitutional emergency decrees, all of which were approved by an obligatory referendum. Between 1949 and 1970 only three such decrees had been issued. Similarly, between 1971 and 1976 the government issued fifteen constitutional emergency decrees, about 10 percent of the total number of bills passed and about 15 percent of the significant political issues, none of which was appealed by the optional referendum stipulated by the constitution. Between 1949 and 1970 only seven such decrees had been issued.[45] Expressed in numerical terms, in the 1970s the annual average of these two forms of emergency decree increased by factors of 11 and 8 respectively. Rule by emergency decree increases state power by reducing the number of points of intervention in the policy process as well as the number of participants, but because of the collaborative process of policy making that has evolved since 1945, Switzerland stopped far short of moving back in the 1970s all the way to the crisis pattern of the 1930s.

Switzerland's consensus politics strengthens the power of this weak state in relation to nonstate actors. The narrowing of power differences that is essential to the success of political collaboration relies on a combination of collective representation and collective self-discipline. Consensus politics restricts the power of Austria's strong state and enhances that of Switzerland's weak state. In the temptations it holds and in the transformations it affects, cooperation thus has a different impact on the state in different systems. In both Switzerland and Austria cooperative arrangements are a mechanism for reintegrating conflicting class interests in a broader conception of national welfare informed by the vulnerabilities that beset open economies. The inclusionary character of these political arrangements makes possible the narrowing of power differences that affect differently the character of the state in Switzerland and Austria.

The experience of the 1930s made the Austrians wary of political arrangements that would give full control of the levers of state power to only one of the two major parties. That perilous decade forced the Swiss to grant the state emergency powers that threatened to transform their system of direct democracy. Although memories of the 1930s have faded in Austria and Switzerland, institutional arrangements that spawned cooperation have acquired their own momentum. The pressure to remain competitive in the international economy makes acceptable political arrangements that closely link in one policy network the state, business, and labor.

The effect of multiple links is to diminish the power of the state in Austria and to increase the power of the state in Switzerland. On questions of state power, then, present-day political relations have become divorced from the historical reasons that gave rise to them.

Consequences for Policy

State power in Austria and Switzerland is conditioned by both divergent and convergent historical developments. Historical differences explain why in their politics these two societies epitomize, respectively, democratic socialism and liberal capitalism. Historical similarities explain why a collaborative politics emerges from the political relations among actors of relatively equal standing. The consequence of both developments can be traced in the economic and social policies that Austria and Switzerland have adopted in the past several decades.

Switzerland has followed a consistently liberal foreign trade policy, has invested heavily abroad, and has imported foreign labor on a large scale. It has limited public expenditures, developed a privatized social welfare system, and generally adhered to a market-oriented economic policy. Conversely, Austria has cautiously pursued a liberal foreign trade policy, has heavily subsidized domestic investment, and has been fully committed to full employment and an active labor market policy. It has large public expenditures, a generous publicly funded social welfare system, and an incomes policy regulating wages and prices that is agreed on by both unions and business. These differences in policy show that the Austrian state tends toward activism, the Swiss toward passivity. State activism agrees with the central importance of the labor movement in Austrian politics, and a passive state suits the central place of the business community in Swiss politics. In neither country does there exist any fundamental political tension over the role that the state plays on the political stage.

Of equal importance is the fact that collaborative political arrangements require a relatively equal distribution of power among political actors. This tends to restrain state activism in Austria and encourages it under special circumstances in Switzerland. State activity in both societies is not geared primarily to the task of economic development and social redistribution. Instead, its primary purpose is to relegitimize the collaborative arrangements that Austria and Switzerland have evolved in response to external pressures.

On questions of social redistribution, Switzerland's and Austria's experiences are rather similar. As is true in the case of most other industrial states, we do not have an adequate body of data on which to base this judgment with any degree of precision or confidence, but the evidence that is available points in this direction. In the case of Switzerland this fact is not surprising. Switzerland is a bastion of private business and the home of an electorate that defends personal liberty and property energetically through the institution of direct democracy. Because Switzerland's trade unions and Social Democratic Left have failed in mounting a substantial offensive against this strong coalition defending the status quo, social redistribution is not an issue seriously debated or acted on by the Swiss state.

More surprising is the fact that questions of social redistribution have remained dormant in Austria even though the Left has implanted itself increasingly in positions of power since 1945. In hoping to further the objectives of social democracy through a strategy of growth rather than through distributional struggles, the Austrian union movement was prepared to accept in the late 1960s and early 1970s substantial losses in the relative share of the gross domestic product accruing to labor. Noted several times in the OECD's *Economic Surveys,* this was characterized as "an atypical development" in the prolonged upswing of the business cycle then experienced by the industrial world.[46] The gains of 1974–75 stemming from very large real wage increases in the face of a world recession that had not been accurately projected by Austrian economists were offset by the sharp drop in the wage share in 1978–80. Even if we correct for changes in the structure of Austria's employment, it remains the case that a decade of Socialist rule has not altered the size of the wage share in national income.[47] Moreover, Austria's growth policy has, at best, left unaltered the inegalitarian distribution of income and wealth. More likely, that policy has reinforced an inequality that, at least in principle, the union movement is committed to erasing.[48] Instead of emphasizing the goal of social equality in programmatic demands and ideological debates, the Austrian union leadership has chosen instead to involve itself politically at the very highest levels in the arenas of economic and social policy most critical to Austria's political strategy in the world economy.

The similar positions that Switzerland and Austria occupy in the international economy leave the transformation of the economic structures of these two countries primarily to international markets rather than state initiatives. Because of the stronger position of the unions and the political Left, questions of social redistribution are more relevant in Austria than in Switzerland, where the strength of the business community and a conservative electorate block most possibilities for redistribution. But in Austria the requirements of economic efficiency and considerations of maintaining the political balance between Left and Right have severely constrained the interventionist impulses of the state. Conversely, in Switzerland the political requirements of maintaining social consensus occasionally have prompted state interventions in economy and society that deviate from efficient market solutions.

This essay has argued three different points. First, historical developments dating back to the eighteenth century have left Austria and Switzerland with differences in the character of their business communities, labor movements, and state structures. In Austria the state is relatively strong and centralized and has a broad scope of action. In Switzerland the state is relatively weak and decentralized and enjoys only a narrow scope of action. These differences must be understood against the backdrop of historical contrasts in the constitutions of the two polities, in the timing and nature of the process of industrialization, and in the geopolitical paths the two nations followed into the postwar world. They are reflected, in turn, in the social and economic policies of the two countries.

The second point complements the first. Historically grounded differences in the state's role persist side by side with strong convergent tendencies. The principal pressure toward convergence comes from the problems the two countries share. Both are small, committed to economic openness, and inextricably involved in the international economy. In each, increasing involvement in a liberal international economy has reinforced the political lessons of the 1930s and 1940s, encouraging far-reaching political collaboration. One of the most important correlates of their consensus politics is a narrowing of power differences between actors, which in Austria tends to diminish and in Switzerland to enhance state power. Just as the differences in the character of these states are reflected in social policy, the convergent tendencies are reflected in some surprising similarities in the political strategies by which Austria and Switzerland have solved their economic and social problems in the postwar world.

Finally, the attempt to interpret simultaneously the divergent and similar characteristics of Austria and Switzerland points to the value of looking at the state from more than one perspective. Two perspectives have been employed here. The state has been examined as an actor on the political stage and also as part of a policy network that links it with other social actors. The first perspective served to highlight differences between the two states, the second to illuminate surprising convergences. Each of these interpretations offers an important half-truth about Austria and Switzerland. Taken together, they point to the intersections of political forces that in the Alps, and perhaps elsewhere, continuously modify state capacities and state structures.

Notes

This chapter draws on some of the material published in my *Corporatism and Change: Austria, Switzerland, and the Politics of Industry* (Ithaca, N.Y.: Cornell University Press, 1984). I would like to thank the Rockefeller Foundation and the German Marshall Fund for their financial support of this project and the editors of this volume for their critical comments on earlier drafts of this chapter. I also benefited from the criticisms and suggestions of Mary F. Katzenstein, Stephen Krasner, T. J. Pempel, Martin Shefter, and Sidney Tarrow.

1. Alexander Gerschenkron, *An Economic Spurt That Failed: Four Lectures in Austrian History* (Princeton, N.J.: Princeton University Press, 1977).

2. David Klingman, *Social Change, Political Change, and Public Policy: Norway and Sweden, 1875–1965* (Beverly Hills, Calif.: Sage, 1976).

3. B. Beedham and G. Lee, "Even in Paradise," *Economist*, February 22, 1969 (Survey), p. v.

4. Ulrich Klöti, *Die Chefbeamten der schweizerischen Bundesverwaltung* (Bern: Francke, 1971); Thomas A. Baylis, "Collegial Leadership in Advanced Industrial Societies: The Relevance of the Swiss Experience," *Polity* 13 (Fall 1980): 33–56.

5. Hanspeter Kriesi, *Entscheidungsstrukturen und Entscheidungsprozesse in der Schweizer Politik* (Frankfurt: Campus, 1980), p. 35.

6. Jean Meynaud, *Les organisations professionelles en Suisse* (Lausanne: Payot, 1963), p. 313; as quoted in Roland Ruffieux, "The Political Influence of Senior Civil Servants in Switzerland," in *The Mandarins of Western Europe: The Political Role of Top Civil Servants* ed. Mattei Dogan (New York: Wiley, 1975), p. 250.

7. Raimund E. Germann and Andreas Frutiger, "Role Cumulation in Swiss Advisory Committees" (Paper prepared for a workshop, Interest Groups and Governments, European Consortium for Political Research, Florence, March 25–30, 1980), pp. 1–3.

8. Organization for Economic Cooperation and Development, *Public Expenditure Trends* (Paris: OECD, 1978), p. 90.

9. Gottfried Berweger and Jean-Pierre Hoby, "Typologien für Wirtschaftspolitik" (Sociology Institute, University of Zurich, 1978), pp. 6–8.

10. *New York Times,* June 5, 1979, p. D4.

11. *Wall Street Journal,* April 27, 1982, p. 31.

12. Jonathan Steinberg, *Why Switzerland?* (Cambridge: Cambridge University Press, 1976), p. 156.

13. Harold L. Wilensky, *The Welfare State and Equality: Structural and Ideological Roots of Public Expenditure* (Berkeley: University of California Press, 1975), pp. 10–11.

14. Ferdinand Lacina, *The Development of the Austrian Public Sector since World War II,* Technical papers ser. no. 7 (Institute of Latin American Studies, Office for Public Sector Studies, University of Texas at Austin, 1977), p. 8.

15. Oskar Grünwald, "Austrian Industrial Structure and Industrial Policy," in *The Political Economy of Austria,* ed. Sven W. Arndt (Washington, D.C.: American Enterprise Institute for Public Policy Research, 1982), p. 136.

16. Sarah Hogg, "A Small House in Order," *Economist,* March 15, 1980 (Survey), p. 8.

17. Ferdinand Lacina, "Zielsetzung und Effizienz verstaatlichter Unternehmen," *Wirtschaft und Gesellschaft* 4(2) (1978): 143–54; Manfred Drennig, "Vermögensverteilung in Österreich – ihre politische Relevanz," in *Das politische System Österreichs,* ed. Heinz Fischer (Vienna: Europa Verlag, 1974), p. 481; Volker Bornschier, *Wachstum, Konzentration und Multinationalisierung von Industrieunternehmen* (Frauenfeld: Huber, 1976), p. 206.

18. Karl Socher, "Die öffentlichen Unternehmen im österreichischen Banken- und Versicherungswesen," in *Die Verstaatlichung in Österreich,* ed. Wilhelm Weber (Berlin: Duncker & Humblot, 1964), pp. 393–400; Hogg, "A Small House in Order," p. 8.

19. Leonhard Neidhart, *Plebiszit und pluralitäre Demokratie: Eine Analyse der Funktion des schweizerischen Gesetzesreferendums* (Bern: Francke, 1970), pp. 313–19.

20. See my *Small States in World Markets: Industrial Policy in Europe* (Ithaca: Cornell University Press, 1985), chap. 3, for a full statement of the argument and supporting evidence.

250   Peter Katzenstein

21. Margaret Sieber, *Dimensionen kleinstaatlicher Auslandabhängigkeit,* Kleine Studien zur Politischen Wissenschaft no. 206–207 (Forschungsstelle für Politische Wissenschaft, University of Zurich, 1981), pp. 156–59; Peter J. Katzenstein, *Corporatism and Change,* chaps. 5 and 6.

22. Uwe Kitzinger, quoted in Andrew Shonfield, *Modern Capitalism: The Changing Balance of Public and Private Power* (London: Oxford University Press, 1965), p. 194.

23. Christof Gaspari and Hans Millendorfer, *Prognosen für Österreich: Fakten und Formeln der Entwicklung* (Vienna: Verlag für Geschichte und Politik, 1973), p. 117.

24. Christian Smekal, *Die verstaatlichte Industrie in der Marktwirtschaft: Das österreichische Beispiel* (Cologne: Heymanns, 1963), p. 55.

25. Quoted in Dennison I. Rusinow, "Notes towards a Political Definition of Austria," part 4, *AUFS Reports,* June 1966: 20.

26. Erich Andrlik, "Labor–Management Relations in Austria's Steel Industry" (Unpublished paper, May 1982), pp. 12–13.

27. Organization for Economic Cooperation and Development, *Industrial Policy of Austria* (Paris: OECD, 1971), p. 66.

28. Siegfried Hollerer, *Verstaatlichung und Wirtschaftsplanung in Österreich (1946–1949)* (Vienna: Verband der Wissenschaftlichen Gesellschaften Österreichs, 1974), p. 2; Rusinow, "Notes," part 4, p. 5. Rupert Zimmerman, *Verstaatlichung in Österreich: Ihre Aufgaben und Ziele* (Vienna: Verlag der Wiener Volksbuchhandlung, 1964), p. 78.

29. Rusinow, "Notes," part 4, pp. 11–12.

30. "The Austrian Lesson in Economic Harmony," *Euromoney* (supplement), May 1979; Socher, "Die öffentlichen Unternehmen," pp. 381, 385–88, 437–39, 444–46, 451, 454.

31. Hogg, "A Small House in Order," p. 3.

32. Socher, "Die öffentlichen Unternehmen," p. 372.

33. "The Austrian Lesson," p. 9.

34. *Jahrbuch der österreichischen Wirtschaft 1976/1: Tätigkeitsbericht der Bundeswirtschaftskammer* (Vienna: Bundeswirtschaftskammer, 1977), pp. 30–34.

35. For this information I am indebted to Irirangi Coates Bloomfield, "Public Policy, Technology and the Environment: A Comparative Inquiry into Agricultural Policy Approaches and Environmental Outcomes in the United States and Switzerland" (Ph.D. diss., Boston University, 1981), especially pp. 181–82, 194, 221, 235, 242, 249–50, 257.

36. Ibid., pp. 225, 232.

37. Benjamin R. Barber, *The Death of Communal Liberty: A History of Freedom in a Swiss Mountain Canton* (Princeton, N.J.: Princeton University Press, 1974).

38. *Jahrbuch der österreichischen Wirtschaft 1976/1,* p. 110; Paolo Urio, "Parliamentary Control over Public Expenditure in Switzerland," in *The Power of the Purse: A Symposium on the Role of European Parliaments in Budgetary Decisions* ed. David L. L. Coombes (New York: Praeger, 1975), p. 319; Kriesi, *Entscheidungsstrukturen und Entscheidungsprozesse,* p. 36; *New York Times,* February 1, 1981, p. 13.

39. Dietrich Thränhardt, "Ausländische Arbeiter in der Bundesrepublik, in Österreich und in der Schweiz," *Neue Politische Literatur* 20(1) (1975): 68–69; Hans-Joachim Hoffman-Nowotny and Martin Killias, "Switzerland," in *International Labor Migration in Europe,* ed. Ronald E. Krane (New York: Praeger, 1979), pp. 49, 54, 55–58, 61.

40. Peter J. Katzenstein, *Capitalism in One Country? Switzerland in the International Economy*, Occasional papers 13 (Western Societies Program, Cornell University, January 1980), pp. 100–103.

41. Guido A. Keel, "L'influence des groupes d'intérêt politiques sur la politique étrangere Suisse," in *Handbuch der schweizerischen Aussenpolitik* ed. Alois Riklin, Hans Haug, and Hans C. Binswanger (Bern: Haupt, 1975), p. 313.

42. André Jäggi and Margret Sieber, "Interest Aggregation and Foreign Economic Policy: The Case of Switzerland" (Paper prepared for a workshop, Interest Groups and Governments, European Consortium for Political Research, Florence, March 25–30, 1980), p. 46.

43. Jane Kramer, "A Reporter in Europe," *New Yorker*, December 15, 1980, p. 140.

44. Jörg P. Müller, *Gebrauch und Missbrauch des Dringlichkeitsrechts* (Bern: Haupt, 1977), p. 8; Klaus Schumann, *Das Regierungssystem der Schweiz* (Cologne: Heymanns, 1971), pp. 175–78.

45. Müller, *Gebrauch und Missbrauch*, pp. 12, 15. Kriesi, *Entscheidungsstrukturen und Entscheidungsprozesse*, p. 138.

46. Organization for Economic Cooperation and Development, *Economic Surveys: Austria* (Paris: OECD, 1971), p. 11.

47. Wilhelm Hankel, *Prosperity amidst Crisis: Austria's Economic Policy and the Energy Crunch* (Boulder, Colo.: Westview Press, 1981), pp. 56, 69.

48. Hannes Suppanz, "Einkommensverteilung in Österreich," *Journal für angewandte Sozialforschung* 20(3–4) (1980): 40–45.

Part III

States and the Patterning of Social Conflicts

The introductory essay to this volume argued that "bringing the state back in" not only means analyzing states as organizations that may pursue distinctive goals. It also means spelling out the ways in which states influence the meanings and methods of politics for all groups and classes in society. Social cleavages and interests are *not*, as received wisdom too often implies, primordial givens that affect the state through politics "from without." Rather, the organizational arrangements of states, the existing patterns of state intervention in economic and social life, and policies already in place all influence the social interests pursued in politics. Some potential group identities are activated; others are not. Some lines of social conflict are politicized; others are not. Some demands are pressed; others are not imagined or are considered inappropriate given the kind of state structure and established policies with which social actors must deal. In turn, these political realities partially affected by the state feed back to affect future struggles over state structures and policies.

These "Tocquevillian" ideas were illustrated in the introduction with the aid of recent literature about political culture, parties, corporatist arrangements, issue agendas, and class formation in the United States and Western Europe. In addition, since the essays in each of the sections of this volume are hardly sealed off analytically from one another, all of the previous chapters have to some degree made use of this perspective on the state in relation to politics and society. In particular, several earlier essays highlighted ways in which the impact of states on sociopolitical conflicts affects the capacities of states to formulate or implement economic strategies. Rueschemeyer and Evans pointed out that autonomous, effective state interventions might inspire social classes to press new political demands and to capture parts of the state apparatus. Weir and Skocpol discussed how pioneering British unemployment policies tended to channel later working-class and Labour party demands toward calls for extending those benefits rather than toward launching deficit-financed public works. Similarly, Katzenstein's study of Switzerland and

Austria probed the corporatist interlocking of class organizations and class demands with state interventions aimed at constantly readjusting national economies to the requisites of openness to international markets.

The three studies in this part carry forward the Tocquevillian vision of states and politics. The concern here is not so much state capacities to act, although this problem never recedes far from view. These essays focus more directly on the matter of political conflict, tracing how state structures and activities play major roles in determining which social conflicts and demands will become politicized, how, and to what effect for the social groups involved.

Ira Katznelson's "Working-Class Formation and the State" extends the analytical and comparative scope of the argument about the United States in his book *City Trenches*. Very pointedly in this contribution, Katznelson grounds his causal argument about working-class political orientations in state-centered variables. These variables refer to the historical timing of electoral democratization in relation to industrialization, to patterns of centralization and bureaucratization of the administrative structure of the national state, and to legal conditions facilitating or repressing working-class organization at work and in residential communities. Katznelson shows how both the organization and operation of political parties and the meaningful concepts through which industrial workers understood their collective identities as political actors were influenced by these aspects of state formation, state structure, and public policy.

Katznelson's essay is especially valuable because it contrasts two countries, Britain and the United States in the nineteenth century, that are usually understood to be *similar* instances of "weak" states. Most students of working-class politics in Britain and America have taken for granted that these were similarly "weak" liberal states and have concentrated their analytical attention on community arrangements or socioeconomic or ethnic differention. Katznelson shows, however, that the British and U.S. states were sufficiently different to account for the emergence among English workers of a global "class politics," bridging identities and conflicts at work and in residence communities, versus the development among American workers of economically centered "labor struggles" at work along with ethnic mobilizations in the democratized electoral politics of residential communities. Thus, Katznelson helps to move us beyond any simplistic, global dichotomy of "strong" versus "weak" states and toward more differentiated specification of particular dimensions of state structure and policy that affect political culture and the formation of collective identities.

Like Katznelson's essay, David Laitin's intriguing "Hegemony and Religious Conflict" deals with the issue of which of alternative social cleavages will become politicized. Laitin greatly extends the purview of analysis by examining new kinds of cleavages and by carrying the discussion into the non-Western colonial world, well beyond the industrial-capitalist democracies that have been the grounds of our discussion of the Tocquevillian perspective so far. In Katznelson's comparison, both class and ethnic (especially Anglo versus Irish) divisions really existed in the social circumstances of nineteenth-century England and American workers, but the operation of states and parties favored the politicization of class in England versus the politicization of residential–ethnic identities in the United States. Analogously, Laitin shows us that, among the Yoruba of what is now northern Nigeria, there are cross-cutting social identifications both with Christianity versus Islam and with different "ancestral cities" within Yorubaland. Only the latter cleavage has become politically consequential, however, and current theories of "primordial loyalties" or of "economic rationality" cannot account for the surprising nonpoliticization of the religious differences.

Laitin argues that the selection of social identities on which political conflicts will be elaborated can depend on the strategies of domination used by "hegemonic states" that have the motivation and capacity to structure, or restructure, the patterns of group formation in society. In the Yoruba case, he concludes, only by reference to the historical modes of social control used by the British colonial state can we account for the politicization of orientations to ancestral cities rather than religious differences. Laitin suggests that this finding is consistent with other research on "tribal" identities in Africa and on the politicization of religious identities in British-colonized India.

Obviously, neither Laitin nor Katznelson argues that political cleavages can be created "whole cloth" without any prior foundation in social reality. Nor does either view the impacts of states on political cleavages in any simple Machiavellian or instrumental way. Their findings do, however, reinforce the notion that states encourage certain forms of political identity and conflict rather than others, both by virtue of direct state interventions in social relations such as those practiced by colonial authorities using tactics of "indirect rule," and by virtue of indirect consequences of state structures and policies even when authorities do not necessarily consciously construct or reinforce selected social identities.

Finally, Alfred Stepan's essay, "State Power and the Strength of Civil Society," takes us to contemporary Latin America and to a different set of issues than those addressed by Katznelson and Laitin. The basic politicization of social identities is not Stepan's concern, for he begins with a polarizing political issue already on the agenda in Brazil, Uruguay, Chile, and Argentina: the possible transition from bureaucratic authoritarian rule to democracy. Given the reality of resistance by already constituted groups in civil society to the continuance of repressive state authority, Stepan probes the various ways in which social resistance affects state strategies and, reciprocally, the ways in which the structures and strategies of the southern cone states have influenced the options and strategies of groups politically opposed to them.

On matters of central interest in this volume, Stepan offers a number of provocative findings and ideas. For one thing, he argues that the economic projects undertaken by bureaucratic authoritarian regimes can have as much impact as their repressive capacities on the prospects for social resistance, yet in surprising ways. A comparison of Brazil and Chile suggests that active and reasonably "successful" state interventions to promote economic development can reduce the state's ability to domi-

nate and control civil society, whereas deliberate state efforts to shrink
the public sector can disorganize social forces and undercut effective political opposition, even when economic difficulties grow apace.

Stepan explores the impact of bureaucratic authoritarian rule and policies on class conflicts, which may, if exacerbated, undercut possibilities
for unified social resistance or dominant-class willingness to risk a transition to democracy. He also probes for internal splits among elites and
agencies within the bureaucratic authoritarian regimes. When present,
such splits may allow openings for social opposition, as in Brazil, or they
may simply weaken a regime's capacity for coherent action, as in Chile.

In setting up his analysis and carrying through the case studies and
comparisons, Stepan avoids the mechanical assumption that states and
civil societies are monolithic actors locked in zero-sum struggles for
power. He deliberately looks for non-zero-sum ways in which states and
civil oppositions can disintegrate in tandem or experience parallel gains
in capacities for coherent political action. In fact, Stepan finds that Brazil,
above all, is a case in which the projects and structure of the bureaucratic
authoritarian regime have allowed recent "recomposition" of autonomous, oppositional forces in civil society. Much of the empirical interest
of Stepan's essay lies in his elaboration of this finding. Its analytical interest lies in the fully dialectical approach Stepan takes to unraveling the
interactions between state organizations and societal organizations and
between state projects and the political aims of social groups.

As much as, if not more than, the other essays in this volume, the
three in this part embody strategies of analysis and hypotheses about
state–society relations that open up new agendas for research and invite
investigations of parallel issues in other times and places. What is more,
these essays demonstrate better than any others that taking states seriously as institutional structures and as potentially autonomous actors
does not mean regarding them as all-encompassing, let alone all-power-
ful, entities. Social identities, social conflicts, and collective group action
– including social resistance to the repressive power of coercive states
themselves – may continue to rivet our scholarly attention. It is just that
we must take seriously the impacts of states to understand the forms and
dynamics of these phenomena.

8. Working-Class Formation and the State: Nineteenth-Century England in American Perspective

Ira Katznelson

When the House of Representatives investigated election fraud in New York City in 1868, it uncovered a massive scheme organized by Tammany Hall to sell counterfeit naturalization papers in order to register immigrants, who were not yet citizens, to vote. The committee report revealed that neighborhood saloons provided the locations for most of this activity. The testimony of Theodore Allen, the owner of "St. Bernard's" on Thompson Street in Greenwich Village, was quite typical:

I keep a public house, and a man by the name of James Goff and his brother, who were engaged in procuring naturalization certificates, used to come to my house a great deal. . . . I suppose 1000 were sent to Brooklyn that I saw them have. They contracted for these papers, they said, at 50 cents a head.[1]

Each Sunday evening, from the mid-1850s to the late 1880s, a debating society met at the Hope and Anchor Inn on Navigation Street in England's Birmingham. Some twenty to forty speakers would argue their cases on a set topic. From the vantage point of the middle classes, Brian Harrison has noted,

there was much to frighten the outside observer: the motion of 23 January 1859 for working class enfranchisement was unopposed, and the monarchy lost by thirty-nine votes to sixteen in a debate on republicanism on 22 March 1863. On two occasions, 26 August 1866 and 21 April 1867, the Society was visited by prominent London Reform Leaguers: these included George Howell who joined in the debates. . . . By twenty-three votes to fifteen, on 11 June 1871, the Society supported the Paris Communists. Nor was its radicalism exclusively political. On 21 August 1859, the strikers in the London building trade were supported by twenty-two votes to two; on 16 October 1864 the midlands miners, on strike at the time, were supported by forty-five votes to eighteen.[2]

The puzzle I wish to identify and explain can be discovered in the working-class saloons and pubs of nineteenth-century city neighborhoods in

England and the United States. In both countries drinking places were important centers of transportation before the widespread introduction of steam-powered streetcars and trains; and after, they were places of refreshment for short- and long-distance commuters. Sometimes plain and sometimes extravagantly decorated, public houses were places of entertainment, especially for men. Some were music halls, some underworld hangouts, some houses of prostitution. All were places of dense sociability, embedded in the fabric of street and community. And, especially after midcentury, most were gathering places for crowds that were increasingly homogeneous in terms of social class.

In both England and the United States public houses became the most common location of working-class political activity. In the United States, saloons provided hospitable gathering places for political parties. Saloonkeepers often acted as political entrepreneurs who built modestly durable and intensely local partisan machines capable of delivering votes in a predictable way in exchange for patronage. As an important study of party organization in the nineteenth and early twentieth centuries concluded, "The saloons were the nodal points of district organization of both parties. In the back rooms the bosses met to discuss their plans for carrying the districts, while out in front before the bar the captains were building up good-will among the patrons."[3]

These political parties, I have argued elsewhere,[4] were organizations the political mobilization activities of which were disconnected on the whole from the trade union and work dimensions of working-class life. The manifest content of saloon politics was not that of class but of ethnicity and territoriality. It was concerned with the links between the citizens of a specific residential area and the local level of government.

Working-class pubs in England, by contrast, were part of a network of values and organizations that reflected and promoted the view that class pervades all social relationships, not just those at the work place. For the middle classes, pubs came into their own, much like American saloons, as places of mobilization of voters at election time, but for the great majority who could not vote, the meeting rooms of *their* pubs provided refuge for a host of oppositional political activities, including, most notably, trade union and Chartist groups.

The contrasting political content of working-class activity in pubs and saloons in England and the United States is indicative of a general pattern that has been overlooked in most treatments of working-class formation in England. Implicit in much of this scholarship is a Continental contrast that makes problematic the cautious, reformist quality of workers' collective expressions and actions, especially after the demise of the Chartist movement. By contrast, the class character of working-class dispositions, organization, and activity is taken for granted as the virtually inevitable product of capitalist-industrial development. The important, but in this respect typical treatment of the emergence of class in the early nineteenth century by

Asa Briggs thus begins by reminding us (no doubt correctly) that "the concept of social 'class' with all its attendant terminology was a product of large-scale economic and social changes of the late eighteenth and early nineteenth centuries" and stresses that "the change in nomenclature in the late eighteenth and early nineteenth centuries reflected a basic change not only in men's ways of viewing society but in society itself."[5]

A comparison with the United States demonstrates the dubious quality of even such an innocuous formulation and its confusion of necessary and sufficient conditions. As in England, American workers eschewed class struggle outside of a gradualist, constitutional framework. In the United States, however, a split consciousness came to divide the working class: as laborers at the work place and as ethnics or residents of this or that territory in their residential communities. In England, by contrast, there was no equivalent divided consciousness, nor was class as a category of social understanding limited to the realm of work and labor. "Class" joined rather than divided the realms of work and off work. Especially characteristic of working-class struggles in early industrial England, Stedman Jones has argued, was "the closer intertwining of industrial and political demands. . . . It is difficult to separate political and industrial demands in the thirties and forties because working class leaders themselves rarely did so. Universal suffrage, according to Doherty, the spinners' leader, 'means nothing more than a power given to every man to protect his own labour from being devoured by others.' "[6] Such rhetoric would have been quite unusual in the United States, and the talk of suffrage gives us a first hint as to how to think about why.

These differences in the degree and character of class understanding and activity, captured in microcosm in the differences between the rhetorical and organizational content of political gatherings at the drinking places of working people, indicate how the dominant tradition of English working-class historiography debilitates our understanding by assuming what must be explained and, in so doing, makes comparative studies of English and other instances of working-class formation very skewed. At the extreme, this perspective simply treats England as the paradigmatic case of class formation: As the first working class to be made *and* to make itself, it revealed the ineluctable logic of the capitalist mode of production. In this way, historical analyses of the English working class have tended to mimic Marx's identification of England at the economic level as heralding the path of Western capitalist development more generally.

Historical treatments of American working-class formation have suffered, not without irony, from an imitation of this approach. A good number of radical social historians in the United States (who are better described as neoprogressives in the Beardian sense than as neo-Marxists) have sought to recapture and reconstruct the long-neglected past of the working class. The large, suggestive literature they have produced too often assumes the aptness of the "making" teleology in English work. The important issue is not whether class was made at all in America or in England or elsewhere, but rather the *terms* on which a working class was formed.

How shall we go about the task of explaining the puzzle of variation between English and American patterns of working-class formation? My starting point is an aphorism of Irving Howe's: "The working class is a reality, the proletariat an idea."[7] Approaches to problems of class formation that are too structural and too teleological are unable to deal with real working classes, precisely because they address theoretically constructed proletariats expected by imputation of interest to appear and act in history in particular ways.[8]

But which concrete *historical* factors shall we place our explanatory bets on? This essay develops a state-centered explanation. I argue in a brief examination of "labor aristocracy" approaches to English working-class formation that economy- and society-centered explanations tend to make unwarranted teleological assumptions, overemphasize the place of work, and underestimate the significance of spatial arrangements, especially as they concern the connections between work and home. I next show that even when we compensate for the shortcomings of such explanations by stressing the reorganization of city space under the impact of industrialization, by underscoring activities in working-class residential communities, and by making contingent what some theorists assume to be "natural," they still fail to account for the kinds of variations we find in the politics of the neighborhood and the saloon. On key dimensions, especially the consequences of capitalist and urban development for working-class residential spaces, the United States and Britain were very similar. The differences in English and American patterns of working-class formation, I try to show, are best accounted for by the impact of the organization and public policies of their respective states.

This is an essay, in short, about how states and their policies shape and inform the creation of meaning about class expressed in language, dispositions, and organizations. At issue is how the political contexts created by state authorities established the vocabularies and institutional forms that workers would develop to shape and represent their demands directed both to employers and to the state in the early industrial period. In explaining the contrasting cases of England and the United States, I stress the importance of variation in patterns of interest representation and repression rather than the similarities between the two states (porous bureaucracies, constitutional continuity, and the significance of the law), which are often lumped together too crudely under the macrocomparative rubric of the "weak" state. Without attention to the differences between these states' organizations and public policies, I argue, it is not possible to understand the key differences in class formation. How and why the state provided a major source of variation in key features of the development of the English working class, considered in contrast to the American, is the analytical centerpiece of the essay.

Society- and Economy-Centered Explanations

If working classes are expected to develop "naturally" in certain militant or revolutionary ways but do not, historians are tempted to search for alibis.[9] Since most treatments of working-class formation in England take working-class moderation as the object of their explanations, they characteristically try to explain why the counterfactual of a revolutionary class has not been realized. Although this puzzle and this approach are very different from my own, I begin here for three reasons: It is the dominant approach; attention to it will help us to clear some important analytical ground; and some work in this tradition will help us to reformulate a precise, if dissimilar, object of analysis.

"Labor aristocracy" explanations of both a crude and subtle variety are the most common "alibi" approaches. Using such diverse criteria as wage levels, regularity of work, trade union membership, styles of consumption and culture, and commitments to distinctive sets of norms and values, scholars have sought to find a fault line dividing the working class. The analytical payoff is a political one. As Henry Pelling has observed, "It is an essential feature of the Marxist theory of the labour aristocracy that this supposedly small section of the working class was conservative in politics and imposed its conservatism upon working class institutions, thereby concealing but by no means eliminating the underlying militancy of the mass of the workers."[10]

This approach is beset by a number of fundamental empirical and analytical flaws. The term "labor aristocracy" is inexact. It shifts in meaning from one treatment to another. A number of microlevel treatments of the relations of craft and manual workers in specific industrial settings indicate just how difficult it is to specify work locations where aristocrats of labor actually confronted a mass of workers. Contrary to expectations of the theory, empirical evidence, especially for the late nineteenth century, suggests that "it was the more prosperous workers who were the more politically militant and radical, while the lower ranks displayed either apathy or conservatism."[11] And if the leadership of unions did display a certain narrowness of focus, stressing immediate gains in wages, working conditions, and in public policy rather than more fundamental social transformations, what were their strategic alternatives?

The labor aristocracy approach invites comparison with continental Europe rather than with the United States. This orientation highlights certain questions and obscures others, especially those with which this essay is concerned. Leaving this problem aside for the moment, we might note that the construction of a European foil for the English case depends on an entirely problematic vision of what actually happened across the English Channel. Reformism is not just an English issue. There are quite remarkable similarities in all the capitalist societies of Western Europe and North America with respect to the limits in practice of working-class challenges to the existing order. The implicit Continental contrast in much scholarship about the English working class operates on an entirely misleading model of sustained, heroic, protorevolutionary activity by European working classes.[12]

Perhaps an even more basic problem in the labor aristocracy position (one stressed in an important critique by H. F. Moorhouse) is its tendency to assert a priori the significance of a segment of the working class. Such a designation is not possible to assess unless working-class culture as a whole is examined. At most, an explanation stressing a privileged stratum of labor would have to be the outcome of a historical analysis of causes of variation in patterns of working-class formation in specific settings rather than a model of cooptation and sellouts imposed on historical analysis.[13]

This reading and critique of the labor aristocracy approach, and, by extension, other equivalent answers to the question of why the working class did not behave as an essentialist class model predicts, begins to clear the ground to an alternative approach. It beckons us to shift focus away from the gradualist *problématique* of the Continental contrast toward a focus on the emergence of a holistic, or global, kind of class consciousness in England that an American comparison implores us to explain. It insists that we look in the first instance not at a fragment of the working class but at the language and activity of the group broadly conceived, and it demands that we reject the notion that there is one most likely course of working-class development. Instead, we must turn to history and its variations, even as we understand that each case of working-class formation is one of a family sharing common traits – but what history and what traits?

Let us return to St. Bernard's saloon on Thompson Street and to Birmingham's Crown and Anchor for some guidance about how to proceed. These public houses shared a number of traits that highlight basic features of capitalist industrialization and urbanization that are directly connected to the variations in patterns of working-class formation we have identified in the English and American cases. These public houses were located in neighborhoods that were predominantly residential. Such local places of work as existed were outside the home. The communities in which they were found were segregated by class. The pubs – like local fire companies, gangs, burial and insurance societies, and other neighborhood-based organizations – were part of the fabric of new kinds of working-class residential communities. Unlike preindustrial city neighborhoods, where people tended to work in home-based settings and where the social classes were jumbled together, the new urban space separated work from home and the classes from each other.

The significance of this spatial reorganization is apparent when we realize that what distinguished the early development of the English from the American working class concerned primarily patterns of culture and activity, not at the place of work, but at the place of residence. In both countries working people constructed tools where they lived to respond to the bewildering environments in which they found themselves. Although the forms assumed by working-class organizations in the two societies were virtually identical, however, their rhetorical and institutional contents diverged radically. The contrast between the American pattern of divided consciousness and the English pattern of a more holistic understanding of the significance of class is, at its core, a difference in understanding about the meaning and role of working-class neighborhoods and their links both to work places and to the political process. For this reason, before we attempt to account for this divergence we need to look closely at the spatial reorganization of the early industrial city.

First, however, I should like to make a small detour. An important book, Patrick Joyce's *Work, Society, and Politics: The Culture of the Factory in Late Victorian England*,[14] provides a coherent alternative to the labor aristocracy position on post-1840s working-class gradualism by focusing on the working class as a whole. His treatment differs fundamentally from this essay not only in the puzzles it explores but also in its explicit rejection of the spatial dimension I think so important. By detouring briefly through Joyce's book, I will be able to clarify my argument and meet the most cogent objections I know to it.

Joyce focuses on the factory rather than on the residential community in Lancashire and the West Riding. Building on a distinction originally proposed by Stedman Jones between artisans subject to the formal control of capitalists and factory workers subject to "real" substantive control in the work process, he tries to show how the consolidation of the industrial factory system created a common reality for workers and how their experience of work shaped their institutions and mentalities outside of work. A culture of deference forged in the factory, he argued, was extended to all facets of social and political existence.

Joyce acknowledges that the factory and the neighborhood had become separate entities, but he maintains that the factory and its social relations were at the heart of neighborhood feeling and that the class segregation of working-class housing areas was nestled into a larger, well-ordered system of deference. In this view, working-class subcultures were but an aspect of an elaborate network of exchanges between the classes presided over by manufacturers who dominated not only the politics but the cultural expectations of their town and whose sway over working-class life was the product of their deeply rooted, factory-based hegemony. He maintains that as the industrial process became more developed factory life penetrated more deeply into other spheres of life; the less complete the mechanization of production, the less powerful was the hold of the paternal culture of the factory.

In advancing this claim, Joyce challenges not only the view, which I hold, that the growing separation of place of work from place of residence made possible an autonomous working-class cultural and political life, a matter I shall return to, but also the core argument of the labor aristocracy position, which he turns on end (and in so doing reproduces its corporeal shape). "Far from being the 'moderates,' " he writes, "the labour aristocrats were in the forefront of radical politics in this period. . . . The politics of labour . . . were chiefly the concern of those outside the cultural environment of the factory, and especially the craft and skilled sectors in the working class. If these were a labour aristocracy then it was independence rather than reformist 'collaboration' that was their political legacy."[15]

In turning upside down the labor aristocracy position, Joyce adopts its tendency to overstate the divisions between craft and factory workers at the work place (writing about France, William Sewell has shown how factory transformations may in fact provide for new definitions and extensions of craft labor) and leaves unaccounted for the immense number of workers, like those in the engineering trades, who fall neatly into neither broad category.[16] Furthermore, although it is clear that the "aristocrats" *by definition* provided leadership to the trade union and party politics of the late nineteenth century, it is by no means clear that they were "radical" as opposed to "gradual," nor is it obvious that they represented an elite without a mass, factory-based following. For the trade unions such a claim borders on the ridiculous, and for the electoral process the question must remain opaque because most factory workers could not vote until the end of the First World War.

From the perspective of the argument I am developing, Joyce's mimetic treatment of the aristocracy thesis is not merely a matter of secondary interest. It points to the failure of both positions to make crisp distinctions among three axes of differentiation of working-class members: (*a*) workers relatively privileged at work (whether because of their wages or the character of the labor process); (*b*) workers with different styles of life in residential communities segregated by distinctions not only between the working class and other classes, but within the working class itself; and (*c*) workers who provided the political leadership for trade unions, pressure groups, and political parties. The various attempts to collapse all of these axes into one grand axis of internal working-class division obscure the interesting contingent questions about the relationships among these three (sometimes overlapping) sets of actors. From my point of view these distinctions are crucial, because without them it is impossible to ask why, and under what circumstances, political leaders make demands at work directed at employers and, off work, directed at the state in the same terms (as broadly was the case in England) and when they press their demands in utterly different terms in each arena (as broadly was the case in the United States).

Transformations of Urban Space

What of Joyce's challenge to the stress on the spatial separateness of work and community and its implications? He takes some pains to deprecate the significance of this separation. The factory town of the mid-nineteenth to late nineteenth century, he writes, "retained more of the village than it acquired of the city. Understood as the 'walking city' the factory town grew by cellular reproduction, the town slowly absorbing factory neighborhoods in its expansion." Until the introduction of tramways and bicycles at the turn of the century, he continues, "the link between home and work remained firm until these severed it."[17]

If Joyce is correct, then a state-centered explanation of the single, rather than divided, quality of class understanding in England is not necessary. We might then argue that differences in class formation between the United States and England simply are reflections of different patterns in the objective organization of spatial relations. In this approach the split consciousness of the American working class would be explained by changes in city space in the antebellum period, a subject I have tackled elsewhere.[18] The more unitary English pattern, by contrast, would be accounted for by the more tight integration of work space and home space.

It is not possible to sustain this line of reasoning, because Joyce is wrong. There was a major reorganization of space in the very large and middle-sized industrializing cities and towns in the middle decades of the nineteenth century. The most dramatic changes came about in the largest cities; indeed, one cannot help but wonder if the exclusion of Liverpool and Manchester (Lancashire's most important centers of working-class concentration) did not bias Joyce's view of the relationship of work and off work. But even in smaller cities (we shall look at the Lancashire factory town of Chorley later) it would be difficult to overstate the importance of changes in and about space.

The large-scale urbanization of British society is one of the most striking features of the nineteenth century. None of the ten largest cities less than doubled in population between 1801 and 1851 (compared with only one of the top French cities in the same period). At this moment of astounding growth, Leeds and Birmingham tripled in size; Manchester and Liverpool quadrupled. All of the ten largest cities had populations of over 100,000 by 1851, with Liverpool and Manchester well over 300,000. By midcentury Liverpool's upper and middle classes "who could afford to do so had moved from their place of work or business or even beyond it into adjacent townships." Their residential areas in new suburban rings were divorced from both the work and the residence places of workers. Within the heart of the city there were "distinctive zones of different economy and society." Dividing the city into eight areas, Lawton has shown with great clarity how Liverpool space had become sorted out into spatial divisions of the classes from each other.[19] Other research has carefully established that most of the housing constructed in early-nineteenth-century Liverpool was built for the new working classes in class-segregated residential neighborhoods. By midcentury, workshop houses had become domiciles of the past for the majority of Liverpool residents and those of other industrializing cities.[20]

Joyce might suggest that the big-city pattern is atypical, but very fine recent studies would put such an assertion in question. A. M. Warnes, for example, has studied the Lancashire town of Chorley between 1780 and 1850. In the manner of Sam Bass Warner's study of Philadelphia, he takes three "snapshots" of the town in 1780, 1816, and 1850.[21] Before 1780 the town was an agricultural township, serving the market and commercial functions of its rural environment. Its growth began to accelerate around 1780 as a result of the weaving trade stimulated by the mechanization of spinning. Even so, its landscape continued to be defined by its preindustrial functions: "Nowhere had large employing units been formed; most people still lived at or immediately adjacent to their place of employment."[22]

Between 1780 and 1816 the town's population increased by 50 percent to 6,000, a growth stimulated mainly by employment in early, small textile mills. At this date factories and clusters of houses around them became part of the town's topography, but the growth of the textile industry can be accounted for more by the enlargement of existing workshops than by their replacement by factories, and "residential location was still to a great extent determined by the location of employment and not usually by the social differences among the population."[23]

Nevertheless, the 1816 social geography of the town was rather more complicated than that of 1780. A somewhat more differentiated pattern had developed, characterized by a more well defined commercial core, a more rapid pattern of growth in outlying parts, and scattered but discernible clusters of settlements associated with specific new occupations, including calico works and cotton spinning factories.

By 1850 the town had been radically transformed. In the years since 1816 Chorley had become a factory town. Reporting on the same transformation stressed by Joyce, Warnes notes that handloom weavers, once the majority of the population, were reduced to under 10 percent of the work force. Using the enumerators' books of the 1851 census, he estimates that "over one half of the economically active were engaged in branches of the textile industry that necessitated a journey to work." Furthermore, he finds not only that there was a dramatic shift from domestic employment, but that "by 1851 the proximity of home and workplace was breaking up, at least for certain sections of the workforce," and "the conditions for a recognizable pattern of social segregation were beginning to develop."[24]

It is important not to overstate the modernity of this pattern. Only a negligible number of workers (about 4 percent) lived more than a mile from their work, and over half of the 1,813 people Warnes examined lived within a quarter-mile of their work places. Of the two in three workers who no longer labored where they lived, the majority had to move only short distances to overcome the separation. "Nevertheless there is no doubt that the average distance travelled to work had sharply increased since 1816, not only because more workers lived away from their work but also because of the increasing variety of employment." In a striking finding Warnes reports that, the newer the factory, the farther away were the locations of residence of its workers.[25]

He also hypothesizes (contra Joyce's emphasis on tied loyalties) that with the diversification of work places there may have been a reduction of commitment by workers to a particular factory or employer, as well as a diversification of family employment in different factories. These changes probably increased the average distance of family members from work. Residential differentiation based on occupation was being replaced by a "tendency for those with similar incomes, educational levels, or other status variables, to congregate in limited parts of the town."[26] Paradoxically, belonging to certain occupations (spinning, printing, and bleaching) made such a divorce between occupations and residence possible.

Joyce concludes his treatment of the residence community with a caution. The impersonality and class segregation of the twentieth-century town are so often read back into the nineteenth century that we forget just how unlike the towns of these two centuries were. As words of prudence these imprecations are well taken, but for the purposes of our discussion they largely miss the point. Writing about the industrial revolution more generally, Sewell has shrewdly observed that "what now appears as the hesitant beginnings of a long and slow development seemed to be a major departure to contemporaries: Even a few steam engines or blast furnaces or spinning mills could make a powerful impression on people who had never seen them before. From their point of view, modern industry was a distinctive feature of their age; theirs was an industrial society as no previous society had even seen."[27]

So with the spatial concomitants of industrialization. What mattered not at all to contemporaries of the nineteenth century was the degree of difference between the nineteenth- and twentieth-century city; impressed on their lives and consciousness was the new urban form that introduced patterns of separation between work and off work not just for the very wealthy but for the majority. In some towns places of work and residence may have been only a short walk away, but they were places *apart*, and except in the case of employer-provided housing (by best estimates only a small fraction of working-class housing, even in single-factory towns) workers came to cluster in communities separate from the locus of work, from other classes, and from other workers with different (Weberian) class attributes.

This revolution in space produced a fundamental change in relationships of authority and in forms of local organization. With the exception of company towns, where factory masters held sway over the totality of working-class life, the role of capitalists was constricted to the work place, freeing workers to live without direct supervision by their bosses in their neighborhoods. This new freedom was undergirded by a new division between markets for labor and markets for housing. In the workshop structure of employment and residence, the two had moved together to the same rhythm. With the sundering of this link, working-class communities came to be shaped more and more by real-estate speculation and by the strategies of builders and landlords. They became stratified by income and styles of life. And they came to be conscious environments that people of all classes sought to shape and control.[28]

In these new environments, working-class people created new institutions, new relationships, new patterns of life. The *contingent* connections between these and broader patterns of politics and class formation have too long been neglected in favor of such explanatory shortcuts as the labor aristocracy hypothesis.

There is, however, one major exception to the rule of the neglect of space in this approach to class formation. It is worth our attention, because it gives us important clues about how to shape our analytical questions and our approaches to answering them. This exception is John Foster's *Class Struggle and the Industrial Revolution*,[29] the most explicit (I would say rigid) Leninist version of the aristocracy thesis. Its great merit is to have introduced social space into its arguments about working-class reformism. Foster's study of Oldham is rich with hypotheses about cross-class alliances, demographic and production patterns, and the formation of a specific kind of labor aristocracy. I shall leave most alone, but I do wish to highlight Foster's unusual sensitivity to the implications of spatial transformations in the early industrial town and his attempt to incorporate space as a constitutive element of the social structure.

The transformations of the textile industry in Oldham were not merely changes in the organization and techniques of production. When production was organized in cross-class households, where work and off work were tightly integrated, a patriarchal model of class and authority based on face-to-face paternal relations and the direct supervision of the various spheres of social life integrated the social order. The material and ethical claims of this system could not survive the industrial process that shattered household patterns of production.

Foster shows that during the first half of the nineteenth century Oldham's workers came less and less frequently to live where they worked. As the town's districts came to be designated increasingly either as places of work or as places of residence, members of the working class came to live apart from their employers and their supervision. By devising their own social and cultural institutions where they lived, working people fashioned an independence from the patriarchal claims of their employers. These institutions, rooted in the relatively free space of the working-class community, provided the potential basis for the construction of relatively independent sources of class and group dispositions and collective action.[30]

Although Foster's contribution more than shares in the dubious features of the labor aristocracy position, his joining of space, class, and politics has the particular merit of making *conditional* the role that working-class neighborhood institutions might play in the larger story of working-class life.

Because of his focus on the traditional historiographical problem of working-class reformism, Foster stresses the contingent aspects of these social and cultural institutions with respect to whether they became autonomous organizations capable of building working-class solidarity against capitalists and the state in spite of divisions among workers or whether they became differentiated between the community institutions of the "aristocrats" and the rest of the working class (with the former becoming closely tied to bourgeois ideology, politics, and authority).

What Foster does not deal with are the related, but different contingent questions of whether and under what circumstances workers will utilize their newly autonomous institutions in the residence community to mount demands not only against their employers but against the state in class terms. Put another way, what will be the relationship between the politics of labor and the work place and the potentially separate emerging politics of community?[31]

Of all the Western industrializing countires, the urban–spatial histories of the United States and England in the nineteenth century were the most alike.[32] So too was the array of territorially based working-class institutions that provided a dense infrastructure to community life.[33] As workers in both countries experienced the separation of work and community, they developed ways of construing and acting on these experiences in their new residential spaces and institutions. Precisely because of the relatively tight controls that employers continued to exercise in the posthousehold factory (a point stressed by Joyce), the residence community came to loom so important as the place where workers could create meanings and practices in partial freedom.

Let us return once again to some of these local institutions. Historians of American neighborhood and political party life have long been impressed by the combination of sociability and political action of the local party machine. The same dual role of leisure and instrumental activity characterized Chartist meetings in workingmen's clubs, friendly societies, and public houses. Rowley writes, for example, of annual dinners held to "commemorate the birthday of Tom Paine, enlivened by radical songs, toasts, and recitations," and, more generally, of heavy drinking during business meetings.[34] Whereas such activities underscored a divided working-class consciousness in the United States, they helped promote a more global consciousness of class in England.

Quite unlike the American patterns, where even early trade unions developed meeting places at or very near work places, English trade union branches, many secret and illicit, usually met in working-class neighborhoods, most frequently in pubs. The organization of industrial disputes was often pub-based, and pub landlords frequently acted as strike coordinators or union treasurers. Many unions were identified with specific public houses, and some important Chartist pubs (like Nottingham's Seven Stars and the King of George on Horseback, the landlords of which acted as treasurers of their local Chartist cells)[35] simultaneously were prominent meeting places for industrial and political organizers.

Friendly societies, the main self-help community organizations of English workers, also gathered in ale houses. Intensely local in character, many of these societies were trade unions by other names that sought to protect their funds and their members from legal recrimination.[36] The quality of the "trade union consciousness" created by this compressed set of working-class organizations in the residence community obviously is rather different from the "trade union consciousness" that came to prevail in the United States, where from the very earliest moments of trade union history labor unions were disconnected from other institutions and locations of working-class life and political activity.

From the vantage point of the United States, the key issue for studies of English working-class formation is whether we can account for the broad cultural pattern identified by Pelling as a combination of political and social "conservatism, associated however with a profound class consciousness and quite commonly a marked sense of grievance."[37] This distinctive mix of political caution, stressed by most historical analysts, and a keen, pervasive sense of the relevance of class divisions to all spheres of life (a situation described by Eric Hobsbawm in the language of "high classness")[38] was very different from the American pattern with respect to the second, but not the first, characteristic. Obviously, the English pattern was the result of a historically contingent process. What were its causes?

One way to approach this question is to ask why both trade union and political agitation in England but not the United States were pressed into institutions of residence community. There, in the voluntary organizations created in the "free space" of communities separated from work places, English workers learned to put claims to their employers and to the state in a rhetoric and idiom of class.

What accounts for this development? Obviously, the industrial urban, spatial, and organizational patterns that English workers shared with their American counterparts cannot explain the divergence between the two histories of working-class formation. Equally clear is the inability of society- and economy-centered explanations, rooted more in what these societies share than in their differences, to account for these variations. In the remainder of this essay I propose that important differences in the organizational structures and the public policies of the states in the two countries account for the key divergences we have identified. The claims I shall make, I hasten to add, are provisional – in Charles Tilly's words, "more solid than working hypotheses, perhaps, but less firm than theses one nails up, to challenge all the world, at the end of a long inquiry."[39]

State Structures and State Policies

A focus on the state as a major source of variation in patterns of class formation in the English and American cases at once confronts an important feature of the macrocomparative literature on the state: the tendency to lump these two countries together under the rubric of the Anglo-American "weak state." J. P. Nettl's seminal essay proposing that "stateness" be treated as a variable cites Marx favorably for observing that the United States and England were excluded from the "necessity of violent overthrow of the state because there was no state as such to overthrow." In neither country is the state "instantly recognizable as an area of autonomous action," and in both, the law, rather than being an emanation of the state, has a great deal of autonomy.[40]

Most analyses of the "weak" American state, from Tocqueville's *Democracy in America* to more recent treatments such as Huntington's well-known analysis of the diffusion of the Tudor polity,[41] root the U.S. experience in the British for the obvious historical reasons. In this largely persuasive line of analysis, England is understood to be an aberrant case of state formation in early modern Europe. The Glorious Revolution of 1688, though radical from a Continental perspective, ratified the traditional prerogatives of Parliament against those of an absolutist alternative. Sovereignty was defined not by a conflation of the civil and the civic within the state but in terms of representation and, ultimately, a system of political parties linking state and society through electoral mechanisms.

Although English sovereignty crystallized in a single representative body, indicating a pattern of centralization very different from the American federal system, where sovereignty ultimately resided in the "people," both countries shared a very clear contrast with the state patterns of continental Europe. These states, unlike those of Prussia or France, did not have a monopoly of access to technical, professional information. Furthermore, for reasons Barrington Moore explains, "England's whole previous history, her reliance on a navy instead of an army, on unpaid justices of the peace instead of royal officials, had put in the hands of the central government a repressive apparatus weaker than that possessed by strong continental monarchies."[42] Colonial America, of course, shared in and inherited the characteristics of the British state, whose Crown bordered on an abstraction and which was relatively undeveloped as an autonomous entitity demarcated from civil society.[43]

Although one might be tempted to point to an apparent correlation between strong states and militant working classes in continental Europe and to the seeming correlation between weak states and reformist tendencies within the working classes of England and the United States, the consequences of the weak states in both England and the United States compared with the absolutist and bureaucratic regimes of the Continent are not self-evident. Propositions along these lines would have to depend on caricature to the point of distortion. Continental working classes have hardly displayed a uniform propensity for revolutionary or protorevolutionary activity, just as the English working class has known moments of militant contention (E. P. Thompson, for one, thinks that in 1832, as in 1819, the year of Peterloo, "a revolution was possible" because "the government was isolated and there were sharp differences within the ruling class"),[44] and American workers have challenged capital at the work place with great courage and at high risk and cost.

If it is difficult to move directly from an assessment of a given state as "strong" or "weak" to statements about revolutionary versus reformist working-class orientations to the regime, it is even more difficult to make this kind of causal claim if we want to explain whether class, as a category of understanding and action, joined the spheres of work and community or was limited to the sphere of work.

The main attempt I know of to apply this line of reasoning to the English case, that of Kenneth Dyson, is flawed in ways that an American comparison reveals. In his view, England's weak state "helped to cement polarization in the industrial and political systems. . . . Accordingly, the experience of a relatively 'unbridled' capitalism gave it a bad reputation, created a powerful and isolated working class culture, and undermined willingness to cooperate both in industry and in politics. Britain acquired a peculiar class structure: the obstinacy and distrust associated with attitudes of 'them' and 'us' were not directed at the state but at bastions of privilege and exclusiveness associated with society."[45] We shall see, from an American vantage point, that it is misleading to say that working-class dispositions and structures of feelings in England were not honed in opposition to the state. The American experience, moreover, in which "we"–"they" distinctions based on class were constricted largely to employee–employer conflicts at the work place, appears to belie this line of argument.

But appearances can be deceptive, for if we inquire about the precise organizational forms that the "weak state" took in England and the United States; if we examine the different clusters of political rights the two working classes possessed in the early industrial period; if we look at other bundles of public policies; and if we explore the effects that these differences had on the content of working-class organizations located where workers lived, we shall be able to make more persuasive connections between the characteristics of these states and their activities and divergent patterns of working-class formation.

The most important political right in the nineteenth century, of course, was the right to vote. Here the differences between the United States and England were marked. Virtually all adult males in the United States could vote by the early 1830s, but in England only one in five adult males composed the eligible electorate after the reforms of 1832, one in three after 1867, and only three in five even after 1885. How important was this difference for our puzzle?

Accounts of the genesis of the franchise and the story of its expansion have long been familiar themes in treatments of the formation and civic incorporation of Western working classes. Reinhard Bendix, elaborating the scholarship of T. H. Marshall, has suggested that there is a common sequence of the extension of voting citizenship in the West that helps to explain the shared political gradualism of the various national working classes. By contrast, H. F. Moorhouse explains English reformism (the standard object of analysis), not so much by civic incorporation through the franchise, but by the long period of exclusion of workers. The differences between the protagonists of this debate, however, represent two sides of the same coin,[46] since all the participants in the discussion agree on what is not in doubt: that franchise extensions and their timing have had an important effect on working-class propensities to act in certain ways. They disagree only about how. Here, too, a comparative American perspective is chastening, for the history of the franchise in the United States reminds us that gradualist outcomes do not depend only, or necessarily, on a protracted period for the extension of citizenship rights to individuals.

What is so striking about the familiar discussions of the franchise and class is their avoidance of the questions about class formation that are at the heart of the comparative puzzle with which we are concerned. The quick, nearly conflict-free extension of the franchise to men in the United States and the much more protracted, conflict-ridden expansion of the right to vote in England are central to explanations of the differences between the global consciousness of class on one side of the Atlantic and the divided consciousness of class on the other.

But the impact of the variation of political rights on class formation was not a direct or simple one. To understand it, we have to take up the franchise in combination with another key difference between the two countries concerning the organization of the state: that of a federal versus a unitary state.

Nettl, it will be recalled, who introduced the concepts of "weak" and "strong" states into contemporary comparative-historical political sociology, stressed that the United States and England shared relatively diffuse state organizations, but he paid insufficient attention to the differences in the ways their states were organized. The diffuse federal organizational structure of the United States took much of the charge out of the issue of franchise extension, for there was no unitary state to defend or transform. Once suffrage restrictions were lifted (in tandem with other democratizing reforms, such as an increase in the number of public offices and in the regularity and frequency of elections), the United States had the world's first political system of participatory federalism.

Within this framework of state organization and democratic political rights, new kinds of political parties with a mass base were constructed. These political organizations, reaching into virtually every ward and neighborhood in the country, put together the spatial, ethnic, religious, and political identities of the various subgroups of the American working class. This act of organization and social definition took place where workers and their families lived. It created direct links between the political system and voting citizens, who were organized into politics on the basis of many identities but rarely those of class as such, and this pattern created an institutional and participatory structure that was set apart from the organizations workers created to put their demands to their employers.

American participatory federalism was not just a system of voting based on intensely local solidarities. It was also a system of governance, taxation, and delivery of services. During the antebellum years in the cities, where the bulk of working people lived, municipal services provided the main content of a local politics of patronage and distribution. This period saw the introduction of professional police forces, the bureaucratization of municipal charity and poor relief, and the establishment of mass public school systems, as well as a massive program of publicly licensed construction. Political parties focused on the connections between these services and the various neighborhoods of the city. Local politics became a segmented and distributive politics of community. In this politics, workers appeared in the political arena not as workers but as residents of a specific place or as members of a specific (nonclass) group. Although there were many class-related economic issues on the national and state political agendas, including internal improvements, tariffs, control of banking, and slavery, the process of voting for most workers was insulated from these concerns, because it was focused elsewhere.

By contrast to the United States, the interplay of state and class in England was radically different in each of the respects I have noted. The unitary (not federal) English state concentrated distributive public policies at the center as a result of the passage of such public acts as the Poor Law of 1834; the Public Health Acts of 1848, 1866, 1872, and 1875; the Police Acts of 1839 and 1856; and the Food and Drug Acts of 1860 and 1872. Whether this growth was mainly the result of the initiatives of humanitarian and Benthamite civil servants and parliamentarians or the result of attempts to defuse class-based opposition of industrial capitalism (these are the two main poles of a lively historiographical debate),[47] the growth of the *central* government was staggering. In 1797 most of the 16,000 employees on the central government payroll were customs, excise, and post office personnel. By 1869 this number had grown to 108,000, reflecting the new activities undertaken by the administrative agencies of the state. For the century as a whole, public expenditure grew fifteen times in real terms.[48]

If patronage and property were the two hallmarks of the pre-nineteenth-century civil service, by midcentury patronage had been sacrificed to "save the main pillar, property."[49] The professionalization of governmental administration at the center, a process that marked the period from 1830 to 1870, further focused attention by members of all social classes on the center of the state apparatus in London. As Parliament and Whitehall took on new responsibilities for social policy and the regulation of working conditions and as they reorganized their affairs to rationalize the enforcement of regulations and the delivery of services, they potently reached into and affected working-class life, at the work place but especially in the residence community. Each new parliamentary act and each new wave of administrative expansion and reform focused ever the more sharply the attention of the working class on the state and its activities.

From the perspective of a working person (and from an American perspective), the state that he or she confronted was not a "weak state." The comparative intensity of the tie between the working class and the central state was powerfully reinforced by the second aspect of what Harold Perkin has aptly called the nineteenth-century "battle for the state": the struggle for the franchise.[50]

Just as the services and the regulations of government penetrated working-class life and thus reinforced class identities at the residence place as well as at the work place, so the demand by English workers for the right to vote could have been constructed on no other basis than that of class, for the working class was excluded on explicit class criteria. Only with universal suffrage, Heatherington wrote in the *Poor Man's Guardian* in December 1831, would "the term *classes* merge into some comprehensive appellation, and no bloodshed will ensue."[51] Although working-class reform organizations before and after 1832 were local in organization, unlike American political party machines they directed their claims of citizenship *to the center*, that is, to Parliament.

One effect of the interplay between the state and workers where they lived was the creation of a common fault line, based on class, in all parts of English society:

One of the distinguishing features of the new society, by contrast with the localism of the old, was the nationwide character of the classes, in appeal if not always in strength. At some point between the French Revolution and the Great Reform Act, the vertical antagonisms and horizontal solidarities of class emerged on a national scale from and overlay the vertical bonds and horizontal rivalries of connection and interest. That moment . . . saw the birth of class.[52]

When every caution has been made, the outstanding fact of the period between 1790 and 1830 is the formation of the working class. This is revealed, first, in the growth of class-consciousness: the consciousness of an identity of interests as between all these diverse groups of working people and as against the interests of other classes. And, second, in the growth of corresponding forms of political and industrial organization. By 1832 there were strongly based and self-conscious working class institutions – trade unions, friendly societies, educational and religious movments, political organizations, periodicals – working class intellectual traditions, working class community-patterns, and a working class structure of feeling.[53]

English working-class voluntary organizations turned outward in two respects. Rather than reinforcing local particularities based on intraclass differences of territory, income, or craft, they linked the activities and sensibilities of workers to each other across these lines. Furthermore, they joined to the concerns of the residence community the class issues of political participation, public policy, and trade unionism. In this respect, the

Chartist movement provided the most important post-1832 concretization and deepening of these tendencies, which contrast so sharply with the role played by neighborhood-based working-class voluntary organizations in the United States.

Chartism provided the unifying pivot of English working-class dispositions and organization. This movement took a working class that had oscillated from the turn of the century between economic and political action and fused both kinds of action in a national network of community-based associations. For some two decades, Chartism created a distinctively English global consciousness of class harnessed not only to the campaign for votes, but to poor law agitation, to trade unionism, to factory reform, to Owenite socialism, to an unstamped press, to millenarianism, and to machine breaking.

In all these activities Chartism reflected the great diversity of a differentiated working class. Where there was a substantial number of artisans, Chartist associations tended to stress values of self-help and independence. Where handloom weavers predominated, as in Lancashire and the West Riding, the form and content of agitation tended to be more strident. Where domestic industry predominated, as in the East Midlands, workers were more likely to seek allies and guidance from middle-class reformers.[54]

Overall, however, there were consistent themes to Chartism. These included the attempt to build an independent political voice for laborers based on class understanding, as well as the regular elaboration of links between economic problems and political representation. At its most vigorous, Chartism swallowed up other working-class movements and gave them a common definition. Its key feature, J. F. C. Harrison has argued, was "its class consciousness and temper. . . . Chartists of many shades of opinion emphasized their movement was concerned to promote the interests of working men as a class." They "assumed the need for class solidarity and their leaders talked the language of class struggle."[55]

From the point of view of the historiographical *problematique* of gradualism, Chartism seems to be another instance of working-class reformism. From the vantage point of the American comparison, the important feature of Chartism is its scope and depth as a class institution and its posing of a democratic, egalitarian alternative to the existing political and economic order based on a class analysis. As Trygve Tholfsen has stressed so tellingly, the People's Charter was not just a political document but a coherent class-based set of demands connecting all spheres of society. "Implicit in the Charter was both a demand for the transformation of the structure of politics and the broader principle that working men ought to exercise control over every aspect of their lives. . . . What set Chartism ideologically apart from middle-class liberalism . . . was the conviction, often only tacit, that class was the crux of the problem of progress and justice."[56] This view was reflected at the level of organization. Unlike American political parties, which were class specific in the neighborhood but were otherwise interclass institutions, the Chartist "party" was entirely independent of the Whigs and Tories, and over time, the Chartists drew away from middle-class allies.

If Chartism disconnected the working class from other classes, it joined the political to the economic aspirations of workers, and it was affected as a movement by economic conditions and struggles. The dominant classes and politicians who successfully managed to use the state to deny workers the vote in 1832 tried to crush trade unions both before and after. As a consequence, it was possible for Chartism to become the common core of the working class and thus to impose itself as the common sense of a ho-listic rather than a divided kind of class consciousness, in tandem with a trade unionism quite different from its American counterpart. Just as the absence of political citizenship pressed political agitation into the autono-mous institutions of working-class localities, so the state's stance with re-spect to union activity produced relatively weak unions and compelled workers to bring their work-place organizational efforts into the protected space of the residential community.

The Combination Acts of 1799 and 1800 made union organization very risky and thus drove labor organization underground, to the pubs and friendly societies of hospitable neighborhoods. Even after the acts were repealed in 1825, the state used the common law to interdict strike activity.

After 1825 trade unions were harassed, though not legally suppressed; unions, as such were no longer unlawful, but action in restraint of trade was. The Combination Act of 1825 did not by itself make strikes illegal, but it left to judicial opinion whether a strike was in restraint of trade. This legal situation did not prevent the development of unions; on the contrary, there was an explosion of public unionization attempts, sometimes on a grand scale, in the late 1820s and 1830s. But the fact that "after 1825 the common law was invoked against trade unions to an unprecedented ex-tent" produced a situation that compelled unions to keep their planning and activities as secret as possible, hidden from the authorities in commu-nity-based associations.[57] Moreover, the legal climate of repression com-bined with the pressures on union continuity provided by the operation of business cycles made unions especially fragile institutions. At moments of economic depression the state could leave to economic forces the role of restraining unions, but when the cycle proved favorable and unions grew more bold, the state could invoke the doctrine "to the effect that any overt positive action by groups of workers was likely to be a wrong in the nature of Conspiracy, even where the strike was quietly conducted."[58]

As a result of these political forces, English organized labor was too frag-ile to provide an independent basis of action against capital. English work-ers were pushed out of the arena of work into politics and into the resi-dence community at the same time. Although the trade unions themselves never joined Chartism, "the greater number of trade unionists," Slosson found, "declared for the Charter."[59]

In the United States, by contrast, the comparatively mild character of state repression against trade unions made a clearly defined, public, workplace-based organization of workers possible. There, too, workers were liable for combinations under the common law, but in the American federal system there was no national legislation or central direction to antiunion prosecutions. Charges brought in one locality were not brought in another, and prosecutors found convictions difficult to obtain in a system of trial by peers rather than by magistrates. American unions were buffeted by economic crises throughout the nineteenth century and, in the century's later decades, were faced with a wave of public as well as private attempts to repress labor organization. In the early period of class formation, however, the problems that unions had with the law were quite secondary. In times of economic prosperity workers were not inhibited on the whole from joining unions at the work place; in the middle 1830s, for example, some two in three craft workers in New York City were unionized.[60]

The organizational forms of the American and English states and their constitutional and public policies, in short, had very different consequences for the political content of local working-class associations and, by extension, for patterns of working-class formation in each country. In the United States, political agitation for the vote was unnecessary, and the community provided the location for the organizations at the base of interclass political parties that appealed to voters by mobilizing nonclass solidarities. Unions, in turn, were allowed a separate existence. In *their* embrace a working class was formed as labor.

Not so in England, where only the institutions of the residence community were available to workers through which to put demands to employers and to the state. Pressed together by the exigencies of law, repression, state organization, and public policy, the locality-based voluntary organization fused the separate facets of working-class life into a common, deeply felt consciousness of class.[61]

Notes

I am pleased to acknowledge the many helpful comments I received on earlier drafts of this chapter from the participants at the Social Science Research Council Conference, "States and Social Structures: Research Implications of Current Theories," held at the Seven Springs Conference Center, Mount Kisco, New York, February 25–27, 1982, where it was first presented (especially those of Ken Sharpe and Theda Skocpol) and also from J. David Greenstone, Michael Harloe, Richard Harris, and Henry Pelling.

1. M. R. Werner, *Tammany Hall* (New York: Doubleday, Doran, 1928), p. 135.
2. Brian Harrison, "Pubs," in *The Victorian City*, ed. H. J. Dyos and Michael Wolff (London: Routledge & Kegan Paul, 1973), p. 180.
3. Roy V. Peel, *The Political Clubs of New York City* (New York: Putnam, 1935), p. 38.

4. Ira Katznelson, *City Trenches: Urban Politics and the Patterning of Class in the United States* (New York: Pantheon Books, 1981).

5. Asa Briggs, "The Language of 'Class' in Early Nineteenth Century England," in *Essays in Labour History*, ed. Asa Briggs and John Saville (London: Macmillan, 1967), p. 43. Briggs has also written one of the few well-crafted comparisons of English and Continental patterns of class formation. See his "Social Structure and Politics in Birmingham and Lyons," *British Journal of Sociology* 6 (January 1950): 67–80.

6. Gareth Stedman Jones, "Class Struggle and the Industrial Revolution," *New Left Review*, no. 90 (March–April 1975): 56, 58.

7. Irving Howe, "Sweet and Sour Notes: On Workers and Intellectuals," *Dissent*, Winter 1972: 264.

8. I might add that many scholars who find themselves on the culturalist side of the structuralist–culturalist debates raging among social historians share with Briggs the idea that a working class that *experiences* a society arranged in class ways will be made, and will make itself, into a class. This formulation is implicit in E. P. Thompson's magisterial volume, *The Making of the English Working Class* (London: Victor Gollancz, 1963), just as it inhabits lesser contributions that take working-class reformism as the main object of analysis. The three journals in which these discussions are most accessible are *History Workshop*, *Radical History Review*, and *Social History*.

9. One of the problems this approach to English working-class formation poses is worthy of comment in passing. By taking the class orientations of workers for granted, debates about reformism and militancy are oddly divorced from the actual content of the society's discourse, organizations, and competing capacities of classes. The result, as Eley and Nield acutely observe, is an imitation by Marxist historiography of the liberal "intellectual schematization – if workers go on the barricades they are 'revolutionary,' if they do not they are 'reformist' or 'integrated,' " a perspective that "misses the realities that drive workers to action or condemn them to inaction." In accepting this dichotomy much Marxist historiography has appended to it the assumption that a formed working class *should* develop in certain ways. If it does not, a "theoretical alibi" for the working class as a whole has to be found (Geoff Eley and Keith Nield, "Why Does Social History Ignore Politics?" *Social History* 5 [May 1980]: 260–61, 258).

10. Henry Pelling, "The Concept of the Labour Aristocracy," in *Popular Politics and Society in Late Victorian Britain*, ed. Henry Pelling, (London: Macmillan, 1968), p. 41. Rooted in an article by Engels in 1885 and in Lenin's treatment of imperialism, the concept of a labor aristocracy was introduced into contemporary historical scholarship by Eric Hobsbawm. Work in this tradition has examined wages and conditions of work (including the divide between craft and factory workers), urban neighborhood differentiation (emphasizing spatial segregation, housing conditions, voluntary organizations, and leisure activities – the focus I find most congenial), and politics (with a look at the positional location and world views of labor union and party leadership). For the development of the concept of the labor aristocracy, see Friedrich Engels, "England in 1845 and 1885," in *On Britain*, ed. Karl Marx and Friedrich Engels (Moscow: International Publishers, 1934), pp. 67, 99; and E. J. Hobsbawm, "The Labour Aristocracy," in *Labouring Men*, ed. E. J. Hobsbawm (London: Weidenfeld & Nicholson), 1964.

The classic treatment of working-class reformism is that of Walter Bagehot,

The English Constitution (London: Collins, 1971). Other approaches include a stress on value systems and political culture, understood in the limited sense of the aggregation of individual orientations to politics (see Gabriel Almond and Sidney Verba, *The Civic Culture* [Boston: Little, Brown, 1965]); a macrohistorical emphasis on the distinctive sequence of British political development (see Otto Kirchheimer, "The Transformation of the Western European Party Systems," in *Political Parties and Political Development,* ed. Joseph LaPalombara and Myron Weiner [Princeton, N.J.: Princeton University Press, 1966], pp. 177–200); and on the debilitating character of available class alliances and ideologies (see Perry Anderson, "The Origins of the Present Crisis," in *Towards Socialism,* ed. Perry Anderson, and Robin Blackburn [Ithaca, N.Y.: Cornell University Press, 1966], pp. 11–52).

11. Pelling, "Concept of the Labour Aristocracy," p. 56.
12. See H. F. Moorhouse, "The Marxist Theory of the Labour Aristocracy," *Social History* 3 (January 1978): 61–82; H. F. Moorhouse, "The Significance of the Labour Aristocracy," *Social History* 6 (May 1981): 229–33.
13. Moorhouse, "Marxist Theory," p. 73.
14. Patrick Joyce, *Work, Society, and Politics: The Culture of the Factory in Late Victorian England* (New Brunswick, N.J.: Rutgers University Press, 1980).
15. Ibid., p. xv.
16. William H. Sewell, *Work and Revolution in France: The Language of Labor from the Old Regime to 1848* (Cambridge: Cambridge University Press, 1980), pp. 154–61.
17. Joyce, *Work, Society, and Politics,* pp. 118–119.
18. Katznelson, *City Trenches,* chap. 3.
19. R. Lawton, "The Population of Liverpool in the Mid-Nineteenth Century," *Transactions of the Historical Society of Lancashire and Cheshire* 197 (1955): 93, 94.
20. James H. Treble, "Liverpool Working Class Housing, 1801–1851," in *The History of Working Class Housing: A Symposium,* ed. S. D. Chapman (Newton Abbot, United Kingdom: David & Charles, 1971), pp. 167–209. Other studies confirm the Liverpool pattern. Pritchard, for example, has treated the spatial transformation of Leicester, where in 1840 the integration between work and residence was very tight but by 1870 had been shattered and a modern form of spatial organization had developed. Vance has done the same for Birmingham, and Prest for Coventry. Olsen, Wohl, Sheppard, and a good many others have shown that even in London, where craft production survived as the dominant form through the nineteenth century, there was a "systematic sorting-out of London into single-purpose, homogeneous specialized neighborhoods," an increased crowding of the working classes into wholly separate neighborhoods, and, overall, the large-scale separation of work and home (R. M. Pritchard, *Housing and the Spatial Structure of the City [Cambridge: Cambridge University Press, 1976];* James Vance, Jr., "Housing the Worker: Determinative and Contingent Ties in Nineteenth Century Birmingham," *Economic Geography* 43 [April 1967], pp. 95–127; John Prest, *The Industrial Revolution in Coventry* [Oxford: Oxford University Press, 1960]; A. S. Wohl, "The Housing of the Working Classes in London," in *London 1808–1870: The Infernal Wen,* ed. S. D. Chapman and Francis Sheppard [London: Secker & Warburg, 1971]; Harold Pollins, "Transport Lines and Social Divisions," in *London: Aspects of Change,* ed. Ruth Glass [London: Macgibbon & Kee, 1964], pp. 27–51; Donald Olsen, "Victorian London: Specialization, Segregation, and Privacy," *Victorian Studies* 17 [March 1974]: 267).

21. Sam Bass Warner, Jr., *The Private City: Philadelphia in the Three Periods of Its Growth* (Philadelphia: University of Pennsylvania Press, 1968); A. M. Warnes, "Early Separation of Homes from Workplaces and the Urban Structure of Chorley, 1780 to 1850," *Transactions of the Historical Society of Lancashire and Cheshire* 122 (1970): 106.

22. Ibid., p. 111.

23. Ibid., p. 119.

24. Ibid., pp. 120, 122.

25. Ibid., p. 132.

26. Ibid., p. 133. A parallel discussion can be found in T. C. Barker and J. R. Harris, *A Merseyside Town in the Industrial Revolution: St. Helen's, 1750–1900* (Liverpool: Liverpool University Press, 1954).

27. Sewell, *Work and Revolution in France*, p. 143. In this reminder of the danger of reading modern patterns into the past, he echoes geographer David Ward, who tells us that the social geography of English and American cities in the nineteenth century was one of comparatively weak patterns of spatial differentiation as compared with twentieth-century cities (David Ward, "Victorian Cities: How Modern?" *Journal of Historical Geography* 1[2] [1975]: 135–51).

28. For a discussion, see Vance, "Housing the Worker." One of the few textbook histories to recognize the importance of spatial transformations is that of Eric Hopkins, *A Social History of the English Working Classes* (London: Edward Arnold, 1979). Its first two chapters are called "Life at Work" and "Life at Home."

29. John Foster, *Class Struggle and the Industrial Revolution: Early Capitalism in Three English Towns* (London: Weidenfeld & Nicholson, 1974). A suggestive discussion of these issues can be found in the review of the Foster book by Mary Anne Clawson in *Contemporary Sociology* 6 (May 1977): 289–94.

30. This division between employers and workers in space was accompanied as well by another division: between workers themselves. With the separation of labor and housing markets as a concomitant of the division between work and community, workers with different capacities to consume goods and services (the hallmarks of class for Max Weber) came more and more to be segregated from each other in different areas of the city. The result, Foster argued, was the development of a geographically segmented working class that produced a tendency toward fragmentation and, in his terms, false consciousness. In this view, the ties of occupation, income, and space conjoined to make possible the development of a distinctive privileged stratum of the working class, an aristocracy of labor, whose propensity for alliances with the bourgeoisie undermined the "revolutionary consciousness" that had prevailed in the age of Chartism.

31. The spatial dimensions of a labor aristocracy approach have also been developed suggestively by Geoffrey Crossick and Robert Gray. Crossick's study of artisans segregated in space from industrial workers in mid-nineteenth-century Kentish London illuminates the contradictory elements of the values and language structure of these "aristocrats" whose emphasis on sobriety, thrift, and respectability seemed to imitate dominant middle-class Victorian values yet who also asserted an independent, even insular, working-class culture. Gray's work likewise stresses the corporate class consciousness (here he borrows from Gramsci) of the spatially separate "superior" artisans, whose neighborhoods, housing conditions, and styles of life reflected "feelings of exclusiveness and

superior social status" intertwined with "a strong sense of class pride." There followed, in this view, a complicated pattern of implicit negotiated accommodations between this stratum of the working class and the middle classes that established the terms of incorporation of the working class into social and political life (Geoffrey Crossick, "The Labour Aristocracy and Its Values: A Study of Mid-Victorian Kentish London, *Victorian Studies* 20 [March 1976]: 301–28; Geoffrey Crossick, *An Artisan Elite in Victorian Society* [London: Croom Helm, 1978]; R. Q. Gray, *The Labour Aristocracy in Victorian Edinburgh* [Oxford: Oxford University Press, 1976]; Gray, "Styles of Life," p. 429).

32. For my ability to make this comparative claim I am indebted to discussions with members of the Research Planning Group on Working Class Formation, funded by the Council for European Studies. For recent U.S. evidence, see Theodore Hershberg, Harold E. Cox, Dale B. Light, Jr., and Richard R. Greenfield, "The Journey to Work: An Empirical Investigation of Work, Residence, and Transportation: Philadelphia, 1850 and 1880," in *Philadelphia: Work Space, Family and Group Experience in the 19th Century*, ed. Theodore Hershberg (New York: Oxford University Press, 1981, pp. 128–73.

33. For comparisons see the discussions in Thompson, *Making of the English Working Class*, and in Amy Bridges, "A City in the Republic: New York and the Origins of Machine Politics" (Ph.d. diss., University of Chicago, 1980). Also see Ronald Aminzade, *Class, Politics, and Early Industrial Capitalism: A Study of Mid-Nineteenth Century Toulouse, France* (Albany, N.Y.: State University of New York Press, 1981), pp. 82, 94. Another complementary discussion of the importance of residence community ties is that of Michael Anderson, *Family Structure in Nineteenth Century Lancashire* (Cambridge: Cambridge University Press, 1971), p. 103.

34. J. J. Rowley, "Drink and the Public House in Nottingham, 1830–1860," *Transactions of the Thoroton Society of Nottinghamshire* 79 (1975): 76.

35. Ibid.

36. P. H. J. H. Gosden, *The Friendly Societies in England, 1815–1875* (Manchester: Manchester University Press, 1961).

37. Henry Pelling, "Then and Now: Popular Attitudes since 1945," in *Politics and Society*, ed. Pelling, p. 165.

38. E. J. Hobsbawm, "From Social History to the History of Society," *Daedalus* 100 (Winter 1971): 20–45.

39. Charles Tilly, "Reflections on the History of European State-Making," in *The Transformation of National States in Western Europe*, ed. C. Tilly (Princeton, N.J.: Princeton University Press, 1975), p. 47.

40. J. P. Nettl, "The State as a Conceptual Variable," *World Politics* 20 (July 1968): 577, 584.

41. Samuel P. Huntington, *Political Order in Changing Societies* (New Haven, Conn.: Yale Univeristy Press, 1968).

42. Barrington Moore, Jr., *Social Origins of Dictatorship and Democracy: Lord and Peasant in the Making of the Modern World* (Boston: Beacon Press, 1966), p. 444 (cited in Tilly, "Reflections," p. 632).

43. The discussion in this paragraph was stimulated by my reading of Kenneth Dyson, *The State Tradition in Western Europe* (New York: Oxford University Press, 1980), especially pp. 36–44 and 186–202. Also see Alastair Reid, "Politics and

Economics in the Formation of the British Working Class: A Response to H. F. Moorhouse," *Social History* 3 (October 1978): 347–61.

44. Thompson, *Making of the English Working Class* p. 737.

45. Dyson, *State Tradition*, pp. 249, 250. Recent work on the French working class (here I am thinking of Hanagan as well as Aminzade and Sewell) strongly suggests that it is not possible to think about the impact of the state on class formation and mobilization without considering political rights and repression over time (Michael P. Hanagan, *The Logic of Solidarity: Artisans and Industrial Workers in Three French Towns, 1871–1914* [Urbana: University of Illinois Press, 1980]).

46. Reinhard Bendix, *Nation-Building and Citizenship: Studies of Our Changing Social Order* (New York: Anchor Books, 1969).

47. For discussions, see Oliver MacDonagh, *Early Victorian Government, 1830–1870* (London: Weidenfeld & Nicholson, 1977); Harold Perkin, *The Origins of Modern English Society* (London: Routledge & Kegan Paul, 1969); Paul Richards and R. A. Slaney, "The Industrial Town and Early Victorian Social Policy," *Social History* 4 (January 1979): 85–101; Robert D. Storch, "The Policeman as Domestic Missionary: Urban Discipline and Popular Culture in Northern England, 1850–1880," *Journal of Social History* 9 (Summer 1976): 481–97; D. C. Moore, "Political Morality in Mid-Nineteenth England: Concepts, Norms and Violations," *Victorian Studies* 13 (September 1969): 1–16; John Milton-Smith, "Earl Grey's Cabinet and the Objects of Parliamentary Reform," *Historical Journal* 15 (March 1972): 63–82; Henry Parris, "The Nineteenth Century Revolution in Government: A Reappraisal Reappraised," *Historical Journal* 3 (March, 1960): 1–37; and David Roberts, "Jeremy Bentham and the Victorian Administrative State," *Victorian Studies* 2 (March 1959): 193–210.

48. Perkin, *Origins of Modern English Society*, pp. 123–24.

49. Ibid., p. 310.

50. Ibid., pp. 308–19.

51. Cited in Patricia Hollis, ed., *Class and Class Conflict in Nineteenth Century England, 1815–1850* (London: Routledge & Kegan Paul, 1973), p. 80.

52. Perkin, *Origins of Modern English Society*, p. 177.

53. Thompson, *Making of the English Working Class*, pp. 212–13.

54. J. F. C. Harrison, *The Early Victorians, 1832–1851* (London, Weidenfeld & Nicholson, 1971), p. 156.

55. Ibid., p. 157.

56. Trygve Tholfsen, *Working Class Radicalism in Mid-Victorian England* (New York: Columbia University Press, 1977), p. 85.

57. D. F. Macdonald, *The State and the Trade Unions* (London: Macmillan, 1960), p. 23.

58. Gerald Abrahams, *Trade Unions and the Law* (London: Cassell, 1968), p. 28.

59. Peter William Slosson, *The Decline of the Chartist Movement* (London: Frank Cass, 1967; originally 1916), p. 46. Also see David Jones, *Chartism and the Chartists* (London: Allen Lane, 1975); and Brian Brown, "Industrial Capitalism, Conflict, and Working Class Contention in Lancashire, 1842," in *Class Conflict and Collective Action*, ed. Louise A Tilly and Charles Tilly (Beverly Hills, Calif.: Sage, 1981).

60. Katznelson, *City Trenches*; also see Sean Wilentz, *Chants Democratic: New York*

City and the Rise of the American Working Class, 1788–1850 (New York: Oxford University Press, 1984), p. 220.

61. For an important treatment of these issues, see Tholfsen, *Working Class Radicalism*. Also useful is H. I. Dutton and J. E. King, "The Limits of Paternalism: The Cotton Tyrants of North Lancashire, 1836–1854," *Social History* 7 (January 1982): 111–41. For a fine-grained comparison of Birmingham and Sheffield that shows important variations in class formation *within* England, see Dennis Smith, *Conflict and Compromise: Class Formation in English Society, 1830–1914* (London: Routledge & Kegan Paul, 1982).

9.   Hegemony and Religious Conflict: British
     Imperial Control and Political Cleavages
     in Yorubaland

David D. Laitin

> There is a *hierarchy of cleavage bases* in each system and these orders of
> political primacy not only vary among polities, but also tend to undergo
> changes over time. Such differences and changes in the political weight of
> sociocultural cleavages set fundamental problems for comparative re-
> search: When is region, language, or ethnicity most likely to prove polar-
> izing? When will class take the primacy and when will denominational
> commitments and religious identities prove equally important cleavage
> bases? . . . what we want to know is when the one type of cleavage will
> prove more salient than the other, what kind of alliances they have pro-
> duced and what consequences these constellations of forces have had for
> consensus-building within the nation-state.[1]

A Puzzle

The Yoruba, a nationality comprising some 10 million people who dominate the political scene in the five states of southwestern Nigeria, have
experienced three generations of religious differentiation. Since the late
1890s, when nearly everyone shared a common allegiance to a religious
framework, about 40 percent of the Yorubas have converted to Christianity
and about the same percentage have become Muslims. In a previous publication,[2] I reported that, in the past century, two religious subcultures have
indeed emerged. Christian Yorubas conceptualize authority relations, responsibility, and the meaning of participation differently from Muslim Yorubas, but when it comes to issues on the political agenda of the day, the
two subcultures hold virtually identical views. I questioned members of
both groups on items in which views of authority relations, participation,
and responsibility would be determining. Surprisingly, I could not differentiate the answers of the Christian and Muslim Yorubas. This became for
me a thorny theoretical problem. Another problematic issue concerned the

fact that Yorubas organize themselves politically on the basis of their membership in "ancestral cities" even though many Yoruba families have not lived in "their" cities for generations and derive few material benefits for their continued allegiance. More perplexing still was the counterintuitive finding that, although religious differentiation among the Yorubas did account for discernible differences in socioeconomic opportunities, religious adherence had no bearing whatsoever on political alignments in Yorubaland. This anomaly, especially in light of the contemporary Islamic awakening that has compelled scholars to reassess the importance of religious differentiation for politics, compelled me to reopen the question so poignantly posed on Lipset and Rokkan (in the epigraph) some fifteen years ago. Why, after a century of differential religious institutionalization, constituting a new basis for social and economic cleavage, had religion not become a focus for political identification in Yorubaland?

In the analysis of this anomalous case, it will become apparent that conventional theories of the politicization of ethnic cleavages are inadequate. According to theories that rely on Shils and Geertz,[3] certain aspects of identity are "givens" and cannot easily be shed. Any individual develops a sense of self based on kinship, language, and racial ties. These ties, called *primordial*, become fundamental bases for political attachment, especially in preindustrial societies. This theoretical perspective would lead us to postulate that, in Yorubaland, ancestral city ties are "given" but that religious ties are "taken." But, as this essay will show, Yorubas have for a long time strategically reformulated their ancestral city identities in order to position themselves for economic and political benefits. Ancestral city identities are therefore "taken" as much as they are "given"; they are hardly more primordial than religious ties.

Theorists who have highlighted the strategic manipulation of identities as an alternative to the primordial perspective provide a second answer to the puzzle posed by the pattern in which cultural identities are politicized in Yorubaland.[4] These theorists assume that all people are rational investors seeking the greatest return from their identity choices. This perspective helps us to explain how and why Yorubas attach themselves to different ancestral cities. It is less helpful, as we shall see, in providing an answer to the puzzle of why so few Yorubas have calculated the possible returns of changing the dimension on which they divide themselves from ancestral city to religion. Political organization based on religious affiliation has provided a plausible opportunity for identity investment that is not part of the calculus of Yoruba political entrepreneurs.

In light of the failures of primordial and rational-actor theories, this essay postulates an alternative explanation for the nonpoliticization of the religious cleavage in Yorubaland. I shall argue that the modes of control used by the British colonial administration in Yorubaland successfully influenced which sociocultural cleavages would become politicized and which would remain politically irrelevant. When a central administration has the motivation and power to structure the pattern of political group formation in society, that administration can be considered to be *hegemonic*. I shall therefore argue that the pattern of political cleavages that I observed in Yorubaland are best explained by a focus on the actions of a hegemonic state.

For the purposes of this chapter, "hegemony" can be defined as the political forging – whether through coercion or elite bargaining – and institutionalization of a pattern of group activity in a society and the concurrent idealization of that schema into a dominant symbolic framework that reigns as common sense. Whereas Gramsci[5] used "hegemony" to refer to the coercive and ideological power of a historical bloc coming from *within* a society, I shall extend that concept to include the activities of an external (colonial) state. In the course of this essay, I shall argue that the British colonial state, interested in political control at low cost, found it useful to resuscitate the declining fortunes of the kings of the Yoruba ancestral cities. Amid considerable socioeconomic changes in the nineteenth century, city-kingdoms ceased to exert social control over their members. The kings, without traditional sources of revenue, could easily be coopted by the colonial forces. Colonial administrators drew boundaries, processed political requests, and paid salaries as if ancestral cities were the only real form of political attachment in Yorubaland and, for that, earned complete loyalty from the ancestral city kings. To be sure, Yorubas themselves certainly felt the kings of the ancestral cities to be legitimate leaders, but the colonial state built on those feelings to institutionalize a political system in which ancestral city identities remained predominant, at the top of the hierarchy of cleavage bases.

Both the primordial and rational-choice perspectives focus on variables within the society in order to explain the pattern of group activity in a country. Neither of them provides a theory of how government activity itself may structure opportunities in such a way as to determine the nature of social cleavages within the society. Yet any state must come to terms with the cultural commitments of the members of the society that it attempts to govern. Because the stance toward culture generally transcends particular governments within a country, the stance itself is best conceived of as an attribute of the state. Therefore, the model of hegemony presented in this chapter is a contribution to the perspective of bringing the state back into political explanation.

Historical Background

Contemporary Yorubaland has its roots in the Oyo Empire (1600–1836). Oyo became one of the great savannah empires in West Africa because it was able to take strategic advantage of its geographic location. Because Oyo bordered on the Sahara, its traders could purchase horses and slaves from the desert caravans. North of the forest region where the tsetse reigned over the horse, Oyo military elites could support a large cavalry that made short and sharp escapades into the forest areas to maintain political dominance. Moreover, Oyo was close enough to the Atlantic so that its traders could sell slaves for guns, cloth, manufactured goods, iron, and cowries. Oyo merchants therefore profited greatly by serving as middlemen between two great international trade networks.

The political coalition that governed this trade empire consisted of the leading city-kingdoms, units that I call "ancestral cities." Oyo-Ile, the dominant ancestral city, was governed by a king, called *alaafin*, and a council of chiefs, the Oyo Misi, headed by the *basorun*, the army commander. The *alaafin* received from the kings of the subject ancestral cities gifts and obedience in exchange for protection in long-distance trade. The *basorun* received booty and slaves from the military conquests of the expanding empire.

In the seventeenth and eighteenth centuries a common framework became consolidated. A "nation" began to form. Oyo-Ile attempted to legitimate its military and political domination through an appeal to common values among the imperial domains. In collaboration with Ile-Ife, a declining commercial center but once a preeminent power, Oyo-Ile consecrated Ile-Ife as the religious center of the empire and the ancestral home of the founder of the common religion. One consequence of establishing Ile-Ife as the *religious* center of the Oyo Empire was that Oyo's *political* supremacy became legitimated. Another was that the seeds of a Yoruba nation were planted.[6]

By the end of the eighteenth century, the political balance began to tip. The *basorun* and the *alaafin* could no longer avoid their divergence of interest. The long period of peace enhanced the wealth of the traders and of the civilian kings who collected tolls but threatened the status and wealth of the military. With constant internal battles between civilians and the military in the city of Oyo, other ancestral cities began to challenge Oyo. In Ilorin, the military commander of Oyo's foreign legion made an alliance with one of the commanders of the Islamic *jihad*, which had recently and successfully united the vast area that today comprises northern Nigeria. This alliance successfully challenged Oyo, and in the 1820s the *alaafin* was forced to abandon Oyo-Ile and set up his realm in an inconsequential village some 100 miles south. Thus, began an intra-Yoruba war that lasted until 1893, which was to change profoundly the basis of authority in Yorubaland.

The consequences of this war were manifold. For one, the large army that fought against Ilorin emerged out of a coalition of commanders from a number of ancestral cities. This army was successful in holding back the Ilorin forces and in establishing the basis for a new centralized authority in Yorubaland. Eventually, the army was stalled in Ibadan, formerly a small village. It soon became a major new city, populated by Yorubas from a cross section of ancestral cities. Ibadan represented a challenge to the political legitimacy of ancestral cities, since domination in Ibadan was legitimated not by lineage but by military success. Succession to leadership in Ibadan therefore opened mobility opportunities for Yorubas of many ancestral cities.[7]

The second major consequence of the civil war was the opening it created for British imperialism. British traders who wanted direct access to palm products in Yorubaland were anxious to have the flag precede them. Their argument, that the anarchy in the hinterland was inimical to trade, had far greater cogency when Yorubaland was in fact at war with itself. British officials helped to create a truce in the early 1890s, and in 1895 they bombed new Oyo into submission and ultimately brought Yorubaland into the British Empire. British authority, as we shall see, not only overwhelmed Ibadan's, but also helped to establish new Oyo as Yorubaland's center.

A third consequence of the civil war was the creation of a vast number of refugees – Yorubas who escaped from their ancestral cities to become immigrants in other ancestral cities or to establish new towns. Free from the social control of their compounds, these refugees began to establish new social networks. Most significantly, Yorubas began to affiliate with the Christian and the Muslim religious communities in large numbers. Within a half-century, about 40 percent of the Yoruba population considered themselves Christian and about the same percentage considered themselves Muslim. Both religions won converts from each of the ancestral cities and from all social groups within Yorubaland. When the wars ended, many of the refugees returned home and began to establish mosques and churches in their ancestral cities. Many others became permanent residents in "foreign" ancestral cities.

A final consequence of the war and its aftermath was the consolidation of a Yoruba nation. Although the seeds had been planted centuries earlier, it was not until the late nineteenth century that the nation itself became a social reality. The war was a factor, for as the Oyo Empire crumbled, Yoruba-speaking peoples within that empire recognized their common culture. Perhaps more important for national development were the war captives who were sold into slavery. This was the period of the British antislave blockade, and many of these people became "recaptives" and were given their freedom in Sierra Leone. There, in recaptivity, other African groups recognized the common identity of the Yoruba speakers, and they were all classified under a single rubric. When some of these people returned to Nigeria, they identified more with the Yoruba nationality than they did with their particular cities. One of them translated the Bible into the Yoruba language, and this act itself was a crucial development in the Yoruba nation. Whatever cleavage patterns subsequently emerged in Yorubaland, it is clear that by the late nineteenth century those cleavages would be socially perceived to be intranational.[8]

At the turn of the twentieth century, cleavage patterns in Yorubaland were diverse. Ancestral city identification continued to matter, even with the great movements in population. Military factions within the Ibadan system were a newer, but more powerful source of authority and formed another set of cleavages. Finally, religious identification presented a new source of cleavage among the Yoruba. In retrospect, it was unclear which pattern would provide the framework for subsequent political mobilization. What did emerge is that, although ancestral city identification continued to decline as a source of social cleavage in the course of the twentieth century, it never lost its basis for political identification among the Yoruba. And although religious identification became an increasingly important indicator of social status, it has never become a basis for political identification or action. Why this pattern held requires me to reopen the question posed by Lipset and Rokkan and to provide a new theoretical basis for addressing that question.

Competing Cleavages: Ancestral City and Religion

Although the ancestral city has always been associated with ties of blood, it is hardly an overriding objective basis for distinguishing people in Yorubaland. There are regional variations among the Yoruba to be sure, but the ancestral city is not the stuff of Tamil–Sinhalese, Waloon–Flemming, Yoruba–Igbo, or even Scots–English politics. Very little sociocultural differentiation is discernible among Yorubas from different ancestral cities. Common language, a common set of political institutions (nearly all Yoruba cities have comparable political offices with similar domains of authority), a common pantheon in the religion centered at Ile-Ife, and a shared myth of creation made the Yoruba a single nation. This nation was sustained by centuries of an integrated trade network, consolidated through war, and reconsolidated politically in the nineteenth century. In a situation of this sort, where there is a nation, one might expect a weakening of traditional sources of political cleavage.

Furthermore, with the collapse of old Oyo and the rise of Ibadan, one would further expect a decline in the social meaning of the ancestral city. Refugees were establishing themselves in new cities, thereby dividing their loyalties. Ibadan was creating a new basis for authority, and progressive forces throughout Yorubaland began to emulate Ibadan. The traditional legitimation of authority, essential to the sustenance of ancestral city domination, was losing its compelling force.

As the twentieth century progressed, social processes continued that would lead one to predict the further decline of the social significance of the ancestral city. The amalgamation of Nigeria (in which Yorubaland constituted one of three regions) created pressures for unity among all Yorubas. Obafemi Awolowo, the leading Yoruba politician of this century, was born in Ijebu, a city-kingdom barely incorporated into the Oyo Empire. Nonetheless, he found it useful to emphasize the unity of the Yorubas. He organized a society, Egbe Omo Oduduwa, that symbolized their common ancestry. This movement, along with the ever-increasing geographic mobility of Yorubas amid the Pax Britannica, further eroded the social significance of the ancestral city.

Despite these social trends, the ancestral city remains today the central basis for political identification and mobilization within the Yoruba states of the Nigerian Federation. In each city, the myth of common descent is sustained by regularly scheduled rituals honoring the gods of special importance to that city. The festivals associated with those rituals bring back many emigrants and their families.[9] During the festivals, successful members of the city's diaspora are showered with status rewards, especially if they have performed services in support of their "home" cities. Yorubas who live in anomic cosmopolitan centers like Ibadan or Lagos derive great pleasure on return to their ancestral city from seeing people bow to them at every encounter and having "praise singers" follow them through the town, immortalizing their origins and their worldly successes. These sons of the ancestral city want to keep alive to the king of their town their claim for a prime plot of land for a retirement home or for a status home for their relatives. No less important is the fact that despite the Pax Britannica, which virtually ended the Yoruba civil wars by 1892, Yorubas remain security conscious and consider their ancestral cities their own true safe haven.[10]

During the civil wars, Yorubas in the merchant trade at Lagos were expected to develop links with the international arms traffic and to become suppliers of the latest military material to the leadership of their ancestral cities. This pattern of loyalty to one's ancestral city over one's city of residence persisted into the era of nationalist politics. The early battles between Awolowo's Action Group and Azikiwe's NCNC in Yorubaland can be understood only in terms of conflicts between ancestral cities. Awolowo was associated with the Ijebu kingdom, and the NCNC used anti-Ijebu propaganda to recruit the Oyos, especially in Ibadan. (Azikiwe is not a Yoruba, but he knew well how to fight intra-Yoruba political battles.)

The race for civil service jobs in Yorubaland has also been marked by intercity rivalry. At the University of Ibadan, the conduit for the social mobility of educated Yorubas, student unions based on attachment to one's ancestral city compete for placement and success. In one recent study of Yorubaland, in which the idea of social class was the dominant focus, the author found instead that his working-class respondents perceived the most important differences among the Yoruba to be those of ancestral city.[11]

In the 1979 elections, the first after thirteen years of military rule, the Yorubas achieved a united front for electoral purposes, and there was no organized opposition to Awolowo's Unity Party of Nigeria in the Yoruba states of Oyo, Ondo, Ogun, and Lagos. In Bendel and Kwara, two states with large Yoruba populations, the Yoruba voters were also united behind Awolowo's party. Yet beneath the surface, Yoruba unity is threatened most deeply by divisions due to identification with the ancestral city. The only real threat to Awolowo's electoral base in those elections came from Og-bomoso, an Oyo town the leaders of which had long fought against the Ijebu domination within Yoruba political organization.

My guess is that the most incendiary conflict within Yorubaland today concerns the legitimacy of the land tenancy of "strangers" (i.e., Yorubas of different ancestral cities) in Yoruba towns. Although the pattern of land-lessness is complex in Yorubaland, in the context of Yoruba politics, issues concerning rent and ownership are usually interpreted solely as battles between ancestral city "natives" and "strangers."

Social processes have reduced the objective relevance of the ancestral city in Yorubaland, but identification with one's ancestral city is the lens through which most Yorubas interpret politics; it remains the core political cleavage. The mirror situation, the increased social meaning of religious identification conjoined with its political irrelevance, remains to be established.

Conversion to Christianity and Islam did not acquire significance as a social force until the late nineteenth century in Yorubaland. Both religions presented "modern" alternatives to ambitious young traders. Each of the religions made selective challenges to traditional practices. Christian evangelists pushed for monogamy, church burials, hatlessness during prayer, and the elimination of divination rituals. Muslim preachers demanded a rigid monotheism, abstention from liquor, and a reduced significance for the celebrations associated with family milestones. Neither of the world religions brought instantaneous social change, but both developed an institutionalized leadership that could refer to the Bible and the Qur'an and seek adjustment of group behavior on the basis of an independent reading of the religious corpora. Yoruba Christians and Muslims spent a significant portion of their disposable incomes building magnificent churches and mosques and devoted a significant portion of their free time to participation in religious services and organizations. To speak of Yoruba "syncretism" in order to diminish the religious significance of Yoruba conversion is to miss an essential point. All religious adherence represents some sort of historical synthesis, and the Yoruba converts have found themselves in social patterns based on religious adherence that go far beyond their original commitments.

The two subcultures – Yoruba Christians and Yoruba Muslims – were hardly distinct in the early twentieth century, but the social cleavage has indeed grown. In the race for jobs in the civil service sector, the key to social mobility in the colonial world, Yoruba Christians were able to out-pace the Muslims. Largely because the education provided by the Christian missionaries was tied to job requirements in the colonial civil service, Christian converts had an immediate advantage. Students at Christian schools soon developed a monopoly of access to the English language, which assured young Yorubas of good jobs in the modern sector and provided a crucial skill in combating colonialism. The anticolonial battle against liberal Europe in most of middle Africa was fought by lawyers and not guerillas. So Christian Yorubas were at the forefront of modern education, procured the first jobs in the modern sector, and captured leadership positions in the nationalist movement.

Data on educational development in Lagos bear this point out. In 1870, only 9 percent of the students in the Lagos missionary schools (virtually the only places to acquire English literacy) were Muslims; by 1893, the figure was only 13 percent. The Muslims tried to counteract this inequality by building their own schools, but their efforts brought only marginal improvements. Other data collected in rural Ile-Ife show that, even in this era of government schools and free education, Christians maintain their advantages in school enrollments. Among the farmers interviewed, 58.7 percent were Christians, but their children accounted for 63.7 percent of those attending school.[12] In a comprehensive study of education in Yorubaland, Fafunwa wrote, "It is perhaps safe to say that at least one out of three Christians has been to school while the Muslim ratio is likely to be one out of five or six." At the University of Ibadan, where Yoruba students predominate, some 92 percent of the students claimed to be Christians, whereas only 6 percent claimed to be Muslims.[13] Many Yorubas have used their salaries or retirement benefits from their modern sector jobs as investment capital. It was access to the skills provided by missionary education that provided the opportunity for capitalizing on new trade opportunities.[14]

Available data on farm wealth are sparse. It appears however, that in landownership Christians have not achieved supremacy. This is due largely to the fact that, until now, there have been considerable constraints on the open sale of land. In a survey of 267 farmers in the periphery of Ile-Ife, there was found to be no difference in the average size of farms belonging to Christians and Muslims. For example, 84.2 percent of the Christians and 82.3 percent of the Muslims had less than 10 acres of land. In studies of elite farmers, however, a different picture emerges. Beer has shown that, in the politically important cooperative committees, the Christian Yorubas accounted for 63.4 percent of the members and 100 percent of members who were literate. Berry's data demonstrate that it was the Christian Yorubas who were the first to take advantage of, and to continue to profit by, the investment potential in cocoa. The Christian–Muslim cleavage, then, is not manifest in the ownership of land but is so in the pattern of wealth and political influence among farmers.[15]

The socioeconomic preeminence of Christians in Yorubaland is clearly demonstrated in Donald Morrison's massive survey conducted under the auspices of the University of Ibadan with a subsample of nearly 2,000 Yorubas living in Yorubaland. Whereas 48 percent of the Muslim respondents were illiterate, with 2 percent completing a university degree, only 36 percent of the Christians were illiterate, with 10 percent having a university degree. Only five of the respondents' parents had completed university, but all of them were Christians. A higher percentage of the parents of the

Christian respondents were literate than the parents of the Muslims. Sixty percent of the Christians but only 35 percent of the Muslims claimed to read a newspaper every day. A higher percentage of Christians claimed to have a radio, a wristwatch, a gas cooker, a refrigerator, a sewing machine, an electric iron, a car, a house or land, an electric fan, and a clock. On no consumer items did the Muslims report an advantage.[16]

Not only economic opportunity but political opportunity as well has gone to Yoruba Christians. Of the sixty-one inaugural and executive members of the Action Group, there were only two Muslims. Only three Muslims were identified among Sklar's tabulation of 33 Western Regional personalities in the Federal Executive Council of the Action Group in 1958, and only one Muslim was among the twelve regional ministers. Finally, there were only five Muslims among the seventy-five constituency and divisional leaders of the Action Group. Among the members of the delegations from the Yoruba states in the Nigerian Constitutional Drafting Committee in 1977, 74 percent (of those delegates I could identify on the basis of religion) were Christian.[17]

In Ile-Ife, where Christianity and Islam have developed at comparable rates, the pattern of Christian dominance in the elite holds. In a dissertation on political power in Ile-Ife, using Robert Dahl's techniques to identify the political elite, Oyediran enumerated eight leaders, all of whom were Christian. The only prominent Muslim who appeared to play a role in the political conflicts within the town was illiterate and could not sustain himself on the political stage.[18]

In my own observations in Ile-Ife, where I regularly attended both the central mosque and a central Anglican church, I found the weekly voluntary contributions at the church to be commensurate with the quarterly sum of the mosque's capital improvement fund. Within six months, the Anglican church was able to raise N 26,000 for a new marble floor, whereas the mosque was well behind in its goal for N 10,000 to build a second story. The differences were quite conspicuous: The Anglican church compound on Sundays looked liked a Mercedes-Benz showroom.

To be sure, Nigeria has provided substantial mobility opportunities for its citizens with any wit or will. A growing civil service since the completion of the railroad in 1911, the expanding educational opportunities in the wake of independence, the presence of multinational firms seeking alliance with "bridgehead elites," and of course the new oil economy have all worked to provide outlets for many Nigerians with ambition. Nonetheless, the relative advantage of Christians in capturing those opportunities among the Yoruba is clear. There is, then, a discernible social cleavage based on religion in Yorubaland.

Most Yorubas deny vigorously the idea that there is a real religious cleavage. They uphold the myth that, in religious matters, "we are all one family." In interview after interview with Yorubas in all walks of life, the most common explanation for the nonpoliticization of religion in Yoruba society concerned the cultural importance of the family, which is divided by religion but tied together by blood. Again and again, I found examples of religious conflict being ameliorated by cross-cutting family ties, the most interesting being one in Abeokuta, in which the bishop and chief *imam* were from the same family.

There is indeed some truth to this myth. Since "family" is a socially constructed rather than a biologically constructed reality, however, it is worth asking, to the extent that the myth is true, why Yorubas do not realign their families to make them religiously homogeneous. They do so for the ancestral city: The children of women whose ancestral cities are different from their husbands' are unambiguously attached to the ancestral cities of their fathers. In any event, the data I collected in the town of Ile-Ife suggest that to a considerable extent Yoruba families *are* religiously homogenous. I interviewed seventy elders from the Anglican church and central mosque and found that despite their protestations of being socially mixed in religion, there was remarkable religious homogeneity within their close social network. An examination of Table 9.1 should establish that, in Ile-Ife, religious homogeneity within the family is as much a social reality as is the ancestral city. More than 90 percent of the respondents' wives were affiliated with the same religious group as their husbands, and members of the wider family also were of the same religious group. In the cases where there were differences (e.g., part V, Table 9.1), conversion brought homogeneity. Friendship patterns also reflect the reality of religious affiliation. Although the data in part VII suggest that a higher percentage of the respondents had friends of a different religion, in only three of the seventy cases did a respondent mention more than one friend who affiliated with a different world religion. Furthermore, since the respondents lived in neighborhoods that are religiously heterogeneous but homogeneous with regard to ancestral city, the startling finding of part VII is the low percentage of friendships that cross religion. Despite a myth of religious heterogeneity within Yoruba social networks, the reality is one of religious homogeneity.

All that is required now is complete the sociological puzzle is to demonstrate that despite the socioeconomic cleavage in Yorubaland that is based on religious differentiation, this cleavage has no resonance in the political arena. Although external observers have often interpreted Yoruba politics in a religious frame, Yorubas themselves never have.

The civil wars of the nineteenth century set the pattern. A common interpretation of Ilorin's challenge to Oyo supremacy concerns the Islamization of Ilorin and the concomitant continuation of the Fulani *jihad* into Yorubaland with Ilorin as the base camp.[19] This interpretation ignores the social realities in Ilorin and Oyo. First, Afonja, the king of Ilorin, was not himself a Muslim, and he refused to destroy the sacred groves and other symbols of the Yoruba traditional religion. Second, after Ilorin's victory, Muslims in Oyo suffered no discrimination, nor were they seen to be traitors. Many

Table 9.1. *The Yoruba Family in Ile-Ife: Religious and Ancestral Homogeneity Compared*

Part I

| | Those who have a wife of a different: | | |
Religion of respondent	Ancestral city (%)	World religion at birth (%)	Religion (%)
Christian	14	9	11
Muslim	37	40	6

Part II

| | Sister's religion at present | | |
Religion of respondent	Christian (%)	Muslim (%)	Traditional (%)
Christian	89	3.6	7.4
Muslim	19	76.1	4.8

Part III

| Brother's religion at present | Brothers with wives of a different: | |
	Ancestral city (%)	Religion (%)
Christian	13	4.3
Muslim	8	0

Part IV

| Sister's religion at birth | Sister's husband's religion at birth | | |
	Traditional (%)	Muslim (%)	Christian (%)
Traditional	<u>61.5</u>	15.4	23.1
Muslim	2.5	<u>68.8</u>	18.8
Christian	17.6	11.8	<u>70.6</u>

Part V

| | Same as father's religion: | |
Religion of respondent	At birth (%)	Now (%)
Christian	11	69
Muslim	11	77

Part VI

| | Sister's husband of the same: | |
Religion of respondent	Ancestral city (%)	Religion (%)
Christian	84.2	85.7
Muslim	88.9	78.6

Table 9.1. *(cont.)*

Part VII	Of three friends mentioned, at least one of a different:	
Religion of respondent	Ancestral city (%)	Religion (%)
Christian	14	29
Muslim	17	37

Note: All parts of this table are drawn from the same data base. I interviewed thirty-five Muslims and thirty-five Christians in Ile-Ife, Nigeria, in 1980. After 5 months of regular attendance at the church and mosque from which these two samples were drawn, I recruited an elder to escort me to the homes of senior members of their congregations. I made no further stipulations. My desire to obtain accurate information led me to choose a sample biased in the direction of my escort's circle rather than one more randomly chosen. The bias of this sample overemphasizes the social cohesion of coreligionists in that those people most associated with the church and mosque were obviously chosen by my escort. But since I chose the central mosque and church, I did not interview the vast number of Yoruba migrants in the town, who attended other churches and mosques. Therefore, the solidarity based on ancestral city is also overemphasized by these data. The significance of the data lies in their demonstration that even in central Ile-Ife, the most "traditional" of Yoruba towns and most committed to the idea of the reality of the ancestral city, religious solidarity has become a social reality. A full discussion of the methodology of this survey will appear in my forthcoming book, *Hegemony and Culture: Politics and Religious Change among the Yoruba.*

Oyo Muslims eventually supported the Ilorin forces, but their actions were perceived to be anti-*alaafin* rather than pro-Muslim. Third, Solagberu, the military commander of Ilorin, a Yoruba Muslim, was liquidated by the Fulani advisers. The war was perceived to be one of Fulani control over Ilorin rather than Muslim control over Oyo. Robin Law concludes that Islam was central to this rebellion only insofar as "it provided a basis upon which disparate elements – Fulani, Hausa, and Yoruba – could be united in a common loyalty for an assault upon the established order." But even this is too strong, because the alliance was ephemeral and hardly induced any social integration between Fulani and Yoruba Muslims.[20]

This pattern of the nonpoliticization of religious differentiation in Yorubaland persisted into the twentieth century. In the 1950s, when Yoruba Muslims complained that they were relatively disadvantaged in the race for jobs and considered the mission schools to be the culprits, the Western Region government enacted an education law that contained a formula for special funding for Muslim educational agencies.[21] In that same period, Chief Awolowo, a Christian, worked out an inventive program to subsidize Yoruba Muslims on their pilgrimages to Mecca, without a complementary program to mollify the Christians.

One place in Yorubaland where Muslims might have become mobilized as Muslims was Ibadan. (Ilorin, which became administratively a part of the non-Yoruba Northern Region, requires separate treatment.)[22] In 1953, Awolowo's Action Group attempted to wrest control over Ibadan from the rival NCNC. The Action Group surreptitiously supported a prominent Muslim from Ibadan in the development of a United Muslim party. This turned out to be a disastrous failure, because Adegoke Adelabu, the Yoruba leader of Ibadan's NCNC and a Muslim, decried the strategy and defeated the Action Group at the polls. By 1956, Adelabu, now in a weakened position politically, attempted to revive his political fortunes by making the pilgrimage to Mecca himself and then mobilizing Yoruba Muslims as Muslims. This time, Awolowo copied Adelabu's rhetoric of 1953, and the National Muslim League felt compelled to change its name to the National Emancipation League in the 1958 election. Even still, it polled less than 1 percent of the total vote in the local government elections that year and failed to win a seat in the 1959 federal election. In 1965, the last election before military rule, and in 1979, the first election after military rule, there were no parties that attempted to bifurcate the Yoruba on the religious dimension. Of even greater significance, in the 1977 debates on the role of the Sharia courts in the new constitution, Yoruba delegates, both Christian and Muslim, were the most moderate in the entire federation. In fact, they provided the constituency for a compromise that saved the country from yet another constitutional failure. They did this, not for the sake of political payoff, but rather because making political use of religious differentiation was inconceivable to the Yoruba delegates.[23]

The actions of the Yoruba delegates in the Constitutional Drafting Committee appear to be nonrational. Should they not have exploited their indifference on the Sharia courts issue by extracting benefits from the Muslim northerners in areas where they, the Yorubas, were not indifferent? Yet the behavior of the delegates was representative of the political framework in Yorubaland. In my research in Ile-Ife, I informally explored the political alternatives for electoral action with my interviewees. The Yoruba-dominated party, the UPN, could not build an electoral alliance with any region and lost to the National Party of Nigeria (NPN). The NPN originated in the populous northern states, and although it was able to win in two non-Muslim southeastern states, it was perceived to be the party of the northern Muslims. The NPN tried a variety of strategies to incorporate Yoruba groups into its electoral coalition, but outside of a few prominent figures with virtually no electoral base, the NPN failed completely to develop a foothold in Yorubaland. I asked my Muslim interviewees whether they thought about aligning with the NPN. I pointed out to them that joining the NPN might entail a variety of payoffs to Yoruba Muslims that would not be available to them if they remained loyal to the UPN. Their response was not that my calculation of benefits was incorrect, but rather that organizing politically as Muslims was not in their realm of calculation at all.

In the 1983 elections, the NPN did, in fact, make significant inroads in Yorubaland; yet its successes were based entirely on the exploitation of ancestral city fissures. Yorubas who identified with Oyo were mobilized again to counter Ijebu domination of the UPN. In Ibadan, violence between Oyos and Ijebus broke out in the wake of the voting. In Ile-Ife, where the dominant Ifes are closely allied with Awolowo and his Ijebu constituency, there is a ward of Oyo refugees who settled in Ile-Ife a century ago. The NPN penetrated that ward rather completely, and in one electoral contest, the ward produced more NPN votes than the estimated population of the entire city. Ancestral cities – Oyo, Ijebu, and Ife – remain the categories within which Yorubas think and act politically. Religious affiliation had no discernible bearing on political alignments in the 1983 elections.[24]

The *problematic* of this section can now be restated: Although the social significance of religious differentiation among the Yoruba has increased in the past century, its political manifestations have been weak. Meanwhile, the relative social significance of the ancestral city has declined markedly in the past century, yet its political centrality persists. At the top of the hierarchy of cleavages in the political realm, the dominant metaphor for political interpretation within Yorubaland is the ancestral city. What is the explanation for this outcome?

Explaining Religious Toleration

The Reality of Primordial Ties

The predominant explanation by Yorubas for this outcome is that ancestral city identification is real, whereas religious identification is artificial. In my discussion of religious penetration and the data on religion and the ancestral city within Ile-Ife families, I hope to have demonstrated that the ties of the ancestral city are hardly more "real" than the ties of religion. Here, I shall press this argument further, because the data demonstrate, not the "givenness" of primordial ties, but rather their changeability.

Consistent with data presented by theorists of the rational-choice perspective, the Yoruba case provides abundant evidence of the fluidity of the social definition of identity. The development of Ibadan, discussed earlier, is an excellent example. Originally a military camp with refugees from a variety of ancestral cities, Ibadan soon began to develop its own "tradition," and its leaders fostered an Ibadan consciousness. Soon these leaders were making claims for higher status titles in the "traditional" hierarchy. Ibadan, through the efforts of ambitious politicians, became an ancestral city. Manipulation of the ancestral city "tradition" was in fact common. Yoruba kings from peripheral areas held regular negotiations with the king of Ile-Ife in order to rearrange their status in the "ancient" hierarchy of kings. The British colonizers paid kings their salaries on the basis of their positions in the hierarchy, and Yoruba kings had little difficulty in recreating their tradition to garner economic payoffs.[25] Neither the presumed weakness of the hold of the world religions, nor the presumed "givenness" of blood ties to the ancestral city can explain the pattern of politicization of social cleavages in Yorubaland.

The Rationality of Cleavage Patterns

On the basis of overwhelming evidence that tradition is less a constraint on action than a resource for political engineering, social scientists have developed a neo-Benthamite paradigm in which the politicization of social cleavages is seen to be the rational pursuit of goals by value-maximizing individuals. In the African setting, the new paradigm works in the following manner. First, exogenous social and economic changes yield a new pattern of rewards. Groups who live on mineral-rich land, or who can produce crops in high demand elsewhere begin to gain relative to their neighbors. Groups who are on new trade routes or whose urban areas become important new administrative centers also gain. Sometimes gain comes from a willingness to put up with missionaries: European evangelists opened up job opportunities for their literate students in the colonial states. For a set of reasons, the broad social changes of the past century have brought a new pattern of rewards.

Second, rewards and resources are inevitably scarce, and competition for jobs, for status, and for other manifestations of "modernity" is intense. Individuals from areas that are not spatially favored migrate to other areas in order to reap the benefits of the changed environment.[26]

Third, political entrepreneurs find it cheaper to organize people on the basis of their ethnic identities than on the basis of their class identities. This is the case because people who share ethnic identities often have a common language, so that translation costs are low; and they share a myth of kinship, so that the symbolic basis of solidarity is already available. The logic of collective action therefore favors the mobilization of particular migrant groups and, in opposition to them, the sons of the soil; but it does not favor the mobilization of the lumpen proletariat.[27]

Finally, the ambitious entrepreneur will attempt to broaden the boundaries of the ethnic group he leads in order to enhance the geographic scope of his authority. This is not an impossible task. Since "tribal" identities are fluid and the myths of kinship are subject to manipulation, the boundaries of ethnic identification (and the symbolic core of the ethnic group) are subject to rearticulation by both entrepreneurs and members – in both cases to enhance the opportunity for the successful pursuit of resources.[28] Therefore, primordially based political action is not a result of "givens"; rather it is the result of strategic identity readjustments by self-interested individuals.

This instrumentalist perspective can be, and has been, formalized. For my purposes, however, its importance is that it has generated interesting, nontrivial hypotheses of the emergence of tribalism and the politicization of tribal identities.[29] The reasoning behind these hypotheses is that, under conditions of imperfect access to information, high risk, and uncertainty, individuals will adopt short-run political strategies to maximize their status, wealth, and power. Tribalism is the macrosociological outcome of rationally pursued strategies by individuals. In the Yoruba case, the politicization of the ancestral city cleavage would be explained by the inexpensiveness of political communications and the preexistence of an infrastructure for political organization in the ancestral cities and their networks in the larger urban centers.

But just as the theory focusing on primordial identities faces the anomalies of identity readjustment and the apparent rationality of ethnically based political organization, the neo-Benthamite theory faces its own anomalies. These must be confronted if the theory is to be refined and advanced. The first problem that the rational-action theory faces is the *persistence* of communal identities. In another context, responding to arguments that political identities in Europe may, under certain conditions, be transferred from the nation-state to the Continent, Stanley Hoffmann pointed out that national identity is not like an onion, which can be peeled away into nothing, but rather like an artichoke: People will transfer their loyalty for purposes of political advantage only so far – until it reaches their heart.[30] Of course, the primordialists often assume that the heart has an immutable reality. The data do not support this view, but once the rational-action perspective perspective is adopted, what was obvious to the primordialist and therefore not requiring explanation becomes problematic to the instrumentalist.

Robert Bates, who is of the instrumentalist tradition, has argued that "ethnic groups persist largely because of their capacity to extract goods and services from the modern sector and thereby satisfy the demands of their members for the components of modernity."[31] Brian Barry, in a similar vein, has stated, "I would guess that ethnic groups will survive in the US just so long as it is a source of satisfaction."[32] In addition to the fact that no data have been presented to support these propositions, one easily sees how strained and unconvincing they are. People do not leave their ethnic groups as they do their jobs; nor do they change their ethnic identities in the same way they change their brands of beer. Because one aspect of ethnic identity involves the belief that it does indeed represent a biological "given," most people at most times do not calculate how much satisfaction they derive from their ethnic identities. Without calculation and the weighing of satisfactions, economic paradigms lose their explanatory power. Persistence of ethnic identity without concomitant calculation concerning benefits is, then, a thorny problem for students of the rational-actor paradigm.

The second problem in the instrumentalist paradigm is its inability to explain the puzzle of this essay, that is, why some communal groups mobilize politically whereas others do not. One way to pose the problem is to examine the tension between two neo-Benthamite points: that tribal identities have lower organizational costs and that tribal identities are fluid. If they are fluid, then their organizational costs must be higher than assumed. If they are higher than assumed, why are they so easily mobilized in the African context? But whether high or low, we still lack a theory that tells us which identities will become politicized.

Rational-choice theorists can address this problem by arguing that the success of a group in forming a viable political organization is contingent on political entrepreneurs who understand the "Olson" problem of organization. Since political entrepreneurs are offering their constituencies a "public good," why should any follower be willing to incur a specific cost? Should not all prospective followers want a "free ride" while others pay for what all will have to share? A good entrepreneur, from this point of view, is one who knows how to provide "selective incentives" to particular individuals to join in the group effort. Communal groups will politicize when there is an entrepreneur who (perhaps instinctively) understands the constraints to organization of rational individual behavior.[33] This is a powerful response, and it would be considerably enhanced as a theoretical contribution if it were possible to establish from independent data the quality of the strategic calculations of entrepreneurs before one assesses whether their organizations were successful.

Nonetheless, the response that emphasizes selective incentives tends to miss broad contemporaneous patterns over a number of similar countries. Why were religious entrepreneurs in sixteenth-century Europe able to politicize religious differences in virtually all the states? Why did entrepreneurs of peripheral nationalities in Europe suddenly become moderately successful in the same period of the 1970s? Meanwhile, why are religious entrepreneurs without large constituencies in Europe today, whereas they cannot be contained in the Shi'ite world? In the case under discussion, why in postindependence Africa have tribal entrepreneurs been successful in mobilizing political constituencies, whereas religious entrepreneurs have been less successful? Certain aspects of identity become crucial at certain times and politically irrelevant at others. These global patterns cannot be successfully addressed by the instrumentalists, who focus on the logic of individual cases.

Especially problematic for the instrumentalists in the case studies here is the apparent quiescence of the Muslim Yorubas. Morrison's survey demonstrated that Yoruba Muslims were less critical of the distribution of wealth than were the Yoruba Christians and saw themselves as benefiting from government services more than did the Christians. Muslims were more likely to point to improvements in Nigeria over the past ten years and were equally optimistic as the Christians about their children's opportunities.

Given the data on their educational and economic positions presented earlier, these attitudes hardly represent rational calculation.[34] My inability to induce Yoruba Muslims to *calculate* the potential satisfactions of politically identifying with the Muslim-dominated NPN suggests that the ancestral city cleavage enjoys dominance for reasons that transcend the incentives provided by tribal entrepreneurs.

Rational-choice theorists are prudent when they set theoretical limits to their paradigm and remind us that microeconomics has always concerned itself with marginal decisions but not structural transformations. A theory embedded in microeconomics might be able to explain why a Yoruba emphasized his attachment to his mother's ancestral city over his father's, but it could not explain his decision to identify himself on a new dimension entirely. A different theory is required to explain structural transformation. This response begs the question of how one determines whether an identity readjustment is marginal or structural. Without a mechanism for making such a determination, the claim that for an Ijebu man to consider himself an Egba is marginal, whereas for an *Ijebu* Christian to consider himself an Ijebu *Christian* is structural, has no foundation. The model of hegemonic control is an attempt to remedy this problem through the development of a theoretical explanation of how political control can create structural barriers to what may well have been marginal changes.[35]

The Model of Hegemonic Control

Not Bentham but Gramsci provides the solution to the puzzle presented in this essay. The logic of imperial action can help to explain the reification of the "tribe" in African politics – both why that cleavage became the dominant metaphor for political action and why that cleavage persisted.

In the late nineteenth century, Lord Lugard, who helped to define and articulate the mechanisms of British administrative control over Nigeria and elsewhere in Africa,[36] developed a strategy of "indirect rule." The core idea was to preserve local authority structures but to grant colonial authorities the power to "overrule," that is, guide and manipulate local authority. In certain areas of Africa, this idea had some basis in reality, as in the emirates of northern Nigeria.[37] In others, it made no sense, because there was no semblance of hierarchical authority through which the British could rule. This was the case in much of eastern Nigeria, especially among the Igbos.[38] With the Yorubas, the idea of indirect rule was neither realistic nor irrelevant; it was merely reactionary. What the British did in Yorubaland, as has been chronicled by J. A. Atanda, was to create the "New Oyo Empire."[39] New Oyo, a refugee encampment virtually powerless against upstart Ibadan, was given a new lease on life by the British colonialists.

The relationship between Oyo and the British, from the beginning, had aspects of common interest. In 1888, Alfred Moloney, the governor of Lagos, attempted to enlist the support of the *alaafin* in keeping French traders out of Yorubaland. The seeds of indirect rule were planted in his message, which was addressed to "Adeyemi, Alaafin of Oyo, the Head of Yorubaland, the four corners of which are and have been from time immemorial known as Egba, Ketu, Jebu, and Oyo, embracing within its area that inhabited by all Yoruba-speaking peoples."[40] The provisions called for a nice "dash" (payoff) for the *alaafin* if he used his influence to keep trade open to the British. Even the treaty ending the Kiriji War, the last of the great battles of the Yoruba civil wars, a treaty that was secured by British influence and power, gave the *alaafin* the responsibility of managing the final settlement between Ibadan and Ilorin. (He failed).[41] That there was a mutually productive relationship between the *alaafin* and the British was clear to both.

In 1895 the British nonetheless had to prove their superiority; one short bombing of the town forced the *alaafin* to flee and the town to submit. Despite this inauspicious event, the Oyos were quick to see the advantages of submission. To the eyes of the colonialists, Ibadan's power was thin, whereas Oyo's legitimacy was deep. Ibadan was noisy and rough; Oyo stable and orderly. When in 1898 the resident at Ibadan, F. C. Fuller, visited Oyo, he described the *alaafin* as "the most 'royal' native" he had "seen in Yorubaland." Atanda noted that "it was thought that great administrative advantages would be derived if the Alaafin's 'empty' appellation of 'Head of Yorubaland' was given some reality. The first step was to increase the territorial responsibility of Oyo at the expense of Ibadan."[42]

When W. A. Ross became district commissioner for Oyo in 1906, the consequences of indirect rule for the relative status of Oyo and Ibadan became apparent. Ross was an ardent advocate of indirect rule and a Yorubaphile who deeply wished to enhance and protect the Yoruba tradition. He was an age-mate and friend of Oyo's crown prince. In fact, Ross was instrumental in getting the crown prince appointed *alaafin* when the latter died, even though it took some creative reinterpretation of the Oyo tradition.

In implementing his grand scheme, Ross first had to overcome a treaty of 1893 in which the British conceded to Ibadan that it would be autonomous from Oyo. He waited until he became acting resident over the whole region in 1912 and then rearranged authority relations so completely that even the white missionaries found themselves subordinate to the *alaafin*. When Lugard became governor of Nigeria that same year and his doctrine of indirect rule became enshrined, Ross preempted Lugard's thrust by intervening in a succession battle for the leadership of Ibadan by making "loyalty to the Alaafin a *sine qua non* for election."[43]

Ross's next move was to make Oyo the seat and headquarters of the entire province, with the *alaafin* considered the "paramount chief." When the leader of Ibadan protested, Ross had him deposed. Lugard gave Ross permission to grant the *alaafin* the authority to impose the death sentence on rebels and to exert judicial control over a wide range of issues. He could send his own residents throughout the province, who became high-handed marauders. Nonetheless, Ross overlooked the complaints against them, arguing that it was the *alaafin's* duty to discipline them.[44]

The implications of Ross's version of indirect rule for the structure of cleavages in modern Yorubaland are wide. First, Ross's policies enhanced the position of those elites who considered themselves "traditional authorities" in Oyo, and this helped to sustain an Oyo identity even though the people were living far away from their ancestral home. If the notion of an Oyo identity was becoming more ambiguous in the wake of the civil war, that identity was reified and restored by British authority.

Second, other groups found that the only "legitimate" claims they could make within the colonial political system were ones based on traditional and historical rights. The king of Ife received considerable benefits from the British because he represented an ancestral city that had special religious meaning. Soon, even Ibadan played the game, and its leaders petitioned the British to grant ever higher titles in the Yoruba framework for the leader of their city. The British, then, not only gave new power and meaning to the Oyo identity, but they also provided benefits to other groups who made claims in terms of their "traditional" identities.[45]

Third, the system of indirect rule led groups that had no special claims by virtue of their authority in the old Oyo Empire to challenge the advances by Oyo and Ile-Ife. The only way they could succeed, however, was by making alliances with other cities or with outsiders (in the case of Ekiti and Ijebu, alliances were made with missionaries) to garner more resources. Catching up with Oyo became a dominant theme, but that theme itself acted further to reify identity based on the ancestral city. It is interesting that the Ijebu and Ekiti alliance with missionaries paid off in the long term, for their sons procured civil service jobs more effectively than any other Yoruba groups, and the sons of Oyo found themselves trying to catch up. Not Oyo's preeminence, but the very game of intercity competition became enshrined.

Meanwhile, claims based on religious identity were expunged from the political arena by British administrators. Indirect rule as an administrative philosophy guided the British away from their original effort to promote Christianity. They became instead arbiters among the interests of Muslims and Christians. In 1875, for example, the government attempted to settle an internal Islamic dispute in a sense of "fairness and freedom of worship," and again in 1902–03 a factional dispute among Muslims in Epe induced the governor to bring in a group of Lagos Muslims to arbitrate. These actions probably enhanced the governor's prestige.[46]

In education as well, the governor agreed to subsidize Christian schools if they would accommodate their curricula to meet the needs of Muslim students. When this failed, the governor began to subsidize Muslim schools. In return for these funds, Muslims helped the governor to bring peace to the country. Governor Carter recruited the chief *imam* of Lagos to appeal directly to the *emir* of Ilorin to make peace with the British, and Carter found himself an intermediary among Muslims in their internal disputes. Despite the protestations of the Christian missionaries that the government was giving "excessive deference" to the Muslims, it is clear that the preemption of political claims based on religion was the British goal.[47] To defuse religious antagonism rather than to support religious hierarchy was the British strategy. This is in marked contrast to British policies regarding ancestral cities, where antagonisms were exacerbated in order to establish a ruling hierarchy. The British, then, politicized one cleavage and depoliticized another.

The Problem of Persistence

The colonial structure in Yorubaland made indirect rule an efficient strategy of control. Indirect rule involved the infusion of resources to politically defunct but socially legitimate leaders. This strategy led to the reification of the tribe and the depoliticization of religion. But why does this pattern persist, especially after a generation of political independence and a very fluid political scene in Nigeria, of which Yorubaland, no longer administratively unified, is only a part? How does a model of hegemonic control explain the persistence of social cleavages after the hegemon leaves the scene? Must we rely on rational-choice theory to claim that the transition costs are too high?

The discussion up to this point has alluded to material and ideological forces that have acted to sustain the present pattern of cleavages in Yorubaland. Let us first examine the material forces. The structure of the modern Nigerian state was built on the Lugardian system of reified identities. Battling groups – Igbos against Hausas, Yorubas against Igbos, minority tribes against the regionally powerful tribes – all used criteria of group membership that were nourished by indirect rule. As Yoruba politics entered the federal realm, politicians found that the idea of a "Yoruba" interest could most easily be articulated on a foundation of sub-Yoruba (i.e., ancestral city) interests. Independent Nigerian politics based on regions therefore helped to sustain colonial cleavage patterns based on city-kingdoms.

Furthermore, ancestral cities are still able to provide valued goods. They provide protection to Yorubas escaping from troubled situations elsewhere, and they can provide land as well. Until the 1978 Land Decree, which gave some strangers the right to claim title to land their families had worked, Yoruba kings could promise land to non-resident sons of the town. The ability of kings to offer protection and land also helped to sustain the political relevance of ancestral cities.

Another material factor consists of the interests of the first generation of political elites in independent Nigeria. Chief Awolowo, who developed the earliest electoral strategies in Yorubaland, remains the dominant political force in Yorubaland at the time of this writing. He is identified by all Yorubas as an "Ijebu man" and by all Nigerians as a "Yoruba." He is more than 70 years old, and many Nigerians argue that when both he and his elder, Azikiwe, the Igbo patriarch, pass from the scene, there will be a new opportunity to change the basis of political coalitions in Nigeria. Those elites who gained power during an era of tribalism have an interest in sustaining its vocabulary.[48]

Finally, the comparative theory of ethnic political arousal suggests that, as long as the hegemonic coalition is not faltering economically, it is not likely that the disadvantaged groups will turn their latent hostility into political action.[49] Only a long period of relative economic decline for the Yorubas vis-à-vis the rest of Nigeria would make it worthwhile for Yoruba Muslims to seek redistributions from their Christian counterparts. Only then would they begin to refocus their political identities.

However reasonable these explanations seem to be, they do not do justice to the pattern of cleavages that presently exists in Yorubaland. Given the existence of the new land decree, the fact of Awolowo's advanced age, and the deep problems facing Nigeria since its budget cutbacks in the wake of declining oil revenues, a look only at the material forces would lead one to forecast a potential realignment toward religion in the near future.

But there is no Muslim political movement on the Yoruba horizon. This is largely because ideological forces have combined with material forces to sustain colonial cleavage patterns. Yoruba towns have turned old religious rituals into a civic religion. Lagos elites are invited back to recite the chants formerly reserved for the traditional religious elites, and the rituals have turned into public holidays.[50] Rituals act to sustain personal identification with towns, even when the towns are less able to provide material resources to the individual. Stereotypes of people from other towns abound in Yoruba vocabulary, and this too sustains personal identification with the ancestral city.

Most important, however, has been the creation of a "common sense" as the ideological force of hegemony. The fact that the ancestral city represents "blood" whereas religion represents "choice" is so deeply embedded into common-sense thinking that experience to the contrary will not easily disabuse the Yoruba people of this "truth." The colonial state infused Yorubas with a common-sensical framework for self-understanding. This framework infused ancestral cities with an immutable reality. Rational-choice theorists are correct when they point to the high transition costs of changing one's political identity, but they are unable to grasp the nature of these costs. Primordial theorists correctly point to the strong power of traditional identities, but they cannot make sense of the political basis of primordial identities. The model of hegemonic control comprehends the material basis of cleavage patterns, but in the case at hand its major contribution is a plausible explanation of the way in which primordial identities become politically forged and how, once forged, these identities become common-sensically real.

Colonial Hegemonic Control in Comparative Perspective

This discussion of indirect rule in Yorubaland focuses on an important social force missed by theories of both primordial attachment and rational choice: the role of a hegemonic state in fashioning a cultural product. Colonial Britain is a special kind of hegemonic state, to be sure, but like all hegemons, Britain had an interest in efficient social control. The need for efficient social control led British colonial administrators to create incentives for certain groups to form and to repress other groups. In any state, but especially in colonized states, the political organizations that make demands on the state are themselves partly a function of state actions. Although patterns of social stratification may be a function of a range of social and economic variables, the patterns of politicized cleavages may be better understood to be largely a function of the strategies of political control by hegemonic states.

Because the discussion thus far has focused on a single case, it would be useful to point out the range of applicability of the model of hegemonic control. In his contribution to the volume edited by Lipset and Rokkan, whose statement of the general theoretical problem opened this essay, Immanuel Wallerstein argued that the colonial ruling elites upheld an "essential doctrine": "The meaningful social entity remained the tribe. . . . By upholding this traditional definition of the situation, they hoped to maintain their power by control via their clients, the chiefs." With the parameters of the colonial situation set, nationalist parties found themselves faced with tribal claims and, by addressing those claims, recognized their reality.[51] Wallerstein's evidence demonstrates that (a) "tribe" was a convenient category through which colonial powers could rule and (b) once chosen, the existence of tribes as a social reality, a reality that could not be denied by anyone with common sense, was reified. Lemarchand's more recent discussion of state building in Africa provides abundant evidence that colonial states restratified African society for purposes of social control.[52] The strategy of reproducing African culture so as to impress the local population with the obvious and eternal legitimacy of the political order is the benchmark of colonial control. The colonial reproduction of culture complemented military repression to yield short-term political order but long-term patterns of political cleavage. It is the hegemonic state that seeks to combine military repression with ideological infusion in order to restructure society.

The case of Yoruba political organization is consistent not only with other research on colonial strategy in Africa, but with recent studies of hegemonic control in India and Israel as well. Let us first consider the exciting and sophisticated historiographical debate concerning the emergence of violent Hindu–Muslim conflict in twentieth-century India. Both parties to the debate, Paul Brass and Francis Robinson, agree that owing to the patterns set by Akbar in the late sixteenth century, in which "affirmative-action programs" for Hindus helped many of them achieve equity with their Muslim rulers, there was no unambiguous social or political cleavage between Muslims and Hindus in the early nineteenth century. As Robinson points out, "Muslims had little in common with each other apart from their religion; Hindus were fundamentally divided even by their faith. Many Muslims and Hindus had more in common with each other than with their co-religionists, and in late-nineteenth-century [United Provinces, today the State of Uttar Pradesh in northern India] the political connections which really mattered were based on the common outlook and interests of Hindu and Muslim landlords and government servants." Brass would no doubt accept this statement, and he sought a theory that would "reveal the process by which the pre-existing differences separating Muslims from Hindus were emphasized, communicated, and translated into a political movement."[53]

Brass's answer is consistent with the rational-choice model discussed in the previous section. He notes that Indian Muslims in the early twentieth century were socially mobilized at a faster rate than Hindus, but this only made them depressingly aware that the numerical majority of Hindus in the United Provinces, which was the seedbed of the religious conflict, would continue to work in the Hindus' favor under the electoral formulas then being developed. Muslim elites, sensing clearly their weakening political position, began to make claims to the British. They used data from Bengal, where Muslims were in fact relatively deprived in social development, to make claims for preferential treatment throughout India. They demanded secure seats in legislative assemblies to protect their own privileges. These actions induced a creative response by Hindu elites to mobilize themselves for political action. Part of the reason for the movement to promote the Hindi language (and to differentiate it from Urdu – no easy task since the languages were basically the same save for some vocabulary and the orthography) was a strategic reaction by Hindu elites to create a Hindu consciousness for the purposes of political action. The more the elites on either side could manipulate symbols to differentiate their community from the other, the more were the opportunities for political success. This political dialectic snowballed unmercifully. The rational pursuit of power within India, Brass concludes, led to the irrational holocaust of partition.

However elegant Brass's presentation, it fails to explain why there was a greater number of political enterpreneurs selling religious symbols than of those selling symbols that would divide the population in other ways. Or, even if there were an equal number of entrepreneurs trying to mobilize constituencies on a variety of dimensions, why were the religious entrepreneurs far more successful in rallying supporters? To answer questions such as these, Robinson has focused his attention on the United Kingdom, whose colonial civil servants had a clear image of Indian society and who set the "context" for subsequent political mobilization. "The British," Robinson suggests, "insisted on discussing Indian politics and society in terms of Muslims and Hindus. . . . They had done so from the beginning of their contact with Indian society. . . . Religious differences were the most apparent and the most easily understood so they were the most readily employed by those who wished to describe the society and its politics."[54] And so, despite much evidence to the contrary, the Mutiny of 1857 was seen to be a product of Muslim conspiracy. Reinterpreting Indian politics in terms of Muslim–Hindu differences made British civil servants open to political claims based on these attachments, which thereupon created the incentive for political entrepreneurs to make such claims. That the British were not too far wrong concerning Indian emotional attachment to religion made those entrepreneurs very successful. The actions of the United Kingdom in asking Muslims "to help in the business of ruling in return for which their interests would be given consideration"[55] were structurally similar to its actions in Yorubaland in ruling through the Oyos. A colonial hegemon, whether in India or in Yorubaland, can instill in certain cleavage patterns a sense of reality and objectivity that is not fully supported by the social structure.

The role of a hegemonic state in fashioning and reifying culture can also be observed in regard to Israel's strategy to control its Arab population. Ian Lustick describes a set of strategies formulated by Israeli authorities for the purpose of reducing the costs of social control over a potentially subversive Arab sector. To this end, they reified and sustained socially defunct categories within Arab social structure in order to "segment" the controlled population, and then they purchased support from the newly created "primordial" leaders through a strategy of "cooptation." The Israelis appear to have been even more self-conscious in their hegemonic strategy than the British in either Nigeria or India. They appeared to recognize the need to recreate the power of those Arab elites who had maintained their legitimacy but had lost the resources to sustain their authority. The Israelis, by providing these "traditional" elites with resources for coercive power, won their allegiance and then allowed them to establish themselves over more radical counterelites.[56]

To be sure, the rule adduced from the British actions in Yorubaland and India and the Israeli strategy concerning its Arab citizens are not the only examples of rational strategies for states seeking hegemonic control. France, for example, engaged in a different strategy of political control with different consequences for political cleavages in the postcolonial state. Instead of reifying "ancient" authority structures, French colonial administrators coopted leaders who assumed French identities. Because the French were less prone to impose an ethnic map of their own design in Africa than were the British, institutionalized conflicts between "tribal" groups have been less important in postcolonial French Africa.[57]

Furthermore, the strategy of a hegemonic state discussed in this essay does not assume that the hegemon is aware of its overarching power. British administrators hardly appreciated their hegemony. Many thought they were hanging on a thread. Furthermore, even Lord Lugard, perhaps the most prescient and sophisticated designer of British colonial strategy in Africa, did not see the ancestral city as a socially waning source of cleavage that, if strategically supported, would become reified and thereby yield political quiescence. He had an evolutionary view of the state and felt that at a low level of civilization, which he believed to be the condition of the Yoruba, "tribes" were the *only* possible legitimate grouping. Ruling through religious elites, in Lugard's view, required a more developed colony.[58] The "rule," then, describes British colonial behavior even though British administrators were not conscious of the implications of their choices.

Conclusion

This essay has focused on the model of hegemonic control in order to make sense of the nonpoliticization of the religious cleavage in Yoruba society. It has demonstrated that an exogenous power interested in creating order in a weak state would find it attractive to seek out a set of elites that had high legitimacy in the society but declining resources with which to exert authority. The hegemon could then support the expansion of power and control by those elites but, through cooptation, control them. (In this sense, the policy would not be one of "divide and rule," but rather one of "divide and recombine so that one can rule through a vigorous and legitimate elite.") Viewing the situation in this way, one sees the power of the reification of the primordial. The strategy would not be successful unless there were a real basis in the symbolic repertoire of the society for such a pattern of cleavage. The hegemonic rulers would get a "free ride" by reinfusing with coercive resources political elites who were both poor and legitimate. Those challenging the hegemonic power would then be forced to attempt a very difficult task: delegitimating what their own society thought to be obviously and eternally legitimate. The hegemonic state would buy short-term control at low cost and set long-term patterns of political cleavage by reifying traditional culture and ensuring that traditional culture would be spun into a web of significance that neither the hegemon nor the dominated society could easily escape.

The Yoruba case study (supported by the vignettes from India and Israel) suggests that colonial administrations have employed their power to structure the hierarchy of cleavages in the societies they control. Within Yorubaland, the pattern of societal inputs into the present Nigerian state is not so much a function of biological affinities or of rational-group calculation.

It is more a function of resource manipulation by the colonial state and the infusion of an ideology that ancestral city ties are real. This combination of resource manipulation and ideological infusion by a powerful administrative apparatus is the defining characteristic of hegemony.

Lipset and Rokkan, in their volume quoted at the beginning of this essay, argued that contemporary political cleavage patterns in European states were a function of the dominant social cleavages in the earliest electoral periods. The early electoral coalitions became institutionalized and were thereby perpetuated by the political system.[59] In the Yoruba case, however, to claim that ancestral city identification has become institutionalized is to beg the question of the source of that institutionalization. To accept uncritically the institutionalization paradigm is to accept implicitly a society-centered view of politics. Political cleavages are seen to be the outcome of rationally pursued strategies of societal groups. This case study has demonstrated the importance of state actions in shaping long-term political cleavages within the society. I have shown how a state apparatus, in this case a colonial state, can structure the hierarchy of sociocultural cleavages. A hegemonic state can decisively influence the nature of the societal inputs that it must subsequently process.

Notes

An earlier version of this chapter was delivered at the 1982 annual meeting of the American Political Science Association, Denver, Colorado, September 2–5, 1982. The author would like to thank A. I. Asiwaju, Robert Bates, Peter Cowhey, Peter Gourevitch, Ernst Haas, Daniel Hallin, Mary Katzenstein, Peter Katzenstein, Ian Lustick, Anthony Oyewole, and Crawford Young for helpful comments. This research was supported by a grant from the National Endowment for the Humanities.

  1. Seymour M. Lipset and Stein Rokkan, *Party Systems and Voter Alignments: Cross-National Perspectives* (New York: Free Press, 1967), p. 6.
  2. David Laitin, "Conversion and Political Change: A Study of (Anglican) Christianity and Islam among the Yorubas in Ile-Ife," in *Political Anthropology Yearbook*, ed. M. J. Aronoff (New Brunswick, N.J.: Transaction Books, 1982).
  3. See Edward Shils, "Primordial, Personal, Sacred and Civil Ties," *British Journal of Sociology* 8 (1957): 130–45 and Clifford Geertz, "The Integrative Revolution: Primordial Sentiments and Civil Politics in the New States," in *Old Societies and New States*, ed. C. Geertz, (Glencoe: Ill.: Free Press, 1963), pp. 105–57.
  4. See M. C. Young, *Politics in the Congo* (Princeton, N. J.: Princeton University Press, 1965), especially his discussion of the Bangala people, pp. 242–46; Robert Bates, "Ethnic Competition and Modernization in Contemporary Africa," *Comparative Political Studies* 6(4) (1974): 457–84; Nelson Kasfir, "Explaining Ethnic Political Participation," *World Politics* 31(3) (1979): 365–88; Abner Cohen, *Custom and Politics in Urban Africa* (Berkeley: University of California Press, 1969); and Joseph Gusfield, "The Social Construction of Tradition: an Interactionist View of Social Change," in *Traditional Attitudes and Modern Styles in Political Leadership*, ed. J. D. Legge, (Melbourne: Angus & Robertson, 1973), pp. 83–104.
  5. For a translation of Gramsci's writings, I relied on the edited volume of Quintin

Hoare and Geoffrey Nowell-Smith, *Selections from the Prison Notebooks* (London: Lawrence & Wishart, 1971). The secondary sources on which I relied are Perry Anderson, "The Antinomies of Antonio Gramsci," *New Left Review* 100 (November 1976–January 1977): 5–80; and Walter L. Adamson, *Hegemony and Revolution: Antonio Gramsci's Political and Cultural Theory* (Berkeley: University of California Press, 1980). For definitions of "hegemony" I found Raymond Williams, *Marxism and Literature* (Oxford: Oxford University Press, 1977), chap. 6, to be excellent. I also relied on David Kertzer, "Gramsci's Concept of Hegemony: The Italian Church–Communist Struggle," *Dialectical Anthropology* 4(4) (1979): 321–28. On the idea of the reification of culture, I conjoined Marshall Sahlins, *Culture and Practical Reason* (Chicago: University of Chicago Press, 1976), and Andrew Feenberg, *Lukacs, Marx and the Sources of Critical Theory* (Oxford: Robertson, 1981), especially p. 157.

6. This assessment is based on a controversial paper by Robin Horton, "Ancient Ife: A Reassessment" (University of Ife, Spring 1976).

7. The seminal study of the rise of Ibadan is that by Bolanle Awe, "The Rise of Ibadan as a Yoruba Power, 1851–1893" (Ph.D. diss., Oxford University, 1965).

8. J. H. Kopytoff, *A Preface to Modern Nigeria* (Madison: University of Wisconsin Press, 1965), discusses the role of the recaptives. See B. Weinstein, "Language Strategists: Redefining Political Frontiers on the Basis of Linguistic Choices," *World Politics* 31(3) (1979): 345–64 for a discussion of the implications of the translation of the Bible into Yoruba.

9. An excellent discussion of the contemporary role of ancestral cities can be found in Akin Mabogunje and J. D. Omer-Cooper, *Owu in Yoruba History* (Ibadan: Ibadan University Press, 1971), p. 83.

10. P. C. Lloyd, *Power and Independence* (London: Routledge & Kegan Paul, 1974), p. 121. See also, O. Awolowo, *Awo* (Cambridge: Cambridge University Press, 1960), for a magnificent discussion of how Awolowo's family used its village as a sanctuary. J. S. Eades, in *The Yoruba Today* (Cambridge: Cambridge University Press, 1980), p. 63, provides some recent examples.

11. Lloyd, *Power and Independence*, pp. 141, 169.

12. For Lagos, see G. O. Gbadamosi, "The Establishment of Western Education among Muslims in Nigeria, 1896–1926," *Journal of the Historical Society of Nigeria* 4(1) (1967). I. H. Vanden Driesen kindly supplied me with some of the data on Ile-Ife from his research. The full sample, unfortunately, was not available. A complete discussion of the data base is available in his "Patterns of Land Holding and Land Distribution in the Ife Division of Western Nigeria," *Africa (London)*, 41(1) (1971): 42–53.

13. A. B. Fafunwa, *History of Education in Nigeria* (London: Allen & Unwin, 1974), p. 72. See also Pierre Van den Berghe, *Power and Privilege at an African University* (Cambridge, Mass.: Schenkman, 1973).

14. Richard Sklar, *Nigerian Political Parties* (Princeton, N. J.: Princeton University Press, 1963), p. 285. On the differential performance of Ijebu Christians and Muslims, see also D. Aronson, "Cultural Stability and Social Change among the Modern Ijebu Yoruba" (Ph.D. diss., University of Chicago, 1970).

15. Vanden Driesen's data (see note 12) for landownership. See also C. E. F. Beer, *The Politics of Peasant Groups in Western Nigeria* (Ibadan: Ibadan University Press, 1976); and S. S. Berry, "Christianity and the Rise of Cocoa-Growing in Ibadan and Ondo," *Journal of the Historical Society of Nigeria* 4(3) (1968).

16. On these data, I compared Muslim Yoruba respondents with Yoruba Protestants. Morrison also obtained responses from Catholic and "Independent Christian" Yorubas. The results would not have been markedly different if I had included the latter two groups along with the Protestants. I wish to thank Professor Morrison for his willingness to provide these data.

17. Sklar, *Nigerian Political Parties*, pp. 248–49; David Laitin, "The Sharia Debate and the Origins of Nigeria's Second Republic," *Journal of Modern African Studies* 20 (September 1982).

18. O. Oyediran, "Political Change in a Nigerian Urban Community" (Ph.D. diss., University of Pittsburgh, 1971).

19. The source of this conventional view is Samuel Johnson's epic, *The History of the Yorubas* (London: Routledge & Kegan Paul, 1921), p. 194. It is reflected in Margery Perham's biography, *Lugard* (Hamden, Conn.: Archon, 1968), vol. 2, p. 439.

20. See Robin Law, *The Oyo Empire* (Oxford: Clarendon, 1977), pp. 255–58; R. A. Adeleye, *Power and Diplomacy in Northern Nigeria, 1804–1906: The Sokoto Caliphate and Its Enemies* (London: Longman, 1971), pp. 35–37; and Johnson, *History of the Yorubas*, p. 194.

21. David Abernethy, *The Political Dilemma of Popular Education* (Stanford, Calif.: Stanford University Press, 1967), pp. 153–54.

22. The fascinating story of religious conflict and cohesion in Ilorin cannot be recounted here. An excellent source on this city's development is C. S. Whitaker, Jr., *The Politics of Tradition: Continuity and Change in Northern Nigeria* (Princeton, N. J.: Princeton University Press, 1970), chap. 3.

23. On Adelabu, see K. W. J. Post and George D. Jenkins, *The Price of Liberty* (Cambridge: Cambridge University Press, 1973). On the elections of 1958 and 1959, see Sklar, *Nigerian Political Parties*, p. 251. On the Sharia debate, see Laitin, "The Sharia Debate."

24. *West Africa (London)*, August 22, 1983, pp. 1927–28.

25. A. I. Asiwaju, "Political Motivation and Oral Historical Traditions in Africa: The Case of Yoruba Crowns, 1900–1960," *Africa (London)*, 46(2) (1976): 113–27. For an excellent example of the instrumental management of the "tradition," see T. Chappel, "The Yoruba Cult of Twins in Historical Perspective," *Africa (London)*, 44(3) (1974): 250–65. Evidently, severe population loss engendered by the civil wars led many Yorubas to accept a relatively new cult – one that rejected the "traditional" view of twins as abnormal and saw them, instead, as a sign of grace.

26. See Myron Weiner, *Sons of the Soil: Migration and Ethnic Conflict in India* (Princeton, N. J.: Princeton University Press, 1978); Mary F. Katzenstein, *Ethnicity and Equality: The Shiv Sena Party and Preferential Policies in Bombay* (Ithaca, N. Y. Cornell University Press, 1979); and Paul Brass, "Class, Ethnic Group, and Party in Indian Politics," *World Politics* 33(3) (1981): 449–67.

27. The organizational costs of effective political action are fully considered in Mancur Olson's seminal *The Logic of Collective Action* (Cambridge: Harvard University Press, 1965).

28. Paul Brass, *Language, Religion and Politics in North India* (Cambridge: Cambridge University Press, 1974), chap. 1.

29. For a wide range of hypotheses, see Robert Melson and Howard Wolpe, "Modernization and the Politics of Communalism," *American Political Science Review* 64(4) (1970): 1112–30; Alvin Rabushka and Kenneth Shepsle, *Politics in Plural*

Societies: A Theory of Democratic Instability (Columbus, Ohio: Merrill, 1972); and Ronald Rogowski, "Understanding Nationalism: The Possible Contributions of a General Theory of Political Cleavage" (Unpublished manuscript, September 1980).

30. Stanley Hoffmann, "Obstinate or Obsolete? The Fate of the Nation-State and the Case of Western Europe" in *International Regionalism*, ed. J. S. Nye (Boston: Little, Brown, 1968), pp. 200–201.

31. See Robert Bates, "Modernization, Ethnic Competition, and the Rationality of Politics in Contemporary Africa," in *Ethnicity, State Coherence, and Public Policy: African Dilemmas*, ed. Victor Olorunsola and Donald Rothchild (Boulder, Colo.: Westview Press, 1982).

32. Brian Barry, "Ethnicity and the State," in *Politics and Language: Spanish and English in the United States*, ed. D. J. R. Bruckner (University of Chicago, Center for Policy Study, 1978), p. 46.

33. I owe my colleague, Samuel Popkin, a great debt for teaching me to respect this approach and for listening to me as I tried to rebut it. See his *The Rational Peasant* (Berkeley: University of California Press, 1979), pp. 259–66. On the "Olson" problem, see Olson, *Logic of Collective Action*.

34. Morrison, note 16.

35. In "The Problem with Neoclassical Institutional Economics: A Critique with Special Reference to the North/Thomas Model of Pre-1500 Europe," *Explorations in Economic History* 18 (1981): 174–97, Alexander J. Field argues that epistemological problems make a satisfactory explanation of political outcomes through the use of economic variables impossible. I remain agnostic on the issue, but Robert Bates has helped me see the ways in which microeconomics can be complementary to the model of hegemonic control.

36. This theory is outlined in Frederick Lugard, *The Dual Mandate in British Tropical Africa* (London: Frank Cass, 1922), chaps. 10 and 11.

37. See Murray Last, *The Sokoto Caliphate* (London: Longman, 1967), but Adeleye, *Power and Diplomacy*, discerns less hierarchy in northern Nigeria than the conventional wisdom holds.

38. See A. E. Afigbo, *The Warrant Chiefs* (London: Longman, 1972).

39. J. A. Atanda, *The New Oyo Empire* (London: Longman, 1973).

40. Johnson, *History of the Yorubas*, p. 574.

41. Ibid., p. 584.

42. Atanda, *The New Oyo Empire*, pp. 101–102.

43. Ibid., p. 118.

44. Ibid., p. 203.

45. Ibid., p. 258; see also Post and Jenkins, *Price of Liberty*, p. 22.

46. See T. G. O. Gbadamosi, *The Growth of Islam among the Yoruba* (Atlantic Highlands, N.J.: Humanities Press, 1978), pp. 161–63.

47. Ibid., pp. 164–77, 215–16, and app. III.

48. This is the argument of Olatunde J. B. Ojo, "The Impact of Personality and Ethnicity on the Nigerian Elections of 1979," *Africa Today* 28(1) (1981): 47–58.

49. Peter Gourevitch, "The Reemergence of 'Peripheral Nationalisms': Some Comparative Speculations on the Spatial Distribution of Political Leadership and Economic Growth," *Comparative Studies in Society and History* 21 (July 1979): 295–314.

50. See, for example, W. B. Schwab, "The Growth and Conflicts of Religion in a Modern Yoruba Community," *Zaire* 6(8) (1952): 829–35. Not Schwab, who al-

ready saw the secular aspects of traditional ritual eight years before independence, but anthropologists in the Durkheimian school tend to seek the "real" tradition and thereby focus on people who have been least influenced by European culture. See, for example, E. E. Evans-Pritchard's cavalier dismissal of Islam in his classic study, *The Nuer* (Oxford: Oxford University Press, 1940). In my observation of Yoruba festivals, I, like Schwab, was struck by the role of high-ranking bureaucrats, visiting from Lagos for the occasion, *reading* the "traditional" praise songs to their king.

51. Immanuel Wallerstein, "Class, Tribe, and Party in West African Politics," in *Party Systems and Voter Alignments,* ed. Lipset and Rokkan, pp. 501–502, 509.

52. René Lemarchand, "The State and Society in Africa," in *Ethnicity, State Coherence, and Public Policy,* ed. Olorunsola and Rothchild.

53. Francis Robinson, *Separatism among Indian Muslims* (Cambridge: Cambridge University Press, 1974), p. 33; Brass, *Language, Religion and Politics,* p. 124.

54. Robinson, *Separatism,* p. 99.

55. Francis Robinson, "Nation Formation: The Brass Thesis and Muslim Separatism," *Journal of Commonwealth and Comparative Politics* 15(3) (1977): 226. See Brass's reply that follows. The debate continued in David Taylor and Malcolm Yapp, eds., *Political Identity in South Asia* (London: Curzon Press, 1979).

56. Ian Lustick, *Arabs in the Jewish State: A Study in the Control of a Minority Population* (Austin: University of Texas Press, 1980).

57. The best controlled comparison of the strategies of the British and French in West Africa is that of A. I. Asiwaju, *Western Yorubaland under European Rule, 1889–1945* (New York: Humanities Press, 1976). The nonpoliticization of the potential Arab–Berber cleavage in Morocco is linked to French colonial strategy in Ernest Gellner and Charles Micaud, eds., *Arabs and Berbers* (Lexington, Mass.: Heath, 1972).

58. See Lugard, *Dual Mandate,* chap. 4.

59. Lipset and Rokkan, *Party Systems and Voter Alignments.* Suzanne Berger, in *The French Political System* (New York: Random House, 1974), pp. 65–68, comes to a conclusion with regard to the perpetuation of the clerical–secular political cleavage in French politics that gives credence to the Lipset and Rokkan formulation.

10. State Power and the Strength of Civil Society in the Southern Cone of Latin America

Alfred Stepan

Society-centered views of political and economic transformation have never held the unchallenged sway in Latin America that they have in North America. The prevalence of "organic statist" models of society that assume a central and relatively autonomous role for the state has affected both policy makers and social scientists.[1] Beginning in the late 1960s, focus on the state became particularly intense. The erosion of the intellectual credibility of the society-centered "modernization" model of political and economic development coincided with the apparent exhaustion of both industrialization based on import substitution and the associated populist and parliamentary political regimes that were associated with it.[2] The assumptions of modernization theory that liberal democratic regimes would be inexorably produced by the process of industrialization was replaced by a new preoccupation with the ways in which the state apparatus might become a central instrument for both the repression of subordinate classes and the reorientation of the process of industrial development. This new concern is perhaps best exemplified in the seminal work of Guillermo O'Donnell on bureaucratic authoritarian (BA) regimes.[3] A BA regime was associated with (if not necessarily responsible for) an impressive episode of industrialization (in the Brazilian case). Such regimes also proved to be extremely effective at fragmenting, atomizing, and inhibiting potential oppositional collectivities. The initial period of the BA was one in which the civil society lost its capacity to generate new political and economic initiatives while the power of the state grew. Thus, analysis of the actions and initiatives of groups operating within the state apparatus became a central focus of social science research. In my own case, for example, I focused on the military as an institution: first, on the forces that led it to take on the role of military as government and then on the contradictions involved in its attempts to carry out this role while simultaneously maintaining its coherence as an "institution."[4]

Bureaucratic authoritarian regimes are still with us, but if the 1960s was the decade of the exhaustion of the easy stage of import substituting industrialization and parliamentary democracy in the southern cone, the 1980s appears to hold the promise of the "exhaustion" of the BA regime. These regimes are currently beset both by problems of political legitimacy and by an apparent inability to deal with the international economic context of the 1980s. Their difficulties have stimulated new interest in the interaction between civil society and the state in authoritarian contexts. The state itself, the goals of those who control it, the contradictions within it, and its continued capacity for repression and economic transformation remain tremendously important. At the same time, however, initiatives for change, insofar as such initiatives exist at all, are coming increasingly from within civil society. The role of the political opposition in shaping the future strategies of the state must be taken more explicitly into account. Likewise, the ways in which state structures and strategies define the options and strategies of the political opposition must be given close attention.

The aim here is to look at the reciprocal relations between the power of the state and the power of civil society. At the grossest level of abstraction, there are four possibilities. The first, and most obvious, has already been noted. The growth of state power may be accompanied in zero-sum fashion by a diminution of the power of civil society. It also is possible for the power relations between the state and civil society to be positive-sum. The interaction may also prove to be negative-sum. The state's capacity to structure outcomes may decline while the opposition's capacity to act in concert also declines. Finally, of course, there is the possibility that the power of actors operating outside the state apparatus may grow while that of those working within the state declines.

In this chapter, I explore variations in the power relations between the state and civil society through a consideration of the four countries of the southern cone in Latin American, namely, Chile, Uruguay, Argentina, and Brazil. As a group they share some important characteristics. In the 1960s or 1970s all four countries witnessed the advent of new, more pervasive forms of authoritarian rule. The new authoritarianism in all four countries followed periods of extensive but faltering industrialization and was installed in an atmosphere of growing class conflict. In each country the bourgeoisie provided the social base for the new authoritarian regimes, whose first political acts were the use of the coercive apparatus of the state (located institutionally in the army) to dismantle and disarticulate working-class organizations. In all four countries there was a major effort to restructure capitalism, though the concrete means of achieving such restructuring varied greatly from country to country.

All four of these regimes began with periods in which the institutions of civil society were emasculated while the state enhanced its ability to pursue its own goals, but the subsequent history of the relations between the authoritarian state and civil institutions has differed considerably among the four cases.[5] Only in Brazil do we find even a brief positive-sum period in which civil society began to reconstitute its institutions while the state continued to acquire additional capacity. In Chile, eight years of authoritarian rule passed without significant movement out of the initial authoritarian situation; civil society remained debilitated in the face of the strength of the state, though recently there seems to have been some weakening of the relative power of the state. In Uruguay, the initial period was followed by a period of stagnation in which neither the state nor civil society increased its capacity to achieve its goals. Finally, Argentina from 1979 to 1981 moved in the direction of a negative-sum interaction in which the power of civil society and the state declined simultaneously. Only after the defeat in Malvinas did civil institutions begin to recompose themselves, and then in the context of a dramatic decline in the capacity of the military regime.

It is not my purpose in this essay to provide a complete and balanced comparative history for each of the BAs, and thus there is no attempt to make observations at "comparable" moments of each BA. Rather, I am using the four countries to illuminate different dilemmas that the democratic opposition faces in its struggle against quite different BA state alliances. In the discussion that follows I hope to provide some heuristically fruitful suggestions as to the ways in which variations in the nature of the state apparatus and in the structure of civil society have led to such different outcomes in each of the four countries.

By discussing four authoritarian states that share some important characteristics, I also hope to illuminate how the relative autonomy of the authoritarian state apparatus is highly fluid and is affected by certain factors. For example, how much direct political (or, in extreme cases, economic) power are the state's bourgeois allies willing to abdicate in a brumairian sense[6] in return for defensive protection? Since coercion is a major component of an exclusionary authoritarian regime such as a BA, why and how can some types of fused or divided power among the chief executive, the three branches of the military, and the major intelligence forces increase or decrease relative state autonomy? How and why can struggles within these elements of the state apparatus create space for the opposition? Since bureaucratic routines and statutes are an important dimension of state control of civil society, is it possible that some routines or statutes adopted for a particular set of state purposes in fact also facilitate new forms of collective action and power creation in civil society?

Growth of State Power and the Decline of Civil Society: Chile, 1973–81

In 1973–81, in only one of the four authoritarian states in the southern cone, namely, Chile, did state power grow while the power of civil society declined. The possibility of such a trajectory depended on several interrelated factors. First, the intensity of class conflict during the period that preceded the regime made it relatively easy for the regime to gain acceptance of its "project" in the upper and middle classes. Equally important, fear of the possible recomposition of the Marxist opposition helped maintain the internal cohesion of the state apparatus itself. The nature of the state's "project" was also important. By focusing on the problem of domination and carefully designing its efforts at economic transformation so that their primary effect would be to reinforce the project of domination, the Chilean state managed to enhance its power over civil society.

In any regime, but especially in a BA regime, the capacity to lead the regime's political allies depends on the degree to which the regime has both "defensive" and "offensive" projects that potential allies consider to be feasible, crucial for the preservation and advancement of their own interests, and dependent on authoritarian power for their execution. Since coercion is a particularly important part of the regime's power, the degree of internal institutional cohesion of the repressive apparatus is also a key variable. The Chilean regime was strong in all these respects for almost the entire period between 1973 and 1981.

In Chile, the social and institutional groups in control of the state convinced their potential allies that they had a vital "defensive" project (continued repression of the Marxist Left and its "Kerenskyite" Christian Democratic forms). They also convinced their allies that they had an "offensive" *foundational* project that, if fully implemented by the turn of the century, would restructure Chilean capitalism and civil society so that a stable market economy would emerge, one capable of withstanding the reintroduction of some representative features of government.[7] This "radical" liberal market project included a modified constitution giving the state apparatus residual emergency powers to repress civil society and enforce the economic rules of the game. From 1973 to 1980 both the economic team and the coercive core of the state apparatus demonstrated a surprising degree of internal unity under the leadership of General Pinochet, who showed considerable ability to integrate diverse groups of the power bloc.

The regime's capacity to lead its allies was manifest in the plebiscite called by General Pinochet to ratify the highly authoritarian constitution in September 1980. Among other things, the new constitution called for the beginning of an eight-year "constitutional" term for Pinochet, from 1981 to 1989, with extremely easy procedures for renewing the term for another eight years.

The plebiscite was announced on August 10 and was held on September 10. In the first two weeks following the announcement, virtually all of the more than twenty major producer groups in Chile issued a manifesto urging an affirmative vote to ratify the constitution and paid to have their manifesto published in *El Mercurio*. Most major opposition groups issued manifestos urging a no vote in the plebiscite, and these, too, were published in *El Mercurio*.

Analysis of the newspaper in the thirty days leading up to the plebiscite fails to reveal a single producer group urging a negative vote or even a somewhat qualified yes. The language of the producer groups' manifestos was replete with references to the necessary defensive and offensive tasks of the regime. Most manifestos referred to what were seen to be the chaotic and threatening conditions of 1973 and indicated that a return to such conditions would follow a no vote. In almost all the manifestos it was argued that the social and economic project of the regime constituted a structural attack on the pre-1973 conditions and required a substantially longer period of exceptional rule to make the regime's changes irreversible. Most of the rightist groups in civil society, especially women's organizations and professional associations, remobilized their followers during the plebiscite campaign. Gallup Polls taken before the plebiscite showed that, of seven possible categories of satisfaction with the general direction of the regime's policy, 100 percent of the upper class (but only 45 percent of the middle class) located themselves in the top three categories. The level of upper-class fear was likewise high. In answer to a multiple-choice questionnaire by the Gallup Poll of Chile on the consequences of a no vote on the new constitution, 58.8 percent of the upper class (and only 33.2 percent of the middle class) indicated that the worst outcome would result, namely, "return to the year 1973."[8]

The persistence of fear within the upper bourgeoisie was an important element in the bourgeoisie's willingness to accept individual policies that hurt the upper class (there were numerous bankruptcies of domestic firms following the drastic tariff reductions and the decline of consumer purchasing power) but were seen to be the necessary cost of protecting its overall interests. It is impossible to understand the passivity of the industrial fraction of the bourgeoisie in Chile (a passivity that, of course, increased the policy autonomy of the state) outside of the context of fear.

An important indication of the upper bourgeoisie's willingness to abandon some of its independent political instruments for advancing its interests was its closure of the traditional party, the Partido Nacional, in 1973. For almost a decade there was virtually no effort by the high bourgeoisie to create any party mechanism. An interview with the former president of the conservative Partido Nacional during the plebiscite campaign underscores this "Eighteenth Brumaire"–like abdication to the authoritarian state. In answer to a journalist's question as to how he viewed the loss of power of such parties, the former president of the national party said, "I don't regret anything, neither the absence of political parties, nor the absence of parliament for the last seven years, because I believe that the construction of a free society could only have been achieved without them. . . . We were at war and what you have to do in wartime is defend yourself. . . . I simply believe that a government of authority is required for the entire period needed for Chile to be converted into a modern nation."[9]

Turning more explicitly to the issue of the potential for concerted action by opposition groups in civil society, it is clear that this potential is related in part to the internal unity of the state apparatus, the degree of support the state apparatus receives from allies in civil society, and the degree of coercion the state is able and willing to impose on opposition groups. In the case of Chile, as we have just seen, all these factors were such as to make concerted action by the opposition difficult in the 1973–81 period.

Two other factors are important to consider. One is the degree of ideological, class, and party tension *within* the opposition. In Chile, in the period under analysis, these tensions were high. The major components of the party opposition were the Christian Democrats, the Socialists, and the Communists. In democratic Chile, the greatest degree of party polarization occurred during the national elections of 1964 and 1970 and during the congressional elections of 1973. In all three elections the Christian Democrats were on one side, and the Socialists and Communists on the other. At the beginning of the plebiscite campaign, all three parties joined in an informal oppositional alliance, but the history of past party conflict and the different class and ideological bases of the parties made concerted action extremely difficult. Within three weeks, part of the Christian Democratic rank and file, fearful of the consequences of cooperating with the Marxists, refused to support the party leader, Eduardo Frei. For his part, Eduardo Frei became engaged in an extremely bitter condemnation of what he thought was Communist betrayal of the informal understanding. In turn, the Marxist parties were disillusioned by what they viewed as the absence of rewards for their ideologically costly cooperation with the Christian Democrats.[10]

The second factor consists of the structural changes in the political economy and their effect on the capacity of the opposition in civil society to work in concert against the state. The Chilean program of "libertarianism from above" (especially in its halcyon days of 1978–81) was an extreme form of liberal economics imposed by a highly coercive state. Tariffs were reduced to a uniform 10 percent, robbing the "national industrial bourgeoisie" of protection from imported manufactured goods. One result of the extremely rapid reduction in tariffs was the absolute reduction in the size of the industrial working class.[11] The structural base of potential oppositional collectivities in this very important arena of civil society was thus weakened.

Furthermore, whereas the initial control of working-class collectivities came about by direct coercion by the state, after 1978 there emerged a much more sophisticated attempt at policy-induced structural fragmentation of existing and potential oppositional collectivities. These policies reflected the ideas of Friedrich A. Hayek, the author of *The Road to Serfdom,* and such radical libertarian, antistatist, "public-choice" political economists as James Buchanan and Gordon Tullock.[12] In fact, the continuing labeling of the regime's theorists as "Chicago boys" missed important theoretical, historical, and political nuances. The Chicago school of economics was most influential in 1973–78. In 1979–81 the "Virginia school" of political economy (Buchanan, Tullock, and to a lesser extent Brunner) had the most impact.[13] The Virginia school was not concerned primarily with a general theory of the market. The major preoccupation was with the "marketization" of the state, with turning the state into a firm, and with atomizing civil society into an apolitical market. For their part, the "Santiago boys" went beyond the Virginia school in praxis. They represented a new phase in rightist political economy in the world, in that they actually used their privileged positions in the state apparatus to devise and apply a policy package aimed at dismantling, and then restructuring, civil society in accordance with their radical market views.

Pinochet's Santiago was not going to Washington, London, or Chicago. Reagan's Washington, Thatcher's London, and the University of Chicago economists were going to Santiago to see the future. In the area of social security, the pilgrims envisoned multiple private firms, each advertizing a slightly different program; these programs would virtually assume the resources and the role of the public sector in the social security area. The architect of this plan was quite clear about the political purpose of the new social security system: By setting a single nationwide social security rate, the state provided a systematic incentive for groups in civil society to mobilize collectivities against the state. The intention was to remove this incentive.[14]

The new union code created in 1979 had a similar goal. The intent of the code, according to its author, was to "create rewards and structures that depoliticize automatically" by the systematic insistence on market and individual-choice principles.[15] Thus, the right of any group to form its own union and engage in bargaining was restricted to the plant level, and conflicts were in theory to be resolved by workers and managers without the involvement of the state. Of course, if the market then operated only in a context in which the state apparatus forbade a closed shop, industrywide negotiations, or an active role for union leaders in political parties, the state would hardly be kept out of union life. Nevertheless, by fragmenting union collectivities, by passing large parts of the social security apparatus and public health into the private sector, and by imposing "free-choice anti-monopoly rules" on unions and professional associations, the Pinochet state apparatus launched a long-range attack on the organizational potential of the opposition in civil society.

If our focus on the state is the state's share of the economy, the Chilean state can be said to have shrunk. The changes in the role of state enterprises that took place under the Pinochet regime between 1973 and 1981 provide a good example. In sharp contrast to the Brazilian BA model, which involved a dramatic expansion of the role of state enterprises, the Chilean version entailed an equally dramatic reduction in their role. By 1981, state enterprises had been reduced from around 500 to fewer than 20. If, however, our focus is on the role of the state in the domination and imperative coordination of civil society, then in Chile the program of "libertarianism from above" resulted in a "small-state, strong-state" project for the domination of opposition in civil society.[16]

The theory of those in command of the Chilean state in this period might be paraphrased as follows. By eschewing the capacity to produce economic outcomes different from those that flow "naturally" from the operation of the market in a class-divided society, the state may increase its capacity to dominate civil society. One might even go so far as to argue that the Chilean state represents a step beyond Bonapartism. Instead of exchanging the right to rule for the right to make money in the classic Bonapartist transaction, significant fractions of the Chilean bourgeoisie abdicated the right to rule and severely jeopardized their right to make money in the short run in the hope of preserving class privilege in the long run. This is not an unusual occurrence in itself. It characterized, for example, the early period of the Brazilian BA, which was economically difficult for the Brazilian bourgeoisie. What is unusual about the Chilean case is that the state was able to persist in this strategy for almost a decade.

The question raised by the Chilean case, then, was how long the state could continue to find support for a project that stood in objective contradiction to the requirements of local capital accumulation. The fact that it did so for as long as it did must be considered a strong challenge to theories of the "capitalist state." But even the extremities of the Chilean situation seem unlikely to support such a state indefinitely. It might be noted that the first major economic crisis of the Santiago boys' model occurred in November 1981, when three banks came so close to defaulting that the state, in violation of its own model, rescued them and imprisoned some officials. The "natural" operation of the market may adversely affect not just the working class but also important segments of the bourgeoisie, especially in a dependent capitalist country.[17] Nonetheless, the Chilean state has been remarkably successful at "turning a deaf ear to the national bourgeoisie."[18]

Clearly, the foundational offensive project of the Chicago, Santiago, and Virginia schools increasingly disintegrated after November 1981, and the range and intensity of oppositional activities increased. However, the state apparatus remained relatively powerful throughout the 1982–83 crises for three reasons. One was the de facto unity of command of Pinochet over the army, navy, air force, and intelligence service. No other BA had one-man presidential control over the coercive apparatus remotely comparable to that in Chile. Second was the fact that important sectors of the bourgeoisie, even though they could no longer believe in the offensive project of the authoritarian state or even in Pinochet, still harbored sufficient fear of the Left to be unavailable to the democratic opposition and therefore gave tacit support to the defensive project of the coercive apparatus.[19] The third reason was that there remained major divisions – deeper, as we shall see, than those faced in Brazil, Chile, or Uruguay – within the active opposition itself.

Power Stagnation and Standoff: Uruguay, 1978–81

Uruguay presents a very different system of power relations between the authoritarian state and civil society. Historians date the installation of the BA regime in Uruguay with the closing of Congress in June 1973. This event, however, only capped a long period of rule by fiat that extended back to 1968. From 1968 until 1978, the state gained power relative to civil society.[20] In fact, in Uruguay the percentage of the population detained for questioning by the police was higher than in any other country of the southern cone, press and intellectual censorship more complete, and repression of guerrillas and labor more severe. Civil society shrank drastically in Uruguay in 1973–78. However, in the three years from 1978 to 1981 there was a noticeable decline in the regime's capacity to lead its original allies in civil society (but absolutely no loss of its capacity to coerce any working-class or leftist opponents), and the opposition began to show greater capacity to formulate an alternative program (though not to challenge the government directly). Why was there this difference between Uruguay and Chile?

I shall start with the "defensive" projects of the regimes. If we contrast Chile and Uruguay before the installation of their respective BA regimes, we see that the Chilean bourgeoisie believed far more strongly than its Uruguayan counterpart that its economic and social survival was threatened. The Chilean bourgeoisie developed numerous vehicles of class mobilization and protection. This element of bourgeois mobilization was virtually absent in Uruguay. In Uruguay, in fact, the military had destroyed the major radical claimants to power, the Tupamaros, months before the military finally closed Parliament and installed the new regime. In sharp contrast to Chile, therefore, the Uruguayan military had a relatively weak "salvationist" relationship to the bourgeoisie when the military closed the classic instrument of the bourgeoisie in Uruguay – Parliament. Since 1975, the Tupamaros have had no visible existence and are simply not a credible threat. Communist-controlled trade unions were certainly a source of resistance to the bourgeoisie and could reappear as a force in some form, but the repression was so massive that the unions did not launch a single important strike for almost a decade.

If we contrast the offensive projects, we see that in Uruguay the state announced an ambitious economic liberalization program that was similar, on paper at least, to that in Chile. In the period from 1978 to 1980 the macroeconomic indicators went in the direction the state planners wanted. The budget, even after the inclusion of the country's capital expenditures, was almost balanced. Inflation was greatly reduced, and, most importantly, the gross domestic product, which had virtually stagnated at 0.3 percent per year from 1961 to 1968, grew at 6.4 percent per year from 1978 to 1980.[21] However, market liberalism as a long-term project that would change the political economy and society lost steam early on.

The less frightened Uruguayan bourgeoisie defended its specific interests much more forcefully than its Chilean counterpart. Thus, the Uruguayan state planners never had the degree of relative autonomy from the Uruguayan bourgeoisie that their counterparts had in Chile. The Uruguayan state planners' lack of autonomy was further diminished by the collegial decision-making formula used by the Uruguayan BA. Virtually all major decisions were made by the Junta de Oficiales Generales, which by statute contained all four-star officers from the army, navy, and air force. This decision-making formula was chosen by the military to ensure the participation of all three services, but it engendered significant internal veto power, opened up multiple lobbying points for civil society, and reduced the capacity of the state planners to implement the sweeping policies they proposed on paper. Thus, tariffs, instead of being reduced to a uniform 10 percent as in Chile, were still hovering around 90 percent in Uruguay by 1981. Likewise, although the regime in Uruguay initially made pledges to privatize many state enterprises as in Chile, not a single major state enterprise was abolished. Before 1973 it was rare for the presidency of one of the eight largest state enterprises to be held by a military officer, but after five years of BA rule, it had become the norm for the presidencies of the largest state enterprises to be held by active-duty officers. The chief economic architect of the original Uruguayan model acknowledged that the division of power within the state apparatus made the implementation of his privatizing goals unrealistic. As a consequence, he did not make a great effort to push his initial goals. He also judged that the same balance of forces made it unlikely that Uruguay could ever reduce tariffs much below 80 percent. He observed in passing that Uruguay did not have a commanding single figure like Pinochet, but rather that Uruguayan "collegiality slows decision-making and occasionally introduces differences in policy implementation."[22]

By 1980 in Uruguay it was no longer clear that the regime had an unfulfilled sociopolitical offensive project. Offensively and defensively, the regime seemed to have completed its initial agenda. If this is so, on theoretical grounds it would seem that the bourgeoisie would not see a continued need to abdicate to the military the direct articulation of its interests, which would otherwise take place via some representative institutions. This would be even more true if the bourgeoisie had reason to think that the prolongation of a regime of exception might set into motion reactions in civil society that could present long-term threats to its core interests – threats that would be substantially more severe than those presented by the inevitable uncertainties of representative politics. Let us look for evidence related to these issues.

In November 1980 the military government in Uruguay held a plebiscite to ratify a constitution similar to that in Chile. In sharp contrast to the situation in Chile, however, in Uruguay during the campaign, *not one* producer organization issued a manifesto urging a yes vote. Although none

Table 10.1. *Public Opinion in Urban Uruguay Concerning the Effect of Political Opening on the Economy, May 1980*

	Upper class (%)	Middle class (%)	Lower class (%)
Speed up	35	48	53
Slow down	16	16	12
No effect	28	20	12
No response	14	12	14

Note: The question was worded as follows: "In your judgment, would the reestablishment of political practices – elections, parties, and parliament – speed or slow economic recuperation, or have no effect on recuperation?"
Source: Gallup Poll, Uruguay Indice Gallup de Opinión Politica.

Table 10.2. *Public Opinion in Urban Uruguay Concerning the Effect of Political Opening on Public Order, May 1980*

	Upper class (%)	Middle class (%)	Lower class (%)
Improve	43	37	29
Worsen	6	12	6
No effect	36	37	53
No response	12	10	7

Note: The question was worded as follows: "In your judgment, what would be the immediate effects of a political opening on tranquility and public order?"
Source: Gallup Poll, Uruguay Indice Gallup de Opinión Politica.

issued a manifesto urging a no vote, the lack of active support for the authoritarian state by producer groups was one reason the new constitution was rejected in an election that amazed outsiders.

Although the overlap between producer groups and the group the Gallup Poll of Uruguay calls "upper class" is not exact, the results of the poll were interesting. They indicated that the original allies of the authoritarian regime in Uruguay no longer believed that they could further their interests only within an authoritarian, politically closed system. In May 1980 the Gallup Poll of Uruguay explored opinions about a political opening. Whereas in Chile a large section of the upper class in that year was still certain that a political opening would hurt the economy and set off potentially dangerous conflict, in Uruguay the Gallup Poll revealed a dramatically different response on the part of the urban upper class. By a margin of 2 to 1, upper-class respondents believed that a political opening would speed rather than slow economic recuperation (Table 10.1). Even more significantly, by a margin of 7 to 1, upper-class respondents believed that a political opening would improve rather than worsen tranquility and public order (Table 10.2).[23]

Turning to the question of the potential for concerted political opposition in civil society, the contrast between Chile and Uruguay is also striking. The major difference is that the two main political parties in Uruguay, the Blanco and the Colorado parties, are not highly differentiated in terms of programmatic content, ideological discourse, or class composition. Furthermore, between them, the two parties have never received less than 80 percent of the votes cast in any election in the twentieth century. Although the parties have a tradition of intense electoral competition, they also have a history of power sharing that has gone so far as to include some consociational practices. The leadership of the two parties cooperated on the no vote in the plebiscite without any recriminations of the kind that surfaced in the brief attempt at collaboration between the Christian Democrats and the Marxists in Chile.

In fact, the absence of threat and the presence of party alternatives that they found tolerable explained why producer group leaders, in extensive interviews conducted in 1981, voiced the opinion that the return to electoral politics in the near future might be their safest option. In interview after interview, they worried aloud about the risks of a prolonged regime of exception to Uruguay's "safe" party structure. In their opinion, the two traditional parties still retained the allegiance of around 70 to 80 percent of the electorate. Because the regime had no long-range offensive sociopolitical project that seemed attractive or credible, they were afraid that, if there was another decade without party elections, the workers and the Left would seek, and possibly find, other vehicles. For political as well as economic reasons, therefore, the Uruguayan bourgeoisie was becoming less and less willing to abdicate the management of its affairs to the coercive apparatus of the state (the armed forces). In this sense the BA state had lost a significant degree of the autonomy it once had in Uruguay.

However, a close examination of the state–civil society relations in Uruguay during this period illuminates some sobering limitations to oppositional power. First, the upper bourgeoisie, though it did not give active support to the state authoritarian regime, by and large did not join (as many did in Brazil) the active opposition. Second, although the two traditional political parties joined together in opposition on a purely electoral issue, neither party had forged powerful links with the trade unions or attempted to mobilize active resistance to the regime. Thus, the costs of rule for the state apparatus were not very high. There was some division and a major scandal within the army, the key component of the state coercive apparatus, but not enough to shake the military's will or capacity to retain control.

The military did announce an election for 1984. However, on the basis of interviews with the political secretariat of the armed forces, two issues emerged clearly. First, the military did not feel that they were under great pressure from civil society to withdraw from power. In the absence of impelling societal or corporate reasons to withdraw, they prepared a rather elaborate agenda of "participatory prerogatives" for the armed forces in any future democracy. Second, the absence of any effort by the political parties to talk with or organize within the working class weakened Uruguayan civil society, and some key military leaders openly expressed the opinion to me that the barriers to subsequent military reentry and control of the state apparatus were quite low.

Overall, the case of Uruguay reinforces the lessons of the Chilean case regarding the relation between conflicts in civil society and the ability of the state to achieve uncontested domination. The level of class conflict in Uruguay was reduced to the point that the bourgeoisie was no longer willing to give a *carte blanche* to the authoritarian state. Nonetheless, at least until late 1983, elite perceptions of the potential for conflict within civil society were still sufficient to obviate any attempt to build significantly higher barriers to military reentry after the scheduled transfer of state power in 1985.

Decline of State Power and Decline of Civil Society: Argentina, 1978–81

I shall be even more schematic for Argentina. From 1976 through 1978 the authoritarian regime in Argentina was characterized by four elements that increased state power vis-à-vis civil society. First, although Argentina never had the fusion of rule found in Chile (indeed, the regime institutionalized a decision rule whereby virtually all administrative and political units such as provinces, ministries, state enterprises, and even central bank directorates would be allocated one-third to the army, one-third to the navy, and one-third to the air force), there was at least a reasonable degree of harmony between the military as an institution (represented by the junta, which considered itself the ultimate source of authority) and the military as government (represented by the president). Second, the military as an institution and as government used its impressive coercive powers to repress any signs of opposition in civil society and, to a somewhat lesser extent, to support the technocratic team in its economic project, the initial phases of which hurt not only the working class but, with the exception of the financial groups, most sectors of the bourgeoisie. Third, the high bourgeoisie was sufficiently frightened by previous conflict to accept the stated goals (if not yet the actual implementation) of the state program.

In 1980–81, with the exception of the capacity of the state apparatus to coerce the opposition, which remained strong, the situation changed considerably. State power had clearly begun to decline. Critical to this outcome was the growth of contradictions within the state, more precisely between the military as an institution and the military as government. After considerable debate within the military institution, a new military president was selected whose authority was questioned by the military within months of his inauguration. Economic policy indecision, a chaotic series of devaluations, and a dangerous run on reserves cast doubt on the entire economic program. Anyone who analyzed regime power as a capacity not only to coerce but to use the resources of the state apparatus to structure outcomes would have to conclude that in the period 1979–81 there had been a decline in state power.

In contrast, analysis of civil society in Argentina in the period from 1976 to mid-1981 shows that virtually all the components necessary for independent oppositional life in civil society – unions, political parties, and student organization – also declined in power, despite the signs of state decomposition by 1980–81. Certainly, civil society showed few signs of being able to achieve concerted action over an alternative project. Argentina by mid-1981 was a country in which both the state and civil society had experienced major losses of power.

The Argentine case enlarges on the lessons of the Chilean and Uruguayan cases. Conflict within civil society does not by itself provide the preconditions of a growth in state power. In the Argentine case, the absence of cohesion within the heart of the state apparatus had led to a negative-sum game in which the overall capacity to structure either economic or political outcomes, from either inside or outside of the state apparatus, had declined markedly. The Argentine case, even more than the Chilean case, also posed serious problems for conventional theories of the capitalist state. Argentina was a state that was clearly "relatively autonomous" in a society that was clearly capitalist; yet the state was not "organizing capitalist interests" and overcoming problems of capital accumulation, as some theories presuppose.[24] On the contrary, the actions of the state apparatus were a prime factor in the vigorous "underdeveloping" of Argentina, labeled by some the "Bolivianization of Argentina."

The power relations between the authoritarian state and civil society were slowly beginning to change before Malvinas. Beginning in July 1981, the political parties began a public search for a common position called La Multipartidaria Nacional. Indeed, in February 1982, an impressive set of proposals was published in Argentina.[25] The invasion of Malvinas gave the military enormous instant support. However, the unprepared Argentine public reacted with extraordinary revulsion to the news of the military surrender at Malvinas. I attended a number of mass meetings in the aftermath of the surrender, and charges of cowardice, dishonesty, and incompetence were hurled at the military with a vengeance. The high bourgeoisie, with its extensive ties to English commercial and financial networks, also realized that its alliance with the military was extremely dangerous. For our purposes, however, the most important point is that after Malvinas rapid extrication from state power was seen to be an institutional imperative by many military officers. For example, the vice-director of the Escuela Nacional de Defensa bitterly acknowledged that the parceling out of provinces, ministries, and state enterprises by thirds might possibly have been a way for the military to rule domestically, but Argentina went to war with "three political parties," which were completely unable to perform professionally. He argued that the military had to extricate itself from government, sharply de-emphasize its internal security orientation, and professionalize with a NATO opponent in mind and that democratic parties needed to rule. He stated, "If that option fails, Argentina may face a Russian revolution."[26]

Until Malvinas, fear of Nuremburg-like trials and reprisals was a strong disincentive to military extrication. However, after Malvinas, officers' fear of military and state collapse was so great that it, in fact, made them more willing to accept harder terms from the opposition. This was underscored in an interview with an active-duty brigadier general. In answer to my question as to whether military fear of reprisals would impede extrication, he emphatically shot back, "There *has* to be an exit or we will disintegrate."[27]

State power is relational. The near collapse of the state coercive apparatus increased the relative power of civil society even though many leaders of civil society wanted to contain attacks on the military to give themselves time to reconstitute civil and political society. After the defeat in Malvinas, state power was clearly in disintegration, but civil and political society still faced tough problems of democratic recomposition. Raúl Alfonsín saw the task with startling clarity: "We should not confuse the self-defeat of the regime with the triumph of the democratic forces. The first is happening, the second depends on us."[28]

From Parallel Growth to Conflict: Brazil, 1970–81

Brazil raises the most theoretically interesting and complex questions of the four cases. Without supplying full documentation, I would like to claim that from 1970 to 1973 both the power of the authoritarian state and the power of the opposition increased. There are two major caveats. Obviously, the power of civil society started its growth from a very low base. The years 1969–70 were the years of maximum repression. In contrast, the power of the state to impose its solution on its allies by 1973 was great, yet already generating contradictions that would later limit state autonomy.

State power grew in the period under consideration under two special conditions. First, in the atmosphere of armed struggle against urban guerillas, the state security apparatus achieved unprecedented independence in its repression of any activity in society believed to be related to "subversion." Second, there was extraordinary economic growth. In the years 1967–70 the gross domestic product (GDP) rose at an average annual rate of 9.3 percent. It had risen by 11.3 percent in 1971, by 10.4 percent in 1972, and by 10.0 percent in 1973. In the same period, the power of the state enterprises at the apex of the economy also grew rapidly. For example, if we rank Brazil's thirty largest nonfinancial firms by net assets, thirteen of these were public enterprises in 1967, seventeen in 1971, and twenty-three in

1974. Coupled with the rapid growth of the GDP, the state's tax revenues expressed as a percentage of GDP also increased, from 8.4 percent in 1967, to 10.2 percent in 1971, and to 10.8 percent in 1974. The financial role of the state was reinforced still more by the growth of state banks and the state's ability to grant subsidies.[29]

Surprisingly, the growth of the state's role in the economy did not damage its relationship with its allies in the private sector. Even though the private sector's share of the gross national product (GNP) declined, attacks on "statism" did not appear because the state gave generous subsidies to the private sector and the private sector experienced high rates of absolute growth. For example, the capital goods and consumer goods sectors, both of which were predominantly private sector–controlled, grew at an annual average rate of 22 percent in the 1969–73 period.[30] The first response of the state apparatus to the oil crisis in 1973 was to centralize decision making even more within the state apparatus and to increase its relative autonomy vis-à-vis its allies. Thus, this was a period in which the state appeared to have a "credible, violent enemy" and therefore a continuing defensive project, as well as a credible offensive project.

In what sense can we argue that civil society also gained in power in the same period? Many of the elements that became striking later in the 1970s had their origins in this earlier period. The most important of these was the change within the Catholic church. The church supported the military coup in 1964, but by 1970 the church hierarchy, offended (but not directly affected) by the coercive force of the state's "defensive project," became increasingly critical of human rights violations in Brazil. In the sphere of its internal life, the church had a high degree of autonomy from the state.

The church made particularly good use of this autonomy in the steady development of base community organizations (Comunidades Eclesiais de Base). These base communities did not confront the state directly in the period 1970–73 but began to build up their ideological, human, and organizational resources, resources that eventually could be transferred horizontally from one sphere of civil society to other spheres in which the members of the base communities worked. In the late 1970s, this was an important ingredient in the emergence of stronger urban unions, especially in the critical area of greater São Paulo, and it helps to explain the unprecedented growth of rural unions, which also had a surprising degree of autonomy.

Until the late 1970s, unions had been encapsulated in state-crafted corporatist structures, which reduced the autonomy of worker organizations in civil society. The emergence in this period of a new brand of trade unionism that began to challenge the limits of these structures is seen by a number of labor specialists to have been a vital step in Brazilian labor history. According to José Alvaro Moisés, "It is beyond doubt that from the beginning of the 1970s there began to be developed efforts to create a new structure for representation of the rank and file factory workers in their unions. . . . It is now clear that the organizational structure of the new unionism is quite different from the unions of the past."[31]

The growth of the new unionism in the period, like the growth of the church base communities, represented an increase in the autonomous actions of a part of civil society. Like the base communities, the unions did not initially come into direct conflict with the state. This appears to have been because the transformations that were occurring were related primarily to internal organization and ideology and were not immediately reflected in challenges to capital or the state.

By 1973–74, representatives of the new unionism began to negotiate for a series of changes at the factory level. For example, on May 1, 1973, the Metallurgical Federation of São Paulo sent a demand to President Médici for the right to establish factory committees, to negotiate collectively with owners, and to by-pass the state and for greater autonomy from the Ministry of Labor.[32] In fact, before the first wave of strikes in 1978 that brought the unions into direct conflict with the state, the metallurgical unions steadily broadened the scope of their direct, collective negotiations at the factory level.[33]

The emergence of a stronger trade union movement was due not only to changes within the unions themselves, or even within civil society as a whole. It was also, to a significant degree, the unintended consequence of the past actions of the state itself. We have seen how the "success" of the state's defensive project helped generate new forms of church-based opposition in civil society. The success of the "offensive" project also had the unintended consequences of generating new potential for opposition in civil society. The "economic miracle" substantially increased the size of the industrial labor force. Between 1960 and 1970 the number of workers employed in industry grew by 52 percent, and between 1970 and 1974 again by 38 percent.[34] Moreover, the state's policy of relying on multinational corporations and allowing industrial concentration to take its course unimpeded contributed to the tendency of the growth of the working class to concentrate around the city of São Paulo. Industrial growth in itself does not entail a growth in the autonomy of working-class organizations, as the history of Mexican labor illustrates, but the quantitative growth of the Brazilian working class, especially in greater São Paulo, clearly contributed to the generation of the working-class movements that came to be so important in the opposition. Finally, it should be added that in 1976 the minister of labor relaxed the accounting procedures by which the state monitored union funds. In the vast majority of unions this probably meant that the state-approved union officials had access to some discretionary funds for personal and cooptive uses. For his part the minister of labor was able to make an ideological claim that union *abertura* (liberalization) preceded the political *abertura*.[35] For the key São Bernardo union, however, these discretionary funds were actually vitally important in enabling a new generation of unionists like "Lula" to build up the infrastructure that in 1978 helped launch Brazil's first serious strike in a decade.[36] The strategy of the Brazilian state with regard to the working class stands, therefore, in sharp contrast to that of the other BA states, most strikingly to that of Chile.

Those in charge of the Brazilian state also took a very different tack from Pinochet's in their strategy toward Congress, fixed presidential terms, and parties. In order to bolster their ideological claims that the military coup was executed to save democracy, they purged but did not close Congress, they controlled but did not eliminate elections and parties, and they adhered to the existing norms of presidential rotation with fixed terms. All of these initial state decision rules, which in Brazil precluded from the beginning a long-term fusion of power such as Pinochet attained, contributed to a dynamic that increasingly constrained authoritarian state autonomy but that would have been costly (even for the internal unity of the state coercive apparatus) to abrogate.[37] The willingness to tolerate political parties as long as "subversive" individuals were removed probably reflected the generals' prior experience in Brazil in which parties as such were organizationally weak and depended on the charisma of individual leaders or on traditional patronage structures. Parties as organizations were, in short, thought to be much less threatening in Brazil than in Chile. The decision to allow parties to exist at all, however, had unintended consequences for the stability of Brazil's BA regime.

An official opposition party was created in 1965, only to be weakened with the closing of Congress in 1968. In 1970 the officially sanctioned opposition party, MDB, had very little respect within the Left, and it was not felt to represent in any serious way opposition opinion in civil society. For example, in the city of São Paulo in 1970, blank and defaced ballots were twice as numerous as votes for the MDB. By 1974, however, under conditions of less censorship on television, more open elections, and four years of MDB protest activity in Congress, null and blank votes decreased from 33.7 to 10.9 percent of the votes cast in the national election.[38] In the country as a whole, the MDB won only 39.5 percent of the senate votes in 1970 but 59.1 percent in 1974.[39]

Of course, the election of 1974 falls outside our period of 1970–73 and occurred under conditions of government-initiated liberalization, an initiative that began in the second half of 1974. Nonetheless, the stunning results of the elections can be understood only by realizing that in the period from 1970 to 1973 as a whole, the authoritarian state had failed in its attempt to win ideological hegemony in civil society and that the opposition had made real organizational and ideological gains in their long "war of position" against the BA state. A case can thus be made, I believe, for considering the period from 1970 to 1973 to be one in which both the state and civil society increased their power within the spheres of their major activities.

The following period, from 1974 to 1981, was a very different one. The state's economic strategy remained very similar, but the international context in which it was operating changed dramatically, and the accretionary changes that had occurred in the period 1970–73 began to make themselves felt. By the end of 1973, the urban guerrilla movement had virtually been extinguished as a threat to the bourgeois order and the oil crisis began to curtail the Brazilian economic miracle. Without a credible threat and with technocratic planners having to sail against, rather than with, the prevailing economic winds, two of the major forces that had enhanced the relative autonomy of the state in the period 1969–73 began to flag. The predominant state response to the oil crisis of 1973 was one of (*a*) further grandiose development projects in which state enterprises were programmed to play a major role and (*b*) greater centralization of the economy in the hands of the planning and finance ministries in such areas as price setting, criteria for imports, and special export subsidies. In short, the administration of General Geisel followed in the footsteps of previous military administrations in assuming that a strengthening of the economic role of the state would put the economy back on its trajectory growth, enhance the regime's legitimacy, and reduce its political problems. Unfortunately for Geisel, the state's efforts in the economic sphere did not produce the growth rates of the earlier period; instead, Brazil began to experience slower growth and rising debt. Moreover, this time the reaction of the bourgeoisie to the expansion of the state's role was strikingly different. "Antistatism" became a major political issue.

The campaign against "statism" launched by Brazilian business groups in 1975 must be analyzed in a more political context. As we have seen, state enterprises grew at an extremely rapid rate from 1967 to 1973; yet this growth generated little protest. We must therefore qualify the purely doctrinal elements of the antistatist movement that began in 1975. The antistatist movement is best seen as a movement that began when the state had less disposable surplus to pass on as political and economic subsidies to its domestic allies. In the case of Brazil, by 1975 the state had, with the defeat of the guerrillas, lost its most credible defensive project, and although it had its own offensive project of economic growth, it was not a project that the domestic bourgeoisie would accept *carte blanche*. My interviews in Brazil indicate that Paulista entrepreneurial arguments against statism were arguments not against the state as a producer but rather against the state as a regulator. The antistatist campaign was thus the first clear signal of the declining capacity of the state to lead its allies. By 1978, with the issuing of the famous "Manifesto of the Eight" entrepreneurs, an important fraction of the state's initial allies had in fact joined the movement in civil society for liberalization.

Hand in hand with the growth of political opposition in the bourgeoisie came mounting evidence that the state could not carry out its economic project in the new international context. Inflation, which had been reduced from over 60 percent in 1964 to less than 20 percent in 1972–73, rose again to 29 percent in 1974, 38 percent in 1976, and over 100 percent in 1980. The foreign debt soared from U.S. $12 billion in 1973 to over $70 billion in 1982.[40] With mounting inflation and a severely constraining debt/service ratio, state planners in 1975–76, and again in late 1980, had to abandon key aspects of their development project. From 1974 to 1981, then, we can talk of a significant decline in the state's power to lead its allies and to execute a coherent development project, but unlike Argentina, the state never appeared to be in the process of disintegration, and like Chile and Uruguay, it still retained a high capacity to repress.

Finally, the capacity of civil society to formulate new goals and structure political outcomes, which had been nascent in the earlier period, began to mature. The union movement by 1978 was in a position to organize the most important wave of strikes in over a decade, starting in the most industrialized sector of greater São Paulo and then spreading to much of the southeast and south of Brazil. The ecclesiastical base communities developed in number, fervor, and breadth as they became a major force not only in São Paulo but in the northeast and the north of Brazil as well. The Brazilian Bar Association and the Brazilian Press Association launched sustained campaigns against some of the procedural rules crucial to the autonomy of the authoritarian state. The bar association centered its campaign around demands that the state apparatus adhere to the rule of law and especially habeas corpus. The press association campaigned against state censorship. By a dialectical process of societal demand and state concession, both associations helped to increase the sphere of civil society that was relatively free of direct state repression. In this atmosphere, the number and quality of publications advancing ideas, information, and projects stemming from critical sectors of civil society grew impressively.

The simultaneous development of new organizations and energies in diverse sectors of civil society had a more than additive effect. As developments in each sector progressed, horizontal ties between sectors also grew. As a result of these horizontal ties, changes in each sector helped to speed and reinforce changes in the others.[41]

This "horizontal dimension" is sufficiently critical to the overall growth of the power of civil society to warrant some elaboration. Almost all the sectors in civil society have been helped by the reorientation of the church. The trade union movement has benefited particularly. Union activists stress the extent to which the emergence of a more independent trade union movement in greater São Paulo has been helped by the ecclesiastical base community movements, not because these movements are involved directly in trade union activities (they are not), but because they have helped to nurture a sense of social injustice in community members who are also trade unionists and have convinced them of the need for more participatory organizational styles. In addition, of course, the church has provided concrete assistance by allowing critical union meetings to be held inside local churches.

Unions have also been helped by the increased boldness of the press, which has given union positions extensive coverage. It was the press, after all, that made Lula, the new leader of the São Bernardo do Campo metal-workers union, a national figure *before* the first major strike. The Brazilian Bar Association's campaign for the legal rights of organizations and individuals, which also came before the strike movement, contributed to undermining the legitimacy of the state's repressive efforts once the strikes began.

The interaction between the revitalization of the press and the emergence of political opposition among industrial elites is particularly interesting. In 1977, despite growing private reservations about the military regime among entrepreneurs, there was no organization or set of publically recognized leaders to transform these sentiments into a politically effective statement. The *Gazeta Mercantil* (Brazil's equivalent of the *Wall Street Journal*) came up with an ingenious plan. It sent out a request to 5000 businessmen to choose "the ten most representative spokesmen of the business class."[42] Unlike elections for official business confederations, this "election" included no mechanism for the vetoing of potential candidates by the government. Significantly, almost none of the presidents of existing state-charted business groups were elected. The ten businessmen who were selected, however, became legitimated as public spokesmen for the industrial elite. Eight of them signed the highly critical "Manifesto of the Eight." One of the signers reported to me later: "Once we issued the manifesto, civil society entered right into my office by the window. We received numerous invitations to participate in public forums about Brazil's problems and future with members of the church, trade unions, intellectuals, and students – groups we had almost never worked with before."[43]

Without the growth of horizontal ties within civil society, the kind of political evolution that Brazil experienced would not have been possible. Nonetheless, the state played a central role in setting the conditions that allowed these crucial developments in civil society to take place at all. In fact, it might be argued that the initial decision to allow greater space for organization in civil society was as much as anything else an attempt to resolve certain contradictions within the state apparatus itself.

In 1974, the Geisel regime began to promote an *abertura*. One of the prime architects of this liberalization process, General Golbery, argues that an important motivation for the strategy was that of reducing the autonomy of the secret service apparatus vis-à-vis the military as government. During the period of intense fighting against urban guerillas, the Serviço Nacional de Informações (Brazil's peak security organization), along with the individual security forces maintained by each of the three branches of the armed forces, gained a great deal of power. By 1974 the security apparatus had acquired such autonomy and insulation from the regular military that it was perceived to be generating corporate threats to the military as an institution. At least some of those within the military as government wanted to move in the direction of a rule of law in order to reduce the space of "legal exceptionalism" within which the secret service thrived. Liberalization was also seen to be a tactic for generating civil society resources (a freer and more critical press) and movements (protests against torture) that would be useful to the military as government in their "intrastate" effort to gain control of the security forces.[44]

Insofar as the growth of the power of civil society in Brazil served interests within the state apparatus, it was obviously a more robust development, but the nature of the shifting balance of power should not be exaggerated. The state apparatus continued to be very powerful and continued to have a strong interest in domination. For example, in November 1981 the top members of the coercive apparatus determined that they would risk dangerous losses if the rules for the 1982 elections were not changed. President Figueiredo changed them overnight. In the crucial five days after this state fiat, *not one* protest demonstration was held.

In Brazil, as in Uruguay, it was by no means clear that the military was preparing to abdicate. This should not, however, obscure the fact that the evolution of events in Brazil were dramatically different from that in Uruguay. The growth of the power of civil society, fostered in part by state policies, made the tension between the BA regime and the opposition much more dynamic in the Brazilian case. Events subsequent to the period under consideration here, most prominently the elections of 1982, in which the opposition won control of ten states, including the three key states of São Paulo, Rio de Janeiro, and Minas Gerais, and the massive campaigns in 1985 for direct elections, reconfirmed this dynamic.

Unlike Argentina, the Brazilian state in 1982 and 1983 was not threatened with disintegration. The leaders of the state apparatus in 1982 had fewer active supporters and more active opponents in civil society than at any time since the regime began in 1964. Nonetheless, they retained sufficient room for political initiative to make significant changes in the rules of the game for the opposition parties in 1982. Brazil is a clear case in which a lack of civil society support is not a sufficient cause for the military as an institution to yield its share of control over state power. By 1983 it was clear that one of the vital tasks of the democratic opposition would be to forge more organic links between the new organizations in civil society and the political parties. In this way, demands for redemocratization would become a continued social and political force to raise the cost of rule for the authoritarian state apparatus and to present at the same time a clear governing alternative for Brazil's growing political and economic crisis. This happened in 1984 and prepared the way for a candidate of the unified opposition to preside in 1985.

Conclusions

This examination of the variations in relations between the state and civil society in the four BA regimes of the southern cone, however cursory, has suggested several interesting generalizations regarding the way in which the character of the state affects the evolution of opposition politics.

That the state's definition of its "project" affects the possibilities for opposition is clearly evident in the contrast between Chile and Brazil. In Brazil, the BA's appeal to many active supporters came to be based in large part on its association with the improved rate of capital accumulation that characterized Brazil in the late 1960s and early 1970s. "State strength" was thereby identified in important ways with a capacity for effective economic intervention. Repressive capacity was also important, but it was, in addition, a divisive issue within the state because it implied excessive power in the hands of the security apparatus (relative to the rest of the state apparatus and even to the rest of the military). The Brazilian state's concern with promoting capital accumulation did more than simply leave more space in which the opposition could move without repression. It had the unintended consequence of generating conditions that promoted the development of the structural base of the opposition, most notably in its effects on the growth of the working class in São Paulo.

In Chile, capacity for economic intervention was not simply absent from the regime's definition of state strength; reducing the state's capacity for economic intervention was a positive goal. This did not mean that the state had no impact on the course of economic change. Efforts to extricate the state from the economy had a number of important structural consequences, all of which had the intention of lessening the possibility of mounting a political opposition. One of the most important of these was the reduction in the size of the working class and also its fragmentation through the removal, wherever possible, of suitable targets of economic grievances beyond the level of the firm. In short, until the crisis of the economy in late 1981, the Chilean regime's economic strategy reinforced its strength as an instrument of domination quite independently of the state's (very effective) direct efforts at coercive control.

Looking at Chile and Brazil, it would seem that the "common-sense" hypothesis that state strength defined in economic terms naturally reinforces the state's capacity for the political domination of civil society should be reconsidered. State economic intervention, by politicizing "economistic" issues, may increase the potential for political organization in civil society. Conversely, in the setting of dependent capitalist development, the fight against public sector encroachment may be both antihistorical and antipopular – antihistorical in the sense that it undercuts the belief that continued state presence is an essential component of continued capital accumulation and antipopular in the sense that the major beneficiaries of a reduced public sector role are likely to be a small number of tightly interconnected oligopolists.

The second lesson to be drawn from these four cases involves the importance of the threat of class conflict in creating the conditions for domination of civil society by the state. O'Donnell has already pointed out the importance of this factor,[45] but the analysis presented here reinforces his argument. In Chile, where the possibility for a fundamental reordering of the class structure seemed real to the bourgeoisie, the latter accepted un questioningly many state policies that were detrimental to its economic interests and acquiesced completely in the state's project of relatively autonomous domination of the political sphere. In Uruguay and in Argentina (until after Malvinas), fear of opening the door to changes in the class structure kept dominant civilian elites from pressuring more strongly for an opening in the political system. In Brazil, it was only after private elites became convinced that they could manage their economic and political future more effectively within a more open political environment that they began to mount a serious attack on the degree of autonomy that the state had achieved.

Overall, the most important lesson to be derived from these cases may be a methodological one. The power of the state as an actor and institution cannot be analyzed in isolation from an understanding of the nature of the cleavages that rend civil society, on the one hand, or the growth of horizontal ties that bring different sectors of civil society together, on the other hand. At the same time, the evolution of opposition to the state within civil society is shaped by the way in which the state defines its project and by the contradictions and conflicts that emerge inside the state apparatus itself.

Notes

1. Alfred Stepan, *The State and Society: Peru in Comparative Perspective* (Princeton, N. J.: Princeton University Press, 1978), chap. 1.
2. See Fernando Henrique Cardoso and Enzo Faletto, *Dependence and Development in Latin America* (Berkeley: University of California Press, 1979).
3. See Guillermo O'Donnell, *Modernization and Bureaucratic Authoritarianism: Studies in South American Politics*, Institute of International Studies, Politics of Modernization Series, no. 9 (University of California, Berkeley, 1973). See also G. O'Donnell, "Reflections on the Patterns of Change in the Bureaucratic-Authoritarian State," *Latin American Research Review* 13 (1978): 3–38. He later elaborates what he considers the eight principal characteristics of bureaucratic authoritarianism as a type of authoritarian state in his "Tensions in the Bureaucratic-Authoritarian State and Question of Democracy," in *The New Authoritarianism in Latin America*, ed. David Collier (Princeton, N. J.: Princeton University Press, 1979), pp. 291–94.
4. See Alfred Stepan, *The Military in Politics: Changing Patterns in Brazil* (Princeton, N. J.: Princeton University Press, 1971); Stepan, *The State and Society*.
5. This essay was written originally in the beginning of 1982. The major part of the fieldwork on which it is based was done in 1981 and 1982. Although I have updated the discussion to include some reference to events in 1983, I have left the analysis of the crucial events of 1984 (e.g., the opposition's electoral victory in Uruguay, the massive campaign for direct elections in Brazil, and Alfonsín's removal of recalcitrant members of the higher command in Argentina) for another occasion.
6. Karl Marx, in "The Eighteenth Brumaire," described as one of the characteristics of the Bonapartist regime the abdication by the bourgeoisie of its right to

rule in exchange for other kinds of protection by the ensuing strong state. Here, I use the word "brumairian" to evoke the kind of relation described in Marx's essay.

7. The best overall analysis of the foundational aspirations of the Chilean regime is found in Manuel Antonio Garretón, *El Proceso Político Chileno* (Santiago, Chile: FLACSO, 1983), pp. 131–72. A useful examination of the ideological dimensions of the foundational project in its early phases is found in Tomás Moulián and Pilar Vergara, "Estado, Ideología y Políticas Económicas en Chile: 1973–1978," *Estudios CIEPLAN*, no. 3 (June 1980).

8. Data supplied by the Gallup Poll of Chile.

9. *El Mercurio*, August 31, 1980, p. D7.

10. These observations are based on my interviews with party activists in Chile in June 1981.

11. Overall employment in the industrial sector dropped from a 1974 index of 110.4 to 92 in 1978. Employment in the economically and politically important metallic products, machinery, and equipment subsector fell from 117.8 in 1974 to 84.3 in 1978. See Alexandro Foxley, *Latin American Experiments in Neo-Conservative Economics* (Berkeley: University of California Press, 1983), p. 76.

12. All three were frequent visitors to Chile and were closely associated with the regime's "anticollectivities" think tank, Centro de Estudios Publicos. The first issue of the center's journal, *Estudios Publicos*, was devoted to the theme "Liberty and Leviathan" and featured articles by Buchanan, Tullock, Hayek, Karl Brunner, and Milton Friedman.

13. The Virginia (actually VPI) public-choice school represented a thorough-going critique of what it saw to be the increasing pathological conditions of modern democracy. James M. Buchanan began *The Limits of Liberty: Between Anarchy and Leviathan* (Chicago: University of Chicago Press, 1975), pp. ix–x, with the following appeal: "When government takes on an independent life of its own, when Leviathan lives and breathes, a whole set of additional control issues come into being. . . . General escape may be possible only through genuine revolution in constitutional structure, through generalized rewriting of social contract. To expect such a revolution to take place may seem visionary, and in this respect the book may be considered quasi-utopian." Chile became such a "quasi-utopian" experiment. Other important books in this school are that of Richard D. Auster and Morris Silver, *The State as a Firm: Economic Forces in Political Development*, Studies in Public Choice, no. 3, ed. Gordon Tullock (Boston: Martinus Nijhoff, 1979); and the influential early critique by James Buchanan and Gordon Tullock, *The Calculus of Consent: Logical Foundations of Constitutional Democracy* (Ann Arbor: University of Michigan Press, 1962).

14. These comments are based on interviews conducted in Santiago in May 1981.

15. Ibid.

16. I owe the "small-state, strong-state" phrase to Manuel Antonio Garretón.

17. See José Pablo Arellano, "De la Liberalización a la Intervención: El Mercado de Capitales en Chile, 1974–83," *Estudios CIEPLAN*, no. 11 (December 1983): 5–49.

18. See O'Donnell, "Reflections on the Patterns of Change."

19. The Santiago weekly published a poll which indicated that, in answer to the question "What would be the best formula of government to solve the problems of the country?" only 8.5 percent of the upper class selected "the present government of Pinochet" and only 0.7 percent selected "an exclusively military

government." However, only 21.7 percent of the upper class said they wanted "a government formed by all the opposition." *Hoy,* December 1983, pp. 12–16.

20. The best general overview of the Uruguay BA is found in Charles Gillespie, "From Suspended Animation to Animated Suspension: Political Parties and the Reconstruction of Democracy in Uruguay," in *Prospects for Democracy: Transitions from Authoritarian Rule,* ed. Guillermo O'Donnell, Phillippe C. Schmitter, and Laurence Whitehead (Baltimore, Md.: Johns Hopkins University Press, forthcoming), vol. 2, chap. 8.

21. See the statistical appendix to Luis Macadar, *Uruguay 1974–1980: Un Nuevo Ensayo de Reajuste Económico?* (Montevideo: Ediciones de la Banda Oriental, 1982), especially p. 280.

22. Interview with Alejandro Végh Villegas, Montevideo, March 1981.

23. Data obtained at the office of Gallup Uruguay in Montevideo. The office also published a special report on the plebicite, "El Plebiscito Nacional," *Indice Gallup de Opinión Pública,* no. 315 (January 1981); for an excellent analysis of this period, see Luis E. Gonzáles, "Uruguay, 1980–1981: An Unexpected Opening," *Latin American Research Review* 18 (1983): 63–76.

24. The most influential and provocative argument as to why and how the capitalist state should perform these roles remains the work of Nicos Poulantzas. See, for example, his *Political Power and Social Classes* (London: New Left Books, 1973).

25. *La Propuesta de la Multipartidaria* (Buenos Aires: El Cid Editor, 1982).

26. Interview with the vice-director of the Escuela Nacional de Defensa, Buenos Aires, July 28, 1982.

27. Interview, Buenos Aires, July 27, 1983.

28. Letter circulated in Buenos Aires, July 2, 1982.

29. GNP figures based on data in *Economic and Social Progress in Latin America: Annual Report* (Washington, D.C.: Inter-American Development Bank), 1972, p. 141; 1973, p. 145. Tax revenue figures are based on data in the same series: 1968, p. 78; 1972, p. 140; and, 1975, p. 167. Data on state enterprises are found in Thomas J. Trebat, *Brazil's State-Owned Enterprises: A Case Study of the State as Entrepreneur* (New York: Cambridge University Press, 1983), p. 59.

30. José Serra, "Three Mistaken Theses Regarding the Connection between Industrialization and Authoritarian Regimes," in *The New Authoritarianism,* ed. Collier, p. 121.

31. José Alvaro Moisés, "A Estratégia do Novo Sindicalismo," *Revista de Cultura e Política,* no. 5/6 (1981): 71. Maria Hermenia Tavares de Alemedia, in her "Tendências Recentes da Negociacão Coletiva no Brasil," *Dados* 24 (1981): 160–64, also discusses the period from 1970 to 1973 as one of the germination of the new unionism.

32. See Amaury de Souza and Bolivar Lamounier, "Governo e Sindicatos no Brasil: A Perspectiva dos Anos 80," *Dados* 24 (1981): 145.

33. See the charts documenting this trend in the article by de Almeida, "Tendências Recentes da Negociacão Coletiva," pp. 182–83.

34. See Ronaldo Munck, "The Labor Movement and the Crisis of the Dictatorship in Brazil," in *Authoritarian Capitalism: Brazil's Contemporary Economic and Political Development,* ed. Thomas C. Bruneau and Philippe Faucher (Boulder, Colo.: Westview Press, 1981), p. 228.

35. "Abertura Sindical Antecede a Política," *Estado de São Paulo,* January 1, 1978.

36. Interview with Almir Pazzianotto, the labor lawyer for the São Bernardo do Campo Metallurgical Workers' Union, on August 13, 1981, in São Bernardo do Campo. The great increase in the number of rural trade unions in the early 1970s, which remains understudied, was due largely to a small change in the social security law, which presented new legal organizing opportunities for rural workers, opportunities that were rapidly and legally exploited by progressive churches, lawyers, and trade union movements. See Wanderley Guilherme dos Santos, *Cidadania e Justiça* (Rio de Janeiro: Editora Campus, 1979), pp. 35–38, 113–23.

37. Two important articles that explore the constraints on the institutionalization of the autonomous state created by the initial self-proclaimed norms and procedures of the leaders are Juan J. Linz, "The Future of an Authoritarian Situation or the Institutionalization of an Authoritarian Regime: The Case of Brazil," in *Authoritarian Brazil: Origins, Policies, and Future*, ed. Alfred Stepan (New Haven, Conn.: Yale University Press, 1973), pp. 233–54; and Bolivar Lamounier, "Authoritarian Brazil Revisitado: O Impacto das Eleições na Abertura Politica Brasileira, 1974–1982" (Paper prepared for a conference, Democratizing Brazil?, Columbia University, New York, March 9–10, 1984).

38. See Bolivar Lamounier, ed., *Voto de Desconfianca: Eleições e Mundança Política no Brasil: 1970–1979* (Petrópolis: Editora Vozes, 1980), p. 72.

39. David V. Fleischer, ed., *Os Partidos Políticos no Brasil* (Brasilia: Editora Universidade Brasilia, 1971), vol. 1, p. 222.

40. *Economic and Social Progress in Latin America: Annual Report* (Washington, D.C.: Inter-American Development Bank), 1973, p. 143; 1972, p. 140; 1974, p. 209; 1976, p. 172; and, 1980–81, p. 193. Foreign debt data from *World Debt Tables: External Debt of Developing Countries, 1983–1984 Edition* (Washington, D.C.: International Bank for Reconstruction and Development, 1984), p. 166.

41. See Paul Singer and Vinicius Caldeira Brant, eds., *São Paulo: O Povo em Movimento* (Petrópolis: Vozes/Cebrap, 1982); see also Maria Helena Moreira Alves, *The State and the Opposition in Military Brazil* (Austin: University of Texas Press, forthcoming).

42. For a discussion of the methodology and results of the elections, see J. P. Martinez, "Os Eleitos pela Empresa Privada Nacional," *Gazeta Mercantil: Balanço Anual*, September 1977, pp. 18–26.

43. Interview with Claudio Bardella, the entrepreneur who received the most votes in the *Gazeta Mercantil* poll, São Paulo, August 21, 1981.

44. Interviews with General Golbery do Couto e Silva, June 16 and July 16, 1982, in Brasilia.

45. O'Donnell, "Reflections on the Patterns of Change" and "Tensions in the Bureaucratic-Authoritarian State."

Conclusion

11. On the Road toward a More Adequate Understanding of the State

Peter B. Evans, Dietrich Rueschemeyer, and Theda Skocpol

An intellectual sea change is underway in comparative social science, so the introductory essay to this volume argued. A diverse set of scholars with wide-ranging substantive concerns has begun to place the state, viewed as an institution and social actor, at the center of attention. Yet the introduction also suggested that the important work of theoretical reorientation is only beginning to be done. To overcome deeply rooted assumptions about the absolute causal primacy of socioeconomic processes and – in measured, appropriate fashion – to "bring the state back in" to our studies of social change and politics require continuing theoretical innovation and comparative-historical research, each closely coordinated with the other.

As the book now draws to a close, we are in a position to look both backward and forward. How have the essays assembled here improved our understanding of states in relation to social structures? Can we find common threads of methodological approach, conceptualization, and analytical strategy that point to fruitful directions for future scholarship? What gaps in our understanding of the state seem most salient? Are there new research topics that could and should be pursued in the future?

In the pages to come, we shall pull together themes and lessons from this volume and identify some promising frontiers of research, moving through a series of topics that encompass both concerns. We begin with reflections on the methodological style of this book and then assess what all of its essays considered together can tell us about state autonomy, state capacities, and the best ways to do further work on these issues. Our attention then turns to questions that must be addressed through comparative research on social knowledge and state interventions and on various aspects of the formation and reorganization of states. Finally, we conclude with some reflections on analysis and prescription in social studies of states and their activities.

Studying States through Analytical Induction and Historically Grounded Comparisons

All of the studies included in this volume might be considered ambitious, yet they have clearly abstained from elaborating, or invoking, all-encompassing, deductive theoretical frameworks. Instead, these studies, both individually and collectively, use approaches resembling what Florian Znaniecki once called "analytical induction."[1] They draw research questions, concepts, and causal hypotheses from a variety of existing theoretical debates, especially from the juxtaposition of Weberian understandings of the state with propositions drawn from recent neo-Marxist theories. Then they explore such ideas through comparative and historical research. Each investigation springs from concern with certain analytical problems, and each provides a testing ground for analytical orientations or causal hypotheses potentially generalizable to other contexts. These studies are therefore highly theoretically engaged, even though they invert the normal priorities of "grand theorizing."

Analytical induction has been employed by the contributors to this volume not only because no preexisting grand theory of "the state" seems adequate, but also because this method works well in comparative and historical research. Comparisons across countries and time periods and an emphasis on historical depth, the tracing out of processes over time, are optimal strategies for research on states. Obviously, without cross-national comparisons, investigations of states, even those with grand theoretical pretensions, become mere case descriptions. Along with other macrosocial phenomena that do not repeat themselves (at the same time) in each nation, states require cross-country or cross-time comparisons if they are to be studied analytically.

Historical depth is also necessary for the study of states because of another feature that they share with many of the societal structures with which they are intertwined: historical persistence and continuity.[2] That is, basic patterns of state organization and of the relationships of states to social groups often persist even through major periods of crisis and attempted reorganization or reorientation of state activities. It is necessary for the analyst to identify conditions of persistence or nonpersistence to explain many outcomes, especially unintended outcomes, of interest.

Even within the bounds of an analytically inductive and comparative-historical approach, broadly construed, a range of alternative investigatory tactics is open to scholars.[3] The essays in this volume nicely illustrate the range, and it is worth surveying the fruitful models for future work that they suggest.

Some essays offer not case explorations but empirically illustrated explorations of concepts or models. In "The State and Economic Transformation," for example, Rueschemeyer and Evans develop general hypotheses about the determinants of state capacities to promote capital accumulation and income distribution and suggest the applicability and permutations of these ideas by referring briefly to studies of particular state interventions in many less developed countries, without delving deeply into any one case. Evans's later essay, "Transnational Linkages and the Economic Role of the State," has much the same character. Tilly's chapter on war making and state making similarly refers to many possible historical instances in the course of discussing a theoretical model that does not attempt to posit universal causes, yet highlights analytical relationships worth exploring in changing circumstances across the entire epoch of modern world history.

Other essays use in-depth comparisons of two to four historical instances to bring out contrasts or to establish causal connections. Peter Katzenstein's piece on Switzerland and Austria offers a holistic portrait of state–society linkages in the two cases, chosen to illustrate opposite extremes within the common framework of European corporatism. Weir and Skocpol restrict their analysis to three cases and, like Katzenstein, make some holistic characterizations, but they also focus closely on selected aspects of state organization, political constellations, and economic knowledge in order to make causal arguments about the determinants of the differing depression-era policies of Britain, Sweden, and the United States. Both Katznelson's study, "Nineteenth Century England in American Perspective," and Stepan's exploration of the interplay of states and civil societies in the four countries of the southern cone of Latin America stand somewhere between the analytically controlled comparisons of Weir and Skocpol and the more holistic contrasts and overlaps of Katzenstein.

The remaining contributions are fine examples of comparatively informed studies of critical cases. Amsden's piece on the state and economic development in Taiwan and Laitin's on ethnic alignments in Yorubaland focus in detail on single instances, yet both have important comparative elements. In each, comparative assessment enters into the selection of the historical instance studied and speaks explicitly to the generalizability of the case study's findings. It is no accident, either, that in these contributions we encounter the most extreme forms of state autonomy found in the range of cases covered in this volume. Laitin examines the legacies of colonial state domination in northern Nigeria, and Amsden analyzes the unusual state that grew out of legacies of Japanese colonialism and the occupation of Taiwan by the Mainland Chinese Guomindang military regime. By exploring the determinants and consequences of state action under deliberately chosen extreme conditions, Laitin and Amsden are able to highlight processes that work more subtly, in combination with other determinants, in a range of other situations.

Finally, it is worth underlining a methodological feature that all of the essays share. They are invariably sensitive to what might be called "world historical contexts" – the epochally specific transnational parameters within which their empirical cases or examples are located. Thus, Katzenstein stresses that he is examining Switzerland and Austria as they are in the post–World War II international setting; in another geopolitical and transnational economic environment, institutional patterns and causal connections that are different from the ones he highlights might shape public policy processes. The other authors of essays in Part II similarly underscore the world historical contexts and the constant or shifting geopolitical and economic parameters with which they are dealing.

Attention to world historical settings must always be central to "historically grounded" analyses of states in relation to social structures. It is not enough simply to trace processes over time within national boundaries. Analysts must take account of the embeddedness of nations in changing transnational relations, such as wars and interstate alliances or balances of power, market flows and the international economic division of labor, and patterns of intellectual communication or cultural modeling across national boundaries. Since states are intrinsically Janus-faced, standing at the intersections of transnational and domestic processes, their structures, capacities, and policies are always influenced by identifiable aspects of the particular world historical circumstances in which they exist.

Yet the essays also explore theoretical issues that are relevant across many times and places. Reviewing some of the arguments that have been raised about state autonomy and state capacities should make this point clear.

Determinants of State Autonomy and State Capacities

One of the most prominent debates in the recent neo-Marxist literature on the "capitalist state" has centered on the question of "state autonomy."[4] Some neo-Marxists have taken the position that states are not autonomous but act as instruments of dominant-class interests and will. Others view states as structures embodying class relations and continually being reshaped by political class struggles. For these theorists the state as such is not autonomous, but balances of class forces and alliances do determine whether given regimes or policies might be at odds with the interests of particular classes or class fractions. Still other neo-Marxists posit that states inherently are organizationally autonomous from dominant classes, yet hold that they still necessarily function to further capital accumulation and to preserve class dominance in the mode of production as a whole. Most of these discussions about the fundamental character of the capitalist state have been carried on at the level of theoretical absolutes meant to apply universally to all societies with capitalist relations of production.

Meanwhile, in what might be called neo-Weberian circles, the habit of speaking of strong versus weak states has flourished.[5] In contrast to Marxists, scholars in the Weberian tradition tend to take for granted that states are potentially autonomous and that the controllers of the means of coercion and administration may pursue goals at variance with dominant classes or any other social group. What more directly interests scholars in this tradition are variations in state capacities. As a first, crude cut at this issue, some Weberian-minded comparativists started labeling states, especially modern national states, "stronger" or "weaker" according to how closely they approximated the ideal type of centralized and fully rationalized Weberian bureaucracy, supposedly able to work its will efficiently and without effective social opposition. Eighteenth-century Prussia, for example, had a strong state according to this perspective, whereas the United States has always had a weak state. This labeling system, of course, stands in considerable tension with neo-Marxist notions of state strength. If neo-Marxists speak of a strong state at all, they typically mean a state with a domestically and internationally potent capitalist class, well served by "its" state organizations. The United States would far exceed eighteenth-century Prussia on such a scale of state strength.

Although the essays in this volume show clear awareness of the perspectives and debates just mentioned, they spend little time debating whether states in general are autonomous. Nor do they dwell on global antinomies between "strong" and "weak" states. Instead, these essays explore differentiated instances of state structures and actions. By so doing, they develop arguments that complement those surveyed in the introduction and improve our understanding of the circumstances under which those who command particular sorts of state apparatuses are likely to pursue autonomous goals and the conditions under which they are likely to be successful in their pursuits.

For the investigation of *state capacities*, a tactic repeatedly employed to good effect is the identification of specific organizational structures the presence (or absence) of which seems critical to the ability of state authorities to undertake given tasks. In turn, the presence or absence of organizational structures is connected to past state policies, thus underlining the need for historical as well as structural analysis if specific state capacities and incapacities are to be understood. To take one example, Amsden stresses the extent to which the capacity of the Guomindang regime on Taiwan to extract resources from agriculture depended on the prior existence of a state monopoly in the production and distribution of fertilizer – a monopoly established through the nationalization of Japanese industrial properties on the island after World War II. Several comparable examples of the analytical tactic of connecting state capacities to the existence of concrete organizational structures and these, in turn, to past public policies also lie at the heart of Weir and Skocpol's piece on Britain, Sweden, and the United States.

Not only have authors discussed state capacities in organizationally specific ways. They have also demonstrated that there is not necessarily a positive relationship among different kinds of state capacities. This builds on the theme introduced in Skocpol's essay, "Bringing the State Back In," that states are not likely to be equally capable of intervening in different areas of socioeconomic life. The very unevenness of a state's existing capacities, either at one moment or over time, may be the most important structural feature to recognize in understanding how it confronts challenges.

That there may be insulation or contradictions among different kinds of state capacities is exemplified in discussions of state capacities to intervene in agriculture in Switzerland and the United States. In Switzerland, as Katzenstein shows, well-developed state capacities to intervene in agriculture have not been duplicated by state capacities for other economic interventions. In the United States, according to Weir and Skocpol, this is also the case. Moreover, the New Deal's initially autonomous interventions into the agricultural economy actually set in motion political processes – the strengthening of the American Farm Bureau Federation and congressional conservatives – that later helped to frustrate possibilities for more comprehensive state capacities to do economic planning or to manage high levels of social spending.

Issues of the relations among different kinds of state capacities are raised to higher levels of analytical generality in the essays by Tilly and Stepan, both of which inquire into relationships between the state's capacity to deploy violence and its fiscal capabilities and means for intervening in the economy. Tilly argues that the development and exercise of the state's basic monopoly of violence are necessarily intertwined with the construction of fiscal capacities that vary in response to the resource possibilities of different domestic and world environments. Such fiscal capacities range from measures to extract taxes from peasants and landlords and supervise tax farmers in early modern Europe, to agencies for taxing exports and obtaining foreign loans or aid in many of today's developing nations. In apparent counterpoint to Tilly, Stepan in his analysis of the Chilean case argues that the regime's strengthening of its repressive capacities has gone hand in hand with a self-conscious dismantling of state capacities for economic intervention.

Of course, these two arguments deal with somewhat different types of problems and situations. Stepan deals with internal repression in an internationally subordinate country with well-established state bureaucracies facing mobilized social groups, whereas Tilly focuses on war making among competitive regimes engaged in laying basic foundations of centralized state power. Nevertheless, the juxtaposition of Tilly's argument with Stepan's points us resolutely away from any temptation to characterize states simply as strong or weak, or even stronger and weaker along some generalized continuum. The juxtaposition reminds us of the need to remain alert to the relationships, sometimes contradictory or paradoxical, among different kinds of state capacities, especially as they are developed and deployed over time.

The overall point is not that specific state capacities are randomly distributed among states or explicable only in terms of idiosyncratic histories. All of the essays, and especially the theoretically oriented pieces by Rueschemeyer and Evans and by Tilly, recognize the importance of certain very basic fiscal and administrative capacities that may be utilized for various tasks. The variations, unevenness, and contradictory relationships among state capacities discovered in these chapters invite the kinds of attempts the authors actually make to explain these patterns in generalized if not universal ways. Yet the overall point remains that possibilities for state interventions of given types cannot be derived from some overall level of generalized capacity or "state strength." More finely-tuned analyses must probe actual state organizations in relation to one another, in relation to past policy initiatives, and in relation to the domestic and transnational contexts of state activity.

Along with the analytical tactics for investigating state capacities, the essays collected here also offer suggestive ideas and fresh questions about the dynamics of *state autonomy*. Are state organizations that are controlled and directed "from within" by their own leading officials necessarily those with the greatest capacity and will to intervene in social and economic affairs? What happens to states when they launch new interventions? Careful attention is paid in these studies to the relationships of potentially, but problematically autonomous states to their socioeconomic environments, to dominant and subordinate classes, and to politically active or potentially mobilized groups.

Received theoretical frameworks tend to direct our suppositions about these matters in some well-worn directions. Poulantzian neo-Marxism, for example, posits that an "autonomous" state, capable of wide-ranging and coherent interventions in socioeconomic relations, increases the social power of both leading state officials and the dominant class, because the state necessarily functions to meet the objective, collective needs of the dominant class.[6] An alternative, crudely Weberian imagery about state autonomy tends to produce more straightforwardly zero-sum propositions. In this perspective, the increased ability of a bureaucratic state to realize internally generated goals supposedly reduces the power of all societal groups "outside" the state; conversely, the existence of well-organized social groups with control over the disposition of politically relevant resources implies a less autonomous state.[7] What the Poulantzian and the vulgar Weberian perspectives jointly posit, moreover, is that state autonomy and state capacities for effective socioeconomic interventions go hand in hand. The studies presented here, however, suggest possibilities that are much more dialectical than either of these perspectives.

In the first place, it is apparent that state autonomy and the power of social groups can increase or decrease together. This can happen, for example, through what might be called challenge and response patterns. One of the central arguments of Evans's essay in Part II is that the presence of powerful social actors, specifically transnational corporations, has stimulated the growth of autonomous states with capacities for economic intervention in many Third World countries. Another instance, referring to domestic political processes involving a nondominant class, is Katznelson's presentation of the historically evolved relationship between the federal democratic state and the political capacities of the industrial working class in the United States. Here, the fragmentation and decentralization of state organization, the absence of an autonomous national bureaucracy, and the lack of any consistent repression of workers' collectivities in localities and work places discouraged the emergence of class consciousness or a labor party tied to trade unions.

As for the relationship of state autonomy to the state's capacities, and willingness, to intervene in economic relations, some counterpoints emerge in Amsden's essay on Taiwan and from her discussion considered in relation to Stepan's on Chile. Especially in terms of its capacities to restructure agrarian property relations and to appropriate resources from agriculture, the Guomindang regime newly arrived on Taiwan was, Amsden shows, strengthened because of its unusual degree of autonomy from domestic social classes. But at the same time, the regime's autonomy initially hindered its capacity to further industrial growth, because that autonomy entailed the preeminence of military men and military goals in the overall state apparatus. Somewhat analogously, Stepan argues that Chile's military rulers deliberately reduced their state's capacities to intervene in market outcomes in order to protect the state's repressive coherence and make state policies and organizations less likely to be a target for groups with economic grievances.

This last point brings us to yet another idea that consistently emerges in the essays. Whether originally autonomous or not, state interventions in socioeconomic life can, over time, lead to a diminution of state autonomy and to a reduction of any capacities the state may have for coherent action. As Rueschemeyer and Evans discuss in general terms, states that increase their interventions into the economy risk this diminution and reduction, because social groups pursuing their own interests will tend to mobilize and focus their attention either on trying to penetrate directly parts of the state apparatus or on attempts to gain veto power over state policies. Stepan's analysis of Brazil (along with his aforementioned discussion of Chile) provides a fine illustration. As the Brazilian state became increasingly involved in the process of capital accumulation, Stepan points out, the working class mobilized to engage the state directly and fight for a reduction of its autonomy.

Katzenstein's discussion of Austria provides another illustration of the same basic point. Although the exceptional weight of state-owned enterprises in the Austrian economy might suggest a high degree of state autonomy, in fact, as Katzenstein shows, close analysis of the operation of these enterprises reveals that labor and business groups have firmly inserted themselves into their directorships through mechanisms of party representation. Historically, the very expansion of the state's role made it almost inevitable that affected economic interests would search for ways of reducing the potential autonomy of the state enterprises, and in the Austrian case such attempts proved to be remarkably successful.

In many ways, therefore, all of the essays reinforce the conclusion that issues of "state strength" – whether conceptualized in terms of the state's autonomy from social groups or in terms of its capacities to intervene on its own or others' behalf – can be fruitfully broached only via thoroughly dialectical analyses that allow for non-zero-sum processes and complex interactions between state and society.

Finally, two of the essays also illustrate that interactions among parts of the state apparatus itself may provide the key to changing state capacities and degrees of autonomy. Weir and Skocpol's discussion of the role of the Treasury in Britain is one example. The increased power of the Treasury over other parts of the British civil service certainly made the British state apparatus more autonomous in relation to the Labour party and, by extension, the working-class as a whole. But the increased power of the Treasury also stood in the way of the development by the British state of capacities for sectoral interventions or for Keynesian macroeconomic management, even though such capacities might well have benefited many industrialists and the national economy in addition to unemployed workers.

Still another example – here showing specifically how relations interior to the state apparatus may affect the dynamics of state autonomy – can be found in Stepan's analysis of state and civil society in Brazil. In Stepan's view, one of the important determinants of reduction in the autonomy of the Brazilian state, through cautious "liberalization" from above, was the conviction of the executive-branch leaders that they themselves could rein in sections of the security apparatus only if the autonomy of the state apparatus as a whole in relation to civil society was reduced! Since state repressive autonomy is often thought to be the most intractable to modification from without, it is intriguing to entertain the possibility that intrastate divisions can lead to its diminution.

The welter of ideas reviewed in this section about the determinants and interrelations of state capacities and state autonomy has taken us a long way from broad neo-Marxist and neo-Weberian suppositions. Further refinement of definitions of "the capitalist state," even if "capitalist" is modified by "advanced" or "monopoly" or "dependent," cannot advance our understanding. As the studies presented here demonstrate, telling variations in state structures and capacities often occur among states that appear to belong to the same broad type. Nor is it any longer helpful to assume a single dimension of "state strength" that conflates different features of state organization and resources or, worse, confounds the matter of state autonomy with issues of the capacities a state has for performing certain kinds of tasks.

We have not ended up with a new overall theory of the state – not even with a complete set of hypotheses. Juxtaposing a range of comparative and historical findings as we have done here has had the effect of opening up new ways of asking questions about relations between states and social structures. Certain heuristic principles have emerged as fruitful pointers for future research, such as the value of starting from the permissive assumption that states *may* be autonomous actors. Whether or not they are depends on conjunctures of state structure, the relations of states to societies and transnational environments, and the nature of the challenges faced by given states. These studies have revealed that tracing out the interrelations among various kinds of state autonomy and state capacities requires careful attention to the formal organizations, informal networks, and shared norms that compose the structure of the state apparatus. Likewise, it is clear that, as we avoid global characterizations of state strength, we must conceptualize specific dimensions of state capacities and a range of possible relationships between state actors and other social groups.

For the purposes of actual research structured in the terms just summarized, the strategy of case selection followed by Katzenstein, by Katznelson, and by Weir and Skocpol may prove to be optimal. That strategy entails selecting countries and historical conjunctures that are similar in important respects and then closely analyzing variations in state organizations and capacities within that context. Two illustrations of potential new investigations are worth sketching as we conclude this section.

One investigation might compare contemporary newly industrializing nations across regions of the world, following up on many of the hypotheses put forward in the chapters by Rueschemeyer and Evans, by Evans, and by Amsden. The role of the state in promoting basic economic transformations, and especially industrialization, is especially salient in such nations as Brazil, Mexico, South Korea, Taiwan, India, and Nigeria. Moreover, such countries share the difficulty of attempting to industrialize in a world dominated by transnational capital based outside their borders. Yet despite these basic similarities in the state's task and the world historical context, newly industrializing nations present very different specific state structures and different relationships of state organizations to domestic and transnational elites. Heretofore, there has been a surprising lack of systematic comparisons of such cases across geocultural regions. A systematic comparative study of this kind might well shed important new light not only on the determinants and consequences of patterns of state-led industrialization in the contemporary Third World, but also on more general issues of state autonomy and capacities.

Whereas a comparative investigation of newly industrializing nations would tend to focus especially on states in relation to domestic and transnational capitalists, our second illustration would highlight questions about state structures and policies in relation to broader arrays of groups active in domestic politics. A comparison of various Western "welfare states" in the current period could shed light on what happens as well-established state programs for dispensing social benefits and services "mature" and appear to reach limits in the context of a transnational crisis of faith in Keynesian economic management. How do administrative arrangements, policy legacies, and the established ties of state organizations to policy intellectuals and to politically active groups help to explain the various responses of Western welfare states to similar strains? Obviously, a careful comparative study such as this could address questions about state capacities in the light of the important suggestions about states and the patterning of political conflicts raised in this volume. One of the most likely themes to emerge from such a study would be the consequences of prior welfare-state interventions for the politicization of various social cleavages, which in turn would affect the possibilities for state managers to reorganize and redirect the policies at issue.

Research Frontiers: Social Knowledge and State Interventions

As we have summed up themes that recur throughout the volume, methodological and substantive leads have been indicated for future research on states and social structures. In this and the next section we shall continue to look ahead. But rather than attempt to spin out more possibilities based on topics that have already received considerable attention, we shall now focus on some future research directions that have been only touched on in the essays and in the literature reviewed in the introduction. In this section, we examine ideas about social knowledge and state interventions; in the next section, we sketch some possibilities for comparative research on state structures as such.

State action creates demands for knowledge about the social processes and structures that state interventions seek to affect. Early modern social science responded in large part to the knowledge needs of the state, as is perhaps best indicated by some of the names under which it made its appearance: "statistics," "police science," and "Staatswissenschaft." In fact, the shift from a largely normative and philosophical approach to society to one grounded in factual knowledge is probably the most important intellectual correlate of the rise of the modern state. The emergence of the modern "public sphere," in which voluntary groups proposed measures in the collective interest, also encouraged the search for information about social problems. Once widely disseminated, such information in turn encourages demands for new state interventions, which require still more social knowledge. Demands for both generalized theoretical knowledge and for information about particular social and economic conditions have dramatically increased with the interpenetration of states and other aspects of social life in both advanced capitalism and state socialism.

Yet the state "stands on earth and so in the sphere of caprice, chance, and error," wrote Hegel, whose name has often been associated with idealizing notions about an omniscient and omnipotent state.[8] The knowledge basis of state action, as well as the processes by which the state itself influences the development and application of social knowledge, are indeed research issues of central importance. Some of the essays included here have indicated major analytical angles to be pursued. Thus, Rueschemeyer and Evans point to the importance of assuming that states are likely to have only partial or incomplete knowledge at their disposal. By attending to that possibility we can arrive at more realistic models of state capacities to formulate and pursue interventions. Laitin offers some fascinating suggestions about ways in which state actions shape basic cultural perceptions of the nature of society. And Weir and Skocpol highlight ways in which the differential access of Swedish, British, and American economists to strategic policy centers in the state influenced both the development and the application of their ideas.

Looking to the future, two different but equally promising lines of comparative research might build on substantive issues raised, however cursorily, in this volume. First, one of the notes in Evans's article on transnational linkages flags the importance of the transnational diffusion of norms and expertise in shaping the capacities of Third World states to bargain with transnational corporations in the extractive sector. This points to an important fact: For contemporary Third World states, as well as for developed nations, transnational diffusion of policy-relevant knowledge has always been important in shaping capacities to pursue various lines of action. Thus, a fruitful series of investigations, encompassing both Third World and developed nations, might focus directly on transnational diffusion of policy-relevant economic knowledge. Throughout the history of the modern system of national states, doctrines and practical models of how states do (and should) affect domestic economic life and transnational economic processes have been developed and propagated. How have relevant ideas and institutional arrangements emerged in close relation to the activities of certain national states; how have they then been spread to additional national states; and what have been the consequences for state structures, state capacities, and state–society relationships?

Investigations of these basic questions would tell us a great deal about how variously structured and situated national states, and the intellectual and social groups associated with their policy-making processes, create, appropriate, and rework transnationally visible economic doctrines and associated institutional practices (such as planning agencies or statistical capacities or norms for dealing with multinational corporations). We may expect to learn more about the "fit," or lack thereof, between given economic doctrines and particular kinds of state structures and state capacities for monitoring and intervening in economic processes. And we should learn about the political and social networks through which economic ideas and practices are, or are not, transmitted and reworked. Perhaps most importantly, we should gain new insights into the often ironic results, both for state activities and for economic ideas, that follow from attempts to transmit theories, models, or institutional forms from state to state. For example, an imported theory may be adopted and then later seen to be serving the interests of its foreign progenitors, thus stimulating the development of a countertheory, as happened with free-trade doctrines and the responses of the "ECLA school" in Latin America.

A second line of possible future research on social knowledge and state interventions takes off from Weir and Skocpol's discussion of economists and state responses to the Great Depression in Sweden, Britain, and the United States. Analysis of economics as a profession in each of these countries would have taken Weir and Skocpol too far afield from their central problem – accounting for the possibilities of Keynesian policies at a particular economic and political conjuncture. Their essay nevertheless underlines the need for a kind of comparative study of states and social structures that is rarely undertaken, given the concentration of most comparative political sociologists on classes or interest groups considered as purely instrumental actors. A full understanding of state capacities for socioeconomic interventions requires a better understanding of the historically evolved interrelations between states and "knowledge-bearing occupations," particularly the modern social science professions.

The contemporary literature on social science and public policy tends to ask nonhistorical questions that take for granted an optimistically progressive view of social science in relation to politics: Are social scientists getting sufficient resources for their endeavors, and from whom? Are public policy makers or the general politically engaged public getting the best, the most up-to-date, theoretically powerful, and technically accurate research results, and are they willing and able to act on this "information"? If not, what explanations can we draw from organization theories or political sociology to explain where the "irrational" blockages lie?[9]

What we need are studies that go beyond nonhistorical analyses of knowledge utilization without becoming grand overviews of the joint evolution of social science and the modern state. Fresh insights are most likely to be found through historical and comparative investigations of the *various* ways in which governmental structures and activities have affected the intellectual development and social organization of the social sciences themselves, as well as their policy applications.[10] Historical and comparative studies of three to six advanced industrial liberal democracies could trace out the ways in which governments and their activities have profoundly affected the emergence and social organization of social science activities and disciplinary configurations, as well as their intellectual orientations. Then, in turn, particular areas of welfare-state policy making could be probed in depth to reveal how variously organized and oriented social sciences have influenced the overall shape and content of governmental interventions for economic and social welfare purposes.

As these brief examples of possible future research directions indicate, many critical questions remain to be explored in the broad area of social knowledge and state interventions – particularly questions about actual policy developments considered not only against the background of the organizational structure of states themselves, but also in relation to the generation and flow of policy-relevant ideas and information within and across national societies. There is a need for comparative studies of the ways in which states use social knowledge to address particular kinds of policy problems. Such studies should attend to the interplay of state agencies with institutions and professions oriented to the production and dissemination of knowledge, and they should examine the interrelations of officials with all groups that advance claims to information and social theories in connection with political struggles over state actions. From research of this sort, including the examples we have briefly sketched, much could be learned about the sociology of policy-relevant knowledge, and in the process, our overall understanding of states would be markedly improved.

Research Frontiers: The Formation and Reorganization of States

Reflecting on the many things the essays in this volume have had to say about the roles of states in policy making and social change, one is struck by the need for more adequate understanding of the various structures of states themselves. Although gross characterizations of "strong" versus "weak" states may have been superseded, better ways of characterizing state structures as organizational configurations remain to be developed. These, in turn, would make it easier to pursue comparative studies of state capacities and the impact of states on economic transformations and political conflicts.

We clearly need to probe the internal complexities of state structures, without going to the extreme of treating states simply as disconnected collections of competing agencies. Along with formal bureaucratic mechanisms, budgetary, legal, and ideological processes can be examined to discover the various ways and degrees to which states achieve overall coordination of their activities. Comparative analyses may also reveal systematic fault lines within state structures. Possibly the older parts of states that have been established for a longer period of time, especially the parts dating back to the foundation of traditional warfare regimes specializing in the maintenance of order and the extraction of resources from domestic populations, differ organizationally and operationally from the agencies these states have established since the late nineteenth century to cope with the growing list of demands from social groups that derive from (and encourage) the expanding scope of state socioeconomic interventions. For both older and newer national states, moreover, there may also be systematic differences between parts of states oriented to transnational environments and those specializing in purely domestic problems. In addition, various quasi-independent "parastatal" bodies, such as public enterprises, might reward close analytical and comparative attention. Often these enjoy legal standing but are removed from regular administrative jurisdictions, and they may in practice be enmeshed in markets or closely tied to political parties and systems of patronage.

Although such possibilities could be further elaborated in general terms, the question still arises as to what sorts of empirical studies might sharpen our understanding of state structures at the same time that they would allow us to grapple with significant substantive problems. In our view, comparative and historical examinations of watershed periods in which state apparatuses are constructed or reconstructed may be the most promising approach. To illustrate the possibilities, we shall briefly discuss three examples: episodes of deliberate reform and reorganization of state structures; examinations of the reorganization of state apparatuses that accompany major wars and their settlements; and studies of the formation of new national states in the twentieth century. Issues in each of these areas have come up here and there in this volume, but they have not been the central focus of any of the essays.

First, we need more comparative investigations of when and how established state structures, especially their administrative and fiscal arrangements, are reorganized and with what effects on policy-making capacities and the patterned relationships of state organizations and actors to social groups. The episodes when such deliberate attempts at reform or reorganization are made within solidly established state structures can be particularly rewarding to study, not only for their successes in achieving declared objectives, which probably are few and far between, but for their failures and unintended consequences as well. Comparative-historical studies of such episodes, especially in the long-established states of Western Europe, North America, and Latin America, may reveal with unusual clarity the structural and operational ties that knit the inner parts of complex modern states together or that link some parts of states into domestic or transnational networks outside the formal authority of state executives. Since many such ties may normally be "invisible" to state officials and society members themselves, the macroscopic study of reorganization episodes may enable the analyst to discover important structural features of states that would not be amenable to such research techniques as interviewing or reliance on the writings of public officials.

Second, there is a particular sort of "reorganization episode" that would reward study both at national levels and in transnational geopolitical contexts. Examinations of the reorganization of states that accompany the end of major wars could be especially enlightening about fundamental issues in understanding state structures. How do military demobilization and the lifting of wartime fiscal measures and economic controls occur and with what lasting legacies for state capacities and political cleavages? How do changed international balances of military power and the accompanying new alliances and flows of coercive and economic resources affect the domestic doings of various states? Such issues could obviously be addressed through comparisons across states involved in a particular war. In addition, they could be examined for various watershed periods in international history, such as the aftermath of the Napoleonic Wars, World War I, and World War II, making it possible in due course to make comparisons across such watersheds.

Finally, studies of national state formation in the twentieth century would broaden our cross-cultural understanding of various state structures and build on important earlier work in comparative politics. The penultimate volume of the series of books published by Princeton University Press under the auspices of the SSRC's Committee on Comparative Politics was a series of essays edited by Charles Tilly entitled *The Formation of National States in Western Europe*.[11] This influential volume opened new vistas for historically oriented analysts of state building. As Tilly made clear both in the earlier volume and in his essay here, the social structural, economic, cultural, and geopolitical circumstances within which the original European modern states emerged, and in many cases came to accommodate constitutional political arrangements, were not the same as those in which postcolonial and other emerging national states have operated in modern times. War making among roughly equal, highly competitive state builders has not (yet) played as great a role in the contemporary Third World. Kinship and local community arrangements have presented different obstacles and opportunities for would-be state builders. Many contemporary state builders have been able to derive a greater share of revenues from links to the world economy than from taxing peasants and landlords. And the international diffusion of models of administrative organization, economic planning, public education, and other indications of what a full-fledged "modern" state should be have obviously affected state-building efforts, especially in "new" postcolonial nations and in state-socialist regimes.[12]

During the past decade, new findings and arguments about states and political systems have been piling up in rich area-study literatures on various regions of the Third World and Eastern Europe. Potentially, one could draw many fresh conclusions about the distinctive structures and capacities, or incapacities, of contemporary national states by linking up the findings of historically and culturally sensitive area studies with analyses of the world ideological, international economic, and geopolitical circumstances that have impinged on such countries in the twentieth century. The time is surely ripe to extend the approach to basic state formation presented in the 1975 volume *Formation of National States*, pulling together research findings from studies of diverse parts of the world. The overall aim would be to determine how various geopolitical, social structural, cultural, and economic circumstances have influenced, most basically, the core administrative and fiscal organizations of recently formed national states, as compared with one another and contrasted with national states formed in earlier eras. Attention should also be paid to the sorts of state agencies through which these nations have achieved – to the extent that they have – capacities to pursue various kinds of public policies. Obviously, studies of this sort could, in the end, link up very well with comparative analyses of the role of states in promoting industrialization and other socioeconomic transformations in the contemporary Third World.

Some Concluding Thoughts on Analysis and Prescription

This volume is dedicated to pushing along the recent upsurge of social scientific interest in the state. It has taken the position that little is to be gained from more grand theorizing about the state in general. Instead, scholars from various disciplines must use the findings of wide-ranging comparative studies to improve conceptualizations and generate new hypotheses about the structures and activities of states (plural) in various social structural and transnational settings. Obviously, all of the possibilities for research along these lines exemplified in the essays and projected in this concluding chapter are rife with theoretical and methodological pitfalls. To attempt to anticipate all the possible difficulties would be both impossible and presumptious, as well as unnecessarily discouraging. There is, however, one metatheoretical consideration so fundamental that it not only deserves explicit discussion, but can provide a fitting closing for this book.

The emergence of the modern state with its rationalized extension of control has been accompanied by analysis, critique, and prescription. To this day, however, critique and prescription have tended to overshadow and constrain analysis. Pronouncements about what governments should and should not do have always dominated intellectual debates on the nature of the state. Toward the end of the nineteenth century, understanding of the state as the servant of the capitalist order and individual freedom culminated for both Herbert Spencer and Karl Marx (albeit in contrasting ways) in visions of an eventual demise of coercive control, of the state as they then knew it. Ironically, Adolf Wagner, working in the tradition of German historical economics and of the more state-centered thought of a social science that called itself "Staatswissenschaften," formulated at about the same time his law of an ever-growing expansion of state activities.[13] In the background of Wagner's empirical generalization, we can discern the reverberations of Hegel's normative vision of the state as the guardian of "universal interests," of the common good.

Since the turn of the century, we have seen developments undreamed of four generations ago. Two horrifying world wars and a number of attempts at totalitarian transformations of social life through state-sponsored mobilization and repression have been the most dramatic extreme manifestations of state power. Less threatening state penetrations of economies and social relations have given rise to welfare systems and public economies that far surpass Wagner's anticipations and absorb from one-third to more than one-half of the total domestic product in the various capitalist countries.

These developments have modified, but hardly overturned, earlier orientations toward the state, which remain thoroughly enmeshed in prescriptive antinomies. Although visions of a vanishing state have been reduced to ritualistic assertion or utopian fantasy, fears of an overpowering state – dystopian visions of 1984 – have given new strength to models of the good society that seek to constrain and limit state action as much as possible. Contemporary theories of the "end of the welfare state" come (in subtler ways) to similar conclusions, conclusions that are not independent of powerful social and economic interests that stand to gain from the curtailment of public welfare activities. At the same time, strong popular demands and social exigencies underlie continuing expansions of state activities in the economies and the social life of both developed and developing nations. That mainstream economists warn, with what at times seems virtual unanimity, against the inefficiencies and distortions that allegedly derive from state interventions, whereas governments in the First and Third Worlds, not to mention the Second, proceed almost without exception against that advice, is not an accidental absurdity. It is but the ongoing manifestation of the normative antinomies and the contradictions of analysis and prescription that have accompanied the modern state throughout its history.

It is past time, we suggest, to distinguish more carefully between analysis and understanding of states, on the one hand, and critique and prescription, on the other. Better understanding of the roots and consequences of state actions and capacities must be developed, free of automatic activations of visions about what states ought to do or ought not to do. It is necessary, for example, for social scientists to become less encumbered by the normative and political assumptions built into much of modern economic theory if they are to grasp more fully the conditions and interrelations of market functioning, corporate command structures, and state actions in relation to economic processes.

Differentiation of intellectual concerns is not, however, the same as discarding either side of an inherited tension. Normative reflection must be kept alive in forms that do not cut short analysis and understanding. Indeed, critical reflection would benefit from transcending old ideological encrustations and basing itself on improved analyses of what states can and cannot effectively do. But critical reflection certainly must not be cast aside.

Quite reasonably, one might argue that careful analyses of the causes and consequences of state actions in various circumstances are more likely to provide the analytical tools necessary to avoid misguided attempts at expanding state interventions than ritualistic reaffirmations of the notion that "he governs best who governs least." At the same time we should acknowledge that those whose studies focus on the state have a special responsibility to take a coldly critical look at the efficacy of state "solutions" to policy questions. Cases in which states deliver "collective disasters" must be examined as closely as those in which they deliver "collective goods."

Instances in which social groups or classes manage to tame the behaviors of parasitic state agencies must be probed as carefully as instances in which autonomous state actions appear to further societal welfare over narrow interests.

In sum, advocates of bringing the state back in to a more central place in the analytical agendas and explanatory approaches of the social sciences must remain vigilant lest the old concatenation of liberal critique of the state with a theoretical underestimation of the capacities of states be repeated in a mirror fashion. Studying state action should not entail either glorifying state power or overestimating its efficacy. It is possible to improve our analyses of states in relation to other social structures without immediately taking sides – and certainly without ever taking only the "statist" side – in the inherited and inevitably ongoing debate about what we citizens of the modern world want our states to do, or stop doing.

Notes

1. See Florian Znaniecki, *The Method of Sociology* (New York: Farrar & Rinehart, 1934).
2. The importance of attention to institutional persistence in the study of states has been highlighted above all in the scholarship of Reinhard Bendix. See his *Nation-Building and Citizenship* (New York: Wiley, 1964) and *Kings or People: Power and the Mandate to Rule* (Berkeley: University of California Press, 1978).
3. For methodological discussions of the alternative approaches illustrated in the following paragraphs, see Theda Skocpol and Margaret Somers, "The Uses of Comparative History in Macrosocial Theory," *Comparative Studies in Society and History* 22(2) (1980): 174–97; Skocpol's conclusion to *Vision and Method in Historical Sociology* (Cambridge and New York: Cambridge University Press, 1984); Samuel H. Beer, "Causal Explanation and Imaginative Re-enactment," *History and Theory* 3(1) (1963): 6–29; and Arend Lijphart, "Comparative Politics and the Comparative Method," *American Political Science Review* 65(3) (1971): 682–93.
4. The best surveys of recent neo-Marxist theorizing on the state appear in Bob Jessop, "Recent Theories of the Capitalist State," *Cambridge Journal of Economics* 1 (1977): 353–73; and Martin Carnoy, *The State and Political Theory* (Princeton, N. J.: Princeton University Press, 1984).
5. Examples of works that employ, as a first analytical cut, distinctions between "strong" and "weak" states are J. P. Nettl, "The State as a Conceptual Variable," *World Politics* 20 (1968): 559–92; Stephen D. Krasner, *Defending the National Interest* (Princeton, N. J.: Princeton University Press, 1978); and Peter J. Katzenstein's editorial conclusion to *Between Power and Plenty: The Foreign Economic Policies of Advanced Industrial States* (Madison: University of Wisconsin Press, 1978). All of these also introduce more subtle conceptual tools for analyzing state capacities, however.
6. See especially Nicos Poulantzas, *Political Power and Social Classes*, trans. Timothy O'Hagen (London: New Left Books, 1973).
7. Alvin Gouldner's perspective on the state versus civil society embodied this zero-sum perspective. See the discussion in Theda Skocpol, "A Reflection on

Gouldner's Conceptions of State Power and Political Liberation," *Theory and Society* 11 (1982): 821–30.

8. Georg Wilhelm Friedrich Hegel, *The Philosophy of Right*, trans. and ed. T. M. Knox (Oxford: Clarendon Press, 1942), addition to sec. 258.

9. For a very able example of this kind of approach, see Robert F. Rich, *Social Science Information and Public Policymaking: The Interaction between Bureaucratic Politics and the Use of Survey Data* (San Francisco: Jossey-Bass, 1981).

10. Examples of the kind of studies we have in mind include Philip Abrams, *The Origins of British Sociology, 1834–1914* (Chicago: University of Chicago Press, 1968); Steven J. Diner, *A City and Its Universities: Public Policy in Chicago, 1892–1919* (Chapel Hill: University of North Carolina Press, 1980); Barry D. Karl, *Charles E. Merriam and the Study of Politics* (Chicago: University of Chicago Press, 1974); Martin Bulmer, "Science, Theory, and Values in Social Science Research on Poverty: The United States and Britain," *Comparative Social Research* 6 (1983): 353–69; and Walter Korpi, "Approaches to the Study of Poverty in the United States: Critical Notes from a European Perspective," in *Poverty and Public Policy: An Evaluation of Social Science Research*, ed. Vincent T. Covello (Cambridge, Mass.: Schenkman, 1980), pp. 287–314.

11. Charles Tilly, ed., *The Formation of National States in Western Europe* (Princeton, N. J.: Princeton University Press, 1975).

12. John Meyer and his associates have explored the worldwide spread of "modern" state forms and practices. See George M. Thomas and John Meyer, "The Expansion of the State," *Annual Review of Sociology* 10 (1984): 461–82; John Meyer and Michael Hannan (eds.), *National Development and the World System* (Chicago: University of Chicago Press, 1979).

13. Adolf Wagner, *Finanzwissenschaft*, 4 vols. (Leipzig and Heidelberg: Winter 1887–1901; originally 1871–72).

Notes on the Contributors

ALICE H. AMSDEN is on the faculty of Harvard University, Graduate School of Business Administration. Amsden's first book is entitled *International Firms and Labour in Kenya* (London: Frank Cass, 1971). Her most recent book, coauthored with Linsu Kim and to be published shortly, explores the industrial revolution in South Korea from a technological perspective. Attention is focused on the role of the state in accelerating Korea's growth and acquisition of a technological capability in six industries (textiles, paper, cement, steel, ship building, and general machinery). Recent papers include " 'De-skilling,' Skilled Commodities, and the NICs' Emerging Competitive Advantage," *American Economic Review* 73(2) (1983): 333–37; "The Direction of Trade – Past and Present – and the 'Learning Effects' of Exports to Different Directions," *Journal of Development Economics* (forthcoming); and "The Division of Labor Is Limited by the *Rate of Growth* of the Market: The Taiwan Machine Tool Industry in the 1970s," *Cambridge Journal of Economics* (forthcoming).

PETER B. EVANS, one of the editors of this volume, is Professor of Sociology and Associate Director of the Center for the Comparative Study of Development at Brown University. He is co-chair (with Theda Skocpol) of the Social Science Research Council's Committee on States and Social Structures. Evans has published *Dependent Development: The Alliance of Multinational, State and Local Capital in Brazil* (Princeton, N. J.: Princeton University Press, 1979) and numerous articles on the political economy of development. He is currently working on a study of the role of the state in the development of the computer industry in Brazil.

PETER KATZENSTEIN is Professor of Government at Cornell University. He is a member of the Social Science Research Council's Committee on

States and Social Structures and the editor of *International Organization* as well as the *Cornell Studies in Political Economy*. He has recently completed two books on the politics of corporatism and industrial adjustment in the small European states: *Corporatism and Change: Austria, Switzerland and the Politics of Industry* (Ithaca N. Y.: Cornell University Press, 1984) and *Small States in World Markets: Industrial Policy in Europe* (Ithaca, N. Y.: Cornell University Press, forthcoming). His current research focuses on a comparative study of the United States, West Germany, and Japan.

IRA KATZNELSON, who has taught at Columbia University and the University of Chicago, is Henry A. and Louise Loeb Professor of Political and Social Science at the New School for Social Research, where he is currently Dean of The Graduate Faculty. His work has been concerned principally with exploring the origins and persistence of structures of racial and class inequality in the United States and in Britain. The author of *Black Men, White Cities: Race, Politics, and Migration in the United States, 1900–1930, and Britain, 1948–1968* (New York: Oxford University Press, 1973) and *City Trenches: Urban Politics and the Patterning of Class in the United States* (New York: Pantheon Books, 1981), Katznelson has recently completed two coauthored works: *Schooling for All: Public Education and the American Working Class* (with Margaret Weir; New York: Basic Books, 1985) and *Working Class Formation: Nineteenth Century Patterns in Western Europe and North America* (edited with Aristide Zolberg; Princeton, N. J.: Princeton University Press, 1985). His current research focuses on social policy and social class in England and the United States. Katznelson is a member of the Social Science Research Council's Committee on States and Social Structures.

DAVID D. LAITIN is Professor of Political Science at the University of California, San Diego. He is the author of *Politics, Language and Thought: The Somali Experience* (Chicago: University of Chicago Press, 1977) and articles on language policy and African politics. The book that will elaborate the essay in this volume and also discuss Islam and Christianity as cultural systems will be entitled *Hegemony and Culture: Politics and Religious Change among the Yoruba*. Laitin is currently a recipient of grants from the Howard Foundation and the German Marshall Fund, which is allowing him to conduct research on language politics in Spain.

DIETRICH RUESCHEMEYER, one of the editors of this volume, is Professor of Sociology at Brown University. Earlier he taught at the University of Cologne, Dartmouth College, the University of Toronto, and the Hebrew University of Jerusalem. Rueschemeyer has written on problems of the sociology of knowledge, the theoretical analysis of development and modernization, and professionalization and the control of experts. In *Lawyers and Their Society* (Cambridge: Harvard University Press, 1973) he contrasts the state orientation of the German legal profession with the business orientation of the bar in the United States and relates these differences and their change over time to the role of the state in the history of the two countries. A theoretical monograph, *Power and the Division of Labor*, will be published by Polity Press, Cambridge (forthcoming). Rueschemeyer is a member of the Social Science Research Council's Committee on States and Social Structures.

THEDA SKOCPOL, one of the editors of this volume, is Professor of Sociology and Political Science at the University of Chicago. She also serves as co-chair (with Peter Evans) of the Social Science Research Council's Committee on States and Social Structures. Skocpol's first book, *States and Social Revolutions: A Comparative Analysis of France, Russia, and China* (Cambridge and New York: Cambridge University Press, 1979) was the recipient of the 1979 C. Wright Mills Award and a 1980 American Sociological Association Award for a Distinguished Contribution to Scholarship. During the past few years, Skocpol's research has focused on the social politics of the United States in comparison with Britain, Sweden, and other advanced industrial-capitalist nations. Currently, she is writing a book on the politics of public social benefits in the United States. This work analyzes developments from the late nineteenth century, through the Social Security Act of 1935, until the current period of debates about the future of America's peculiar and incomplete "welfare state."

CHARLES TILLY teaches sociology and history and directs the Center for Studies of Social Change at the New School for Social Research. His sixteen published books and monographs include *The Vendee* (Cambridge: Harvard University Press, 1964), *As Sociology Meets History* (New York: Academic Press, 1981), and *Big Structures, Large Processes, Huge Comparisons* (New York: Russell Sage Foundation, 1985). His next book to appear will be *La France Conteste, 1598–1984* (Paris: Arthème Fayard). Mr. Tilly works mainly on state making, the development of capitalism, conflict, and popular collective action in Western Europe.

MARGARET WEIR is completing her Ph.D. in the Department of Political Science at the University of Chicago, and in 1985–86 will join the Government Department at Harvard University. She is coauthor (with Ira Katznelson) of *Schooling for All: Public Education and the Working Class in the U.S.* (New York: Basic Books, forthcoming). Weir's current research interests focus on policy responses to unemployment in the United States during the post–World War II era. Her dissertation is entitled "The Political Limits of American Economic Policy: The Federal Response to Unemployment, 1960–1980."

Index